Robert Eadon Leader, John Arthur Roebuck

**Life and Letters of John Arthur Roebuck**

P.C., Q.C., M.P.

Robert Eadon Leader, John Arthur Roebuck

**Life and Letters of John Arthur Roebuck**
*P.C., Q.C., M.P.*

ISBN/EAN: 9783744689090

Printed in Europe, USA, Canada, Australia, Japan

Cover: Foto ©Thomas Meinert / pixelio.de

More available books at **www.hansebooks.com**

# LIFE AND LETTERS

OF

# JOHN ARTHUR ROEBUCK

P.C., Q.C., M.P.

*WITH CHAPTERS OF AUTOBIOGRAPHY.*

EDITED BY

ROBERT EADON LEADER.

EDWARD ARNOLD,

LONDON:        NEW YORK:

37, BEDFORD STREET.    70, FIFTH AVENUE.

1897.

# PREFACE.

—◦◦◦—

It is nearly twenty years since Mr. Roebuck died, and surprise has often been expressed that so long a time has elapsed without any record being given to the world of the career of a man of unique personality, who played a prominent part in his country's affairs for half a century. Into the reasons for the delay it is unnecessary to enter. Circumstances have at length made possible the realization of the determination, ever tenaciously held by those most intimately connected with Mr. Roebuck, to place the story of his life before the public. Although the ranks of those who knew him are sadly thinned, and a generation has arisen to whom he is little more than a name, the lapse of time brings with it this compensation—that the events which engrossed Mr. Roebuck's activities can be seen in larger perspective, and the persons with whom he came in contact can be referred to with less of the reticence that would have been necessary during their lifetime.

My work has been that rather of an editor than of an author, because my chief aim has been to let Mr. Roebuck tell his own story, as far as possible, in his own words. There has, compulsorily, been some departure from this plan in dealing with his later years, but, as a rule, the connecting narrative and elucidatory explanations have been restricted within the briefest compass. I have had the invaluable co-operation of Miss Roebuck, who, besides undertaking much of the labour of transcribing, was good enough to entrust to me a large mass of letters and printed papers, including the fragment of autobiography which forms the opening chapters of the book. These, with Hansard's Debates and newspaper reports of speeches delivered out of Parliament, have formed the basis of the work. Mr. Roebuck wrote regularly to Mrs. Roebuck, but beyond that he was not a voluminous correspondent; and the reason why an appeal for his letters has not met with larger response, is probably because there are not many in existence.

My special thanks are due to Mr. Graham Wallas, and, through him, to the representatives of the late Mr. Francis Place, for giving me access to the systematically preserved papers of that "Radical tailor of Charing Cross," who, for many years, was the power behind the activities of the advanced Liberals. I am indebted to Messrs. A. and C. Black for placing at my disposal letters written by Mr. Roebuck to the late Mr. William Tait, of Edinburgh; to the executors of the late Alderman William Fisher, of Sheffield; to Mr. John Temple Leader, of Florence; and to other friendly helpers.

R. E. LEADER.

*May*, 1897.

# CONTENTS.

—◦◦◦—

## AUTOBIOGRAPHY.

## LIFE AND LETTERS.

# CONTENTS.

---

# ILLUSTRATIONS.

# AUTOBIOGRAPHY.

## CHAPTER I.

I FANCY that I have not long to live; therefore, if I can leave anything behind me in the shape of a life history, it must be written in haste, and certainly without any great regard to accuracy as to dates. The space of time to be gone over is large (nearly seventy years), the scenes, many of them, important, and the individuals to be spoken of occupying a great position, and influencing greatly the welfare of this country.

My purpose is to give a faithful, and perhaps an interesting, picture of a single life—of the life of a man born in the middle rank of society in England in the early days of the nineteenth century, and living to the latter end of that century; taking part in the most important transactions as regarded his country, yet perhaps having little influence upon them, in spite of his great zeal and (I believe I may say it) his perfect honesty of purpose.

Without further preface, I will begin the history of my life. A happy life! I have, indeed, to thank Providence for the many benefits with which I have been gifted. I have been happy as a son, as a husband, as a father; I have been happy in my public career : have I not, then, much for which to be thankful ?

I was born at Madras in the year 1802, December 28. My father was Ebenezer Roebuck, a younger son of Dr. John Roebuck, the founder of the Carron Iron Works, in Scotland, and well known in the scientific world.* My mother was Zipporah Tickell, the daughter of Richard Tickell,† also well known in the political and literary world of Fox and Sheridan.

My father's brother Benjamin was paymaster-general of the forces of the East India Company at Madras ‡ at the time of my parents' marriage, and my father took his young wife to India. She was then about twenty-one, having been married at sixteen. She left three children in England, all boys, in the care of her mother; bore three children in India, all boys; came home in 1807, leaving her husband in India. He then had the almost certain prospect of making a great fortune; but on the very day that his wife and children landed in England he died suddenly. Having unwarily made a journey through some deadly forests,§ travelling at night, he was found in the morning dead in his palanquin. My uncle Benjamin died shortly after. Thus my mother was left

---

* Dr. John Roebuck, the second of the five sons of John Roebuck, manufacturer, of Sheffield, was born in that town in 1718. For an interesting account of the manner in which, laying the foundations of great enterprises, he made the fortunes of other men, but lost his own, see Smiles's "Industrial Biography," p. 133. One of Dr. Roebuck's brothers was the first banker in Sheffield; two others were, among Sheffield merchants, the earliest to open correspondence with mercantile houses of the Continent. One of them built Meersbrook House, adapted in recent years to the purposes of the Ruskin Museum.

† A descendant of Addison's friend and under secretary, Thomas Tickell, poet and translator of the Iliad, 1686–1740.

‡ Chemistry was Benjamin Roebuck's hobby. The natives were inclined to look upon him as something of a wizard, through seeing him perform the simple experiment of making ice in front of a fire.

§ While engaged, for the East India Company, in endeavours to improve the navigation of the river Godavery.

with six children, and with very uncertain means. She had to educate them, put them forward in the world, without assistance from her late husband's family or her own. A truly difficult task, and a trying and dangerous position.

She was very beautiful, very clever, fascinating, and young. It is not wonderful that she was sought for by many, that she married soon. The husband she chose (Mr. Simpson) was, like herself, young and handsome, but of no position. In choosing his wife he was guided more by passion than by prudence. Whatever may have been his defects, I have every reason to respect him, and to be grateful to him for his uniform kindness to us, his stepsons, and to our mother, whom he ever treated with the utmost gentleness and loving courtesy. They were indeed a happy couple, as far as themselves were concerned. Fortune, however, did not befriend him. He was a merchant, and not successful; and after many schemes had been tried and failed, it was resolved that we should emigrate to Canada, which we did in the year 1815.

The first years of my life, and the time I passed in America, so deeply affected my whole character, and went so far in forming the man, that I am induced to dwell somewhat longer on those years, and to describe more minutely the incidents of that time than I otherwise should do.

My early life in England was, in its first years, the life of a child of polished society. My mother, in spite of her unwise marriage, retained her connection with her old friends, and much of my time was passed in the house of Mrs. Anne Boscawen, with whom my Aunt Eliza Tickell lived. Mrs. Boscawen's story was a romance. She, early in life, was engaged to my grandfather Tickell, and was by him jilted. But her love for him survived every disappointment; and when he died she took the children that others bore him, and loved them as her own. My mother was the first. She soon married. My Aunt Eliza succeeded, and remained with Mrs. Boscawen until that lady's death. Mrs. Boscawen had been maid of honour to Queen Charlotte, but left that office on her expected marriage with my grandfather. When this was broken off she became, I think, laundress to the Queen, an office not thought unfit for a peer's daughter.

I became a great favourite with my aunt, and saw, young as I was, much of the society that frequented Mrs. Boscawen's rooms in St. James's Palace. My memory chiefly dwells on the rejoicings of 1814, and the visit of the kings and emperor—all of whom I saw—and their suites. But of the men who visited at Mrs. Boscawen's, the only two I really recollect are Kean, and Charles Young, the actor. My aunt, Eliza Tickell, was a proprietor of Drury Lane, and was the first who brought Kean to the notice of the persons who then governed the theatre. She was on a visit in the south of Devon, and saw Kean act in a barn in the village. Her letter to the directors, or whatever they were called, induced them to send down a Doctor Somebody—I forget his name—to see and decide upon Kean. He saw Kean, and was so much struck with him that he recommended that he should be instantly brought to London. Kean came, and the town went mad. I only saw him once in private; I often saw him act. The occasion of my seeing him in private was upon my aunt asking me if I should like to see him; and upon my answering joyously, " Oh yes," she gave me a letter, which I took. I, to this day, recollect the impression made upon me by his eye. He was reading when I was ushered into the room. He spoke kindly to me. What he said I know not, but I was pleased, and the memory of him, as I then saw him, remains with me.

The other person whose name I have mentioned, Charles Young, the actor, I saw only once, when he came on a morning visit to my aunt. I was a shrewd, precocious child, very much of the *enfant terrible* style, and I saw, or fancied I saw, a sort of flirtation going on. The result of this notion of mine will be seen further on. The opinions of a child are worth nothing, but his feelings may be worth knowing. At this time, and during all the after years of my sojourn in England, I was wild about the theatre. Before I was ten years of age I knew Shakespeare by heart. I had seen John Kemble as "Coriolanus," "Brutus," "Hamlet." Young I saw as "Cassius" to Kemble's "Brutus," Charles Kemble playing " Antony." Young also I saw as " Pierre " in *Venice Preserved*. Then, to my extreme delight, I saw Kean as " Richard III.," "Hamlet," "Othello," "Iago." To my child's judgment, by far the best actor was Kean; his violence and rant seemed to me nature. The studied manner of Kemble did not please me, though, led by what I heard, I fancied that I admired him. Young's agreeable and regulated style went straight home to my heart, but Kean made me wild. We boys used to shout the verses, fight the battles we had seen and heard the night before.

Most unfortunately for me, the year after we returned to England I sprained my right knee by slipping on an oilcloth. This sprain I aggravated by skating; and in the severe winter of 1812 I was a well-known performer on the Serpentine. Being very small, and dressed in a scarlet jacket, I attracted attention. I was able to perform many feats. I was great in the spread eagle, and could make two figures of three on one leg; and the consequence was that a ring used to be made in which good skaters performed, one of whom I was. One day, alas! I was attracted by something at a distance. Going straight to my mark, I found in my way a heap of snow, and jumped over it; but the point of my right skate caught in the bottom of the trouser of the left leg, and I came down on my right knee, which immediately swelled. This lamed me for life, and my weak knee has influenced my fate in many ways. That winter (1812) the Thames was frozen over, and I skated from Westminster Bridge to Putney Bridge.

I have also skated on the St. Lawrence from Augusta, on the Canadian side of the river, to Ogdensburgh, on the American shore, the distance being five miles, and the river there a mile broad. This fact is remarkable, as ordinarily, though the river is always frozen over in the winter, that usually happens by successive frosts during which snow generally falls, and there is no possibility of skating; but on the occasion mentioned the frost was so severe as to make an ice bridge over the river in one night. The snow held off, and the river became passable, and skating possible. The wind was down the river, south-west, and I held my great-coat open. This served as a sail, and took me down rapidly; but I was unable to skate against the wind, and had to walk home by the road on the Canada side. As I went gliding over the ice I saw the weeds at the bottom of the river, and the fish swimming among them. This is, however, an anticipation of my American life.

My feeble health, for the most part, kept me at home. Excepting twice, I was never sent to a boarding school, and upon each occasion the success of the experiment was so small that there was no attempt made to renew it. My education, therefore, was confined to English reading. I read with my mother and grandmother, and thus acquired that love of reading which has been my solace through life. I do not recollect the time when I could not read, neither do I know how or when I acquired that power. My aunt first taught me to read with propriety and effect—the manner being far more considered than the matter. I remember my aunt taking me one morning to my mother, to show how prettily I could read Little's poems—a strange book for a child being taught by a young girl. I have

never read a line of Little since, but from what I have learnt
concerning him, I am sure that I understood him not at all ;
and such, I expect, was the case with my teacher.* My
grandmother taught me to read Shakespeare, but this
was some years after. She drilled me thoroughly, and was,
I believe, the cause of my great admiration for that marvellous poet. Under my mother I learned to *feel* what I
was reading. We read chiefly poetry, not dramatic ; but
with her I went through most of the great English
poets.

Under my mother's care I began also to write—that is,
to compose. For many years it was my habit to go into
her room before she was up, and to lay upon her dressing-
table a letter written upon any subject that suggested itself

* Years afterwards, however, Mr. Roebuck, without knowing it, met the
writer of "Little's" poems. This was Thomas Moore, who, in 1801, had
issued a volume of original verse under the assumed name of Thomas Little—
an allusion to his diminutive stature. "In these pieces," says "Chambers's
Encyclopædia of English Literature," "the warmth of the young poet's
feelings and imagination led him to trespass on delicacy and decorum. He
had the good sense to be ashamed of these amatory juvenilia, and genius
enough to redeem the fault." Thomas Hood plays on Moore's pseudonym in
"The Wee Man : "

> "Loud laugh'd the gogmagog, a laugh
> As loud as giant's roar—
> 'When first I came, my proper name
> Was Little—now I'm Moore.'"

Moore, in his diary ("Journals and Correspondence," vol. vii. p. 253), writes
under date February 24, 1839 : "Bessy and I started for (Sir William)
Napier's on our long-promised visit. Found Roebuck with him, whom I was
very glad to meet, and even more surprised than glad, as nothing could be
less like a firebrand than he is, his manner and look being particularly
gentle. Roebuck stayed but a short time, having to return to Bath by the
boat, which I was sorry for.

"*February* 27.—Young Falconer, brother-in-law of Roebuck, came, and
soon after Roebuck himself joined us. Conversation on various subjects—
America, mesmerism, etc., all very agreeable. Some allusion having been
made to my squibs, Roebuck said I had described him (which I had myself
forgot) dancing a fandango with Recorder Shaw [? Law]. On the subject of
mesmerism I found Roebuck to be much of the same opinion as myself—
that the next folly of swallowing all its marvels, is that of rejecting them
all. Was sorry when Roebuck and his brother-in-law left us."

to my fancy. When she first proposed this to me, I objected, saying I had nothing to say. Her answer was, " Never mind that; write anything, no matter what. Tell me what you have done during the day, what you have seen, what you have read. You may always find something —never mind how trivial. You will find, as time goes on, the task more easy, and by-and-by it will become a pleasure." So it did. During one part of these early days I thought of becoming a poet, and among my letters to her were many specimens of my poetical attempts. But I was taught no Latin, no Greek, and, strange to say, no French, though my mother spoke French fluently and well.

One strange scheme of Mr. Simpson's was to turn farmer, which he did in 1813, and went to Leicestershire, taking all of us and my mother with him. This plan naturally failed, but the time spent in the country showed me a new phase of life, though I was too young to understand all that I saw. I nevertheless perceived that we had come among what was to me a strange class of people, whom indeed I liked, for they were very kind to us children, and the fields were pleasanter than London.

Whilst in Gumley, Leicestershire, we had a visitor— a friend of my mother's—who, in after years, was the cause of a mighty effect upon my whole life. This was Thomas Love Peacock,[*] who excited my curiosity by his conversation. He was at the time studying Greek, was reading some Greek dramatist and a commentator, and excited the wonder of the farmers who came into the house by reading, as they said, two books at once. He used to sit on a chair on one side of the fire, at a sort of shelf, which drew out of the wall, which shelf held his

---

[*] Author of " Headlong Hall," " Crotchet Castle," etc. In succession to James Mill, he was Chief Examiner at the India Office, 1836–56. Died 1866.

books, and in the evening his light. Every day after breakfast he folded about a dozen paper boats, which he told me he was accustomed to sail or set afloat in any piece of water which he found in his walk—which walk he began as soon as his boats were made, and continued till our dinner, which was about five o'clock p.m. These long solitary walks, his paper boats, his books, and the fact that he was a poet, made him a sort of mysterious being to the country people, who certainly were somewhat afraid of him.

While I was at Gumley, I went to my second school— I forget where; but the master was a clergyman, and a coward. My brother Benjamin went with me. After we had been about a week at school, we were surprised by seeing Mr. Simpson enter the room in which we were. He told us he had come to take Benjamin home, as the master of the school had written to say that he could not undertake his tuition. To me he had no objection, so I was to be left where I was. Such a proceeding was necessarily calculated to have a most mischievous effect on Benjamin, who was taught thereby that he need obey no one, and that he might do as he liked.

The boys at the school were accustomed to athletic exercises, leaping being a very favourite game. I must take my part, and by so doing soon sprained my weak knee, and was sent to bed until the swelling subsided, which generally took a week. I asked for books, and chose among those offered to me, Glover's "Leonidas." * When I had finished this, I asked again, and the master

---

* The author of the article on Richard Glover in the "Dictionary of National Biography" did not reckon on the literary craving of young Roebuck on his sick-bed when he wrote: "Glover's ponderous 'Athenaid' . . . is much longer, and so far worse than 'Leonidas;' but no one has been able to read either for a century." For Roebuck, an epic poem in blank verse, in nine books (afterwards enlarged to twelve), had no terrors. Glover sat in Parliament for Weymouth, 1761-68. The "Athenaid" was a sequel to "Leonidas," which had been published in 1737.

brought some grave religious books, of which I could not read a page. I was sorely grieved and greatly disgusted; and therefore wrote home, pressing to be taken away, as I learned nothing, and was very miserable. The letter had the effect I wished; and thus ended the second attempt to teach me scholastically.

# CHAPTER II

THE next change in my life resulted from the determination to emigrate. Shipboard and the sea gave me much knowledge of life.

My mother's brother had been secretary to General Simcoe when he was Governor-General of Canada, and my uncle lost his life in an expedition to the great lakes. As he was crossing the Niagara River in a small boat, a short and severe *flurry* of snow came on. When this cleared away, the boat and its occupants had disappeared for ever. The English Government gave my mother five hundred acres of land in Upper Canada, near York (now Toronto), in requital of my uncle's services. This land led, I have no doubt, to the scheme of emigration.

The year we left England was 1815. The passage was in a barque named the *Dorothy*, one of three vessels ordered to the Clyde to ship emigrants to Canada. As the war was now renewed, I suppose this plan was adopted in 1814, upon the defeat of Napoleon and his imprisonment in Elba. When the war ceased in that year, doubtless means were taken to relieve the overburdened Empire. The population was too large for peaceable times. But the war was suddenly renewed, and no one could say when it would end. I imagine the plans of 1814 were not put aside, but carried on as if peace still continued. The news of the battle of Waterloo arrived while we were lying in the Clyde. The ships were dressed in flags, and there were great rejoicings. While still lying before Greenock, the whole of us made an excursion to a house, lately built by the Duke of Argyle, at Roseneath—a charming spot, which in the warm summer days seemed like fairyland.

We went on board in the Clyde, the vessel being the *Baltic Merchant,* which, proving uncomfortable, we left her, and went on board the more roomy and convenient *Dorothy.* I am surprised that I remember the names of these ships and the incidents of those times, things of far greater importance which have happened later having passed away from my memory. The captain of the *Dorothy* was a bluff, good-humoured sailor, of no education, and of low breeding. The calibre of the first mate may be judged by the information he gave us inquisitive boys. He told us the voyage to America would necessarily be a slow one because, from the shape of the earth, we were what he called " climming " uphill; whereas, returning from America, vessels ran downhill, and came faster home.

I was then, and have been all my life, a poor sailor. Sea-sickness never leaves me while I am aboard. After a voyage of eight weeks I have been as ill the last day as the first. I nevertheless employed myself during the voyage in reading and drawing, which have always been with me great means of solace and pleasure.

Our passengers, the emigrants, were chiefly Highlanders. One of the chiefs—his name was MacNab—came on board, and had a lachrymose leavetaking with his clanspeople. " They are all as good as mysel'," he said to us in tearful accents, and as an excuse for his tears, which were plentiful, and seemed sincere. The people, however, were a wild set, particularly the women. But many of their habits were to us most interesting. For hours I have seen four men seated on the deck, each one holding the corner of a shepherd's plaid, and swinging it to and fro, singing, in a low chanting tone, an interminable song in Gaelic, often during the time shedding tears. All the music seemed to me to be in a minor key; but of this I am not sure, as I know little—I may say nothing—of music. They often danced, the women as well as the men, all dancing well. They grew by the exercise very excited, when there often appeared a feeling of anger and hate against the English. Once, there being some trifling dispute with the captain, upon a complaint made by the passengers, an oldish woman, somewhat tipsy, called upon the men to right themselves by their *skenes,* which we were told signified knives. Upon another occasion, a wild-looking Highlander rushed upon deck. Running to the capstan, he dashed his hand upon the top of it, and threw down a cockroach, saying in broken English, " Are these the things ye have on board, and do ye treat us in this way?" The captain, as may be supposed, laughed loudly upon this, and dismissed him and his insect with some rude sailor's answer.

We boys soon took an interest in the working of the ship, and the mizzen-mast was given up to us. We merely worked the yards—that is, on deck—never being allowed to go aloft. I think I made a mistake in calling the vessel a barque, as she had a mizzen top-sail, which a barque has not.

I may mention here a matter which may be a warning to any future emigrant family. A woman-servant, who had lived with us in England many years, and who professed to be warmly attached to my mother, joined us in our plan of emigration, and went with us in the ship to Canada, being treated rather as one of the family than as a servant. When arrived at Quebec, she told my mother that she had promised to marry the captain of the ship, and was to return with him. She left us after eight or nine years of service, and we never heard of her afterwards. This led to engaging the two daughters of an emigrant named Fergusson, Margaret and Katharine.

The passage up the river St. Lawrence was trying to our patience, but agreeable, as the weather was fine, and the wind, though generally unfavourable, yet being south and west, the climate was pleasant. When we arrived at Quebec, the vessels were ordered up to Montreal, upon which we proceeded onwards, and the first day ran aground. The laden vessel could not be got off. Then a fine large steamer came and took us from the ship, baggage and all. When we got on board the steamer we found, among the passengers, Sir Sydney Beckwith. We boys were all clad in barragon,* dressed as we supposed was fitting for a wild country. My mother and Mr. Simpson were dressed as gentlefolks ought to be. Sir Sydney was attracted by my mother, and the large family of boys, and soon entered into conversation. Learning that our name was Roebuck, he made some inquiry which led to his being informed as to who we were. "Good God!" he exclaimed. "What, nephews of Benjamin Roebuck of Madras?" He then put his hand before his eyes and bent towards the table. When he raised his head, which he did directly, there was a glitter in his eyes very like tears. "When I knew their uncle," he said, "he was living in a state of princely magnificence." The contrast evidently shocked him, but he said nothing more. However, the result was, that we were kindly treated by the Government, and every facility afforded us to get up the country.

Mr. Simpson, before leaving Montreal, bought an estate at Augusta, midway on the banks of the St. Lawrence, between Prescott and Brockville, about sixty miles below Kingston, and below the Thousand Islands, the river being, as I believe, nearly a mile broad. The estate had upon it a good stone house, about eighty yards from the river, with convenient outhouses, barns, and a capital orchard

---

* A name in use in Hampshire and Cornwall for fustian. The Lancashire form is "barragan;" in commerce it is "barracan," a strong, thick kind of camlet.—"English Dialect Dictionary."

and garden. I was too young to know anything about the purchase, but I now can see it was a rash act to buy it, and to launch into the expenses which followed. But Mr. Simpson was a daring, sanguine man, and indulged in schemes that would have terrified a sober-minded one. These schemes, and their ultimate failure, I need not describe; the only visible effect of them being, as far as I was concerned, my return to England, and the change that followed in my whole plan of life.

We started on our journey to Upper Canada from the village of Lachine, which is situated on the end of the island of Montreal highest up the river. The Government supplied us with two Canadian bateaux, with five men in each, four oarsmen and a pilot, or steersman. Our baggage and ourselves filled these boats. This, at that time, was the chief mode of conveyance of merchandise and passengers. The Americans navigated the river in a different manner. The American Durham boat was much larger than the Canadian bateau, and had one large fore and aft sail, and was propelled by poles, the men putting the pole to the shoulder and stooping and crawling along a narrow passage on the gunwale, with transverse pieces of wood across it, against which they placed their feet and hands.

In this manner they forced the vessel up the rapids, and against a head wind. The Canadian bateau had a temporary mast and a square sail, which was used when the wind was fair; when it was foul, oars were used where the river was without rapids. At the rapids the boat was forced by poles used in a different manner from that of the American. Sometimes the boat was tracked by a rope, two men remaining on board, one astern, one in the bow, both using poles.

This mode of journeying was necessarily very slow, and we were therefore many days getting to our journey's end. At night we generally had to put up at some house on the bank of the river, being usually very hospitably received, paying, however, for our accommodation. One night—fine, luckily—we were on Lake St. François, and, finding no house, had to rest for the night under an awning in the boat. All this, which was our first experience of our new life, was to us boys a scene of perfect enchantment. The weather was fine; the great river on which we floated, and what to us appeared its wild shores, gave us never-ending delight. Everything was new, and, as far as we could see, all was beautiful. Young as we were, the future did not much trouble us; nor were we yet touched with longing for home, which inevitably wrings the heart of every emigrant. But with minds prepared for adventure, we seemed to ourselves enacting the life of Robinson Crusoe, and nothing prosaic in any way dimmed the brilliant scene before us.

We found the house upon our farm comfortable and roomy, built of stone, and capable of being rendered an agreeable and pleasant residence. That season called the " Indian summer " quickly followed our arrival, and this is perhaps the most beautiful and pleasant part of the whole Canadian year; and we were at first very favourably impressed by the climate.

I remained for the next four years at Augusta, taking my share in all the farm labours. But what I have now to do is to explain the effect that this new life had upon my mind and character.

I may here describe my family, and relate shortly the history of all of them.

The eldest of the emigrant family was my mother's mother. She died at Augusta, and is buried in the grave-yard attached to the Church of England church that is situate about two miles down the river from our house on the road to Prescott. It stands on a pine-barren of about a mile broad, the land being left untilled and the pine trees left standing. It is a wild spot which I have often passed. The perfume of the pines in that wood still lives freshly in my memory. This old lady was to the day of her death of wondrous beauty. I looked on her face a few hours after her death, and then saw the truth of those lines of Byron—

> He who hath bent him o'er the dead,
> Ere the first day of death is fled.

To my startled gaze a flush was upon her cheek; age, and all trace of age, seemed to have vanished, the beauty of youth to have returned, and she whom I had always known as an ancient woman, appeared almost a girl. I did not look again. It would have been a bitter pain to have that fair vision succeeded by the look of age and death—for I loved her dearly.

Of my mother I have already spoken. She died at Coteau-du-Lac, February 9, 1842.

The next is Mr. Simpson, who long survived my mother, and married an American lady. He died at Brookville.

My eldest brother was Richard, who had been sent to sea in his Majesty's service under Sir George Cockburn, who was an old East Indian friend of my mother's. Richard left the navy at the peace of 1814. He was ten and a half years old when he left home; he was, consequently, very illiterate. The care that is now taken of the youngsters in our service was then unknown. When he returned, however, he soon felt his own deficiencies, and became an indefatigable reader, thereby acquiring a good deal of knowledge; but he could never regain the lost time.

William, the second brother, went to Woolwich to study, so as to become either an engineer or of the artillery. He left the Academy in 1818, and joined the emigrant party. He married an American lady, and died, leaving a family, one of whom, the second daughter, I have seen. She is married, and happily settled.

George, the third brother, had not left school when the time for our departure came. He joined us, and, upon the break-up at Augusta, went to the West Indies, to Antigua, where he shortly afterwards died.

Benjamin came next—a bold, daring, harum-scarum boy, who could learn anything he chose, if only he applied his mind to the subject. He also left Canada at the same break-up; through the interest of our family obtained a commission in the East India Company's cavalry, returned to his birthplace, Madras, and died soon after at Seringapatam.

I was the next.

Then came Henry, who remained in Canada, and married. He died, leaving a widow, two sons, and a daughter.

What I desire to do as regards the history of my life in Canada, is to explain the influence upon my character and fortunes of that period of my career. That the state of things in that country had an extraordinary effect upon me, I well know; but I feel it difficult to explain this. A knowledge of the country, of its state and condition, is requisite to the understanding of the sort of influence exercised upon a boy of my antecedents and nature, and even that will hardly give a clue to the effect upon my mind of the circumstances by which I was surrounded. When I went to Canada I was very young, and very ignorant, necessarily, of the world and its ways. I was, besides, in my hidden nature, very romantic, and living most of my time in dreamland.

Never was anything so opposed to this way of thought and feeling as the society made up of my family. The strong, healthy young men and lads, who held in scorn every manifestation of sentiment, who laughed at emotion, constituted but a chilling and depressing atmosphere to anything approaching high feeling and exalted thought. They were, though boys, a set of cynical philosophers. The tone of the conversation was more that of disabused men of the world than a set of boys fresh from school.

From what I then saw, from that example, I am led to believe that English schoolboy life has this tendency—that the general tone of thought and feeling created by an English boy's school damps imagination, chills all ardent aspirations, makes of children cold-blooded beings, who ridicule and contemn all expressions of great and generous maxims. And yet I believe that this mode of conversation was not an expression of the actual state of mind of those employing it, but that a dread of ridicule was the cause of all this cynical bearing.

I was in the habit of constantly writing verse and prose, and I recollect well the dread that I felt lest my brothers should find these effusions, and bring them forward to be laughed at, and myself held up to ridicule. Yet, in spite of the felt and acknowledged difference between myself and my brothers, as years went on, my influence over them and the affairs of the family daily grew, and I was allowed, without much interference, to pursue my own course as it pleased me. My devotion to study met with a tacit approval, the more especially as it never took me away from daily work, which I performed as faithfully as any one of the others, and of which I took my share without shrinking. All my brothers grew to powerful men. I, on the contrary, was from the beginning small, frail, and, before I went to Canada, an invalid. My health there grew assured, but I never became strong. My knee always interfered with any great exertion, and, though I was agile and strong for my size, I could not have held my own with these sons of Anak had not my intellect helped. That came effectually to my aid, and before I left Canada I ruled the family.

----

[Writing, in 1870, to a friend who had lost a brother, Mr. Roebuck said—

I, too, have lost, or am about to lose, my only remaining brother—the loved companion of my infancy and youth, and whose death takes away from me the last member of that once glad party which was made up of six brothers. I, the sickly one, the one never expected to reach manhood, am now left alone, the last and miserable survivor of this once happy band.

Exhorting the working-men of Sheffield to self-culture, in an address given to the Mechanics' Institute of that town (February 1, 1860), Mr. Roebuck sketched, under a transparent veil of anonymity, the mode of life in his Canadian home.

I recollect in my early life meeting a man who had become an emigrant. He was one of a family born to wealth, reared in luxury, and in this country accustomed to all the appliances which luxury can give. He emigrated with his family to America. He was compelled to apply himself to the mere ordinary occupations of gaining a livelihood as a farmer. Now, what did that family do? They were composed of ladies and gentlemen of England. The mother of that family was a woman of great acquirements and ability. I recollect her perfectly well. I had every reason to know her well. She instituted a code in that family that I would recommend to every working man of my country. It was that there should be as much courtesy, good breeding, and every means that could promote the happiness of that family, though now reduced to the position of mere working men, as existed in it when they were of the gentry of England. I recollect that young man telling me that his mother never came into the room but every one of the children rose to salute her. They took out their library from England to America. They passed their time in the day in the ordinary occupation of working-men; the evening they dedicated to intellectual enjoyment. Now, I want to know why the working-men of England cannot do that?]

---

I now desire to give a description of the country and its society, so far as that state of things influenced my mind and our fortunes. This description will be the result of my subsequent experience, reflecting my state of mind when I finally quitted Canada.

The wild country, its great rivers, the vast scale upon

which everything was framed, made on me a profound impression. The freedom in which we lived, the thorough liberty of going where we liked, the new scenes, brought with them a sort of enchantment. All efforts would fail were I to endeavour to describe them.

The great river St. Lawrence lay before us, and was a never-failing source of adventure and delight. We built boats, rigged and sailed them unchecked, save by the nature of things. The primeval forest lay behind us, and in this we hunted and shot, undisturbed by game laws, or even by the will of neighbouring proprietors.

William and myself were given to drawing. William, having a genius for that art, became a very pretty artist. Thus our time was spent in downright hard labour on the farm, and at the same time we retained many of the habits and manners of civilized life.

We had a large and well-selected library of the English classics, which I read completely through, and what I read at that time left an indelible impression upon my memory, and gave whatever of mental power I have possessed in life.

Society, we had little or none. The neighbours were chiefly farmers with some second calling, such as store-keepers of different kinds. What we ought to have done was to have made friends with all these good people, and to have lived on neighbourly terms with them, asserting no airs of superiority, and if we possessed any knowledge or power which might have been useful, to have freely imparted it, and received from them much good advice in return, which their experience enabled them to give. We did none of these things.

The population of the district mostly consisted of the descendants of those Americans who adhered to the side of the mother-country in the War of Independence. These people emigrated to Canada as being still an English possession, and were known as U.E.'s (United Englishmen).

They were in their habits and manners American, it being impossible to find any difference between them and the Americans on the other side of the river. On the Canadian side, however, there came constantly emigrants, chiefly from Ireland, who, though nominally British subjects, hated England and everything English. The natives were not very favourable to the English dominion, and the consequence was, there were constant feuds springing up between us and the people about us. We were extremely English, and not at all backward in giving expression to our opinions.

The life in that wild country had a marked effect upon my character. I never forgot England, and from the first, as a mere child, determined to return home and try my fortunes in the land of my fathers. The effect of the new life, the wild forests, the broad rivers, the roaming and almost wandering habits that were then contracted,—all worked upon my imagination, and made me bold and daring.

No one without experience can appreciate the effect of a life in the forests and wild country of America upon the mind, the character, and the emotions. I, now old (seventy-five years), still feel emotions that result from the days of my boyhood passed in the rapturous freedom of the primeval forest, and on the bosom of the broad rivers of America. Even now when spring comes I sigh involuntarily for the enchanting pleasures enjoyed when winter broke, and joyous spring came with a bound, and loosened all the chains with which frost had bound us. The rivers were again open, and I rushed with wild delight in my canoe over the broad waters of the St. Lawrence. Day and night we fished and followed the wild fowl in the bays of the river, and the many streams that flowed into that magnificent world of waters. The sudden change from the dreary cold days of the winter to the genial warmth of summer was almost miraculous.

At once, and completely, the whole face of nature was changed; the flowers started up in the forest, the birds suddenly appeared, and all nature was alive. The trees in a few days were covered with leaves. The most startling incident, however, was the wonderful change in the great river. To-day and to-night the broad surface was one white sheet, over which horses and sleighs passed as upon the ground. Suddenly the wind came from the south; a deluge of warm rain poured down; a sound as if great guns were being let off was heard; and through the night, commotion, turmoil, and a fierce storm of wind and rain. The morning broke in bright sunshine, and there, where was a desolate white plain, was now sparkling water; the ice was gone, and navigation was free. The summer was come; all the work of agriculture was suddenly resumed. The change was like a stage transformation.

One of my great pleasures was to seat myself under a fence with a book, and dream away hour after hour; and now here in England, fifty years and more having passed over my head, and busy and active life passed away, when the cold spring returns my heart craves for the pleasure of those young days and gay hopes, bright sunshine, and dreamy musing.

These were years of continuous steady study. I read and pored over the English classics day and night. I taught myself French, also a good deal of Latin.*

[Addressing the boys of the Sheffield Collegiate School on June 22, 1861, Mr. Roebuck said—

If I had followed steadily and carefully the business of my own education, instead of pursuing it with the sort of enthusiasm —the madness with which I did, I should not now be what I am, an old man and yet a young one. I recollect perfectly well that I had a window looking upon the expanse of the St Lawrence, and when night came—my studies were usually pursued in winter

* Italian was added some years after.

—from my window I could see the great stars of heaven ; and I recollect to this hour the pleasure I enjoyed in believing and knowing that every other soul was in bed. There is a pleasure to the studious man in the small hours of the morning. He wants to do all that he possibly can to obtain the quiet that is then about him. My good mother used to come up into my room and say, "No, sir, you must go to bed; this will never do." If your mothers will do so to you, they will do you a benefit.]

One thing never left my mind. In thought I constantly reverted to the memory of my ancestors. They had been distinguished in science and literature, and it always seemed to me possible that I might distinguish myself in England. I therefore formed the resolution of returning *home*, and determined to try my fortune at the Bar. How to do this was always in my thoughts, and at last, when I was about twenty or twenty-one, I started for London with £50 in my pocket. That I was allowed to do this seems to me now a wonder, and something worse. That I was not shipwrecked, and cast upon the world without hope, is now to me a marvel. I was indeed supported for some short time by uncertain remittances from Canada, but they failed utterly, and I was thrown upon my own unaided resources.

# CHAPTER III.

In the year 1824 I returned to England from Canada. Among the friends of my mother's was the well-known scholar Thomas L. Peacock,* to whom I took a letter of introduction, and whom I found at the India House acting as what I believe is called a Political Examiner. After a short conversation, he said, " I think I can introduce you to a young friend of mine in this house who belongs to a *disquisition* set of young men "—I remember the word was new to me—"and you may find his acquaintance agreeable and useful." I at once expressed my willingness, and he then took me to the room of John Mill, and after a few words of introduction left us together. Mill and I immediately entered into conversation, in which I laid myself entirely open, having, as I thought, nothing to conceal. Mill, I afterwards found, was cautious, and approached his own peculiar views with great precaution. Among other things, he told me that he was one of a society called the Utilitarian Society, which met about once a week, at the house of Mr. Bentham, for the purpose of discussion. He told me that each member in turn read a paper, upon which a debate followed.

Of the name of Bentham I was utterly ignorant. Of his tenets and philosophy I knew nothing. In fact, I was perfectly ignorant of the political, social, and philosophic

* See *ante*, p. 8.

condition of England and the world.  I had read much,
but without a guide, without a purpose, except the general
one of instructing myself, and I came into this, to me, new
world, without knowing at all what I did by joining this
body of young men.

Mill put into my hands a small octavo manuscript, which
was a description of the principles of the Utilitarian Society,
and its rules.  He offered to introduce me, and if, upon
consideration, I acquiesced, he would propose me as a
member.*

I little knew what an important influence that conversation would have upon my future life.  My reading,
as I have already said, was, for my age, extensive.  Besides
the advantage of my access to the well-selected library
of my mother's husband, I was also free of the public
library of Quebec, which had been founded under the
advice of Priestley.  The consequence was that I was
familiar with the greater part of English literature, had
read all our poets, and many of our philosophers.

I remember well bringing home to Beaufort, where we
then lived, from Quebec a volume of the quarto edition
of Locke, and sitting up late into the night reading it,
when I was disturbed by my mother, and desired to go
to bed.  She looked to see what I was reading, and found
it to be the "Essay on the Human Understanding."  She
turned over the leaves, and asked what possible good there
was in that sort of matter.  I had then, as I should have
now, much difficulty in finding an answer.†

To return to my interview with Mill.  After some

---

* For J. S. Mill's account of the Utilitarian Society see his "Autobiography," p. 79.

† Note by J. A. R.—I put pretty nearly the same question to Grote the last
time I ever conversed with him.  We were dining with the Chancellor of the
Exchequer (Disraeli) on the Queen's birthday.  We were speaking of the
work that Grote was then about, viz. Aristotle, when I asked him if he
thought any real good resulted from that sort of inquiry, and he, as I, was
much puzzled for an answer.

further talk, he asked me if I should like to see the museum, and took me there. In going through it, I was struck with his knowledge—its variety, and, as far as I could judge, its extent. At that time I had not seen his father's "History of India," and though born in India, and connected with it through members of my family, I knew very little about its condition and history. Mill appeared familiar with every subject that the contents of the museum suggested, and explained everything that we came across. I left greatly struck with the remarkable person I had met.

My first visit to the Utilitarian Society I shall never forget. It met in a low, half-furnished, desolate sort of room—I believe the dining-room of the house, not Mr. Bentham's dining-room. The place was lighted by a few tallow candles. A desk was drawn across the end of the room, at which desk sat the chairman, and some half-dozen young men sat in chairs round the room, and formed the society. The essay was a critique for some review of an edition of a Greek author. It was written and read by a young man named Harfield, and appeared to give general satisfaction. Mill told me it was a sort of trial piece, and was intended to test the capacity of Harfield to be the editor of some review.

On that evening I met for the first time the friend of my life, George J. Graham. He walked with me towards my then home, which was in Islington. He lived in Gray's Inn. We were accompanied part of the way by a young man named Place.* We stopped at the door of

* Francis Place, the once well-known Radical politician of Charing Cross. He was a sort of right-hand man to Bentham and to James Mill, and the moving power behind the "Philosophical Radicals." Place, having been born in 1771, was Roebuck's senior by thirty-one years. For an account of him see the article in the "Dictionary of National Biography," by Mr. Graham Wallas, who is also now writing his life. There are some interesting references to Place in Holyoake's "Sixty Years of an Agitator's Life," vol. i. p. 215.

a house in Charing Cross, and I well remember the shock which my pride received when, looking up, I saw the name, " Place, Tailor," over the door!  This was my first experience in democracy.

I eventually became a member of the society, and being greatly struck with the works of Bentham * and James Mill, I, in fact, became also a pupil of John Mill, who, although younger than myself, was far in advance of me in philosophy and politics.

From this time our intimacy increased day by day, and was strengthened by the fact that Graham and myself became sworn friends—brothers, in fact—and with John Mill formed a triumvirate which we laughingly called the " Trijackia," all of us being named John.

I found that Mill, although possessed of much learning, and thoroughly acquainted with the state of the political world, was, as might have been expected, the mere exponent of other men's ideas, those men being his father and Bentham ; and that he was utterly ignorant of what is called society ; that of the world, as it worked around him, he knew nothing ; and, above all, of *woman*, he was as a child.  He had never played with boys ; in his life he had never known any, and we, in fact, who were now his associates, were the first companions he had ever mixed with.  His father took occasion to remark to myself especially, that he had no great liking for his son's new

---

* It is to be regretted that Mr. Roebuck does not tell us more of his association with Bentham.  He became something of a favourite with the old philosopher, who foresaw the mark his young friend would one day make in the world.  The short notes from Roebuck to Bentham, preserved among the Bentham manuscripts at the British Museum, relate only to such matters as invitations to dinner ; but they always contain assurances of the " very great respect " with which the young disciple signs his acceptances to dinner " at the usual hour."  There is a playfully affectionate reference to Roebuck in Browning's " Life of Bentham," vol. xi. p. 81: "I have been catching fish,'' Bentham said one day.  "I have caught a carp.  I shall hang him up, feed him with bread and milk.  He shall be my tame puss, and shall play about on the floor.  But I have a new tame puss.  I will make Roebuck my puss for his article on Canada, and many a mouse shall he catch."

friends. I, on the other hand, let him know that I had no fear of him who was looked upon as a sort of Jupiter Tonans. James Mill looked down on us because we were poor, and not greatly allied, for while in words he was a-severe democrat, in fact and in conduct he bowed down to wealth and position. To the young men of wealth and position who came to see him he was gracious and instructive, while to us he was rude and curt, gave us no advice, but seemed pleased to hurt and offend us. This led to remonstrance and complaint on the part of John Mill, but the result was that we soon ceased to see John Mill at his home. Our chief point of *reunion* was the house of George Grote, Mrs. Grote being the means of bringing us together. She was kind and courteous, and was always ready by kind words and winning, pleasant manner, to render her house an agreeable and really instructive centre of meeting.*

---

[At times interruption to work came in the shape of severe attacks of illness, brought on by a chill in 1825, the effects of which did not pass away for many years, as neuralgia settled in the knee already weakened by injury in childhood, and though Roebuck was active and a swift walker, the long expeditions into the country, taken at this period with J. S. Mill† and others, did not tend to mend matters. One day's walk, especially, of forty miles caused weeks, if not months, of suffering.

On the outbreak of the French Revolution of 1830, after the news of the "three days of July," Roebuck, Mill, G. J. Graham, and others hastened to Paris, filled with enthusiasm and hope for France. Mr. Roebuck, years afterwards,

---

* Mill's account is that the gatherings at Grote's were not meetings of the Utilitarian Society, though consisting largely of the same group (see his "Autobiography," p. 119).

† On these country excursions J. S. Mill would fill his pockets with sweet violet seed, and scatter it in the hedges as he went along.

described how this company of young Englishmen, thinking only of great and wide measures of constitutional government, were taken aback, and not a little disappointed at the state of mind of the French Liberal leaders. One man they found completely occupied with the arrangement of the uniform of the National Guard, especially of what shape the new cockade should be ; others changing the names of the streets, and most of them intriguing for place.

On the occasion of Louis Philippe's first visit to the opera, these young Englishmen happened to be present, and they presently began to shout for " La Marseillaise," in which the house joined ; and then they shouted " Debout, debout ! " until the whole audience, including the king himself, actually stood up during the playing of the revolutionary tune.]

Thus time went on, great events in the world occurred, and our reform opinions seemed about to be tested in earnest. The French Revolution of July occurred. The English Reform Bill followed, and we all three * rushed into the torrent, and were as mad and ardent as youth, energy, and sincere belief in our opinions could make us.

The Reform Bill having become law, and I, having been very active in the many proceedings which attended the passing of that measure, became known to many public men, and, among others, to Joseph Hume, who at that time was a man of great mark and power. Many of the new constituencies created by the Reform Bill had great confidence in him ; among others, the City of Bath showed that confidence by asking him to select for them a man whom they might send as their representative to Parliament. He sent them down three names, of which mine was one, and, I know not for what reason, the choice of the Liberal majority fell upon me. Before this,

* Roebuck, Mill, and Graham.

Hume went down to Bath and introduced me to the constituency.

I had for many years been training myself for a politician, and especially did I study public speaking. I acquired great facility, and striking and incisive powers of speech. I also formed for myself a political scheme, so that I came before the public armed at all points, a trained politician. This procured for me success; and eight years after I had set foot in England, unknown in life's difficult journey, I became, by my own efforts, a Member of the British Parliament.

---

[It will be observed that Mr. Roebuck says he does not know for what reason the choice of the Liberals of Bath fell upon him. Miss Roebuck shows how it came to pass that he enlisted the sympathies of at least one partisan. She writes—

My mother used to tell how one morning, on entering the breakfast-room, her brother, Thomas Falconer, called out, " Here, Henrietta, look at these letters ; they are from candidates for Bath." She took up the letters, looked at each, then, holding out one, said, " This is the one to choose ; the letter is well written, and in the hand of a gentleman." It was signed, " J. A. Roebuck." The day after my father and Mr. Hume arrived in Bath. They were brought in procession, with band playing and flags flying, to my grandfather's [the Rev. Thomas Falconer's] house in the Circus.*

On the way up the hill at the back of the Circus, my father saw a young lady standing with other persons, looking over the garden wall at the crowd. Some one at my father's elbow said, " That is Miss Falconer."

By the time the procession reached No. 29, the lady was in the drawing-room, and there my father and mother first met.

* " We arrived," Mr. Roebuck wrote, " on August 20, and went to the White Hart, where a crowd quickly collected under the windows, shouting. Hume, who was having a cup of tea, said, ' I don't know what to say to these people, Roebuck; just put your head out of window and say something to them,' which I did; and this was my first appearance before the people of Bath."

Thus Mr. Roebuck found at Bath not only a seat in Parliament, but also a wife, who was his loving helper and loyal champion through all the strain and stress of his long and combative life.*

Mr. Mill † gives us a glimpse of the sedulous manner in which Mr. Roebuck cultivated striking and incisive powers of speech. He says—

There was for some time in existence a society of Owenites, called the Co-operative Society, which met for weekly public discussions in Chancery Lane. In the early part of 1825, accident brought Roebuck in contact with several of its members, and led to his attending one or two of the meetings, and taking part in the debate in opposition to Owenism. Some one of us started the notion of going there in a body, and having a general battle ; and Charles Austin and some of his friends, who did not usually take part in our joint exercises, entered into the project.

It was carried out, and many animated discussions with the Owenites followed. This led to Mill and his friends forming a debating society, which held its meetings at Freemason's Tavern. Roebuck was one of the most steadfast members.

Mr. Roebuck was in the habit, at a later period, of referring to the care with which he trained himself for his parliamentary career. At Sheffield, in acknowledging the presentation of 1100 guineas, made to him on September 3, 1856, "in recognition of his great national services, and in memorial of his work as a Liberal, patriotic, and distinguished statesman," he said—

I ask myself what it is that has given me the present occasion of returning you my thanks. It is not talent, it is not name, it is not rank, it is not wealth. What is it, then ? It is steadfastness in that course which I marked out for myself in the beginning. I am proud to say that in the year 1832 I published

* He was married to Miss Falconer on January 14, 1834, at Walcot Church, Bath.
† "Autobiography," p. 123.

a programme of the opinions I then held. I had prepared myself for a public life. I had then formed my opinions. I consigned them to paper. I printed them, and to them I now adhere. That which I said in 1832 I say now ; and it is my thorough and steadfast adherence to the opinions which I then expressed that has won for me the approbation of my countrymen. . . . Going into Parliament, unknown, unsupported, only recommended by that tried friend of the people, Joseph Hume, I determined not to ally myself with either of the great parties that then divided the House of Commons and the kingdom. I was neither Whig nor Tory, and I went into the House of Commons determined to advocate that which I believed to be for the interests of the people, without regard to party considerations. To that rule I have adhered through life.

The following letter is quoted to illustrate Mr. Roebuck's habit of seizing every opportunity of studying political questions, not only in their theoretical, but in their practical bearing. It also throws an interesting light on what would now be called the "Gerrymandering" perpetrated under the Reform Act, as well as the sordid views taken in small southern constituencies of the enlargement of the franchise.

### J. A. Roebuck to Francis Place.

*Mudeford, near Christchurch, Hants, May 2, 1832.*—My DEAR FATHER PLACE, Here I am, poor devil ! in the most doleful banishment. I might almost as well be in New South Wales—at the New Colony that is to be—as here, as to everything respecting politics. I see no papers but the *Examiner*, and my people, poor wretches ! know nothing. However, for my health's sake this am I condemned to, which said health is but a very little, if any, better. The weather has been wretchedly cold, and my pains as great as ever. So I deem myself in Castle Dolorous.

I am living within a stone's throw of Sir George Rose's nomination borough of Christchurch, and if the Bill works no better elsewhere than here, we are making a mighty pother about nothing. The sapient Sir John Romilly was here as

D

Commissioner (I understand) with Colonel Annersley, a high Tory, and from all that I can learn, the Whig Commissioner could not understand the interests of the various parties here. As might be expected, the inhabitants do not wish to be disfranchised, or even to lose one member, and, consequently, Liberals even strove hard to raise the numbers of the inhabitants. The Tory Commissioner took advantage of this, and made the mayor *amend* his report of the numbers of the £10 householders, which he did to the satisfaction of the Tory ; that is, he preserved one of the members by increasing the number of inhabitants a hundred beyond his first report. This was done by much squeezing, including places that ought not to have been included. I vehemently suspect that if the householders of Christchurch alone were numbered, it would prove a very pitiful show. It was Romilly's duty to have made this out, as everything ought to have been done to prove the real disproportion existing between the town and country representation. It is not that I object to including these out places *hereafter*, and increasing to the utmost the constituency ; but I do object to including them now, because every means ought to be taken to lessen the number of boroughs, and the only way to do this was to prove as many as possible utterly insignificant and contemptible as to numbers of inhabitants. Well, now, suppose the borough reformed : the inhabitants are all stout reformers. Why ? Because they hate Sir George Rose. He has tyrannized over them, and they would be freed from his yoke. But they by no means desire to be represented in the hopes of being well governed. What they desire is to be well paid by the candidates, and for this reason they dislike the ballot. Their short-sightedness is wonderful ; they hope to pass from the hands of Sir George Rose into those of Sir George Tapps, who is the greatest landholder here. And so they will. They have so managed the matter that the borough is now made to include his lands and his tenants. Sir George Tapps is a reformer too, after this fashion. He speaks to them fair, promises to lay out money on the harbour, to protect the inhabitants, to get laws passed for them, etc., and the fools believe him. They say he is a good man, not a harsh man like Sir George Rose. And then he will not have the power. No ; nor had Sir George Rose the power when first he came here. (If you see John Mill, ask him to show you my letter to him.

I have there explained how Sir George Rose's power was acquired.) Now, for the chance of a bribe these foolish people are endeavouring to play a game of balance. In doing so, they will trust Whig professions, and again be cheated. One thing I see works strongly with the *bourgeoisie* here. They hate and fear the poor. They have hitherto played the tyrant over the poor in their damned select vestry. They have dinners, etc., all after the old fashion of the select, and are just as great rascals in their way as the aristocracy in theirs. Looking at reform, then, here in the most favourable point of view, it appears a victory of the bourgeoisie over the aristocrats. In my opinion it will be, even to them, a temporary benefit—to the people none at all. I have not yet been able to move about, so that I am in ignorance of the condition of the poor here. The moment I get better I shall hunt them out.]

## CHAPTER IV.

### JOHN STUART MILL.

I HAVE often bethought me whether it was possible to draw the character of Mill intellectually and morally. The difficulties of the task I fully appreciate, but my intimate knowledge and converse with him was just at the most important epoch of his life; and an account of my connection with him may possibly contribute to a true appreciation of the man.

John Mill was the result of a most strict and extraordinary training. He was armed at all points. At that time the mere creation of his father's teaching, with nothing original, yet being endowed with great intellectual power, he was a wonderful product of factitious training. From his childhood to his manhood he received the ideas of other men, and gave them expression in language that was but an echo of those who taught him. Under this guidance, severe and harsh, he acquired a vast quantity of knowledge. He became early acquainted with classic literature, all which he received rather as a knowledge-acquiring machine than as a human being in whom there were emotions. In his childhood and youth he had no playfellows. He walked and talked with his father as if he had been a man receiving all by his head, his heart not being concerned in the matter. When at length nature asserted her rights, he found himself upon a wild, wide turbulent ocean, without a chart, almost without a compass.

But during all this time he never doubted as to his own infallibility. Whatever he thought at the time was right ; but whatever might be the change in him, he was never wrong. A very comfortable condition of things, but not as satisfactory to others as himself. Practical life was to him wholly unknown. He could talk wisely about Man in the abstract ; but of Man, including therein Woman, he knew absolutely nothing.

When Mill began to think for himself, he was anxious to show that his mind was no longer under the dominion of his father, or of Bentham. He therefore placed himself before the world as an independent critic, and took every occasion that offered to enter into disquisition upon the views of Bentham, and consequently of his father, who always agreed with Bentham, and was deemed his chief disciple and exponent.

But John Mill took especial care to confine his criticism to Bentham, and always avoided calling in question the views of his father. This led him, in my mind, to much wavering and uncertainty ; and he wanted one main quality for an original thinker, and that was *courage*.

Among other things, in order to show his severance from his old ideas and mode of thought, he now professed to be greatly swayed by the influence of Poetry.

It is one of the common mistakes respecting the doctrine of *Utility*, and the ideas and feelings of so-called Utilitarians, that they despise and neglect all that softens manners and charms the imagination, and thus they are supposed to contemn Poetry, to take no pleasure in the arts, and, in fact, to be the future of the Puritans of old.

Now, to all this misconception I can give a complete answer in my own case. From childhood upwards I have been passionately fond of and influenced by Poetry. I read the greater portion of our poets to my mother when a boy, and during my life have passed many hours in drawing from nature, and was, I may say, no mean amateur artist.

Mill knew this common misconception, and he took to reading and criticising poetry. But in reality he never had poetic emotions, and the lessons of his early childhood and youth had chilled his heart and deadened his spirit to all the magnificent influences of poetry. In his late biography he has endeavoured to make it appear that our difference arose from our different appreciation of the comparative merits of Byron and Wordsworth. But this was an idle statement ; something far more potent was required to break up so old and warm a friendship.

For, indeed, another new influence came suddenly upon Mill, viz. that of *Woman.* Hitherto he had known only his mother and sisters, and had but a poor and contemptuous opinion of the sex.

As we—that is, Mill, Graham, and I—were always together, and formed a united body, we were generally together in society.

It happened that we all three were invited to dine in the City at the house of a gentleman named Taylor, who was what is called a drysalter, a very respectable and well-to-do man. I do not recollect what passed that evening, but it turned out that Mrs. Taylor was much taken with Mill. From that time I saw little of the Taylor family, but I learned that an intimate acquaintance had arisen between Mill and Mrs. Taylor.

This intimacy went on, I seeing and knowing nothing of it, till on the occasion of an evening party at Mrs. Charles Buller's, I saw Mill enter the room with Mrs. Taylor hanging upon his arm.

The manner of the lady, the evident devotion of the gentleman, soon attracted universal attention, and a suppressed titter went round the room. My affection for Mill was so warm and so sincere that I was hurt by anything which brought ridicule upon him. I saw, or thought I saw, how mischievous might be this affair, and as we had become in all things like brothers, I determined, most unwisely, to speak to him on the subject.

With this resolution I went to the India House next day, and then frankly told him what I thought might result from his connection with Mrs. Taylor. He received my warnings coldly, and after some time I took my leave, little thinking what effect my remonstrances had produced.

The next day I again called at the India House, not with any intention of renewing the subject, but in accordance with a long-formed habit of constantly seeing and conversing with Mill. The moment I entered the room I saw that, as far as he was concerned, our friendship was at an end. His manner was not merely cold, but repulsive; and I, seeing how matters were, left him. His part of our friendship was rooted out, nay, destroyed, but mine was left untouched. My affection for him continued unbroken to the day of his death. For years I saw him not, and had no correspondence with him. For this I was very grieved. My affection for him, as I have said, was very sincere, and I was always grateful for his instruction and kindness. I was also vexed with myself. I thought myself knowing in the ways of men, and I knew, and ought to have acted on that knowledge, that where a woman was concerned, the wisest of men are but fools; and that more especially one so little conversant with women or the world would be a slave to the first woman who told him she liked him. Mill's intellect bowed down to the feet of Mrs. Taylor. He believed her an inspired philosopher in petticoats; and as she had the art of returning his own thoughts to himself, clothed in her own words, he thought them hers, and wondered at her powers of mind, and the accuracy of her conclusions. He, upon the death of Mr. Taylor, married the widow, and when, some years afterwards, she died, he gave expression to his estimate of her in, I believe, a dedication to her memory in some sentences prefixed to one of his works. He fondly loved her, was inconsolable for her loss, and survived her a few years, living a sorrowful life.

When he was returned for Westminster, I approached him in the House, and offered any assistance that my long experience could afford. He received me coldly, though I had taken part in his election and very materially contributed to his return. I asked him to dine with me and Graham, for the sake of "Auld lang Syne;" he excused himself, saying that he was so much engaged he had not time. I felt the meaning of this, and made no further advances. Some short time before his death he sent me an old school Virgil of mine which somehow had come into his possession. On the receipt of the book, I wrote to him, and the wording of that letter took him by surprise, and he said he had been unaware of my feeling of affection towards him. All looked as if our old friendship would be renewed, when, unhappily, this hope was broken off by his untimely death.

--------

The autobiography ends here. Mill's version of the breach not only differs from Roebuck's as to the cause, but places it at an earlier date, for according to Roebuck it occurred after he had entered Parliament. Mill says * the severance arose from a difference of opinion as to the respective merits of Wordsworth, whom he championed, and Byron, whose writings Roebuck regarded as the poetry of human life, while Wordsworth's was that of flowers and butterflies. They fought out the question at the Debating Society, this being the first time when he and Roebuck took opposite sides.

The schism between us widened from this time more and more, though we continued for some years longer to be companions. In the beginning our chief divergence related to the cultivation of the feelings. Roebuck was in many respects very

* "Autobiography," p. 149.

different from the vulgar notion of a Benthamite or Utilitarian. He was a lover of poetry and of most of the fine arts. He took great pleasure in music, in dramatic performances, especially in painting, and himself drew and designed landscapes with great facility and beauty. But he never could be made to see that these things have any value as aids in the formation of character. Personally, instead of being, as Benthamites are supposed to be, void of feeling, he had very quick and strong sensibilities. But, like most Englishmen who have feelings, he found his feelings stand very much in his way. He was much more susceptible to the painful sympathies than to the pleasurable, and looking for his happiness elsewhere, he wished that his feelings should be deadened rather than quickened. . . . He saw little good in any cultivation of the feelings, and none at all in cultivating them through the imagination, which he thought was only cultivating illusions.

## CHAPTER V.

BATH—fashionable, exclusive, sedate Bath—was flung into
a turmoil of affronted indignation when, early in August,
1832, rumours reached its aristocratic ears that its placidity
was to be invaded, and its domestic electoral affairs
disturbed, by the descent upon it of Radical firebrands.
Constituencies are usually jealous of outside interference,
and that Bath, of all places in the kingdom, should be
selected as the chosen striking-point of Radical attack, was
regarded as an unpardonable outrage by all self-respecting
lovers of composure.   The indignation aroused was changed
to absolute fury when these whispers took definite shape,
and it became known that Mr. Joseph Hume cherished the
"inconceivable audacity," as it was called, of attempting to
make Bath his own faggot constituency by forcing upon
it Mr. John Arthur Roebuck.*     Distance lent horror

---

* Although Mr. Hume was held responsible for forcing Mr. Roebuck upon
Bath, the real motive-power behind this, as behind all the then activities of
the Radicals, was Mr. Francis Place.   It is impossible to read his voluminous
correspondence without seeing how largely he inspired and stimulated the
aggressive policy of the militant group.   His was the hand which pulled
unrelentingly the strings in this Bath contest, as in other details of the movement.   For this memorandum is preserved among his papers :—

"*October* 10, 1832.—In consequence of the electors of Bath not thinking
Mr. Hobhouse enough of a reformer, they made application to me and to
Mr. Hume for another candidate, and Mr. Roebuck having been recommended,
he went to Bath and opposed Mr. Hobhouse.   This led to a most furious
attack upon Mr. Hume, and induced me to write a paper, which was printed
in the Bath and Cheltenham *Chronicle*, and a letter also to Simon Barron,

to Mr. Roebuck's personality.   Vaguely regarded as a dangerous revolutionary, he was credited with the championship of every hateful principle.   Associated, as he was supposed to be, with all evil doers, bent on dragging the constitution into the mire, the notion of his candidature was abhorred hardly less heartily by those who had rendered life-service to a timid Liberalism than by the Tories themselves.

Thus it came to pass that, active as was the ferment caused by the General Election under the new suffrage, nowhere was there greater excitement and fiercer animosity than in Bath.   It had been thought that the re-election of General Palmer, who, as a moderate reformer, had represented the city since 1808, was a matter of course.   With him was to be associated, as a colleague, Mr. H. W. Hobhouse, who, besides having local connections, was an estimable member of an influential Whig family.   They were excellent candidates, from the "rest and be thankful" point of view, for General Palmer was supposed to have reaped, in the Reform Act, the harvest of his Radical wild oats, and Mr. Hobhouse was a Whig of the most orthodox type.

This comfortable arrangement was shattered by the action of the Radicals, and the fame of the contest that ensued still remains a living memory in Bath.   From the time when Mr. Roebuck's candidature began, to the announcement of the result of the poll, the city was in a state of constant turmoil.   The new-comer had, among other objections, to encounter the idle criticism of being too young, for his slight figure and extremely fair complexion suggested an age nearer to twenty than to thirty. But his opponents quickly found that, youthful as he looked, they were face to face with a man of power.   From the first he gave forth no uncertain sound.   He quickly showed unusual capacity for stirring up quiet waters, and

chairman of Mr. Hobhouse's committee, with a narration of what passed at an interview with Mr. Hobhouse."

for making dead bones live.  In his various addresses and
speeches he declared himself an earnest supporter of the
most advanced creeds.  He advocated triennial Parliaments,
vote by ballot, corporation reform, an elective magistracy,
free trade, the abolition of the legal monopoly enjoyed by
the Inns of Court, a national system of secular education,
disestablishment of the Church and devotion of its property
to secular uses, repeal of the taxes on knowledge, cheaper
and more efficient administration of justice, equitable
adjustment of taxation—making it direct, and so graduated
as to proportion the burden to the strength of the shoulders
bearing it—the removal of all civil and religious disabilities,
and the abolition of slavery.

All the influences of purse and position were against
him.  His great power lay in the enthusiasm his cause
evoked among the poor.  It is necessary to realize the
bitter hatred against Whig and Tory government which
rankled among the working classes, before we can understand the enthusiasm with which they received the "man
of the people," or the furious violence of capitalists at his
intrusion.  Although steadfastly declining to make any
personal canvass, Mr. Roebuck spent, during the earlier
period of the contest, much of his time in the city, and was
indefatigable in the business of the election.  His speeches
are still remembered as among the best examples of his
pungent eloquence that Bath ever heard.  His genius for
unanswerable invective, provoked by shameful abuse, was
copiously illustrated.  For as there were no limits to the
unscrupulous misrepresentations—including the invention
of a fictitious mad grandfather—of his opponents, so there
was no decency observed in the fashion in which they
imputed to him opinions he had never held.  He was
charged with being a Republican and an Atheist.  He
was subjected to interrogations on his religious belief
which were indecent and almost blasphemous.  The newspapers teemed with lampoons, and the meetings at which

Mr. Roebuck stood at bay against his hecklers, smiting them hip and thigh, were like bear-gardens. All these things are written at length in the history of Bath, and in their details do not concern us here. When Mr. Roebuck was not in the city, the strife hurtled around the heads of his supporters; and of the social and domestic discomforts endured by them we get a glimpse in the following letter addressed to Mr. Alexander Falconer, but evidently intended for his sister's eye.

*J. A. Roebuck to Alexander P. Falconer.*

15, *Gray's Inn Square, November* 3, 1832.—By the regular and interesting despatches we receive through the kind exertions of yourself and Miss Falconer, I am put *au fait* of all that-is proceeding with you, and, being at a distance, am enabled to judge more coolly, and therefore more accurately, than those who are in the thick of the fight, of the complexion which matters have. One thing in all I hear gives me infinite pain, and that is, that your warm and unflinching support of me subjects you to a species of martyrdom. I well know what this is. The rage and bitter disappointment now raging time will diminish, and in the meanwhile lie snug ; let the wind blow and the rain fall till they are tired. The very strength of the tempest ensures a quick end to it. In a very few weeks all will be calm and sunshine. This to me appears the wisest course. You are committed now ; no one can doubt your leanings and wishes, and they will rave and rend at you so long as they are angry. That this will pain you I know ; that you will be subject to much annoyance is but too certain. That this should be on my account, while it makes me grateful, at the same time is exquisitely painful. That your quiet family should be disturbed by political strife ; your calm seclusion invaded and destroyed by raging partisans, is an evil not to be compensated, I fear, by any benefit that I can render to the good and great cause. In my own case, this strife is almost a part of my daily toil ; I am alone, and do not mind it. I have prepared myself for it—have become a species of political athlete, and deem it my business. The abuse, the anger of my opponents, are to me utterly insignificant ; but they cannot be so to you, surrounded as you are. It is this consideration that makes me unhappy ; and I but vainly seek a refuge from the evil. Do we not pay a high price for the benefits we obtain ? If we lie still in dread of all this violence and passion and ill-will, then are we trampled into the earth, bruised and crushed. If we seek to relieve ourselves from this condition, the pleasures of private life are destroyed, and, like troops of fierce horses, we worry ourselves to death. Which is the greater evil ? Mankind have generally accepted the first half of the alternative, and not till they have found that utterly untenable, have they dared to face the second. You are now facing the second, and seem to have a bitter dose. I pray you, my good fellow, to take my advice, and keep out of the way of those who differ from you, and do not let them disturb your peace.

A few weeks now, and the matter will be ended. On the 3rd of December the Parliament will be dissolved, and in a very few days after, the election will take place. The moment the dissolution is declared, I shall be among you. In the mean time state that I am ready to go to you whenever the committee shall desire me to do so.

I feel throughout my writing, as if my letter ought to have been addressed to your indefatigable sister ; 'tis from her letters * that the Bath history comes to me, and, like many other narratives of political deeds, the merits of the style are far beyond the subject matter on which it is employed. Would that she had a pleasanter or more worthy theme. I have a theory on this matter, that I suspect, from a passage in one of her letters, coincides with her views of the question. She says in substance that she believes that women are not fit for politics ; that men alone should take part in them. I do not agree with her here— that is, with the whole of this thus broadly stated. The best and most gentle of women have mingled in politics. Witness many in our own country during the wars against Charles I., and, above all, witness the incomparable Madame Roland. But what may have been in her mind when she said this, and what I suspect from the attending sentence to have been there, I do thoroughly agree in ; it is, that it would be well, if possible, to keep from the sight of women all the bad passions, the many degrading spectacles that political life but too often evinces, and for this reason : men in their commerce with the world become

* Written to her brother, Thomas Falconer, in London.

from use, and from a painful experience, daily less kind, less sympathizing with one another. In order to counteract this necessary tendency, it would be well if they could find a society not thus hardened—a society with all sympathies in their pristine freshness and strength. I would, as much as is consistent with perfect education, keep women out of contact with actual political strife. This is the only argument which I could ever find worth a rush, against giving to women all political rights, and to calling them into active exercise of them. However, I am writing a moral essay, and not a letter.

Did you ever read the letters of Madame de Sevigny, or of Lady Mary Montague? The exquisite tact of women in letter-writing has often puzzled me. I hardly ever saw one written by a man worth reading — Byron's perhaps excepted — while the letters of many women I have known have been perfect specimens of good taste and style. I am, or fancy myself, somewhat of a connoisseur on this matter — there being one curious thing about my education : everything I ever was taught, I was taught by women. However, I have rambled fairly out of my course. Pray give my best and kindest respects to all your family, and believe me most sincerely yours,

J. A. R.

There used to be an old saying current, that most people found that they had an old aunt at Bath; and Mr. Roebuck was no exception, for at this time Mrs. Roebuck, the widow of his uncle Benjamin, was living there. It was in her house at Madras that the new candidate was born, and she became very irate at the abuse showered upon her nephew, in whose progress she naturally took great interest.

This lady is alluded to in a letter to a supporter who thought a reply necessary to some absurd stories set afloat by persons who invented a grandfather for Mr. Roebuck in the eccentric Mr. Henry Disley Roebuck, of Midford Castle, who was not only no relative, but no Roebuck at all, the name having been assumed.

*Gray's Inn, November,* 1832.—I am the grandson of Dr. John Roebuck, the founder of the Iron Works at Carron, in Scotland.

His eldest son was John,* a man well known in the scientific world. Benjamin, his second son, was Paymaster-General of the forces of Madras. The widow of this son is now living in Bath, and his third son, my father, Ebenezer, died in India in 1807, while carrying on contracts with the East India Company. His docks were well known to every person acquainted with British India ; and the name and family of Roebuck must be familiar to every one connected with India between the years 1799 and 1810.

The result of the polling was the return of Major-General Palmer, with Mr. Roebuck as his colleague, Mr. Hobhouse being ninety-eight votes behind.

In the address of thanks and gratulation which he issued to the electors of Bath, Mr. Roebuck explained the spirit in which he interpreted his duties and responsibilities, and he expressed the hope that all animosities would now cease. His opponents lost no time in showing their repudiation of any such desire. A few days after the election the new member had the first of the many physical encounters which marked his public career. This was with Mr. R. Blake Foster, who, after offering himself as a Conservative candidate prepared "not to act the part either of a Bully or a Revolutionist," had retired from the contest. Meeting Mr. Roebuck in the coffee-room of the Sydney Hotel, Mr. Foster was offensive and insulting. Mr. Roebuck demanded his card, and Mr. Foster demurring, the new member promised, failing its production, to knock him down. Mr. Roebuck tendered his own card, and when Mr. Foster contemptuously tore it up, the plucky little man struck

---

* The eldest son of the above-mentioned John was Captain Thomas Roebuck, Public Examiner at the Madras College, and a member of the Asiatic Society. He compiled and translated a collection of Persian and Hindoo proverbs, also one of Hindoo nautical terms; he translated the Persian dictionary, the " Burhan-kati," and several other works. He was associated with Dr. Gilchrist in the preparation of the " British Indian Monitor," and the " English and Hindostani Dictionary." He was born in Linlithgowshire in 1781, and died at Madras in 1819.

him in the face. There was no duel, and valorous threats of legal proceedings ended in empty talk.

More serious was the attempt made to unseat Mr. Roebuck on petition. This was based on the allegation that he did not possess the property qualification then required of members of Parliament. On the hustings, at the nomination, the Mayor of Bath had, on the requisition of two electors, administered to the candidates the nomination oath presented by the Act (9th Anne). Mr. Roebuck, in taking the oath, stated that his property was in the parish of Camberwell, Surrey. The petition, which was promoted by the united Whig and Tory parties in Bath, alleged that there is no parish of Camberwell, and the petitioners, one of whom was Mr. Hobhouse's chairman, said that they had been unable to discover that Mr. Roebuck was seized either by law or equity of any property whatever in the village of Camberwell. The fact seems to be that, prior to the election, Mr. Roebuck had made arrangements for the purchase of a qualification, but the legal formalities were somewhat delayed, so that they were only completed an hour or two before he took the oath. Mr. Roebuck subsequently declared that he himself paid into the hands of Mr. Selby, the vendor, five thousand and odd pounds. The matter was investigated by a committee of the House of Commons, but although Mr. Roebuck was able to prove the truth of his statement made on the hustings, the petition was dismissed only on the casting vote of the chairman, and the committee decided that its presentation was not frivolous or vexatious.

It was at that time a very common practice for friendly arrangements to be made for conferring on candidates artificial qualifications. Mr. Roebuck himself alleged that not one man in ten possessed before his candidature the sort of estate qualifying him to sit. The experience of 1832, with the narrow escape from losing his seat, was not lost on Mr. Roebuck, for when, at a later period, Mr.

E

John Temple Leader * conveyed to him a landed qualification, he was exceedingly punctilious in observing all the forms of purchase.

*John Temple Leader to the Editor.*

*Florence, February* 19, 1896.—As Roebuck had no landed qualification, I gave him one charged on my estate of Burston, in Buckinghamshire. He was so particular in affairs of that kind, that he insisted on having all the legal forms observed, and he actually brought me bank-notes of the requisite value, which had been lent to him by our friend George Grote, and which I, of course, immediately returned to Grote.

---

* Elected member for Bridgewater in 1835, and resigned his seat in 1837 in order to engage in the great Westminster fight against Sir Francis Burdett in May of that year. Though unsuccessful then, he was returned for Westminster at the general election in the following August, and again in 1841. He retired from Parliament in 1847, and has for many years resided in Florence. See *post*, chapter x.

# CHAPTER VI.

THE old order of things had gone. With a widened suffrage there had come new men, new methods, new aspirations, and a marked disruption of the former lines of party demarcation. Nowhere was the revolution more strikingly typified than in the presence, in the House of Commons, of the member for Bath. He concretely personified all the hopes entertained by enthusiastic reformers of the possibilities of the new era. On him was concentrated all the mistrust of those, whether Tories or Whigs, who clave to the past, and who hated change and innovation. Mr. Roebuck lost no time in justifying the fears of his foes and in gratifying the expectations of his admirers. He quickly showed that with the changed conditions there had come a vivifying power into the debates of the House of Commons. On the first night of the debate on the address, there presented itself to the House a thin, slight figure, with clean-cut, thoughtful face, uttering curt, crisp sentences which from the first rang out incisively in clear telling tones, all the more impressive through the absence of gesticulation, and an avoidance of the factitious arts of emotional oratory. In picturing the scene when Roebuck first arrested an attention that never failed whenever, from that moment to the end of his long Parliamentary career, he rose to speak, we must avoid setting it in the chamber

so familiar to us all, in which our legislators now meet.
For the Reformed Parliament assembled not in the building
of to-day, but in that humble historic house where the
great drama of constitutional growth had been enacted,
and where the mighty giants of Parliamentary debate had
struggled for centuries. The Reformed Parliament was as
new wine put into old bottles, for not until the following
year were the ancient buildings destroyed by an act of
reckless folly; not until 1847 were the Lords, not until
1852 were the Commons, able to take up their abode in
Sir Charles Barry's new palace.* In the intervening years
temporary accommodation was provided for the people's
representatives in the old House of Lords, while the peers
were provisionally housed in what is known to history as
the Painted Chamber.

The House of Commons of that time, both as to the
building itself and the manners of its members, seems to
have impressed Mr. Roebuck very unfavourably. In his
"Extracts from the Diary of an M.P.," in *Tait's Edinburgh
Magazine* (July, 1833), he describes it thus :—

A small, ill-conditioned room, with a high-backed chair and
green table on the floor, with benches rising on each side, is the
House of Commons. The Speaker, with his full-blown wig and
flowing gown, occupies the chair; three clerks in wigs sit at his
feet, and around and about, overhead in the galleries, on the
floor, lying at full length on the benches, talking, laughing, hooting, coughing, sleeping, are to be seen the members—the *élite* of
the great nation in the character of legislators ; and one unfortunate wight is, amidst this strange and uncouth assembly,
endeavouring, in the slang phrase, to obtain the attention of the
House—in other words, is making a speech. . . . I often ask old
members whether the Reformed Parliament is worse or better in
point of behaviour than its predecessors. From all I can gather
it is evidently worse ; and the reason assigned is satisfactory. It

* Mr. Roebuck was accustomed jokingly to say that the new houses
were a standing argument against triennial Parliaments, as it took quite
three years to learn their topography.

is not, as the Conservatives would assert, that the more enlarged constituency has made the representatives more vulgar; for, on my knowledge, I can assert that the most rude and boisterous portion of the House are the young fry of Tory nominees. But in former times there were two distinct and organized parties; these parties had well-known leaders, upon whom devolved the business of advocating and opposing the measures before the House. Everybody knew this; and no one interfered with the part assigned to a given individual. The debate then went on quietly, and the House generally listened with something like attention and patience. But now there is no organization. Everybody is at sea; no guides, no rulers, no leaders are acknowledged. Every one sets up for himself, speaks for himself, thinks and acts for himself. The consequence is, that fifty speakers will rise at once, all impatient to be heard; while two or three hundred are around them, impatient to be away—to parties, to the opera, etc. So confusion, riot, calls of "Question, question!" "Bar, bar!"—which is uniformly pronounced "ba, ba," with emphasis— groans and braying are the order of the day. One member possesses the faculty of hooting like an owl, to the great disturbance of the gravity of the assembly and evident annoyance of the Speaker. This rude and boisterous conduct precludes the possibility of deliberation. Nothing is permitted to be discussed. One or two broad assertions of opposition will be permitted; but the moment any argument is attempted—any endeavour made to illustrate or prove—then come yells, and all the many means of silencing an opponent practised in Honourable House.

[After instancing many men who have been actually scared into silence by this behaviour, and citing the attention paid to Mr. Grote's speech on the ballot as a solitary contrary case, Mr. Roebuck goes on]: With that exception, I have never heard in that assembly one generous sentiment, or one logical and really effective argument. All has been passion, ignorance, prejudice. Boldfacedness, however, usually gets a hearing. . . . In sober sadness I must say that the House is very little solicitous respecting the popular feelings; that the members, as a body, have no sympathy with the people, and were it not that they believe that the people have a somewhat greater control than formerly over the electors, we should have them following a course exactly similar to that of the borough-mongers of heretofore.

It was, then, in the old arena, and amid these discouraging surroundings, that the young representative of Bath first obeyed the call of Mr. Speaker Sutton. The description just quoted of the difficulties against which members addressing the House had to contend, explains the justifiable pride with which Mr. Roebuck will be found hereafter referring to the manner in which he had succeeded in compelling the House to hear him—a pride that might seem exaggerated if we measured the assembly by present standards, and forgot the unruly impatience which marked the earlier years of the Reformed Parliament.

When now, sixty-four years later, Ireland still holds dominant place in our National Councils, it is significant to remember that even then the most prominent subject which demanded the attention of the Reformed Parliament was the condition of that distressful country. The harshness of Mr. Secretary Stanley's administration was keenly resented. It was disliked by many, even, of his own colleagues. It was the references to Ireland in the King's Speech that elicited from O'Connell the celebrated denunciation of English rule as "bloody, brutal, and unconstitutional." The fray waged by those giants of vituperation, Mr. O'Connell and the Irish Secretary, Mr. Stanley (the future Lord Derby), was an encounter after Mr. Roebuck's own heart, and he plunged vigorously into the storm. Proclaiming that freedom from party trammels which remained his boast through life, he forthwith fell with great spirit upon Stanley and his policy of force and coercion. In words which might have been appropriately used fifty years later, he said—

The Irish Secretary would take away trial by jury and suspend the habeas corpus. He (Mr. Roebuck) would recommend a thing hitherto untried—honest government. England had never established good government in Ireland. There had been strong governments indeed ; but he did not at present mean such an one, which might be wielded by the hon. secretary at pleasure, which would obey his dictation, and fill the prisons of Ireland. Fears were not the arguments of statesmen, and the only remedy for grievances was to redress them . . . . Government, it was said, must be feared before it was beloved. The proper course for creating affection had not yet been tried. Let the plain and obvious mode of real conciliation be adopted.

So Mr. Roebuck struggled hard against the Irish Coercion Bill, which was subsequently forced through the House. When presenting petitions praying for the rejection of the measure on the day after the third reading had been carried by a majority of 345 to 80, he said—

The members for Ireland had fought their battle in that House manfully, patiently, and with great calmness and discretion ; but that battle, from the votes of last night, was clearly shown to be lost. He felt called upon to say to those honourable gentlemen, if they would take his advice, they would leave that House at once and for ever, as it was plain Ireland could not look for justice from an English House of Commons. If the opinion of the House of Commons were to be judged of by the opinions and votes of its members last night, justice never could be done to Ireland, and the sooner she was separated from England the better. The people of America, having much less grounds than Ireland to complain, had fought nobly for their independence, and had put down the, till then, indomitable pride of England. Unfortunately, Ireland had not followed so glorious an example, and the consequence was that she had suffered oppressions unequalled by any other country in Europe, with the exception of Poland. . . . Irishmen had become the slaves of the despotism of England, and if they wished to continue so, instead of fighting manfully and boldly by every means in their power for their independence, they would passively give way to the provisions of the most iniquitous measure that had ever been brought forward, and they would deserve the execration of every honourable man.*

When charged with preaching open rebellion, Mr. Roebuck referred his assailants to the speeches of Mr. Fox, who had used terms equally strong.

* March 30. Hansard, vol. xvi. p. 876.

The session witnessed other great debates, in which Mr. Roebuck took a prominent part. He assailed the Government, and especially Sir James Graham, in a speech on Mr. Hume's motion for the abolition of sinecure offices and pensions. He flung himself into the indignation caused by the official breaking up of a peaceful political meeting in Coldbath Fields, and into the controversy over the loss of a policeman's life during the disturbance. He attacked ministerial and official interference in Parliamentary elections, and protested against the house and window taxes. Early in the session he had given notice of a motion for a Select Committee to devise a means for the universal and national education of the whole people. This fell through, but in the following July he moved a resolution, pledging the House, early in the next session, to seek a solution of the problem. The motion, being opposed by the Government, was withdrawn, but the speech in which it was commended to the House was praised by Mr. Grote as "able and luminous." In it Mr. Roebuck sketched the methods by which he held that a thoroughly comprehensive scheme of education should be carried out. On this subject, and also on his attitude towards the Established Church, he had left his constituents in no doubt, for he had told them—

I am a member of the Church of England, but I want none but Church of England men to support my Church. With regard to an Established Church, so long as a majority of the people of England wish for an Established Church, let there be one, but for myself I see no necessity for it. I think the property now possessed by the Church is public property, and may be applied as the legislature think fit. If returned I shall advocate its appropriation to national purposes. I would have clergymen properly paid, and apply the surplus to the purposes of education. Private charities I would apply as nearly as possible to the purposes for which they were bequeathed. I consider that all religious disabilities ought to be removed, and that every one who has committed no criminal act should be admitted to all the privileges of the State. In no case whatever ought religion to form part of a national education.

As an object-lesson, exemplifying Mr. Roebuck's views on popular education, a model school was subsequently started in Bath, founded on the principles the honourable member recommended;* but it had to be closed after a career of six months, owing to disputes between the committee and the teacher and superintendent.

An agitation against the Sale of Beer Act elicited the first of a long series of utterances destined to keep Mr. Roebuck in constant conflict with the temperance party. He defended the beer-shops as having greatly benefited the working classes; and he attributed special weight to a petition presented by him from Merthyr Tydvil in their favour, on the ground that it must be the petition of the poor men because almost every person who had signed it was unable to write. He took up the cause of a boy named Barber, who had been imprisoned for selling un-stamped newspapers, and, ever ready to champion the persecuted, and to fly at the prejudices of conventionalism, he presented a petition from Richard Carlile, praying to be released from an imprisonment to which he had been sentenced for writing letters deemed to be incitements to incendiarism. In doing this he made a fierce attack on the Recorder of London, who had tried Carlile. He had never, he declared, heard of a more captious, less careful, calm, and considerate judge, nor one more wholly unworthy and in-capable of performing the duties of his office.†

This session marked the commencement of persistent attempts by Sir A. Agnew to enforce the observance of the Sabbath by legislative enactments. From the first these were met by Mr. Roebuck with irreconcilable opposition.

* See *Tait's Edinburgh Magazine* for 1835, p. 202, for an account of the Bath Education Society, of which Roebuck was the president, and its school.
† See *ante*, p. 7 (chap. i.). The Recorder of London in 1833 was the Hon. C. E. Law, not Shaw, as given in Moore's Diary.

He never ceased to pour upon them bitter contempt and scornful obloquy. By way of *reductio ad absurdum,* Mr. Roebuck was accustomed to threaten to make liable to fine any gentleman whose carriage, or servant, should be seen in the streets on a Sunday. He suggested a penalty of £10 on any one attending a club on Sunday, or sending his servant with messages. He threatened to impose a penalty of £100 on any clergyman driving to church, to be increased in the case of a bishop to £200. He would also endeavour to shut up Hyde Park and the Zoological Gardens, "so that the whole metropolis should be converted into one solemn scene of unmitigated gloom and fanaticism." But a more excellent way, urgently advocated by him, was the opening on Sundays of the British Museum and other places of instructive recreation. Not until 1896 was this done, sixty-three years after Mr. Roebuck pressed it upon the House of Commons.

*June* 21, 1833.—The murder is out, and the ministers are for ever ruined in the public estimation. It is now proved that as men and gentlemen they are unworthy of trust. It was confidently stated that they had determined to give up the integrity of the [Irish Church] Bill, and erase the clause respecting the appropriation of Church property. Matters go quietly until the reading of the 147th clause, when Stanley gets up, and with much calmness and complacency, proposes to leave out the whole clause. The House appeared seriously hurt. He could not get a single cheer. His usual commonplaces were no longer successful, and at length he felt that this hitherto obsequious House was no longer at his command. . . . The usually bold Mr. Stanley shrinks under the fierce cheers of his opponents. The cries of the Opposition were continuous and triumphant. Their scornful laughs made him tremble with rage and shame. . . . He cowers under their well-deserved contumely, and is more than usually pale and ghastly. His proposal was met with undisguised scorn, and shouts of bitter and contemptuous laughter ; and I shall never forget the burst which followed O'Connell's opening remark, which came from him with all that air of truth and burning indignation which he so well knows how to throw into his statements. " No, sir," he said, " I am not disappointed. I am not surprised by the declaration of the right honourable gentleman. I expected that they would break their promise, and they have done so." . . . The House of Commons seemed transformed, as if by magic, from a servile, acquiescent herd ; they appeared at once to have become independent, patriotic, honest. The ministerial influence was annihilated ; and sure am I, whatever may be the majorities obtained by them after this memorable debate, their power, their real influence over men's minds, the strange but hitherto powerful prestige which attended them, is gone for ever.

I wish people would leave off talking nonsense about the return of the Tories to power. They speak as if there were no alternative for the people but Whig or Tory. There is yet one more, viz. an independent, or let us use the strong word, a Radical party. These last are far more in accordance with the popular opinion than either Whig or Tory ; and let their enemies say what they will, the Radicals must be in power before three years are passed, unless indeed the Duke of Wellington should really come into office *à pas de charge*, and bayonet the people into silence. What ! the horrid, the vulgar, the destructive Radicals in office, in this civilized, enlightened, polished, aristocratic country ? Even so, good people. What think you, for example, of the wild, headstrong, destructive propensities of that furious demagogue, Mr. Grote, as Chancellor of the Exchequer ? *

Mr. Roebuck's activities were by no means restricted at this time to his Parliamentary work. Besides the " M.P.'s Diary," he contributed occasional articles to *Tait's Edinburgh Magazine*, on Parliamentary and political subjects chiefly, but not wholly, for on one occasion he advises Mr. Tait of the despatch of an article on children's books, with the remark, " That is my hobby." †

Early in the year 1833 he, with Hume, Grote, Warburton,

* " Diary of an M.P.," *Tait's Edinburgh Magazine*, August, 1833, p. 644.

† The article appears in *Tait's Magazine* for December, 1833. Other articles were, " National Education " (March, 1833); " The Prospects of the People during the Coming Session " (December, 1833, and February, 1834); " Trade Unions " (January, 1834); " Political Mortality of the Tory Ministry " (1835).

and Francis Place, formed a project for establishing a Society for the Diffusion of Political and Moral Knowledge. Place, with his accustomed thoroughness, elaborated the scheme, and Roebuck drew up "a very able" prospectus. The plan which, besides the publication of new and the reissue of standard works of solid instruction, included the establishment of a weekly periodical, was abandoned almost immediately—but not before it had desperately alarmed the *Times* and the *Chronicle* for their advertising revenue—because there seemed some prospect that Lord Althorp was about to fulfil his often expressed desire to abolish the stamp duties on newspapers. When, after some years of impatient waiting, the repeal of the Newspaper Stamp Act seemed more remote than ever, the society, reconstructed, determined to commence, under the editorship of Mr. Roebuck, the publication of a series of Pamphlets for the People. In order to avoid coming under the cognizance of the law affecting periodical publications, these bore no date or number, each forming a separate work. But the idea was to issue one every week, or oftener if needed. "By whomsoever written," said Mr. Roebuck, "my name will appear on the title page as editor, and by this mode they will be known to emanate from the society. . . . By this means the leading matters of present political interest will be brought before the people without any infringement of the existing atrocious law."

The first of these, "On the Means of Conveying Information to the People," was published on June 11, 1835. The first four numbers were wholly from Mr. Roebuck's pen, and out of the entire series of six and thirty, there were few to which he did not contribute some specimens of his pungent thoughts, set forth in an admirably direct and lucid language. Even to-day they cannot be read without delight. The impression they made at the time may be judged by the violent attacks on their author with which the newspapers of the day teem—attacks, it must be admitted, invited by the unsparing plainness of speech in which individuals and institutions were assailed, and unpalatable doctrines proclaimed. But in proportion as they offended the classes, they pleased the masses.

*W. Hawkes Smith to J. A. Roebuck.*

*Birmingham, October* 13, 1835.—I am reading your pamphlets, which I think of and constantly speak of, as ranking among the most important signs of the times—strong and decided, but without vulgar acrimony. Close, practical, and intelligible to all, they give to the people precisely the information they want, on the various divisions of politics as a science, and on the various indications of the state of that science at the present day, which might otherwise escape notice and detection. I prefer them infinitely to Cobbett's *Register*, even in its best days, because I think they have more of the above qualifications than that extraordinary work possessed—have more to do with the people than the *Register* had.

Next to Roebuck, H. S. Chapman * did most of the writing; the contributions of Francis Place and Thomas Falconer (Roebuck's brother-in-law) being less frequent. Grote's name is given in some of the correspondence as having, with Hume, Molesworth, and Warburton, contributed £50 as capital for the undertaking, but this is irreconcilable with the fact that when only two Pamphlets had appeared, Grote wrote to the *Times* to contradict a reference in a leading article to him as connected with them. " This," he said, " is not the fact. You have probably been misled by finding it stated, and correctly stated, by Mr. Roebuck, that I was one of a society projected in the year 1833, for the purpose of disseminating cheap and useful periodicals among the people."

In 1834 we find Mr. Roebuck speaking on education at a meeting of the National Union of the Working Classes.

---

* Chapman, who had previously been resident in Canada, went to the Bar in 1840, and was afterwards a judge in New Zealand and several of the Australian Colonies. He died at Dunedin in 1881.

This speech brought him into sharp antagonism with that able, but curiously erratic politician, William Cobbett, one of whose pet aversions was the spread of knowledge. In a long letter in his *Register* he denounced Mr. Roebuck's views—which is not surprising, as Cobbett declared roundly that in exact proportion as the work of education and the sale of newspapers had increased had the liberties of the nation been undermined and diminished, while crime had augmented nearly tenfold.

Later in the year Cobbett expressed similar views in Parliament, when Mr. Roebuck, returning to the subject he had introduced in 1833, moved for a select committee to inquire into the means of establishing a system of national education. His motion, after an alteration in its terms, made at the instance of Lord Althorp, was agreed to.

His interpositions in debate, up to July, 1834, when Whig dissensions were temporarily patched up by Lord Melbourne's government succeeding that of Lord Grey, were frequent, and the subjects with which he dealt most varied. After that, until the prorogation, Mr. Roebuck was absent.

The affairs of Canada had been in a disturbed condition since 1828, and now, in 1834, they had reached a point that determined the member for Bath to bring them under the notice of Parliament. When moving for a committee of inquiry, he drew a comprehensive and most vivid picture of the evils complained of.* The colonists alleged that these grievances were brought on chiefly by the misgovernment of the home executive, the result being a state of things, even then, amounting to almost open rebellion. Mr. Stanley, on behalf of the Government, having agreed to more limited inquiry into the grievances

---

* For a clear account of the Canadian troubles and their ultimate settlement, see Spencer Walpole's "History of England" (new edition, 1890), vol. iv. chap. xv.

of Lower Canada, excluding the Upper Province, the committee was granted by the House without a division. The committee met, but its report was not made public.

In his earlier elections, Mr. Roebuck made it a point of honour never to canvass personally. He laid down other rules with regard to the relative position of representatives and represented that might usefully be imitated and re-membered. Thus he was attacked at Bath for having refused to subscribe to the Bath and West of England Agricultural Society. His reply was given in a speech made in that city, January 7, 1834, at a meeting on Corporation Reform. He said—

A representative of the people should go to Parliament free and undefiled. If he puts his hands into his pockets to purchase their suffrages, be assured that he will make them pay for it in return. I say, therefore, that, whatever societies I may think proper to subscribe to in my individual capacity, you have no right to expect me to do so as your representative.

Part of the autumn of 1834 was passed in France, where, almost immediately on landing, Mr. Roebuck was seized with a dangerous illness. Two physicians, one French, one English, despaired of their patient, although the French doctor saw some hope if his prescription could be given, but neither he nor the English colleague could muster up courage to give it. When Mrs. Roebuck heard their decision, she said, "I will take that responsibility!" and at once administered the medicine, with the happiest results. The convalescence was long, and the time was chiefly spent in drawing, for which a vigorous and graceful talent had already caused Mr. Roebuck's friends to say that he was an artist lost to the world. The scenes of his first water-colours were taken from the surroundings of the quaint little town of Abbeville, where he was then staying. This pursuit he continued in his leisure moments for years, until eyesight suddenly failed in 1852.

## CHAPTER VII.

"THE queen has done it all," was the spiteful comment, inspired by Brougham, on the announcement, which startled the country on November 15, 1834, that King William IV. had summarily dismissed Lord Melbourne. "Regularly kicked out," Mr. Greville called it; and assuredly no lackey was ever discharged with less ceremony than the king showed in this last dying flicker of prerogative.   His Majesty took the worst possible way of ending a crisis which had long been approaching.   Everything had gone wrong with the ministry during the preceding session.   Ireland—the Irish Church, Irish tithes, Irish coercion—had, as usual, played the part of wrecker. Ministerial divisions had resulted in what Lord John Russell called "the wretched, blundering, wavering course of policy."   "Johnny," in historic phrase, had himself "upset the coach," by publicly dissociating himself from Stanley's views on the appropriation of the revenues of the Church, and thus driving from the Cabinet four of his most influential colleagues.   Then "the pig was killed," in Althorp's bucolic simile.   In the complications arising out of the mistaken confidence of the Irish Secretary (Littleton) of being able to manage O'Connell over the Coercion Bill, Lord Grey threw up the premiership, and left Melbourne to struggle on until the removal of Lord Althorp to the House of Lords, through the death of Lord Spencer, tempted the king to the last and feeblest *coup d'état* ever attempted by a British sovereign. Then Peel, hastily summoned from Rome, began his short and inglorious ministry.

*February* 19, 1835.—The new [temporary] House of Commons opened for the first time for the reception of members. As compared with the old ugly place, it is a beautiful and commodious room. Many mistakes, however, have been made which it is to be hoped will be a warning to the architect of the permanent house. Among the most serious of these was the leaving a large space behind the Speaker's chair for a gossip shop. In fact, all the bad points in the new house arise from a servile imitation of the old one. . . . The table is exactly the size of the old one, as is proved by the appearance of the old oil-cloth covering used in the former house, and saved providentially, as the Speaker would have said, from "the devastations committed by the flames." . . . The Lords are amazingly shorn of their beams. Their now insignificant house is a type of their political condition. Bright colours and much show in an awkward, small, uncomfortable room—in my opinion, however, quite good enough. The whole body being useless, or something worse, it matters little into what place you cram them.

*February* 26.—The division [on an amendment to the address] created little sensation. Whether we were beaten or not was a matter of little consequence, as Sir R. Peel had plainly stated that he would not resign, even if placed in a minority,* and he was right for so saying. We knew the result (ayes, 302 ; noes, 309. Majority for the amendment, 7) before we returned out of the lobby ; and, although a cheer was raised on the declaration of the numbers, very little exultation was felt by the more Liberal portion of the majority. Peel looked painfully downcast. He was as pale as the paper on which I am writing. There was a convulsive motion of his mouth that gave one pain to look at. He seemed to sink under the blow, and walked out of the house as would a man stunned by a fall. He must feel that he is in a false position ; and, doubtless, would give half his fortune to be on the Liberal side of the House. Had

* On the ground that the amendment did not clearly indicate want of confidence in the ministry.

he not bound himself to the Tory party too firmly for retreat, we should have had him as an advocate of the *movement*—a shuffling advocate, without doubt, but still a powerful one.*

This was but the precursor of a constant succession of defeats, against which Peel fought in vain. At length, on April 7, his bark, too, struck on the rock of the Irish Church, and he appealed to the country. At the general election which followed, the Tories of Bath adopted as their Candidate Colonel Daubeney, a tried soldier and one of the most influential of local Conservatives. The Whigs had already summoned Mr. Hobhouse to return to the battle. He had come protesting solicitude for harmonious action in the Liberal camp. The Radicals put their old members in the field. Before the nomination, Mr. Hobhouse retired in order to contest Finsbury. General Palmer, for reasons connected with his private concerns, was absent during the contest; and thus the whole burden of the fight rested upon Mr. Roebuck. The struggle ended in the re-election of himself and his colleague.

In the new Parliament Mr. Roebuck lost no time in returning to the educational problem. He succeeded in obtaining a committee to inquire into the present state of the education of the people, and into the application and effects of the grant made in the last session for erection of school-houses, and to consider the expediency of further grants in aid of education.

The House of Assembly of Lower Canada had appointed Mr. Roebuck as their agent in England, and this session (1835) he continued to give constant attention to the affairs of that colony. He presented a petition from certain members of the Legislative Council and of the House of Assembly of Lower Canada, complaining of their grievances—a document which he described as being as important as any laid before the House of

* "Diary of an M.P.," *Tait's Edinburgh Magazine*, April, 1835, p. 211.

Commons since the disastrous period of 1774. His speech on this occasion, in which the privilege of self-government was demanded, is a clear and interesting statement of the state of the colony and its grievances. This petition elicited rebutting petitions, presented by Mr. Patrick Stewart (Lancaster), and Mr. G. F. Young (Tynemouth). During these controversies Sir Robert Peel made an unfounded charge against Roebuck of having divulged confidential communications. Mr. Roebuck, however, had no difficulty in showing that, so far from having violated confidence, he had earnestly protested against the use, by Canadian delegates, of a conversation with Peel.

Mr. Roebuck's acceptance of the position of agent for the Canadians exposed him to many sneering attacks from opponents who conveniently forgot that Edmund Burke had acted in a similar capacity for the colony of New York at the time of the American Revolution, receiving £500 a year for his services. The vivid imagination of Mr. Roebuck's assailants enabled them to represent him as in receipt of £1100 a year, whereas the Canadians not only failed to pay his salary at the time, but left him to defray the expenses of the defence of Canada in Parliament out of his own pocket, and subsequently repudiated his claim for arrears. Sir John Hanmer, in 1836, asked the House of Commons to affirm that it was contrary to its independence, a breach of its privileges, and derogatory to its character, for any of its members to become the paid advocate of any portion of his Majesty's subjects. The motion was rejected by 178 votes to 67. Mr. Roebuck acted as agent for only a year and a half. When the Canadians became what was termed rebels, he ceased to act for them. Not until many years afterwards was he paid his first claims.

The poor and the oppressed—whether illiterate Irish petitioners, or ill-used paupers, or the London cab-drivers, or the cruelly transported Dorchester labourers, or publishers who had been imprisoned, and printers whose presses had been seized by the Stamp Office—found in Mr. Roebuck a courageous champion. His attacks upon the newspaper stamp were accompanied by his customary fulminations against the newspapers themselves. He said—

There never was a press so degraded, so thoroughly immoral, as the press of this country. . . . From the highest to the lowest, the most paltry corruption, the basest cowardice, and the blackest immorality, were the governing principles of the newspaper press of this country.

He spoke in favour of the relief of Dissenters from the disabilities placed upon them by the marriage laws; against a budget which, while continuing corn laws and other taxes for the benefit of the landed interest, did not even name the taxes on knowledge. He pressed for the ballot. Further attempts at enforcing Sunday observance by legislation drew forth his bitterest sarcasms. Not only was there a Bill against Sunday trading, but attempt was made to introduce into the Great Western Railway Bill a clause prohibiting the running of trains on Sunday. The promoters of the Bill had been sufficiently alarmed to express themselves willing to be bound not to run trains between 11 a.m. and 2 p.m. on Sundays; but their opponents, with a confidence cruelly disillusioned when they found themselves in an impotent minority in the division lobby, loftily declared that the question was one admitting of no compromise. Mr. Roebuck met what he regarded as an attack upon the rights and liberties of the poor by a description of what he had seen of the privileges and proceedings of the rich. He said—

I shall oppose this clause, because it is intended by it to interfere with the enjoyment of the working and poorer classes, while it leaves untouched the recreations of the higher classes. I went a short distance out of town a Sunday or two ago, and

I will narrate to the House what I saw. On that morning I
went first into Piccadilly. At twelve o'clock, the first person
I met was the Duke of Wellington on horseback. I went into
Hyde Park, and there were some men watering the drive for
the comfort of the refined classes that afternoon. A little
further on, at Knightsbridge, I found the soldiers exercising, and
their officers in arms. I pursued my journey over Hammer-
smith Bridge, and there met with the Lord Chief Justice on
horseback, taking a ride into the country. At three o'clock I
arrived at Hampton Court, and there found the right honourable baronet, the member for Tamworth [Sir Robert Peel]. Do
I blame any of these illustrious personages for what they were
doing ? I was doing the same thing as themselves. They had
as much right to travel on Sundays for their health and amusement as I have, and so have the poor. The plain fact is, we
meddle too much with one another. If each individual would
take care of his own goodness, instead of being so anxious about
the goodness of his neighbour, we should have more virtue in the
world, though we might have a little less outward show.

The Municipal Corporation Reform Bill, carried through
the Commons without material disfigurement by the
exercise of Sir Robert Peel's restraining influence on his
more extreme followers, was sent up to the House of Lords
on July 21. The Tory lords at once proceeded to work
their wicked will upon it. They turned it inside out, and
sent back to the Commons a wholly different and re-
actionary measure. Mr. Roebuck, both in Parliament and
in his Pamphlets for the People, declaimed against the Lords.
"Unmixed, then," he wrote, "is the evil which the House
of Lords inflicts upon the nation, whether we view them
as legislators, or judges, or simply as an aristocracy. Such
is my answer to the question, ' Of what use is the House
of Lords ?'" In "The Crisis: What ought Ministers to
do?" he contended that not only ought every change
made to be rejected, and the Bill restored to its original
shape, but that the broader struggle of depriving the Lords
of power to work such mischiefs should be entered upon.

And he spoke to the same effect in the House. When Lord John Russell preached concession, Mr. Roebuck urged defiance. "Let us," he said, "re-enact every one of our original measures, saying that such was the pleasure of the people. Let those who dare resist it."

The following letter to Mrs. Roebuck was written on August 31, during the debate in which Lord John Russell, fresh from a conference with his party in Downing Street, explained which of the Lords' Amendments the Government advised the Commons to reject and which to accept. In this debate, Peel, to the consternation of his followers, threw the Lords overboard on most of the points insisted on by Lord John Russell.

### *To Mrs. Roebuck.*

*London, August* 31.—I am writing in the House in a hurry and against time. I was yesterday at the Grotes', at Dulwich. I found them in high excitement and wishing for me. We had a great talk ; and to-day I went to Lord John Russell to have another talk. We shall not accept the Lords' Amendments as a whole, but only some of them—too many to please me. Still, if the Lords accept the Bill as we return it, it will still be a good one. Lord John [Russell] is on his legs, talking empty nothings in a very pompous tone. Whether the Lords will accept what he proposes is more than I know.

Molesworth I found at Dulwich,* in great glee because he hopes for a row. Grote is in a great rage, and is against all concession. We had Parkes† at dinner, preaching peace, but that was not popular. Strutt and Gaskell were there. Many praises were bestowed on my doings about the Lords, and also on my Canada article.‡ My health is so so.

* Grote's house.

† Joseph Parkes, of the Birmingham Political Union, Secretary to the Municipal Corporations Commission, and in after years in large practice at Westminster as a Parliamentary solicitor. He was one of Bentham's "young men."

‡ "On the Affairs of Canada," in the *London and Westminster Review* for September, 1835

*London, September,* 1835.—I am this moment going to Dulwich with Molesworth. I go because I wish for fresh air. The business here will not be over this week, *oimé!* My motion has excited attention. The next " Pams " I mean to fill with the history of the week.

Mr. Roebuck did, accordingly, devote the next Pamphlet for the People, entitled, " The Conduct of Ministers respecting the Amendments of the House of Lords," to a full description of the proceedings at the Downing Street meeting, and of the debate in the House of Commons. If the Tories were dissatisfied with Peel's conduct in throwing overboard the Lords, Roebuck was furious at what he considered " the unwise, not to say degrading, submission of the Commons of England to a few ignorant, irresponsible, and interested peers." He poured scorn upon Lord John Russell, and he writhed under what he called Peel's " selfish cunning " in taking a line which showed that, while he was the despot over his own party, the ministry was dependent upon him for such portions of the Bill as were saved. Dissatisfied with the newspaper accounts, Roebuck gave in the Pamphlet a full report of his own speech. In this he denounced all compromise, as Grote had also done, both in the House and at the party meeting, and insisted that this latest insulting demonstration of the incompatibility of the existence of the House of Lords with the welfare of England, necessitated curing the evil at its source.

The motion referred to in the foregoing letter as exciting attention was a notice put upon the books for the next session to ask for leave to bring in a Bill proposing that the Lords' veto should be taken away, substituting for it a suspensive power to be exercised only once on any measure in the same session. Mr. Grove Price (Sandwich) intimated that he should meet this with a motion to erase Mr. Roebuck's motion from the paper " as subversive of the principles of our balanced constitution, as derogatory to the character, and an abuse of the privileges of the House." Nothing ever came of either.

The Parliamentary session of 1835 having closed, the Radicals of Bath invited their members and various politicians of the same school to a grand dinner, and welcomed them by a great demonstration of strength. The dinner took place on November 11, 1835.

*To Mrs. Roebuck.*

*Bath, November* 11, 1835.—Lord John [Russell] does *not* come. A Privy Council to-day at eleven is the excuse. The dinner is to be a very splendid affair, I understand. The enthusiasm is extraordinary. Hume preaches mildness, and seems half afraid of my hitting somebody or other very hard. The day yesterday was bitterly cold, but I did not suffer so much as I expected. The country was beautiful beyond description, and I made drawings in my head all the way. I should much like to make some sketches of Salisbury. We have letters from Canada. The Commissioners have already no power, and Lord Gosford tells Papineau as much. They have been doing all sorts of foolish things; among others, they had invited Papineau and Vigier to meet ultra opponents. They all got together by the ears at the governor's table, he being obliged to propose a bumper all round to drown the row.

I have just seen Mrs. Benjamin Roebuck, who says that your mother sings my praises. Mrs. R. was delighted to hear so much good of her " little Johnny "—my old cognomen.

The Bath dinner attracted much attention throughout the country. Its unmixed Radicalism was accepted as an index even of national feeling. Mr. William Hunt was president, Colonel (afterwards General Sir William) Napier *

* Before Mr. Roebuck was selected as candidate for Bath in 1832, Colonel William Napier, who had gone to reside at Freshford, near that city, had been invited to stand, but had refused. An intimate friendship began when, in 1835, he enlisted the Parliamentary aid of Roebuck in a fight he was waging with characteristic heat, against the inhumanity with which the new Poor Law was administered in Freshford. For many years Napier was a prominent and striking figure on Bath platforms, and on one occasion he incontinently knocked down a man who persisted in accusing him of falsehood. His vigorous Radicalism brought him many offers of Parliamentary seats. Seven great constituencies, including Nottingham, Glasgow, Oldham,

boldly indicted the House of Lords. Mr. Roebuck arraigned
their Lordships in equally forcible terms, and Mr. Hume,
though less extreme, joined heartily in the censures conveyed. The general feeling of enthusiasm toward Mr.
Roebuck was remarkable. General Palmer offered the
sincerest homage to his integrity and power, and the
veteran Napier wound up with these words: "General
Palmer is an old friend, but this (laying his hand on Mr.
Roebuck's shoulder)—this is the child of reform; and I hope
that you may live to witness its best results, and until both
you and he have hairs as grey as my own."

Birmingham, and Westminster, competed for the honour of having him as
their representative, but he steadfastly resisted their persuasions, chiefly on
the ground of limited means. Many letters written by him to Roebuck
are quoted in his Life—" Life of General Sir William Napier," by H. A. Bruce,
vol. i. pp. 373, 418, 439, 459, 473; vol. ii. pp. 46, 59, 70, 140, 183, etc. As
usual, Napier got into hot water when Lieut.-Governor of Guernsey, in 1842.
Roebuck visited him, and argued his case before the Privy Council (see *post*,
chap. xiii.). The Napier influence, as will be seen hereafter, was strongly
marked in the part Roebuck took in the debates on the Afghan War and
the affairs of Scinde, 1843, 1844.

# CHAPTER VIII.

### RADICAL RECRIMINATIONS.

MR. ROEBUCK had heralded the session of 1836 by broaching a plan for the government of England by the Radicals. Considering that the staunch and reliable Radicals who were members of the House of Commons numbered not more than twenty, this was a bold proposition. His measures for achieving this object were, however, very carefully taken. The great parties were so nearly balanced in the House of Commons, that a dozen votes would turn the scale; and upon this fact Mr. Roebuck based his scheme of aggression. In the Pamphlet published early in 1836, entitled, "Radical Support to a Whig Ministry," he exposed the selfish indifference with which the Radical pretensions had been treated by the Whigs, and advised that when the question of the Irish Church came on, the Radicals should show their sense of indifference to their demands by their absence.

On the very eve of the session, and in the penultimate Pamphlet, "The Radicals and the Ministers," Roebuck further elaborated this plan of action. Support of the Whigs should, he urged, be continued on promise to repeal the Stamp Duties and to leave the Ballot an open question. If this was refused, the Radicals should abstain from voting on any no-confidence motion proposed by the Tories.

Nothing practical came of the scheme. Radicals like Sir William Molesworth joined with Roebuck in insisting on a more determined and straightforward action on the part of the ministers as the only way to obtain hearty Radical support. Yet the session ran its course with the usual accompaniments of bitter words, but no deeds.

The attempt to galvanize the Radicals into combined revolt was the dying effort of the Pamphlets. Their early promise had not been fulfilled. Refused the support he was entitled to expect, the strain upon Roebuck was too great. Publication was discontinued early in 1836. The conclusion of the story is told in the letters which follow :—

*H. S. Chapman to Francis Place.*

*January* 19, 1836.—You are aware that the Pamphlet did not pay its ordinary, still less its extraordinary, expenses, till towards the close of the session. After the close of the session it ceased to pay, and the result is that we are full £150 on the wrong side. I, on my own responsibility, have carried it on in the face of loss, because I saw it was effecting an enormous amount of good in a public point of view. I saw, too, that it was increasing Roebuck's power and adding to his usefulness ; and if you require a more selfish motive, I also saw that it was making me advantageously known to the public. Thus I had every possible motive to make great sacrifices to maintain it. To such sacrifice, however, there is a limit. I can afford to expend £100—Roebuck can perhaps afford to expend as much—but to go beyond this would not be possible. So much for pecuniary conditions. Now, then, for others not less pressing.

Roebuck is ill. Occasionally he is in a state of nervous excitement which renders writing painful. Such was his state yesterday and to-day. On such occasions it is that he and I feel the manner in which the men who can and ought to have assisted us in this undertaking have left us to our own resources in a matter which should not have been considered merely personal. You, Place, are the only man on whose sympathy and assistance we could rely ; and you know enough of the world to pardon me for now laying a burthen on willing shoulders.

This morning Roebuck was for stopping at once. He urged

that the session was coming on, and that he was unequal to the labour that he would be called on to undergo. Few, he said, would assist us, and John Mill could find time to labour for Fox's Magazine, but not to write a line for the Pamphlets. If four or five good men had been invited at the early part of the session to contribute articles to the Pamphlets, the labour would have been light, and the Pamphlets would have become the organ of the Radical party. It was hard, he concluded, to leave the whole labour and responsibility on our shoulders.

Such, as nearly as I can remember, were his words. Now, what is to be done? Two things are wanted. First, some money; second, the assistance of some writers. At Hume's, on Friday, Perronet Thompson spoke in high terms of the Pamphlets. He said he had purchased the whole volume, and it delighted him, and that he should like to write in it. Now, Perronet Thompson can both write and spare money.

Last week at Buller's, Roebuck met Leader, the member for Bridgewater. Leader stated that he was anxious to render himself useful to the Liberal cause, both in and out of Parliament. Roebuck said, "You go to too many parties to become a hardworking man." Leader seemed hurt—defended himself from the party-going accusation, and again expressed a desire to be useful. Leader also can spare money.

The writer goes on to suggest that applications be made to Sir William Molesworth, Perronet Thompson, John Mill, Hume, and Leader, and—somewhat surprising after the letter to the *Times*, quoted on page 61—to Grote.

*Joseph Hume, M.P., to Francis Place.*

*Bryanston Square, January* 30, 1836.—I hasten to answer your letter of this date, and to return Mr. Chapman's letter to you respecting Roebuck's Pamphlet. It is not my fault that he is in that situation, as I advised him to be quite sure of the means he had of carrying it on before he began. He was quite certain of John Mill and others he mentioned as contributors to the Pamphlet, and he was also quite certain it would more than pay after the first two or three months. When you spoke to me in respect to funds, I spoke to thirty or forty of those members whom I thought likely from their acquaintance with Roebuck, and their support of the cause, to support by subscription the Pamphlet. . . . I only collected about £70. . . . I met with so many rebuffs from those I had expected to find quite ready on principle, that I cannot do more in the money way, though I am most anxious to see it go on. I have recommended it everywhere by special notes, and done all in my power to promote its success, and I consider that the allowing it to drop will be the severest blow to Roebuck that he has had. It will be an admission of failure ; of inability to keep up his work, etc.

I can have no hesitation in saying that when Mr. Roebuck expects the co-operation of others in a general and common cause, he must not be so self-important as to think that every person must give way to him and implicitly obey his mandates. He in reality does so, and yet complains that others will not support him.

I am as ready as any man to speak and to act as I think right ; but when I want the co-operation and assistance of others to carry a point, I am necessarily obliged to yield part of my opinions to those who are to assist me. But Mr. Roebuck has not done so, as you may learn by speaking to Mr. Grote, his longest and most intimate friend, who took the trouble to contradict in the *Times* a statement that Mr. Roebuck had made, and refused, when I asked him to subscribe to support the Pamphlet, on the ground that he could not identify himself with Mr. Roebuck's ultra and startling reforms.

I would also add that if some of my opinions and suggestions had been attended to by Mr. Roebuck, he would have had more friends, and have been in a better condition to support and carry the objects he has in view, than he will be if deserted by those with whom he should act, and on whom he should rely for support on the pinch.

. . . I should think, if you will interfere, the work will go on usefully to the public and with credit to Mr. Roebuck. If it falls now, it will damage him much. . . .

P.S.—You may still command my best assistance, and as I am unwilling to hurt Mr. Roebuck's feelings in any way, you will act accordingly.

The inevitable result followed. The last Pamphlet of

the series, published on February 11, 1836, contained an announcement by Mr. Roebuck of discontinuance, on account of increase of labour consequent on the reassembling of Parliament.

Roebuck again took prominent part in the debates of the session. The peers having introduced such amendments into the Irish Municipal Corporations Bill as compelled the Government to drop that measure, he renewed his attacks upon the House of Lords. However, he said, their Lordships had only acted after their kind. The fault was not theirs, but that of their institution. If the people of England wished to continue a Reforming Parliament, they must aid to put down that irresponsible body.

On the motion of Lord Dudley Stuart, "As to the effect on British interests of the policy pursued by Russia," Mr. Roebuck spoke at some length. He deprecated threatening Russia with denunciations of war, but he equally repudiated the notion that the Government should cower down before her. The true policy of England was openly to avow that she would always be ready to vindicate her interests in any part of the globe whenever and wherever they were threatened or encroached upon. Proudly relying upon her own strength and national sense of justice to safeguard her interests, she should endeavour, as far as was compatible with this, to preserve peace, since the consequences of a war between England and Russia must be a general conflagration among the different states of Europe.

It was in this session that Mr. Roebuck, in a speech against the stamp duties, drew a contrast between the stamped and the unstamped press, very much to the advantage of the latter. Then up jumped Mr. Kearsley, member for Wigan, in a towering rage. He described this as " the most disgusting speech he had ever heard." The chairman of committee (Mr. Bernal) ordered him to withdraw these words. He refused, and, when Mr. Paul

Methuen came to the aid of the chairman, ejaculated, "Paul, Paul, why persecutest thou me?" and attempted to leave the House. This was not permitted, however until, with great difficulty, he had been made to apologize. Sir William Molesworth waited upon him in an ante-room on Mr. Roebuck's behalf, and was treated with such rudeness that he retired perforce with his mission unaccomplished. Mr. Roebuck then related the circumstances to the House, and concluded by saying that he must "forget the drunken antics of this member for Wigan."

Towards the close of the session Mr. Roebuck's name began frequently to be found in the lists of pairs, and eventually he had to leave London on account of ill-health. He returned, though seriously ill, to vote in the last division on the Irish Tithe Bill, and then left for Hampshire, to take that necessary rest which his multifarious duties had prevented ever since he had been a member of the House, and the need of which had prostrated his system. Rest did not accomplish his cure, but he fortunately gained permanent relief in a remarkable manner by a five days' course of treatment under Dr. Elliotson; and when he next went to Bath, in January, 1837, he was able to declare himself in better health than he had been for years.

The neuralgia in the knee returned again and again, and finally yielded to careful and gentle treatment only in 1844.

Another session had increased the disappointment caused by the non-fulfilment of the expectations of great political advances looked for at the hands of a Reformed Parliament. This found angry expression in the autumn, and led to not a little mutual recrimination in the ranks of the Radicals themselves.* Here, as in most of the

---

* Tait, in his *Edinburgh Magazine*, had long before remonstrated with the Radicals on their want of cohesion and co-operation. He had told them plainly that they were impotent because of fatal isolation, every one of them giving himself the airs of a leader, and claiming to take his own line.

advanced movements of the period, Mr. Francis Place was the mainspring. In his incessant endeavours to stimulate the reformers to ceaseless effort, he spared no one; and the manner in which whip and spur were used gives insight into a hitherto unwritten chapter of the hidden influences which mould history.

Mr. John Stuart Mill * speaks of the manner in which the hopes, founded on the presence of the philosophical Radicals in Parliament, had been disappointed. This, as an expression of the outward and general flow of affairs at this time, may appropriately introduce letters which show the under currents.

The men were honest and faithful to their opinions as far as votes were concerned, often in spite of much discouragement. When measures were proposed, flagrantly at variance with their principles, such as the Irish Coercion Bill, or the Canada Coercion in 1837, they came forward manfully, and braved any amount of hostility and prejudice rather than desert the right, but on the whole they did so little to promote any opinions; they had little enterprise, little activity; they left the lead of the Radical portion of the House to the old hands, to Hume and O'Connell. A partial exception must be made in favour of one or two of the younger men; and in the case of Roebuck it is his title to permanent remembrance, that in the first year during which he sat in Parliament he originated (or reoriginated after the unsuccessful attempt of Mr. Brougham) the Parliamentary movement for National Education, and that he was the first to commence, and for years carried on almost alone, the contest for the self-government of the colonies. Nothing, on the whole, equal to these two things was done by any other individual, even of those from whom most was expected. And now, on calm retrospection, I can perceive that the men were less in fault than we supposed, that we had expected too much from them. They were in unfavourable circumstances. Their lot was cast in the ten years of inevitable reaction. . . . It would have required a great political leader, which no one is to be blamed for not being, to have

* " Autobiography," pp. 194-196.

effected really great things by Parliamentary discussion, when the nation was in this mood.

### J. A. Roebuck to Francis Place.

*Christchurch, Hants, September* 23, 1836.—[Respecting a project for bringing forward Sir William Molesworth for Westminster.] His [Molesworth's] absence from the House of Commons would be a great loss—a loss in this way : There are some three or four (not more) men who have courage to say and do what is right in that House. Now, it is of great importance in this wealth-loving aristocratic country to have among those men a *rich* man, of good standing and *rank*. Molesworth filled up this gap for us. Moreover, he did so with great effect, as he is a person of no mean ability and very great industry. He is ever anxious to learn, is studious, and in the right way. Being young, he would soon acquire the art of speaking, which older men cannot.

### To the same.

*October* 2, 1836.—[From Christchurch.] And now, Father Place, a word with you. You are a good hand at a general blow up; but I should particularly like to know in what I deserve blame for my Parliamentary conduct last year. Before the House met I proposed to test the Whigs, and to separate from them if they would not come up to our mark. What was the consequence ? Why, all you prudent politicians went half mad. There was running to and fro, and threats and prayers and remonstrances without end. Even Hume grew frightened. Well, the session came, and did I in one single instance lose an opportunity of giving the ministers a dressing ? Oh, but you will say, you did nothing about the Stamp Act. How could I ? I was here sick, almost at my last gasp ; and then you say one and all deserve a cart-whip. This universal blame is very easy, but exceedingly unjust. No man did what I did last session, and yet you make no exceptions. All are bad because all were not good —this is your logic. You know the House of Commons, and ought to know what *one* man has to face in that House. When you have a party it is all very fine and easy ; but stand alone, and try. I wish some of you that talk so much would make the attempt. You all seem to forget that if a man be poor, unallied to great people, and young, he has a very hard fight to fight. It is something, as any of you would find if you were to try, even to get a hearing. 'Tis something more to have thoroughly cowed the House into respect. All this I have done ; but Rome was not built in a day ; and if I cannot do everything, in the name of justice do not confound me with the fools and cowards who do nothing. But this is the way of the world ; and you, I find, are not above the world in this.

Your distribution of blame is on the same principle as that of the *unstamped.* Agree with them in all things, one only excepted, and you are rogue, thief, and liar. Do all that you can, but fail to effect all you desire, and you instantly call one an ass, a fool, a coward, a rogue. Do you believe that this will conduce to the public good ? Public men have feelings, and justice should be done even to these men. I am heartily sick of my friends. My opponents I expected would abuse me, but I have ever found that the most bitter of all my violent abusers were my intimate friends. This is very agreeable. You want to know something about Stevens. Ask Black to show you the letters he wrote to me in the papers, challenging me to fight.

*Francis Place to J. A. Roebuck.*

*October* 3, 1836.—No, Roebuck, if I am not quite right, I am all but so. I send you a paper I wrote some time ago for Hetherington's *Despatch.* You will there see that in respect to the newspaper tax I excluded you from all censure, on, I am sorry to say, the true cause, your sad indisposition. I hope you are now much better, and that you will tell me so. I know your spirit, your talents, your courage—and I know also your vexatious disposition, which has led you to talk too acutely in the latter part of your letter. I do not look to immediate success in the House. I blame no one because he is not successful. I know all the difficulties a man has to contend with in the House, but he who cannot overcome them is not a man fitted for the present time. You have overcome them, forced attention and compelled respect —which in all such cases must be more the effect of fear than love. I have fought for you all along against all sorts of people, and have maintained that you, and you alone, were the man to be relied on. But you—yes, you, John Roebuck—are not as yet quite up to the mark. I see the greatest possible changes in prospective, and I know how much of good or evil in those changes must be expected from the conduct of the present House of Commons. I should be satisfied if I saw but six men who would despise the opinion of the House when circumstances made it necessary, and stood up for principle, *i.e.* for the people. It was a duty which on no account should have remained unperformed when the English Municipal Bill came back from the Lords. A stand should have been made. Some man should have moved that the Bill be rejected, on the preamble. Had such a motion been made all the backsliders would have been tested, and a considerable impression made upon the public. Hume said he would do it. He wrote so on the morning of the meeting in Downing Street. He went there, and succumbed. To what? To Lord John Russell. And why? Because the Whigs threatened to resign. Men who think the resignation of the Whigs a reason for deserting the people, are of no use to the people; fit only to keep a truckling set of Tories, under the name of Whigs, in office, and thus to drivel down, as low as it can be drivelled down, the whole nation into a state of contemptible imbecility. When the mischief was done, several members condemned their own conduct, but not one of them changed it. They, indeed, changed their tone, complained of the Lords, talked largely of "belling the cat," but no one of the timid mice had the courage to cut the ministers on any occasion. No, they must not even be perplexed, they must be kept in office. Bah! When the time came that the Irish Municipal Bill must go to the Lords, Hume wrote to me. He said, "So surely as the Bill goes to the Lords, so surely will they throw it out; and then what shall we do?" I said, "I will exclude you and three others"—meaning, as he understood, Roebuck, Thompson, Molesworth—"and then I will tell you what the House of Commons will do. They will put up with the flogging the Lords will give them, put their tails between their legs, and crawl away to their kennels like curs, as they are, and the Lords would deserve to be damned outright if they did not flog them." Well, what did the Lords do? They altered the Bill. They rejected the preamble; put another in its place, and made a new Bill of it. They did all it was possible for them to do in their own House to insult the Commons, and yet not one man was found to move that the Bill be rejected—no, not one. They let the Lords act like lords and masters, and they conducted themselves humbly like their liveried servants. . . . No such man was found. The House submitted. It was dragged through the mire by ministers, and the Lords, seeing the plight they were in, treated them with the contempt they deserved. The Lords triumphed simply because no such man showed himself to the people. . . . At the Liberal meetings, as they are called, dinners to shilly-shally members, nothing but misleading treacherous Whiggery is talked ; no symptom of right feeling is shown anywhere—none will be shown while the people are satisfied there are no public men in whom they can place confidence. . . . When I look at the last two sessions, and then think, as the proceedings have often made me do, of the House of Commons' men from the accession of James I. to the shortening of Charles I., and compare them with our House of Commons' men, I feel all but infinitely ashamed, and shuffle off the uneasy feeling as well as I can. Will *you* say that the course I have pointed out, as I pointed out at the times alluded to, and in good time to allow for action, could not be taken—was impossible ? Then I shall say the House of Commons is no place for you, nor can it be for any honest man. It can be useful only to those who are seeking present personal advantage. . . . Had the House acted properly, had the Reformers acted sensibly and boldly, no one can now tell what beneficial changes might have been effected, what in progress. Sure I am that there could have been no chance for the continuance of a Tory administration. And why have not these things been done ? Why but because ministers must be kept in their places. The live lumber, Lord John and Lord Melbourne, and Spring Rice and John Hobhouse, and Glenelg, etc., must not be removed, no, nor made useful in any way. This, Roebuck, "is too bad." Well, well, there goes all my malice. I will have nothing to do with political men, or political matters in connection with members of Parliament, until I see a great change in the right way approaching, and this I at present have no expectation of seeing.

Vanity apart, or vanity indulged—I care not which—but I do believe that were I in the house, you and I could—aye, and would—do much of what ought to be done. Though we should be both bitterly hated, despised we would not be. But the hatred even would not last beyond a session or two. There. If I have expected more from you than from any other man, surely that ought to satisfy you.

The strain on the homogeneity of the Radicals was largely increased by the circumstances under which proposals were launched for a great dinner in honour of the members for Middlesex, Mr. Joseph Hume, and Mr. George Byng. It was intended ostensibly as a demonstration of harmony between the Whigs and the Radicals, and to cement their alliance. Place saw in this a deep design for making the Radicals instruments in strengthening the Whigs, and he spared no effort to prevent his friends from allowing themselves to be used as ministerial tools.

### *Francis Place to Joseph Hume, M.P.*

*December* 30, 1836.—It would be a guinea ill-bestowed in hearing fulsome praises of the Administration and resolutions ambiguously worded in the true Whig style, to secure the assent of those who may be committed by being present, in supporting ministers in breaking down, as far as they can, the energies of the people, in causing them to have no confidence in public men. . . . All the speeches, resolutions, and shoutings, will promote this unless you and Colonel Thompson take a line of conduct precisely the opposite of that which the Whig managers of the meeting will take. It seems to me that you should, on this occasion, place yourselves in a situation which, as matters become developed, will induce the public to look towards, and rely upon, you two, Roebuck and Molesworth, as men on whom they may safely rely, in whom they may place their full confidence. . . . I know no one besides you four in whom confidence can, or ought to be placed; but you are enough if, disregarding present imputations and vexations, you go on upon a broad plan, and trust to time for your justification. . . . This meeting will be a crisis of great importance to the nation, and much may depend on what you and Thompson may say. . . . So general may be the evil, so general and so lasting the good, that I am

7

sure I do not overstep the duty of a friend in calling upon you to give the matter your most serious attention.

*Joseph Hume, M.P., to Francis Place.*

*January* 1, 1837.—You need not be afraid of me as to what I shall say. . . . If you will put down on paper what you would say and do were you in my place, I shall be able to see how far we differ, and in what, and to reconsider all suggestions. You may depend upon it that no arrangement will give other than a Radical character, if the Radicals will attend.

*J. A. Roebuck to Francis Place.*

*Bath, January* 4, 1837.—I have read your letter to Hume with very great pleasure. I wrote him one on the same day, on the same subject, and our views coincide exactly. The dinner appeared to me just in the light it did to you, and I took the liberty of telling Hume so ; in consequence of which he sends me word, as usual, that I am impudent—"union necessary among reformers," and other stuff of the same kind. Now, this is too bad. I had hoped that by this time Radicals would not be as blind as new-born puppies. What will open their eyes if the experience of the last two years have failed to effect that desired object ? I am to see Molesworth and Leader to-night, and shall strongly insist on the course you recommend. Last Monday I met the people here, and pretty plainly stated my mind as to the Whigs, and it took admirably. We had a devil of a row afterwards about the poor laws, in which I did that for the Whigs they would never have dared to do for themselves—to say nothing of their doing the same by us—viz. shared at once, and without circumlocution, the responsibility of the poor law. The fight ended well, and I dealt pretty hard blows on all who yelped a foolish disapprobation.

I am puzzled beyond measure when I endeavour to learn what is meant by Hume and the Prudents. They say, "Do not let *us* destroy the Whigs, but let them fall to pieces." Now, try this statement by a homely illustration. A broken pitcher, kept together by a string, is no bad representation of the present ministry and the Rads. The ministers are the broken pitcher, and the Rads the string. Now, suppose some one to say,

" Let us not break this pitcher to pieces ; no, only let us pull the
string off," what should you say to such a speech ? Why, that
taking the string off necessarily implies breaking the pitcher to
pieces—letting it fall and making it fall to pieces being the same
thing. Thus say I to Hume & Co. : Prudent men, you abuse
the Whigs. You say you are ready and determined to speak all
you think, and divide upon every important question without
reference to the Whigs, and yet you talk of keeping them in
power. Now, this is not honest, or it is very silly. If you do
as you say, the Whigs cannot remain in office. Why, then,
disguise this act of yours by sham names ? This which you
say you will do *is breaking the ministry to pieces*, turning them
out and letting in the Tories. The Whigs know and say this ;
why should we *falsely* deny it, and by lying, glozing words, try
to cheat them and the world ? However, I need not preach
to you.

### Francis Place to J. A. Roebuck.

*January* 5, 1837.—I have had a long but amicable dispute with
Madam Grote. She is by far the best of the party, but she is so
surrounded by the dawdlers that her own strong understanding
gives way, and she is blinded to the fact that to compromise, as
she calls it, is to submit. . . . She and they are for showing at
the dinner on the 23rd that the Reformers and the Whigs will
continue to pull together against the Tories, *i.e.* the Reformers
will consent to be stultified, that the Tories, divided into two
sections under the names of Whigs and Conservatives, may
balance each other and prevent anything useful being done.
This would at any time be a bad game to play, and now especially
it would be a miserably bad game. Madam Grote is wonderfully
pleased with Molesworth's excellent article in the *Review*. She
says that Grote is filled with admiration of its excellent points,
and she talks again of compromising as a proper measure. She
read to me some extracts from a letter from Molesworth ; among
others, this : If Grote speaks out on the ballot he will be silent.
This would be compromising with a vengeance ! He had better
resolve not to compromise at all, nor do anything that has a
tendency to let down the fame the article in the *Review* and his
recent conduct will procure for him. Hold his tongue he cannot.
At the dinner he must be. The people will have a speech from

him, and it must be an uncompromising one. He is a made man if, on this occasion, he talks principles as well as he writes them.

While this correspondence was going on, Mr. Roebuck and his colleague in the representation of Bath, General Palmer, were again entertained by the Reformers of that city at a banquet. At this Sir William Molesworth, M.P., Mr. John Temple Leader, M.P., Colonel William Napier, and Colonel Charles Napier, were present. There General Palmer's speech in defence of Lord Grey and Lord Melbourne was interpreted by Mr. Roebuck into an attack upon his hostility to the Whigs. He retaliated with his accustomed pungency. The speeches of Molesworth, Leader, and the Napiers were all strongly Radical and anti-ministerial. After the loyal toasts, and preceding the army and navy, came the favourite toast of the Bath Radicals, " The People, the only source of political power."

### *J. A. Roebuck to Mrs. Roebuck.*

*Bath, January* 6, 1837.—Our dinner went off admirably. The report of the doings will be a failure, I imagine. Leader and Molesworth's speeches were ready written ; mine was off-hand ; Napier's elaborately prepared, but he seems not to have actually written it. . . . Of Molesworth and Leader I cannot speak too highly. In the former there is by far the more thought, but Leader will be a useful, and by no means a commonplace man. Yesterday Charles Napier was evidently surprised at our fashion of doing things. This " strategy " is new to him, in which mind and not the body fights. You are right as to Mrs. Grote ; she is, and will be for ever, jealous of everybody who puts Grote into the shade. She ought, in truth, to be jealous of Grote, for he himself causes his own eclipse. If he would *do* anything, his reward in praise and esteem would be boundless.

### *Joseph Hume, M.P., to Francis Place.*

*Worthing, January* 5, 1837.—You may depend upon it that the proceedings which you so much complain of in the last session were almost unavoidable. But nothing of the same kind will take place in the ensuing session, as you will see. I think if you had been in the House yourself, you could not have done otherwise than we generally did.

### T. *Perronet Thompson, M.P., to Francis Place.*

*January 7,* 1837.—Having occasion to write to Hume to-day, I have directed his attention to the toast as given at Bath, "His Majesty's Ministers, and may they continue in power as long as they advance the cause of the people," and asked him whether it might not prevent danger of dispute if the toast was to stand so at the Middlesex dinner. As it has been given once at a dinner of Whigs and Radicals, that makes a precedent.

In reply, Mr. Place objected at length for five reasons. "If," he wrote, "the toast be given, I shall turn up my glass and remain seated; as many more as may choose will do the same."

### *Francis Place to Joseph Hume, M.P.*

*January 16,* 1837.—You now see who are to be stewards at the Whig dinner, and among them are the names of leading men who have played you false—men whom you well know would not become stewards excepting on one well-understood condition, namely, that Mr. Hume should not be made the prominent feature of the meeting. The original pretence was "the generally expressed desire of the reformers of Middlesex to give some testimony of approbation to the conduct of their two members." Yet men were at once solicited to become stewards which showed at once that this was a false pretence. Roebuck and Molesworth were especially excluded from any invitation, and a character not to be mistaken given to the meeting. Hume was to be a mere incident, since it was understood that neither Roebuck nor Molesworth was invited, and that they had determined not to go to the feast. All those with whom I have had intercourse resolved not to go, and so did I.

Not long before, Hume had in conversation said that Mr. Byng (his colleague) was then, and had ever since been, his concealed enemy, and had done all he dared to do underhand to oust him.

Notwithstanding this, at the Middlesex dinner, Hume desperately affronted his allies by thus speaking:—

That man must have a flinty heart who could sit unmoved under the speech of my honourable friend [Mr. Byng]. . . . In him our young friends may see the gratifying and honoured consequences of pursuing a straightforward course without turning to the right hand or to the left, by any hereditary prejudices, personal partialities, or selfish interests, but rigidly adhering to the advocacy of those important questions which involve the rights and interests of the people.

*Francis Place to Joseph Parkes.*

*January* 27, 1837.—Well, the Bartlemy Fair Show passed off as became it. Take away the manly, honest speech of Grote, and what will remain? Nothing but glitter and gabble. It was a poorer thing in respect to speech-making—Grote again excepted—than any public political dinner meeting I ever knew in Westminster. To Byng no honour was done ; none could be done. To Hume none was intended, and he did himself none. The Whigs ! Bah ! All the great big bugs staid away. Honour to ministers, none. It showed the public that the so-called friends of ministers were, like themselves, poor things, fit only to be sneered at by the Tories. . . . It has done nothing for ministers. *You* must know that the Tories expect to carry an amendment on the address in the Lords with a large majority, and to lose it in the Commons with a very large majority. May not the king, who refuses to open the Parliament in person, be induced by these circumstances to turn out the imbeciles ? Should he do this, there will be howling enough in the Whig faction, and the people will, I hope, stand aloof, and see the Tory sections worry one another.

Mrs. Grote admitted the extreme mortification the proceedings had caused to her and her husband. She never saw him " so ashamed and contrite," and they spent the next day " covered, as it were, in sackcloth and ashes," mourning a great opportunity lost. Place improved the occasion by urging that Grote should—

Stand upon the knowledge he possesses ; take it as his rule, and act upon it, utterly regardless of what any one may think or say. He may then push the world before him. He would be a host in himself, and would soon be surrounded by a host of the best men in the world, not to advise him, but to carry out his purposes. . . . If he would not fear to make occasional mistakes, as all men must, but relying on his own sound and comprehensive understanding, put himself at once into his high and proper position, he would indeed become *the* people's man, and the cause of there being many other people's men. He and every such man should be, thus far, ambitious.

## CHAPTER IX.

ROEBUCK AS A DEMOCRAT.   1837.

UNDER the influence of these events, Mr. Roebuck seized
the opportunity afforded by the reassembling of Parliament (1837), to deliver, in the debate on the Address in
reply to the King's Speech, an attack upon the Government, directed from the extreme democratic standpoint.
This, while it incurred the wrath of Whigs, brought from
working men's associations, in all parts of the country,
many congratulatory addresses.   The speech was reprinted
in cheap form, and scattered broadcast.   It excited the
more attention because of standing out in marked contrast
with the attitude of other Reformers, whether they abstained from the debate or took part in it.   The press
rang with defences and denunciations of Mr. Roebuck's
conduct.   The *Spectator* drew the following picture of the
House and its attitude :—

Mr. Roebuck startled the House by a speech perhaps the
most remarkable that had been delivered in Parliament since the
times when Lords were voted useless.   Mr. Roebuck's manner
was well suited to the matter of his speech.   It was vehement
without being noisy ; impressive, but not solemn ; plain, but not
vulgar ; contemptuous, but not insolent.   For the most part he
was heard in silence, and when he sat down there was no audible
encouragement.   The feeling of the House was made up of
surprise, displeasure, and apprehension, such as is usually caused
in polite assemblies by the home-thrust of disagreeable truths.
In this way the absence of cheering is accounted for.   But the
House paid Mr. Roebuck a higher compliment than can be

conveyed by shouting ; the representatives of the people listened to him for an hour together, without impatience or fatigue.

Perhaps the most remarkable part of this able speech (wrote one who viewed it from the gallery) was that where Mr. Roebuck loudly proclaimed himself a Democrat. The honourable member over and over again referred to the struggle constantly going on in this country between the democratic and aristocratic parties. He seemed to feel keen pleasure in throwing the word "democracy" in the very teeth of the House of Commons, and told them plainly that, since 1688, the Government of England was not monarchic, as was so often asserted, but an aristocratic republic. I watched narrowly the effect of this speech on the House, and I must say that I never saw men of all parties look more uncomfortable. The truths were cutting and severe, and the language bold and manly to an extent that the walls of St. Stephen's must have been astonished to hear tolerated. Mr. Roebuck's speech, as might be expected, was most disagreeable to the Whigs, and therefore they naturally received it coldly. The Tories were still worse treated, and they gave it no kind look of reception or recognition. Even the Radical party, with very few exceptions, turned their backs on the speaker, and knew him not. But if they reject him, there are others who will joyously hold out the hand of fellowship and support, and take pride in supporting Mr. Roebuck and men resembling him in moral courage and talent. The people want such advocates, and those depending with confidence on the people's support have always been sure of finding it. To account still more fully for the coldness with which Mr. Roebuck's speech was received, it may be well to remind my readers that the last session terminated with a most violent speech from Mr. Hume against ministers. He was still thundering forth when the Commons were summoned to hear the king read his speech. Ministers evidently dreaded the secession from their side of a man so powerful as Hume. They would naturally try to come to terms with him ; and it is supposed, with a great appearance of probability, that during the recess a new compact has been entered into between them and a section of the Radical party. . . Roebuck and some other ultra-Radicals are not, it is said, a party to this agreement, and accordingly we find him fiercely denouncing the conduct of ministers as soon as the Address is moved. Hume got up to speak, not to take part with the member for Bath, not to reiterate the violent speech of the last day of the past session, but to declare that the present moment was not the best for insisting on extreme proceedings on the part of ministers.

The tone Hume took, naturally enough, strained still further the loyalty of his friends. "His doctrine," they said, " was admirably calculated to encourage the Whigs in every species of misdeed. His worst enemy could hardly have wished him to have made a worse speech."

### *Francis Place to J. A. Roebuck.*

*February* 1, 1837.—Words cannot express my admiration of the report of your speech last night in the House of Commons, which I have just now read in the *Constitutional*, in preference to the *Chronicle*. God bless you, my dear boy ! The grovelling hound in the *Chronicle* says you represent yourself. Good, very good ! The stultified beast does not see that unintentionally he bestows the highest possible praise on you. Yes, yes. Be single-minded, single-hearted ; never mind to-day, nor to-morrow ; work on for the time that is coming, and you will not be deserted in the end. Has Hume lost his acuteness that he dawdles and see-saws as he does ? If he can do no better than he did at the Whig Bartlemy Fair dinner, and last night in the House, it is time his night-cap were drawn over his eyes, and he were put away to hibernate the rest of his days.

### *J. S. Mill to Francis Place.*

*Post Mark, February* 10, 1837.—As for Roebuck's speech, it has greatly raised his character, and will do good ; but in so far as it goes beyond Molesworth, I do not agree with it.

A fortnight afterwards, at a dinner given to Mr. Thomas Wakley by the Finsbury electors, Mr. J. Temple Leader in the chair, Mr. Roebuck, in the presence of Mr. Hume, Mr. Daniel O'Connell, and Mr. D. W. Harvey, M.P. for Southwark, bitterly reproached his Radical allies for leaving

him to stand alone in propounding really democratic principles. No Liberal member of a Metropolitan constituency,
he complained, backed him up. He advocated universal
suffrage, and dared to do it in the House of Commons, in
the face of six hundred men who would like to turn him
out of doors. He especially taunted Mr. Harvey, who
preceded him at the banquet, with speaking boldly in
Finsbury truths as to which he kept discreet silence in
the House of Commons. Mr. Harvey, of course, claimed
the right to defend himself, and there ensued a scene of
violence altogether out of place at a convivial meeting.
It is significant of the spirit of the times that the first
toast proposed from the chair was, " The king—his rights,
and no more." The second was, " The people—their rights,
and no less." The third was, " The health of the Princess
Victoria."

Mr. Roebuck not only took prominent part in the most
important debates of the session, but he contributed to a
newspaper " Notes," affecting to be taken by " A Spectator "
from the gallery, descriptive of the proceedings in the
House. He was accustomed in these to discuss his fellow-
members with great frankness. Describing the proceedings on the Municipal Corporations of Ireland Bill, in
which he had spoken incisively, he thus wrote of Lord
Stanley, whose policy he had vigorously assailed from the
moment when he entered the House in 1833, and whom
he had * called "a mere House of Commons debater—a sort
of official prize-fighter "—

To Lord Morpeth followed the renegade Lord Stanley.
Flippant, petulant, and fierce, he showed himself on this occasion
to be passion's slave. He had no argument at hand, but he was
full of threats. " I will," and " I won't," " you shall," and " you
shall not," seemed the sole figures of his rhetoric, his whole butting
of reason. How are the mighty fallen! I remember the time
when men hoped much from this vixen-like stripling—when they

* *Tait's Edinburgh Magazine*, December, 1833, p. 325.

believed his virulence to be satire, and his passion eloquence. He is now esteemed as he ought to be—a weak and petulant boy, too long considered to be a man. *

But Mr. Roebuck, in these sketches, did not exempt himself from his own criticism. Thus, referring to his denunciation of illegal practices in connection with a motion to suspend the issue of a new writ for Stafford, on which there was hot controversy, he described himself as " being laughed at for his pains."

It was on the 8th of February that he had spoken vehemently in favour of the Irish Municipal Corporations Bill, begging and entreating the Government not to abate one jot or iota of a Bill which placed the two parties in the State at issue on matters involving the real democracy of England. They were fighting for the real, right, clear, and definite rule that the people of Great Britain and Ireland were worthy to be their own governors. The Opposition said they were not. That was the true principle before them. To the people of England he would leave the issue of this grand and high debate, certain that the victory would be with the right.

A day or two afterwards Mr. Roebuck was telling the House that its continued disfranchisement of Stafford for bribery was mere hypocrisy. Members did not dislike bribery; they practised it. Their protestations of hatred were a pretence, otherwise they would stop it in the only effectual way—by an extension of the suffrage and by adopting the ballot. On Lord John Russell's Canada resolutions he bluntly informed the House that it was utterly ignorant of everything relating to the question on which it was going to decide; and he renewed the attack he had

* Lord Melbourne and Lord John Russell had both looked upon Stanley as the coming successor to Lord Althorp as leader of the Liberal party in the Commons (Russell's " Recollections and Suggestions," p. 115; Torrens' " Life of Melbourne," i. 420). Stanley had taken the courtesy title of Lord on the death of his grandfather, the twelfth Earl of Derby, in October, 1834. He was created a peer in September, 1844.

made in previous sessions on Sir A. Agnew's "Bill to extend to all classes the privilege of protection in the due observance of the Lord's Day."

On the 9th of June he wound up the attacks upon the Government which he had continued throughout the session by a final assault on their policy, based upon a motion for a committee of the whole House to inquire into the state of the nation.

Even in those days the slowness of Parliamentary procedure irritated the more ardent spirits. Mr. Roebuck, remarking that as, in debate, "the great guns will not go off until after ten o'clock, the hours from five to ten are thrown away," suggested an adjournment from five to ten. "Another plan," he said, "has indeed been proposed, which would be equally efficacious, but this has been rejected—I mean that of regularly adjourning the House every night at twelve punctually. If this were done, the great guns would go off before ten"—a prophecy which, helped by Mr. Gladstone's example of speaking before the dinner-hour, has since been largely realized.

Seldom was due recognition made of Mr. Roebuck's courage and conduct even by his friends. Testimony like the following, coming as it does from the pen of an adversary, is, therefore, all the more valuable :—

His very first speech stamped him as a man of superior talent as a debater, and secured for him a hearing at all times ; of which he availed himself to advocate the cause of the people in their many sufferings. He gave full fling to the democratic tendency of his mind, while at the same time he infused a species of philanthropy into his exertions. Nothing was too arduous for him. On one occasion he stood up and presented a petition from an individual unfortunately too notorious. Other members had refused to present it ; but Mr. Roebuck believed that the party in question had been unjustly treated, and that was enough to induce him to take up the case. . . . It is to his honour that he does not, as some of his compatriots do, wait till a subject is popular before he takes it up. A natural restiveness of temper,

H

and an unconquerable love of justice, which he would secure, even at the peril of social convulsion, urge him with an irresistible impulse to act upon what he conceives to be the abstract merits of the case, with which he will not allow expediency to interfere. Of course, this spirit sometimes carries him to extremes, and betrays him into wild defiance of constituted authority ; but those who would be the most likely to shrink from these extravagancies of an earnest mind cannot refuse to respect the uprightness which sustains Mr. Roebuck against unconquerable prepossessions in the minds of certain classes, and renders him, in respect of many subjects, a model of that very rare character—an independent member of Parliament.

# CHAPTER X.

ON the death of King William IV., Mr. Roebuck and his colleague, General Palmer, offered themselves for re-election as representatives for Bath in the first Parliament of Queen Victoria. Although Mr. Roebuck had, in his five years of Parliamentary life, abundantly realized the hopes of his local Radical supporters, and had strengthened his hold upon them, his uncompromising attacks upon the Whig Government seemed to the official Liberals to have fully justified their original objections to his selection. He had, besides, by his outspoken candour, and especially by the unsparing scorn he had poured on the attempted Sabbatarian legislation, offended large sections of the constituency. There had been long previous preparations for the fight. Lord Powerscourt, a young Irish Orangeman, and Mr. W. H. Ludlow Bruges, a Wiltshire squire, were brought out by the Conservatives. The Whigs put into the field Captain Scobell, a local landowner, and one of the most useful members of the Bath and West of England Agricultural Society. He had shown a generous interest in various movements for the improvement of the lot of the agricultural labourer, and his speeches during the contest contrasted very favourably with the laboured commonplaces of the Tory candidates, who shirked the ordeal of facing public meetings, preferring rather to give unlimited suppers, and to organize disturbances to break up their opponents' gatherings.

1

The contest which ensued is known in local annals as "The Drunken Election." Treating was rampant, and passions ran high. Mr. Roebuck stood at bay against his assailants, refusing to give or to take quarter. Captain Scobell retired from the contest on the eve of the election, declaring afterwards that the wholesale tyranny he had witnessed left him no alternative but henceforth to support the ballot. On the hustings, at the nomination, Mr. Roebuck, by reason of the violence of roughs alleged to have been hired for the purpose, could get no hearing, and his supporters retaliated by preventing Lord Powerscourt from speaking.

The poll from the first hour went strongly against Mr. Roebuck and General Palmer, and by one o'clock the contest was virtually over. Mr. Roebuck did not retire without firing a Parthian shot at his antagonists. Repairing to the hustings as soon as the voting was ended, he said—

Recollect, the minority in which we are placed is caused by Tory gold, Tory intimidation, and Whig duplicity. The Tory has been open in his endeavours—the Whig has been hidden and insidious. You will have cause to remember the event of this day. I am no longer the member for Bath, and the poor man must now, when he has to complain of the bad administration of the Poor Law, or the overbearing conduct of the magistracy apply to the Tory members for Bath. . . . It is the poor man that will suffer. Eight and forty hours will not elapse before you will find the difference. . . . The Dissenters will be the first to suffer. The Tory votes of their representatives will rivet the shackles with which they are bound the more tightly around them. And I cannot but rejoice that my connection with them is so far severed that I shall not have farther to subject myself to reproach in their service. Let them servilely worship their rising sun. Let them crawl before his lordship and sycophantly adore him. I have done with them. I bid you farewell. I have done my duty faithfully by you ; you have not done yours by me so faithfully as you ought.

Mrs. Roebuck has written against a report of her husband's first speech opposing Sir A. Agnew's Lord's Day Bill: "This speech lost Mr. Roebuck his election in 1837 for Bath." The *Spectator*, however, made this explanation, evidently derived from an authoritative source—

There were three important subjects affecting the defeat of Mr. Roebuck. The opinions that he cited of Archbishop Cranmer and of Archbishop Whateley upon the institution of Sunday were placarded and made use of to his prejudice, and many condemned his refusal to permit the "Lord's Day" to be converted into the "Reformer's Day." Secondly, it had been imagined that there really was a union among Reformers, and for the last two years the Radicals in consequence entirely neglected the registration of voters. . . . And thirdly, many of the Radical members of the Town Council, who had afforded active assistance to Mr. Roebuck upon former occasions, had differed among themselves upon municipal affairs, and would not take an active part together in the business of the election committee. . . . The number of electors who polled for him was about 140 less than at the former election; and yet the Tories had employed the most extensive machinery to alienate his supporters from him. Suppers were given, presided over by reputed baronets and reputed gentlemen; treating was frequent; and the constant scenes of many nights of drunkenness and riot in a city distinguished, even during its elections, for its peacefulness, afforded complete evidence of the source of that defeat which ministerial journals ascribe to "going too far" and "impracticable theories." The Liberals gave no suppers; they attempted to debauch no elector; they most honourably refused, upon the last as upon two former occasions, to permit Mr. Roebuck personally to canvass a single elector, and yet the Whigs have no sympathy with a party so honourably distinguished by its conduct.

Mr. Roebuck did not fall alone. Not a few of the prominent men with whom he had been most closely associated also lost their seats; indeed, the elections resulted in something approaching to a Radical rout.

*Mrs. Grote to Francis Place.*

*Berne, August* 16, 1837.—Hume's defeat [Middlesex] cut us up sadly, though he always told us (and told Lord John Russell also) if the magistracy was not purged such would be the consequence at the ensuing election. I see he is in for Kilkenny. But where are Roebuck, Ewart [Liverpool], Thompson [Maidstone], and Hutt [Hull], alas ! and Daniel Gaskell [Wakefield], and Trelawny [Cornwall] ? What havoc surely ! And Grote not secure either ! * Those Whigs have most of it to answer for— that's my belief.

*Francis Place to Mrs. Grote.*

*August* 23, 1837.—Hume's defeat had no such effect upon me as it seems to have had upon you. I cared but little for his being rejected, and wish he had not been returned for Kilkenny. Hume's conduct has not been good during the last two sessions —no, nor that indeed of any of the Reformers in the House of Commons, Roebuck's alone excepted, and his only in the last session. In no one instance did they pull together as they ought to have done. On every occasion they submitted to Lord John. . . . In this they showed want of foresight and of every statesman-like quality. . . . Sure I am that if every one of the Reformers had been rejected it would have been more to the advantage of the nation than some or all of them being returned could be. A session without them would be of great use. It would be seen that the Russells, the Melbournes, the Rices, and the Hobhouses, etc., could not have made headway against the Tories. Thus the value of the Reformers would be seen by themselves and by the public, bringing public acknowledgment of them—although this would be but a negative position, and consequently less imposing than it would be if it had been taken by themselves in a direct and combined opposition in the House of Commons. Had the Reformers done their duty, there would have been a coalition of the Whigs and Tories ; the people would have been roused, and the very name of Whig abolished. There would then be only Reformers and Tories. The battle must thus have been fought on open ground : there could then have been no lagging, no

---

* A petition was threatened against Grote's return for the City of London, where he held his seat by only six votes.

shuffling, no skulking ; and the Reformers, backed by the people, would have conquered. But never mind. The event has only been delayed ; it cannot be prevented coming, and you and I shall live to see it.

### *Francis Place to J. A. Roebuck.*

*September* 10, 1837.—I read your address to the Reformers of Bath with great interest, and I need hardly say that I concurred in every sentiment it contained. You are now the only man having the wisdom to see who has the courage to speak the truth. . . . I did not interfere in any of the elections, not even by advice to any one. I was in hopes that all the Reformers who were members of the last Parliament would have been rejected by the people or beaten by the Tories, Leader alone excepted, and I wished him to succeed merely that the Westminster people might take their own affairs into their own hands again. The Reformers, to a man—you alone excepted—in that House enabled the Whigs to beat the Tories, and I wished to see the two factions fairly pitted against each other, that the country might see the value of a body of Reformers—be taught the value of themselves ; and then, when at the next election there must be a Tory House of Commons, there would really be a popular opposition, and the people might be benefited. But now these " Courtiers " * are all crawling to Lord Melbourne and the queen. . . . Look at Hume, even. . . . being betrayed, as he deserved to be, for meanly becoming subservient to the man (Byng) who had done all he dared to do on previous occasions to prevent him being returned for the county, and then becoming a joint in O'Connell's tail. This conduct I will not forgive in any man. With Hume, however, I will not quarrel. He has done more than any man of his time for the people, and he will yet do more. I will therefore work with him, or for him, in anything I may think worth the trouble it may occasion. I will never give him up unless he joins the Tories. . . .

A pamphlet has been printed by the Ridgeways called " Domestic Prospects of the Country under the New Parliament." This pamphlet has given Brougham great offence, and he says you are the man to write an answer to it, and in this I

* A name given to them by Lord Brougham.

concur with him. I, however, objected to your doing it, on the ground that pamphlets seldom pay their expenses, and you ought not to be called upon to incur loss in the matter. . . . The *Morning Chronicle* says the pamphlet is demi-official. I think that Hobhouse wrote it. . . . The pamphlet is cleverly worded, and will take with nine out of ten of those who think themselves Liberals. . . . It contains much that is true and good, but it very dexterously keeps everything out of sight which could in any way tell against ministers, and puts everything in a strong light which can be made to answer the writer's purpose.

*J. A. Roebuck to Francis Place.*

*Bechton, Christ Church, September* 18, 1837.—I have a great desire to answer the ministerial manifesto, but I do not wish to have the expense of publishing it. . . . I intend this year to set to money-making by law, and shall hang out my sign for election business. Knowing, as I do, so many men of the House, and well understanding their ways, I think success in this line not out of my reach. As for competition, though great in quantity, the quality is of the meanest. Take away Charles Austin, and there is not a man of a grain of common sense among those employed, to say nothing of talent, tact, and power of speaking to a very peculiar and prejudiced judicature. I have hitherto thought little of myself. Now, thanks to the new lights I have received, I shall take care of my personal interests, and shall find, strange to say, that the people will think more of me than if I had looked after theirs. I found when last in Bath that if I had joined the Ministry, and sold the people, my seat would have been safe for life, the people themselves being foremost to honour their betrayer. This is natural among the uneducated. Take the masses separately and talk to them, what do you find? Why, profound ignorance and, necessarily, inveterate prejudice. How, then, can the compound mass differ from the component ingredients? There is no chemical fusion to make a hundred ignorant individuals one instructed body. I heard from Brougham and Hume some time since. Brougham's was a strange composition. Hume is strangely in the dark.

*Francis Place to John Travers.*

*November* 22, 1837.—The Reformers in the House of Commons are not less deserving of censure than the Whig ministers whom they have served. There have been several occasions when it was their duty to their country to have cut ministers and taken a stand upon their own merits. Had they done so, the people would have accepted them, and they would have been eminently popular. I saw these opportunities, and took advantage of them. I conversed with those members who were best known to me, laid the whole case before them, and submitted to them that it was their duty to act in a particular way. They acknowledged it, promised, and, to a man, broke their promises. More than one of them wrote to me, thanked me, and on the very morning again promised to do that which in the evening they wanted courage to perform, yet had just as much courage as enabled them to do just the contrary, and then to be ashamed of their own conduct. At length, and for want of a man of more weight, Roebuck came forward, and then again, to a man, they deserted him. Had they supported him as they ought to have done, he would have found his proper place among them, and the Radicals, as they would then have deserved to have been called, would have gained an importance at the last election which would have saved both themselves and the nation. They were not up to the mark. They had no accurate perception of the solemn duties of men chosen by the people. They threw away the chance of being eminently useful to their country, not wantonly, but cowardly, and became of no importance in the eyes of the people. And now, mark well the consequences. They were treated like slaves by ministers, like dogs by the lords ; and now Lord John and his clique, too narrow-minded to foresee the result, has kicked them from his presence as they richly deserved to be. He has, however, by his great effort to kick them, effectually slipped down himself, and dragged his clique along with himself into the mire.

*Francis Place to Mrs. Grote.*

*November* 25, 1837.—I have read the speeches at White Conduit House. Roebuck's must have told well, but he should have refrained from saying anything about shopocracy. Wakley's

was shuffle—a mean shuffle throughout. Dan's [O'Connell] was
Blather-em-skite roguery at the bottom. People see through his
treachery, and cut him, and then come to him again, and this,
too, time after time. I know him thoroughly, and as thoroughly
dislike him.

From the following we get a glimpse of the society in
which Mr. Roebuck at this time moved :—

*John Temple Leader to the Editor.*

*Florence, February* 19, 1896.—Roebuck and Sir William
Molesworth and Charles Pelham Villiers were, for many years, my
colleagues in the House of Commons, of about the same political
opinions, and my friends. In 1838, and for some years afterwards,
I generally inhabited my villa on Putney Hill, where Edward
John Trelawny (" the younger son ") lived with me, and where I
received my friends who came on Saturday afternoon and left
on Monday morning. My more intimate friends came and went
as they pleased. After an interval of more than half a century,
I remember among them J. A. Roebuck, who was a frequent
and welcome visitor ; and his brother-in-law, the Rev. William
Falconer, called by us "The Rector ;" and Thomas Falconer,
who was afterwards a county court judge, called by us "The
Lawyer ;" and Richard Monckton Milnes (afterwards Lord
Houghton), called by us "The Poet ;" also Rintoul, of the
*Spectator*, and the first Lord Brougham, and Alfred Montgomery,
and the second Duke of Wellington (though an ardent Tory), and
Bickham Escott (also a Tory), and Charles Austin (the successful
lawyer and admirable talker), and his brother, Alfred Austin (who
was one of my electioneering agents) ; the Americans, Charles
Sumner, and General Hamilton, of the South, and James Robert
Black, of Kentucky, for some time my agent, and called by us
"Kentucky ;" the Frenchman, Clement Thomas (who was shot
by the insurgents in Paris), and Godefroy Cavaignac and Armand
Marrast (afterwards President of the French Chamber in 1848).
Some years before, Armand Carrell (who was afterwards killed
in a duel by Girardin) came with me to England, and stayed with
me for a few days at Putney Hill—which, he said, made him
understand the descriptions in Scott's novels. There was also
Prandi and other Italians. . . . My especial connection with

Roebuck was on Canadian affairs—then well known, now probably forgotten. We had the honour to be burnt in effigy by the Tories of Canada. I remember one evening, when driving into town from the country, my carriage was stopped by a crowd all going one way. I asked what it meant, and had for answer, "They are going to see Leader taken to the Tower." I thanked my informant, and drove on. It was a mere idle report. Roebuck was, you know, very irritable, and did not mince his words when speaking of or to an opponent. This made him many enemies. He thought and spoke for himself, and was very little amenable to party discipline.

## CHAPTER XI.

CANADA—THE REPRESENTATION OF GLASGOW.  1838.

ALTHOUGH out of Parliament, public events still claimed
Mr. Roebuck's attention.  He was most especially concerned with the affairs of Lower Canada.  The condition
of that colony had become most serious.  At the moment
when the new Parliament was adjourning for the Christmas
recess, came news of the rebellion—a disaster long foreseen
and predicted, but to eyes that were blind and ears that
were deaf, by the agent of the House of Assembly.

Molesworth and the Radicals in the House, prior to
the adjournment, criticized severely the policy which had
driven the Canadians to despair of the redress of their
grievances by constitutional agitation, and during the
recess, notwithstanding the following caution from Leeds,
there was much plain speaking by Leader, Roebuck, and
others, at a great Westminster meeting, held at the Crown
and Anchor.

*Edwd. Baines, junr. (Leeds), to Francis Place.*

*Leeds Mercury Office, January* 2, 1838.—I wish the meeting at
Westminster on Thursday may do good, but that it may do so it
is exceedingly desirable that Mr. Leader, Sir Wm. Molesworth, and
the other speakers should be less violent and less bitter against
the Government than they were during the late debate in the
House of Commons ; for I assure you that their tone has con-
siderably prejudiced the cause they so ably and so justly espouse,
in the minds of very many people in the country, as well as in
London.

Mr. Place, in reply (Jan. 4, 1838), wholly dissents from this view, and writes—

I, as you know, have seen and conducted many public meetings, yet few that I have seen have equalled that of to-day in numbers, enthusiasm, and perseverance. Never before did I hear, and never did I expect to hear, such a speech as was made by my old friend Roebuck, and never did I see such effects produced by any speech.

*Francis Place to "Fellow Citizen" Samuel Harrison.*

*January* 14, 1838.—Roebuck has done all that any man could do, and more than any other man would do, privately with ministers to prevent civil war, and showed how, even now, arrangements might be made which must be highly beneficial to both countries, and beyond this, he has offered to devote himself to the service ; but he has not been, and will not be, attended to.

On the reassembling of Parliament in 1838, Lord John Russell brought into the Commons a Bill for the suspension of the existing constitution of Canada. Mr. Grote, while opposing the Bill, regretted that there was no one in the House so intimate with all the facts as to be able to reply to the statements of Lord John Russell—one who knew those facts, and who lately represented Bath, being no longer a member.

That evening Mr. Grote presented a petition from Mr. Roebuck, praying to be heard at the Bar on behalf of the House of Assembly of Lower Canada. The request was granted.

Through the columns of the *Weekly Chronicle*, Roebuck (January 17) addressed "The People of England." Referring to the debate which had taken place the previous night, he said—

Some men were in that House who knew the facts of the case, and yet they were silent when Lord John Russell, putting the issue of the debate upon the justice or injustice of the English Government, assailed the House of Assembly of Lower Canada with all the vituperation which malice, unaided by intellect, could supply. Mr. Grote lamented the absence of Mr. Roebuck, but surely the presence of Mr. Roebuck was not needed to refute the calumnies so lavishly employed by Lord John Russell. Mr. Grote knows the whole case, is familiar with the minutest portions of it; had, with his accustomed industry, mastered every detail of this most perplexed and intricate quarrel. Why, then, had he not his knowledge at command? His indignation should have stirred up within him the latent energies of his character, and impelled him to have grappled closely with the many monstrous misstatements of the noble lord, and to have scattered to the four winds of heaven his shallow and miserable sophistries.

*Joseph Parkes to Francis Place.*

*Westminster, January* 18, 1838.—Roebuck has a splendid opportunity on Monday. He has the power, instruction, and taste to take advantage of it if he chooses, and I trust he will. I have been deeply sorry for him, and the sort of proscription under which it has been vainly sought to crush him. But Monday will compensate him for being out of Parliament, and if his advocacy of the question is well done, will place him on a high pedestal. He has begun life at the wrong end, pecuniary independence being essential to an *honest* and successful public man ; but there, he is in this present station, and Monday may elevate him highly, both in his private and public interests.

*Francis Place to Joseph Parkes.*

*January* 18, 1838.—Roebuck is singularly impatient of advice, but still he takes it well from me, and I, as you seem to be, being somewhat apprehensive lest he might not do the best possible, sent him my opinion on several points, and some advice respecting demeanour and management, which I think will be of use to him.

Roebuck accordingly appeared at the Bar of the Commons, and there described the long struggle of Canada for the right to administer her own internal concerns without interference from the Home Executive. It was in vain. The Bill passed, and was sent up to the Lords, where, on February 1, it was read a second time, in spite of Brougham's vehement opposition.

*Francis Place to J. A. Roebuck.*

*January* 24, 1838.—I have heard read to me your speech at the Bar of the House of Injustice, before men nearly the whole of whom have no correct notion either of their own situation or that of the public—before men with pride, contempt, and hatred of all who rank below them, who never perhaps, in the whole course of their lives, felt one serious desire to do justice to the people. On these men your words were thrown away, but they will be recorded, and you will be honoured. Would they could have immediate effect ; but the power of close, deep, *continuous* reasoning is the lot of few, and those few have never yet directly governed mankind. All day yesterday every one whom I saw said you had made a good speech, but some said you had fallen off towards the close of it ; and why ? Why, because you had not abused—for that, indeed, was what they meant—you had not abused ministers. The stand you took was unheeded by them, yet it was the only stand which a sound intellect could take. I, at least, honour you.

I also heard much of your letter in the *Weekly Chronicle.* Every one whom I saw condemned you for having sacrificed your friends, and thus put out of their consideration the other parts of your letter. I wish you had not particularized Grote, because he has done more already in this session than you or I, knowing him as we do, ought to have expected from him, and because you call upon him to say why he did not do that which his peculiar notions did not permit him to do—what, indeed, you as well as I know it was utterly impossible for him to do. I wish you had omitted his name, and put the matter more generally. I always feel uncomfortable when those of our friends who do something or much are *publicly* blamed, while those who do nothing are suffered to go without censure. Now, do not misunderstand me. I concur in everything you have said in your letter, and am pleased with the admirable manner in which it is said, and dissent only from your naming Grote.

I lament as deeply as you do that the so-called Liberals in the House of Commons should be such men as they are—far below the times in which they live. I lament this the more because these are not times when men thus placed by the people should be nullities, since their being so will inevitably lead to great and

long-continued evils.   This, you know, is neither a new nor a
hastily formed opinion, but the result of serious thinking.   It is
not now suddenly expressed as a momentary thought, but has been
said and written time after time, more with pain and shame than
with indignation, great as has been my indignation.

### *J. A. Roebuck to Francis Place.*

*Monday, January* 29, 1838.—I am much obliged by your
kind letter.   The fact of your having written it shows me that
you very correctly understand my position, and that you have
divined my state of mind.   The peculiarly painful consequence
of all my conduct as a public man has been the conduct of my
friends to me on every emergency when their countenance would
have been useful to me..   When all the rest of the world have
discovered that I am right, they have courage to think so also ;
but until the public has come round, they shrug their shoulders,
turn up their eyes, and cry out, " Alas ! he is so imprudent."

In the present case I am not a voluntary agent.   My duty to
my Canadian clients bids me brave everything rather than desert
them.   Now is not the time to turn round.   If they are wrong
now, they have been wrong all along.   The present state of
things is but the necessary consequence of battling for good
government against a powerful and unjust nation.   I saw long
ago the necessary result, and when it was far off, braved it.   I
am not going to turn tail now that it has arrived.   I have acted
with my eyes open, and knew perfectly well what was coming.
Posterity will determine whether I am right, and to that tribunal
I am willing to leave the decision.   In the meantime, the pain
and disgust which beset me are not trifling—pain when I think
with what calumny the right is to be always obtained ; disgust
when I see the pusillanimous leaders, who call themselves the
friends of the people.   I came to town this winter fully determined
to take no active part which was not entailed on me by the past,
in politics.   Unluckily, this Canada business is a part of this
heritage, and I am dragged most unwillingly into public life
again.   This cannot last, however, very long, and I then will follow
out my former determination of leaving the field of politics
entirely for the present.   The people must go through another
probation before men of very decided opinions can be of use.
The sacrifice of quiet is not compensated by any good we can do.

The year 1832 opened a great scene to the Radical party. They have proved themselves unequal to the occasion, and we must wait for another chance. I know not, and for myself care not, how long we may wait.

The letter of which you speak, and the talk about Grote that I hear of, has served more than most things to disgust me. I chose to say that a great opportunity had been thrown away, that no sufficient grounds had been laid to justify those who are supporting the Canadians, and with some praise I mentioned Grote's name, and wondered that he, knowing the whole case, had made so feeble a defence. In doing this I have been accused of base *ingratitude*, and language has been used towards me that would only have been justified by my having deserted Canada and my friends here, and sold myself to the Whigs. Mrs. Grote has utterly severed our friendship for ever. If what she said were true, I am not fit to be her friend ; if it be false, she is not fit to be mine. She is so surrounded by persons who flatter her to her face (while they abuse her behind her back) that the truth never reaches her. Abuse in political papers she rightly sets down as party abuse, and any other blame she never hears, though it is matter of daily occurrence around her. When I spoke out, she thought it criminal. This conduct on my part is very different in all respects from that of her pseudo-friends. It is plain and above-board—very unlike that ribald abuse which I have often rebuked ; but still, this is alone to be condemned. I wish her joy of her discrimination. Had I thought that there was any chance of a misinterpretation such as you mention, I certainly should have avoided mentioning Grote's name, but that there was injustice in my sentiment I cannot see.

I could tell you some strange things, were I to see you, of the thorough-paced cowardice of my friends, but to write them would hardly be worth the trouble.

Leave was also granted to Mr. Roebuck to be heard at the Bar of the House of Lords, and, on the 5th of February, he there recapitulated the Canadian grievances.

*Mrs. Roebuck to her Father.*

*February* 5, 1838.— . . . Roebuck is in high spirits. He has written out his speech to the Lords—eighty-six pages. The

I

speech to the Commons was not written out : all we have of it is the shorthand report by Mr. Gurney ; and whether he sent it to any newspaper, I do not know. Lord Brougham was written to this morning, to ask what time he—Roebuck—was to appear, and also to get me a seat. You must see his answer ; here it is :—

" My dear R.,—You come to our longing arms at a quarter to five, and at five or thereabout, you will begin by saying ' My Lords.' This is the only part of your speech I can anticipate. As for ladies, I have these two days had the most inexorable refusal from the only person that can admit them. Those refused were peeresses."

*February* 6.—Nevertheless, I received a summons to go down hastily to the House of Lords, which summons I obeyed immediately, and found it was not so " impossible." Roebuck went down first, and on his arrival had arranged with Sir Augustus Clifford for my admission. A large chair was pushed before me just to the Bar of the House, where I was requested to sit, and by my side I found two ladies, one rather plain, the other remarkably handsome. The first was the (last) Duchess of Gordon, the other the Duchess of Sutherland. We were the three only ladies admitted on this night only. Roebuck had begun when I came in, and he gave the noble lord at the Colonial Office and Mr. Spring Rice a plain statement. I send you the speech—Thomas [her brother] says the best Roebuck ever made. I remarked, the Lords listened with great attention. The Duke of Wellington and Lord Lyndhurst came down to the Bar, and down below the table there were about a hundred and fifty peers, at least, and their attention was very great. A large number of the House of Commons attended. Lord Brougham sat twitching his nose in great style. The Chancellor [Cottenham] sat with Lord Glenelg, who was red and angry. After the speech was over, I was standing with a crowd of friends round me—in the way, I suppose—and did not see the Chancellor coming. He made a *détour* round me, to my friends' amusement—the Duke of Wellington, amused as the rest, sitting near. The Bill passed its second reading in a very short time—five minutes—without discussion. By the end of the week there will be no constitution in Canada, no Legislative Council, no Assembly, no Agent ; all will be powerless.

This will not please the authors of the row. Instead of getting more, they lose the little they had.

It was not until 1840 that the Canadian troubles were at last ended by uniting the two provinces, and conferring on them legislative independence. By 1843 the province had become quiet and peaceable. Many of those who had been concerned in the rebellion were now loyal subjects, taking honourable part in administrative affairs. But there were still, in penal servitude in Van Diemen's Land, several French Canadian peasants who had been transported during the troublous times. Mr. Roebuck brought their case under the notice of the Government and House of Commons, by a motion " That, as a matter of wisdom, justice, and policy, her Majesty might be humbly addressed to extend that mercy which was the brightest ornament of her prerogative, to these few poor men, and to restore them to their friends and families in their own country." To this Lord Stanley, then Secretary for the Colonies, made objections, chiefly technical, as also did Mr. Charles Buller. The motion was not pressed, its object being partially gained by the promise of Lord Stanley to pay attention to the circumstances of each case. The surviving prisoners were, however, not liberated for nearly two years after. The satisfaction expressed in the colony at their return to America, and their subsequent law-abiding conduct, fully justified the unceasing efforts that at last procured their release. This feeling partially found expression in the following lines :—

> D'autres viendront tantôt saluer leurs chaumières,
> Nous, grâces aux bienfaits d'un enfant d'Albion,
> D'un homme protecteur de notre nation,
> Nous foulons aujourd'hui la terre d'espérance ;
> Béni sois-tu, Roebuck, pour tant de bienveillance!

This, however, is anticipating subsequent events. Reverting to the year 1838, Mr. Roebuck is found, in June, paying a visit to Glasgow, whence had come an invitation from the Liberals asking him to be their candidate at the next election.

*J. A. Roebuck to Mrs. Roebuck.*

*Liverpool, June* 17, 1838.— . . . I arrived here safe at about ten last night. The journey had little that was pleasant, and to me, though the steam made us go fast, it was not agreeable. A villainous smell enveloped us the whole way, spoiled the country air, and overpowered the may that was all around us. At Denbigh Hall the whole posse of us had to leave the train and get into a variety of vehicles, coaches, and 'buses, etc.

*Glasgow, June* 19, 1838.—I arrived here at two yesterday. I shall meet the people on Thursday, and leave behind a legacy to the Whigs, not in hard words, but in plans and principles. . . . Rain, rain, rain—nothing but rain. This is called the wettest place in Scotland, Greenock excepted, and sure enough it has done nothing but rain since I have been here. The journey from Liverpool was not painful, and some parts - of the road were interesting. I should like to pass a few days in the Cheviots. Copley Fielding has been there, I am sure. The day was cloudy, the clouds drifting with gleaming lights. This brought out the round hills capitally, and some of the scenes were strikingly picturesque. The midland part of England surpasses any place I have yet seen in Great Britain for fertility. All around Dunchurch was exquisitely beautiful. Hants cannot compare with Northampton and Warwickshire. For forty miles after you leave London all is cold clay, dry sand, and barren in appearance ; but the rich pastures of Leicestershire and Northamptonshire at once change the scene, and give you a magnificent idea of the beauty and richness of our land. The border country is finely cultivated, but the trees are small, and the soil looks barren and wet. Carlisle is a queer-looking place. I was there at four o'clock in the morning, and found all the people stirring, with flags, etc., to celebrate the opening of the railway to Newcastle. The moment we came to the Cheviots, a new climate, a new country, appeared.

*Glasgow, June* 21, 1838.— . . . As I anticipated, we have certainly beat the Whigs with their own weapons. They are beginning to come in, and to talk of a desire to put aside all differences, and to unite for the purpose of carrying me. Friday Mr. Alex. Dennistoun, whom I knew very well in the House of

Commons, is to introduce me to all the leading Whigs here. He himself is a stout Reformer, and, I find, a great admirer of my doings in *Hon'ble House*. He says people have very erroneous notions respecting me, and he is exceedingly desirous of letting them see or hear me.

Yesterday I was called upon by a person from Kilmarnock, with an invitation to visit their town. Dennistoun wishes me to go, saying that there is another chance there. But I am dubious. You must not flirt with too many places at once, but you love all.

Amongst other things, I saw a cotton-mill—a sight that froze my blood. The place was full of women, young, all of them, some large with child, and obliged to stand twelve hours each day. Their hours are from five in the morning to seven in the evening, two hours of that being for rest, so that they stand twelve clear hours. The heat was excessive in some of the rooms, the stink pestiferous, 'and in all an atmosphere of cotton flue. I nearly fainted. The young women were all pale, sallow, thin, yet generally fairly grown, all with bare feet—a strange sight to English eyes. By-the-by, it rained all day nearly, and in every gutter you might see rows of children standing to wash their feet They looked like so many strings of young ducks. I saw no carriages, no well-dressed women in the streets, but all seem here of the working-class, all dirty, though the town itself, spite of the smoke, is clean. I cannot discover that infernal aristocratic spirit that prevails so fiercely at Bath, for example. A man here has just told me that few people in this place can "count a grandfather." All are newly raised, and by their own exertions; in fact, the only distinction seems to be the degree of wealth. Bad enough this distinction ; but I do not see that mortal terror lest you should come in contact with some one not of your own caste, which besets English people. The same feeling may exist, but as yet I cannot find it. I suspect that trade shakes them all together, and creates a system of hail-fellow-well-met—ridiculous airs of superiority are not openly put on. Mind, I speak from a very small experience, and rather express my wonder at not finding the feeling than a belief that it does not exist.

I am somewhat sanguine now. The Whig party find it impossible to get me an opponent Liberal enough to have a chance, and hating their Tory foes here heartily, they only want an excuse for coming over to me. The real difficulty, I suspect, will be to persuade the Ministry to make an opening. It is circulated here that Lord Melbourne expressed a mortal terror when he heard of my standing. This was sent down in a confidential letter, which, like all confidential communications, was immediately spread abroad. I did hear the name of the writer, but have forgotten it. There may be a spice of truth in this. That the Ministry wish to keep me out of the House I know. They must be sure that they cannot do so for any time, and that opposition will only exasperate me. I have just seen a carriage pass the window—a poor shaky affair. I understand that there are hardly half a dozen equipages in a population of 300,000, the second city in the Empire! The sun shines this morning, but the clouds still look suspicious. I do not by any means seem likely to lose my dislike of the bleak north. There must be something innate, and a love of the tropics in my inward feelings. My health has been capital; not one bad night have I had. I eat and sleep, no pain, and am getting strong. So far this escapade has done well. Ask Alexander [Falconer] if he ever felt a warm day in Scotland. I have a fire at night.

*Glasgow, June* 24, 1838.—I hope to leave Glasgow for York on Wednesday next, but of this I am not sure—the people pulling at me in all ways, and entreating me to remain. I have this moment received a requisition from Kilmarnock with I know not how many hundred names entreating me to go there. I cannot, and yet I fear offence will be taken ; but running about to have gaping crowds look at me is not to my taste. Yesterday I was from ten in the morning till past three walking, talking, seeing all the sights, and all the persons that needed to be seen. At three I left Glasgow with Mr. Reddie (Reddie's father) for his country house down the Clyde. The scene from his house is magnificent. The scene, however, is horribly spoiled by one continual cloud of black smoke vomited forth by steamers passing up and down. Dumbarton was in sight, seated on a solitary hill, the river winding at its base, and the steep sides of the valley closing in the picture thus. [Here followed a sketch.] This with a fine atmosphere would have been beautiful. I was tired by my day's work, and came home, and now I am in the quiet produced by some dozens of preachers thumping away in the various kirks and chapels of this smoky town. Surely I was not made for a leader of the people. I cannot hail people in the market-place and make myself at home among all classes. I hate the idea of canvassing a man's good wishes. If they desire to be well governed, let them, but I am not going to crawl to them in order to persuade them to their own good. It is impossible to divest men of the notion that it is the candidate's interest that is mainly thought of. They will learn otherwise if they know me a little longer.

By-the-by, I had almost forgotten to tell you that we had a great meeting on Friday, and the whole affair went off much to the disgust of the stiff Whigs. My explanation of Radical opinions has thrown a damp upon all who were constantly railing on the wildness of our views and schemes. Every hour proves to me how wise was the determination not to come here with the ——, those wild fellows. My whole difficulty has been to undo what they did, and to show that the thinking Radicals were a very different race from those blatant, ignorant brutes.

The Whigs at the meeting on Friday were compelled to own that *no* such difference existed between my views and theirs, as rendered it impossible for them to support me ; and I see that the Tories are as vexed as their old rivals, because it seems but too probable that the Liberal party will be kept together, spite of all threatening appearances. All parties of the Liberal section confess that my visit has done great good, inasmuch as it has led to a great softening down of asperity among the discordant materials which compose the Liberal party. I shall see the working people to-morrow, *and preach in a church* to them.

Rain threatens again. What a country ! I was right about going north. Every step this way was the wrong way. To the south is my cry ; and would that the Fates would place me within a few degrees of the Line. But I suppose I shall live and die in this bleak place of England—die, too, perhaps in consequence of having swallowed too much mist upon some day which the inhabitants called very fine weather.

I saw yesterday a cotton-mill in which a thousand people were daily employed, the greater part women under twenty. The rooms were lofty and not painfully warm. Barring the monotony of the labour, there seemed no great hardship here ; but fancy one's life passed in a whirr of wheels which prevents the possibility of any hearing, looking at a white wall, tying broken threads, and inhaling cotton fluff and oil stink. Think of this, and then remember that in three weeks all these people might be enjoying the sweet air, the warm climate, and the beautiful scenes of the

New World, free from the terrors of starving, and then say if we be not the slaves of habit, and not the servants of our reason. The quiet *habitant* on the banks of the Mississippi, laughing, dancing away his life, is in my mind a far happier, and a far wiser man than the poor cotton-spinner who spends twelve hours out of the twenty-four in a monotonous labour to get the bare means of existence—aye, and happier, too, than the cotton-spinner's master, whose life is a fear, raised by anxiety and a love of gain. But I will not bore you with my sermon longer; you will say that I am in a melancholy humour.

*York, July* 4, 1838.— . . . The country round York is not pretty, or rather, it is pretty, and pretty only. It is flat, rich in its agriculture and foliage, no hills, not much water, only the little river Ouse, the atmosphere from the rain too grey to be agreeable. In the autumn the dark green will have disappeared, and then perhaps pretty "bits" might easily be found. The lanes are green, and leading I know not where—all mystery, and so far delightful as walks and drives; but my eye is still American, and looks for space and aerial tints.

The scene on the Borders approaching Carlisle, as I saw it, is the finest I have seen on this side the Atlantic. It was grand in its extent and colour, and striking, too, by its historical associations. It was strange to hear the guard of the coach (a character, by-the-by) say, "There, do you see that pointed mountain in the distance? That is England; it is Skiddaw." There is still upon the border a feeling anti-English—the remains of olden time when feuds and fighting were common. Some of the commonplace of life is forgotten at times amid new scenes connected with times past, as those of Scotland are. I was standing on Glasgow Green, and the person with whom I was walking, said, "That hill away to the south-east is Langside Hill, on which Mary stood to behold her army defeated by the Regent Murray." The observation came upon me suddenly. I was looking at, and thinking of, the many tall smoky chimneys of the manufactories round me—of the present world and its woes, the acute, but still commonplace, wretchedness of the poor cotton-spinner, her few shillings a week, and twelve hours' daily labour. The speech of my informant struck a chord that was still, and not in unison with those already touched. The effect startled me. The wretched Mary losing a kingdom, destined to be a prisoner in a foreign land, and at length a victim to a jealous rival's hate, was strangely brought into juxtaposition with the toil-worn, pallid, lowly girl of the cotton-factory, whose forefathers might possibly have battled on that field, little thinking that the result of all the strife and turmoil in after times would be that his children's children would linger away their lives in the dull and dreadful monotony of a prison called a factory. Again and again did I ask myself the question, Have we gained anything by our mighty discoveries? and are we at this moment happier than were our forefathers in the wretched times of the battle of Langside Hill? I fear not. Poor Mary's sufferings, being the sufferings of one in a high place, win sympathy and observation, but the misery of the toiling millions crammed together by the spirit of commerce is unseen. However, I must not punish you by inflicting this tirade upon you at any greater length. Had you seen the chimneys of the Glasgow cotton lords flouting the sky, you would probably have felt as I did. But let us travel back to York, and to our life's commonplaces. . . . Legal advance is slow work to one unconnected with attorneys. I feel assured, however, that time will bring success, and that, if once fairly launched, the ship will not fail to reach her harbour. A competency is all I desire ; so soon as that is gained, adieu to law, adieu to London, coal-smoke, and yellow fog, and all my London life will be a Parliamentary one. We shall see if this hope is to be realized.

I received Papineau's * letter yesterday, and the history of Lord Durham's doings. From this last I augur good. He has taken my advice about the Council, and dismissed them all. This looks well. The calling for the affidavits against the prisoners is also a good sign ; he will learn the frivolous pretences on which many have been thrown into jail, and many driven into exile.

Papineau speaks of coming to Europe. I hope no act of Lord Durham's will drive him here ; but still I desire much that he should be seen and understood. . . . That letter to Howe in Nova Scotia gave me more trouble than anything which occurred during the whole Canadian affair. I wish people would not trouble themselves with my concerns.

Do not believe a word said against me and my doings at

---

* Papineau was a Canadian of French extraction, the leader of the Colonial party in Lower Canada. He desired to sever the connection of the colony with the mother-country (Walpole, vol. iv. 118 and 131).

Glasgow by the Glasgow press. The press is all Whig or Tory, and I, as usual, gave them a *fillip*. They are up in arms, all of them, but the great body of the people have been much undeceived and surprised by my conduct and language. They expected fire and fury, but were agreeably disappointed.

Do you know any books that give a good account of Yorkshire? The forest of Sherwood was up in these parts. I wish to know how far it stretched here away. Do you know York? It seems a dull, stupid, parson-ridden place.

*July* 8, 1838.—I have to-day written a long letter to Brougham, who is evidently all astray as to Lord Durham and Canada, misled by a desire to find Durham in the wrong, and by a passion for talking upon all matters, whether he understands them or not. I have told him the truth, and do not suppose that he will be annoyed. He has no wish to quarrel with me, and will, I dare say, shape his course to meet my views.*

I was to-day (junior) in York, and went to the Minster. That was so full that I could not get into the choir. It was all song and painted glass, with old broken-down fellows in *chapeaux à trois cornes*—breeches and gaiters—who yesterday played the part of javelin men to the judges. What a droll procession! Talk of the lord mayor, and his nonsense, that is downright common sense to the affair of yesterday. The trumpeters, the javelin men, the mounted tenants of the sheriff, the followers of the mayor— a playhouse show surpasses it; and this is the way justice is administered in the most civilized of nations.

The following letter, though of later date, completes the story of the Glasgow candidature:—

*J. A. Roebuck to Mr. A. Purdie, Glasgow.*

*London, June* 11, 1839.—Some time since, having ascertained that a vacancy would soon occur in the representation of Glasgow, I informed the Ministry, through the appropriate channel, that I should contest the honour of being one of your representatives. I received without any circumlocution or hesitation a direct intimation that my return would be opposed by the Government.

---

* Brougham, nevertheless, in the House of Lords attacked Durham with such effect that he immediately threw up his office, and came home without waiting for recall.

This did not deter me; it rather confirmed me in my determination.

My success appeared very nearly assured, in spite of the
opposition of the Whig party. It was, in fact, almost impossible
to find any one to oppose me who could hope to succeed. The
Tory might be let in, but to return the Whig seemed impossible,
and as I was first in the field, the blame of dividing the Liberal
interest rested with the Liberals who opposed me.

From this difficulty the Whig Liberals were rescued by an
accident. There is one who has a claim prior to any that I could
put forward—one whose claim I could not oppose—I mean Mr.
James Oswald, who some time since, with great honour to himself
and satisfaction to his fellow citizens, represented the City of
Glasgow. On my being informed that Mr. Oswald intended to
present himself, I at once felt that duty required of me immediately to withdraw. . . .

Allow me, however, to add one word at parting. It is quite
clear that the business of your representative will be a very
different one from that which it has hitherto been. A reconstruction of political parties is about to take place. A Liberal
Government cannot now be said to exist; in fact, we have no
Government at all; but that party which is nominally said to
govern can lay no further claim to Liberality. The *finality* of
Lord John Russell is the Toryism of Sir Robert Peel with a new-
fangled name, and to support him and his colleagues is to support
Toryism in reality, whatever the name may be. A thoroughly
Liberal representative will therefore now be obliged to hold himself
aloof, and to keep clear of all Ministerial pledges and connections.
Hitherto the Liberal majority have acted as blind partizans of the
Ministry. The country sanctioned this unwise proceeding, and
has at length gathered the fruit from the tree of its own plant-
ing. Lord Melbourne and Lord John Russell have declared in
favour of finality—and finality, be it remembered by the good
people of Glasgow, means continuance of all abuses; and amongst
the other things it means perpetual corn laws, it means extravagant expenditure, war establishments during peace, and further,
it signifies all that ill-blood and uncharitableness which is the off-
spring of an exclusive and dominant Church establishment. Some
of us who call ourselves Liberals may be well pleased in the con-
templation of finality—when we anticipate only a restriction of

the suffrage—but there are few who now lay claim to the name of Reformers who will much admire the doctrine of finality, when viewed under this other aspect. It is to be hoped that the Liberals of Glasgow will make up their minds upon the course which their representative is to pursue. The chief object of their endeavours should be to heal the differences now existing between the middle and the working classes, and to unite them into one band of sturdy Reformers, with common interests, feelings, and sympathies. This is indeed a difficult task, surrounded as we are by sinister interests of every possible description ; whose artful advocates see that their chief hope of a continuation of power and profit lies in creating and maintaining ill-blood between these two sections of the community. He would be a great benefactor to his country who could devise some means of thwarting and defeating the machinations of these chief enemies of the people.

# CHAPTER XII.

Mr. Roebuck, as appears from the following letter, was invited to draw up the people's " Charter."

*Francis Place to Erskine Perry.*

*October* 4, 1838.—The Charter, as the proposed Bill is some-what absurdly called, originated thus : The committee of the Working Men's Association . . . determined to proceed step by step towards the objects they now had in view, and to abandon all old projects (as to division of property, holding in common, and so forth—matters which could have no immediate reference to themselves), and they came to the determination to associate with themselves every one who would go along with them, and, as a test, to draw a Bill for carrying their project into effect. . . . At length application was made to Mr. Roebuck, who promised to draw the Bill ; but extreme ill-health and Parliamentary duties prevented him. Application was then made to me, and I undertook the task upon condition that the points, and as much of the detail as the Association could easily put together, should be prepared, so that in drawing the Bill I might be well aware of their notions. This was done ; and I drew the skeleton of a Bill under appropriate heads, and sent it to Mr. Lovett and Mr. Roebuck to complete, as he had again said he would ; but his sad state of health did not permit him to keep his promise, and I therefore made the Charter, Lovett assisting me as he could.* The Working Men's Association approved of it, and it was printed.

* Holyoake (" Sixty Years of an Agitator's Life "), says William Lovett's was the hand which drew up the Charter, and that Roebuck revised it.

1

Mr. Holyoake has recorded, on the authority of Mr. James Watson, who was often imprisoned for publishing prohibited books and newspapers, that, going on one occasion to Roebuck's chambers to consult him on matters connected with the struggle for a free press, Roebuck was found lying on a rug before the fire, writhing under the pain of neuralgia, from which, in those days, he suffered much. He listened as he lay, then rose, gave shrewd counsel, and forthwith put into writing the steps he advised, or sent letters to others likely to help.

The Charter was received by the Associations everywhere as an admirable epitome of their just political demands. They became "Charterists," or Chartists, and every idea gave way before the Charter. Soon they possessed a press. The *Northern Star*, conducted by their celebrated leader, Feargus O'Connor, and the *Western Vindicator*, which Henry Vincent published at Monmouth and in Bath, commanded in common with the rest of the "unstamped" such a circulation as no papers had ever before boasted.

The first public meeting of the Working Men's Association in Bath demonstrated how fit a soil existed there for the propagation of any democratic ideas. Henry Vincent was present, instinct with the fiery eloquence which distinguished him. Roebuck had been invited, but professional duties detaining him in London, he forwarded to the secretary an outspoken letter of advice and admonition. He wrote—

The working-men do wisely in thus associating together. They have hitherto been excluded from all participation of municipal rights, because disunion has rendered them weak and induced their enemies to contemn their demands. I would say to you, Be united, be firm, learn distinctly what rights you ought to have, and steadily and earnestly demand them. While you do this, however, I would entreat you not to mix up social with political reforms. Social reforms can come only as the consequence

of political ones; and on the one set the great body of the
people are agreed, on the other they are at variance. A good
government, if attained, would conduce to all good social reforms,
and it is not for us to decide beforehand what these last should be.
I give you this warning, because I have been so long in the
habit of advising the people of Bath; and also because I know
that the weakness and disunion of the working classes have arisen
mainly from their unwisely confounding these two essentially
different classes of reforms.

### *Mrs. Grote to Francis Place.*

*October* 27, 1838.—Joseph Hume appears, for once, sensible of
our wretched degradation as a political party. Roebuck, too,
allows that all is, for the present, gloom and darkness. But I for
one will never consent to wag a hand or foot to awaken the great
public up from its lethargy till these base Whigs are sent a-
packing. . . . Roebuck is the only sound Radical qualified to head
a vigorous movement, and I hope I shall see him there ere I die.

Early in 1839 Mr. Roebuck was in Bath, when a service
of plate was presented to him by the electors. Accompanying this was an address full of strong regret and sorrow
for his non-return at the election of 1837. The terms of
the address, though they seem a little exaggerated now,
reflected feelings of disappointment which none but those
who had taken part in the early enthusiasm of 1832 and
1833, and had witnessed the struggle, could fully understand.

### *J. A. Roebuck to Mrs. Roebuck.*

*York, March* 5, 1840.—Last night I had a small body of the
leading Liberals of Leeds, and gave them a specimen, playing
pacificator-general. They have elected me one of their committee
to draw up—in fact, to make—such resolutions for them, as will
serve as an exposition of proper Radical doctrine. They plainly
said (being very moderate Rads, mind), " We want a new *charter*
without the name, which will unite the now conflicting opinions of
the Liberal party." I fancy they must have been a little surprised
at the sort of harangue I gave them—very unlike the ravings of
Messrs. O'Connor and Co.

Things have gone on very well so far as regards law. To-day I feel better in body. My sleep has been much disturbed by pain ; even yet the twinges resist the hydryodate. I hope the fine weather makes our darling flourish. Every hour that I am away from you seems a heavy one.

*York, March* 10, 1840.— . . . While in Leeds I was shown a new manufacture which may work a revolution in the woollen trade in this country. It was cloth made without spinning or weaving—merely from felting. . . . The earliest clothing made from wool alone, was made by matting the fleece together in one homogeneous mass. I was shown the process. In forty-eight hours after the wool is taken from the sheep's back it is perfect cloth, and at half the price. I wanted some, but the patentee said he could not now part with it, as there were strong contending interests against him, and he wished to begin upon a scale to meet them. He is evidently frightened at the greatness of the discovery.

*York, March* 11, 1840.—I spent Sunday with R——. Early in the morning he sent a pony for me, and it being a beautiful, clear, frosty day, I rode out by nine o'clock. As the day advanced it was quite warm and spring-like. The birds sang, the air was soft and sweet, so we determined on a tramp. Setting rheumatism at defiance, away we strode a good six miles, loitering along turfy lanes, till we came to the river Ouse at Poppleton. We then sauntered back, indulging ourselves with all the beautiful things, sweet sounds, soft airs above and around us. I never had a more delightful walk, feeling very little fatigued. The pains in my leg utterly vanished, and I felt myself ten years younger. From this place I shall go to Sheffield sessions, from thence to Liverpool, from thence sessions again at Pontefract.

*York, March* 13, 1840.—I still improve ; last night wholly without pain. Nothing annoys me but my loneliness. It is impossible for me to express my distaste for the society around me. Sarcastic, bitter, shallow, money-hunting, selfish,—such are lawyers. They see so much of the evil part of mankind that they learn to believe in nothing good. They fret me by their eternal sneering at everything noble or exalted, and make me turn cynic in my own defence *par conséquence.* I find some of my bitter sayings in vogue against themselves. They cannot understand that this arises from a very different feeling from that which moves themselves, so I ever let them believe that I am like them. God help me if I were.

*March* 29.—So the ministers have again been beaten, and that, too, upon a serious point.* The very general feeling among the Tories is that a dissolution is to happen. Their wish is father to the thought. O'Connell doubtless will be in a fury, and threaten to put Ireland in a flame. He is the sole cause of the Tories' exclusion from place, therefore do they hate him with a deadly hatred.

*Liverpool, April* 2, 1840.— . . . I stay over the Saturday in order to see some of the leading Liberals. It will be well to do so, as I find there is still a strong belief that I have a tail and horns. One old fellow came to me with a sheet of paper in his hand, and begged of me thereon to write something, as a lady of his acquaintance was very desirous of having my autograph. Rather a strong instance of the lion-hunting mania, seeing that I was just introduced to the applicant. However, I did the thing, as John Kemble said, "handsomely," so he may begin to fancy that the tail and horns may not be wholly true.

*Pontefract, April* 8, 1840.— . . . It appears as if the old experience, viz. "It always snows at Pomfret sessions," were to be continued; bets, I understand, have been laid upon the chance this year. From the appearance of the sky, and fall of the wind, snow does not seem unlikely.

Sir James Graham's motion † will be decided before I reach London, and this is the last real attack upon the Ministry this session. The desire to thump the Chinaman will bring many persons to the side of the Ministry. I do not believe in a dissolution. I find my lawyer brethren do not like the notion of my being in Parliament. This appears by advice, etc., as to the effect it will have upon my professional chances. Of this I am as well able to judge as they. To the dull plodder the game appears a strange and difficult one. Let me keep this rheumatism off, and I fear nothing.

The following relates to an article which shortly after

---

* Lord Stanley's Irish Registration Bill, carried against ministers by 250 to 234 votes.

† Condemning the Government policy towards China. Defeated by a majority of only nine.

appeared in the *Edinburgh Review* on Napier's Peninsular
War :—

*November* 7, 1840.—I have read Harding's letter, and it
completely confirms Napier's narrative.  I have found a passage
in Voltaire, which I mean to quote on the sensitiveness of Napier's
various objectors.

"J'ai honte," says Voltaire, speaking of his "History of
Charles XII.," "surtout d'avoir parlé de tant de combats, de tant
de maux fait aux hommes ; je n'en refers d'autant plus, que
quelques officiers ont dit, ne parlant de ces combats, que je n'avais
pas dit vrai, *attendu que je n'avais pas parlé de leurs regiments ;*
ils supposaient que je devois suivre leur histoire."

Six volumes form a large subject, and I find it difficult to
select or to omit.  Much must be omitted that is interesting ; and
my object has been to create a curiosity about the work, giving
it alone the praise so fully its due.  I yesterday received a letter
from Macvey Napier, begging for the article to be sent.  I hope
to learn next week what Macvey thinks of the same.  The
*Edinburgh* twists round so often, that I am fearful lest I should
mistake its present position.

### *J. A. Roebuck to William Tait, Edinburgh.*

*November* 28, 1840.—Have you still any hankering for our
so-called Liberal Ministry ? or do you think, with me, the sooner
we put them into Opposition the better ?  If they remain much
longer where they are we shall have a Whig war, carried on by
united Tories and Whigs.  What do they say in the North to
all this ?  Does the intrusion question make you all careless even
of a general break-up of the peace of Europe?  Of this quarrel
of yours we in the South know little and care less ; but I fear
it will very fatally influence all elections for some time to come.
Is Edinburgh the passive pocket borough of the Government as
much as ever ? and will a vacancy, if created by Sir John
Campbell's advance to the Irish Bench, be filled without opposition by the Tories or Radicals ?  Opposition by the latter
would indeed appear impossible, but the Conservative party,
growing every day more formidable, will soon attack the Whigs
in their strongholds.  Reformers are becoming faint, and unless
some powerful and sustained effort be made by the really steady

and yet untried friends of improvement, a long Tory reign is inevitable. It is this belief that makes me write to you. I am anxious to unite again the elements of our scattered party ; to persuade all again strenuously to put their hands to the work, and labour as if nothing had yet been done. In the North of England a movement is beginning which, if properly aided, may lead to good results. In order to give this aid, all the means in our power of expressing opinion should be used, and that, too, firmly and earnestly. Now, if you think I can assist in this good work by anything I could write for you, I should be glad to do it. My health is much improved. I have leisure enough for this purpose, and if I could employ it to so good an end, I should be well pleased to do so. I sometimes communicate with an admirer of your magazine—the editor of the *Leeds Times*, who is doing good in the North. He gives me encouragement by describing the spirit of the people as not dead, but sleeping ; while he excites me and all Reformers to action, so that we may sound a trump to awaken these dormant energies. I find so much despondency that any instance of hope is pleasing—and in this case the more so as I scarcely believe he is right—and nothing is wanting but a hearty concurrence on the part of all well-intentioned men, in order to raise up again a strong desire to advance. Does your experience of the North make you think us right ? A budget of news would be acceptable ; for we can only judge of the aggregate by comparing separate opinions, and collating separate pieces of evidence.

### To Wm. Tait, Edinburgh.

*December* 2, 1840.—Have you for your January number an article on the war doings of the Ministry ? If not, I should like to give my poor thoughts upon the question. My purpose would be to expose Lord Palmerston, not by any supposed special know-ledge or gossip, but by showing in what way his interests are forwarded by putting the nation into hot water ; and how the Tories, by a natural instinct, are ready in a moment to support him. The true view as respects France in this matter, I have not yet seen. My belief is that Lord Palmerston has throughout been acting in concert with Louis Philippe. The struggle com-menced in France between the king and M. Thiers, being, in fact, a struggle for the premiership. Thiers forced himself into power against the king's wish. The king and he were consequently deadly enemies, and Thiers well knew that, on the first opportunity, the king would dismiss him. In order to prevent this, he endeavoured to gain popularity. With his old Republican friends he had no ties or correspondence, but he hoped to win these back and gain many others by pandering to the French appetite for military glory. The war party in France is a strong, active, and intelligent party—men who hope to gain more liberal institutions by means of a general " row " in Europe ; and to this party Thiers addressed himself. The king saw the danger, and has done all in his power to excite the terrors of the shopkeepers. Lord Palmerston has aided him, but the thing is about to be carried too far. The response of the war party to Thiers was far more decided and vehement than he had expected. The spirit that was roused has not been laid. The present rulers of France, Soult, & Co., are aware of this, and are secretly but strenuously preparing for war. Palmerston, by his successes in Syria, has crossed the king. Any moment threatens us with an outbreak of the French war spirit ; and an attack on Alexandria, which I see that Palmerston intends, will blow the embers into a flame. If this man be permitted to remain in this Ministry, or be enabled to join the next, we shall have war to a certainty, the result of which will be very much like that which followed the attack on France in 1793, and woe be unto the aristocracy of this country. The people are not now in the state in which they were then. Discontent and knowledge are far more widely diffused now than at that period. A French war will lead to a *propagande*. Italy will rise. Spain will be a republic ; so will Portugal. Poland will be on the alert. Many of the German states will be up against their rulers. Ireland will not be quiet, and England will be fearfully moved. Do you not think a picture after this fashion may do good, and frighten away the utter apathy of the people on this subject ? All are quiet because all fancy war not possible. But it is not only possible, but *imminent*. By showing that it is so we may excite attention, and perhaps ward off the evil.

### *To William Tait, Edinburgh.*

*December* 12, 1840.—I have determined to write, and have commenced my task, " A History of the Ten Years of a Whig Administration "—a fruitful theme, and one which I hope to turn to profit for the public and myself. I shall, according to my present views, make it extend to three octavo volumes ; but have not yet decided whether I shall publish it volume by volume, or all at once. Contemporary history is always valuable, and as I have seen things rather near, and as I know many of the chief actors in the scenes that have been exhibited, I *ought* to have that to say which should be interesting. If what I know, and can learn, be only tolerably well said, the book will live as a testimony ; and if I tell the truth I think some of our Whig people will be handsomely damned to posterity.

*Francis Place to J. A. Roebuck.*

*December* 23, 1840.—I am sorry to find by your letter that you are very ill. . . . You are right. There can be no such move-ment in London as there is in Leeds. It will, however, come to nothing, even there, because it is not in keeping with other circumstances. . . . I concur with you again : "The time for brawling and mere talking men at public meetings is over for the present." The Chartists have done this. Buy the Chartist Almanack, price 3*d.* It contains the constitution of the new Chartist Association. It is as pretty a recommendation of trans-portable offences as either the Whig or Conservative Tories could desire should be made.

I wish you would send me a brief account of what passed when Lovett brought you my draft for the Charter. All I can learn is that you said it was sufficient for the purpose intended.

In respect to your history and my assistance, I do not see how I can comply with your wish ; were I to do so I should be worse off than one of the two tailors who had but one needle between them, because the books—a whole cart-load—could not be readily passed from hand to hand as the needle.

*J. A. Roebuck to Wm. Tait, Edinburgh.* •

*January* 25, 1841.—Our move at Leeds was so important that I think you might find a short account of it not uninterest-ing. If you think as I do, I will send you a short history of what we fancy we have accomplished. It was the first step towards a new movement—that first step being a very successful attempt to unite the middle and working classes, and laying down a principle to which both parties will adhere.

The Ministry begin to fear that their end is near, and wish for pressure from without. This is a very significant symptom.

### To William Tait, Edinburgh.

*February* 9, 1841.—My article will be on the state of parties— at present a very curious theme. The last Tory triumphs have cut down the small majority of the Whigs to something worse than nothing, and now it remains to be seen whether the Whigs intend to go out, looking to come in at some future time on the popular side. If they do not, they are gone as a party ; if they do, they must lay the ground now by proposing some measures of reform that will please the people. Their Irish Registration Bill is of this description. Some half-dozen proposals like that for England and Scotland also, and they may look forward to an early return to power. But I fear their leaders are too much of the aristo- cratic faction for this.

Do you know anything of Perth ? Sir G. Sinclair has been speaking to me thereanent, wishing me to make inquiries as to my chances there. For mine own part, I wish very much to represent a Scots constituency. Once in for a place on proper principles, and the representative is sure of his seat so long as he remains true. This is not the case with us.

### To Mrs. Roebuck.

*York, March* 18, 1841.— . . . The sitting all day in court robs me of power to do anything after the day's work is over, and I usually creep to bed, though not to sleep, as soon as I well can. Yesterday my case came off, or rather on, and lasted from two to eight, ending with the men charged with murder being found guilty of manslaughter, and sentenced to two months' imprison- ment. The attorney, as usual, very profuse of thanks and expressions of gratitude, so I suppose I shall never see him again.

The Chartists from Birmingham have been sending to me for legal advice ! This is rather too much ; they abuse me, and want to use me. But I shall ride rusty. Let them seek aid and counsel from those whom they praise and pay.

I shall be in Sheffield late Saturday. York, however, is more pleasant than the smoke of ten thousand furnaces, so I shall stay here till I am obliged to be at Sheffield. Since I have been here,

during the long hours of the night, I have amused myself with
reading, among other rubbish, "Cecil"—the work of which Lady
Blessington spoke to me. Having got to the last volume, I see
why she was interested in the book. The writer is evidently one
of that scribbling set to which she belongs, and goes out of his way
to abuse her, and sneers at her reminiscences of Byron. He also
alludes to D'Orsay as a broken-down foreigner. You see, these
people who write about others are wonderfully thin-skinned. She
evidently smarted under this, and could not hold her tongue.
Spite of great quotations it is not impossible that it (viz. the
authorship) will turn out to belong to a woman at last.* The
thing has been altogether over-praised.

*March* 21.—A curious thing occurred the other day in Court.
A Canadian, an inhabitant of Lower Canada, of English parents,
was tried for coining in this country Mexican dollars. He said
the dollars were medals intended to be attached to a chain, and to
be worn round the neck, and to be given to the Indians, labourers
of a fur company, of which he was an agent. This fur company
traded on the west of the Rocky Mountains, and went as far
north as the Columbia River; and the question arose, "Where is
the Columbia River?" Nobody knew. The judge, Rolfe, W.,
the prosecuting counsel, B., the defending counsel, the attorneys,
the jury,—all were equally ignorant. W. leaned across the table
and said, "Roebuck, does not the Columbia fall into the Gulf of
Mexico?" I answered, "No, into the Pacific Ocean, and forms
part of the boundary between the United States and British
America." † . . . Yet I have no doubt every one of these persons
had formed some opinion, to which he would strongly adhere,
respecting the justice of our claims to the American territory. . . .
After all, though I am glad of the man's acquittal, I am far from
sure of the intentions with which these dollars were made. The
whole affair was very suspicious.

*Liverpool, March* 28, 1841.— . . . I have at length a quiet
hour to write in. Coming on this pilgrimage of law, I steadily
go through its duties, and sit during the day in the hot, stifling
atmosphere of an abominable and crowded court. The journey
here from Sheffield was one of the most interesting I ever performed in this country. We started for Manchester at half-past

---

* "Cecil" was written by Mrs. Gore.
† Settled soon afterwards by the Ashburton Treaty.

ten, on the top of the coach ; a beautiful day, clear and warm.
The hills and moors which lie between Sheffield and Glossop are
by far the finest I have seen, beating even Blackstone Edge ;
and I hope some fine summer to spend a few days with pencil
in hand among the striking scenes which lie there.   The moors
are preserved by a society of sportsmen, who rent the tract
from the Duke of Norfolk. Through these moors runs the
Derwent, which is also preserved by a set of sportsmen, brothers
of the angle.   This little stream adds much to the beauty of the
scenery, and as we passed I saw many a spot where a painter
might linger for hours.   Glossop is a new town, and bids fair in
time to begrime the beautiful country around it for miles with its
infernal chimneys and smoke.   Suddenly we came to an immense
cutting in the hill—a piece of work like those of the railroads ; it
went clean through the hill (not a tunnel).   I beheld a sight I
shall not quickly forget.   Ashton, Stockport, and half a dozen
manufacturing towns were in sight, if sight it could be called.
On every side tall chimneys were thrusting themselves into the
sky, puffing out huge volumes of black smoke, and for miles the
same horrible view met you—smoke, smoke, smoke ; trees, roads,
the very ground, horses, beasts, and men were black and miserable
to behold.   Every step towards Manchester intensified all these
horrors.   The suddenness of the transition doubtless added to the
sensation of oppression and misery.

*Pomfret, April* 9, 1841.— . . . I have done very well here.
Every day increases my sessions business.   I have had, next to
Lewin, the greatest number of defences.   I passed Sunday at
Frystone.*   There go the bells—ring, ring, almost as bad as
Abbeville of rowdow memory.   We had fine fun with Carlyle, who
talked broad Scotch, and utter nonsense without end.   His
nostrums respecting law reform did not go unscathed.   His pre-
sumption, his dictatorial and positive manner, combined with his
utter weakness, excited in my mind contempt.   Yet this is a
great star in these times of darkness.

I shall be in London on Thursday early ; no poor devil ever
longed for home as I do.   My pains have come upon me, and I
am fighting them with creosote and potass.

* The seat of Mr. Monckton Milnes, afterwards Lord Houghton.

# CHAPTER XIII.

At the General Election of June, 1841, brought about by Lord John Russell's appeal to the country when defeated on the sugar duties and a fixed duty on corn, Mr. Roebuck regained his seat for Bath. Past misfortunes had taught the two wings of the Liberal party there the necessity for co-operation, and although the alliance between the Whigs and the Radicals, to accomplish which strong influence from head-quarters had to be invoked, was by no means firm, or really liked by either section, yet it served its immediate end. The choice of the Whigs was the son of the Earl of Camperdown, Lord Duncan, who, although sitting for Southampton, had wooed the constituency for several years. With him Mr. Roebuck fought. Their opponents were the old members, Lord Powerscourt and Mr. Bruges.

Riot attended the nomination proceedings from their beginning to their close. The occupants of the hustings were assailed unmercifully by missiles of all descriptions. But in the end Toryism suffered the most crushing defeat that ever it underwent in Bath, for the result of the polling was—Lord Duncan, 1223; J. A. Roebuck, 1151; Bruges, 930; Lord Powerscourt, 926.

Soon afterwards Mr. Roebuck went north on circuit. The succeeding letter records a visit to his aunt, Mrs. Stewart, the last surviving member of the numerous family

1

of his grandfather, Dr. John Roebuck, the founder of iron-smelting in Scotland.

### *J. A. Roebuck to Mrs. Roebuck.*

*Birmingham, July,* 1841.—I have just returned from Mrs. Stewart. She is not well, though her intellect is as strong as ever. She is weaker than when you saw her, but at eighty-six what is to be expected? She told me she had written to you her thoughts on various matters, and was anxious to hear from you again.*

In the *Times* of Saturday, July 3, there is a long article on myself—a clever attempt to set the leading Whigs against me. The article is in the shape of a comment on my speech delivered at the declaration [of the poll at Bath], which speech, together with Sir R. Peel's at Tamworth, the *Times* declares to be incomparably the most important of any delivered during the election. They cunningly put Peel and myself forward as the two leaders—Peel of the Conservatives, myself of the Movement party. This is done to exasperate Lord John [Russell]; to wound the vanity of the Whigs, and thus to drive them away from me. Without this fillip they would have been but prone to hate me ; now, that hatred is inevitable—whether it will be openly shown remains to be seen. As yet I feel no doubtings as to my being able to take the position which I ought to take. If my health do but keep as good as it is, I have no fear of the result.

### *J. A. Roebuck to Thomas North, Bath.*

*London, February 15,* 1842.—Lord Duncan was so good as to give me the petition from Bath against the Corn Laws, and in favour of a full representation of the people. I presented the petition yesterday, and stated its prayer to the House. The principles which it advocates will receive a very full discussion, and they will, I have little doubt, be virtually received as just principles by the legislature of this country. We must not, however, relax in our efforts. Our opponents are many, powerful, unscrupulous, and active. With honesty, boldness, and industry, we shall be able, nevertheless, I trust, to conquer them ; but if we fail in any one of these qualities, our present rulers will continue

---

* This lady was the possessor of a guitar made for her when a girl by James Watt.

to govern us. I feel gratified by the approval which my conduct respecting the presentation of petitions has received from all those of my constituents who have expressed an opinion to me on the matter. A more important point as respects the proceedings of the House of Commons was never discussed by it.* All the advances made in favour of civil and religious freedom have been won by means of the continued discussions upon petitions presented to the House of Commons. The effective battery once directed by that means against abuses is now almost destroyed ; but we must endeavour by strenuous and persevering efforts to reconstruct this formidable instrument of offence and protection.

This session of 1842 is remarkable for Sir Robert Peel's great budget, and for the masterly manner in which, by imposing a sevenpenny income-tax and sweeping away the protective duties on 1200 articles of import, he repaired the ravages in the national finances made by long years of deficits. The fierce and protracted debates on these pro-posals, involving the corn laws, the sugar and timber duties, colonial differentiation, and innumerable controversial topics, monopolized the attention both of Parliament and of the country. Mr. Roebuck, while giving a general support to Peel's policy, began an endeavour, which he kept up for many years, to relieve professional men from one-half the burden of the income-tax ; and he fought to equalize the duties on foreign and colonial timber and sugar.

*Liverpool, March* 27, 1842.— . . . My speech † was here before me, and I receive congratulations from people because I am " really a Tory ! " So much are men guided by mere form and party predilections. Because I praise Peel I am a Tory. I praise him because he has really produced a *democratic measure.* The

* Members were formerly permitted, on presenting petitions, to address the House upon them—a privilege still possessed by the Lords. It will have been observed that Mr. Roebuck frequently availed himself of these oppor-tunities. In 1842, however, standing orders were passed restricting members to a statement of the parties from whom a petition came, of the number of signatures attached to it, of its material allegations, and to the reading of its prayer.

† Debate on the Income Tax.

Whigs are, as you may suppose, not backward in aiding the mis-construction. Brougham has written to me again about the pensions. He wants me to attack them, I see.

It was not, however, the Whigs only who disliked Mr. Roebuck's support of Peel's sevenpenny income tax. The Bath Liberal Association sent formal protests, and many warm adherents of the Liberal cause were so disturbed by his action on this and other matters, and by his absence when his colleague, Lord Duncan, was fighting against the window tax, that he found it necessary to go down to Bath, where he addressed a crowded meeting at the Guildhall in justification of his conduct. To complaints of absence from the House of Commons, he pleaded professional duties. He ended thus—

If any one thinks I have done wrong, let him tell me why he thinks so. . . . I entreat you to exercise the same forbearance towards me as I do towards you and others. Believe me, I wish to set a good example to my constituents, and I have brought them together thus to consult with them. But if to-day there should be a difference between us, recollect, I am not come to surrender my right as your representative. You have chosen me for a term, and I shall not give up till that term is expired. When that time comes it will be for you to express your appro-bation or disapprobation by your vote. Till that time you will judge of me by my acts. I shall be always open to, and ready to bear with remonstrance, but let me exhort you not to be hasty in investigating what I am doing ; but chasten the investigation with a calm unbiassed and deliberate judgment, and by so doing you will give me an incentive to the active discharge of my duty, and generously reward me in doing it.

### *J. A. Roebuck to Mrs. Roebuck.*

*York, March* 3, 1842.—Not one day since I have been in Yorkshire have the twenty-four hours passed without a regular downpour of rain. . . . It is so very quiet and determined, it puts me in mind of a pertinacious woman of the demure kind, who, appearing wonderfully subdued and soft in her manner, is, nevertheless, always in the right, and always decided upon having her own way. The waters are beginning to be out. No wheat sown. When I say no wheat, I mean only a small breadth sown. If this continues a week or two longer, Peel's Corn Law will break down the first year.

Labouchere * and Grey have been trading on my capital. I explained to them, at their desire, my view of Gladstone's measure for taxing the colonies,† and they have fired off my constitutional cannon. This shows how they depend upon others for their ideas.

Old Chandler, who is the fiercest Tory here, was very civil; he spoke of you, saying he had often heard of, though he had never seen, you. He asked me to his house. Wortley, when he heard of it, held up his hands and eyes. " Old Chandler ? Why, he is the most out-and-out Tory in the county ! " I myself joked Chandler, reminding him of his black looks at me when I first joined the sessions. He laughed and said, " Aye; we did not know you then—those newspapers lie so." This was the parson who told his congregation that if they would play cricket on Sunday, he would bowl to them.

*York, March* 9, 1842 ; 9 P.M.— . . . We are now in the very throng of the horrible business of trying murders and other dreadful atrocities. My cases will be late. Two are murders. I am for the defence in both, and shall save one wretch, I think, altogether, and prove the other offender guilty, not of murder, but of manslaughter ; so there will be no condemning to death.

At night I have read novels, and, among others, I have again read, after many years, " Corinne "—a beautiful book, spite of everything ; like nothing in nature, perhaps—that is, like nothing we see, but bearing a strong resemblance to much that we feel and think. It agrees with a theory of mine so far. My notion is, that every human being is twin—made up of two sets of feelings and thoughts—the esoteric, and the exoteric man. The last is what we see ; and the description to the many of what is called natural, must be of that outward man. But " Corinne " is a picture of our dreams, of our inward musings—the esoteric existence, which few can discover to their best-loved, best-known friends. As a set-off to " Corinne," I read " Evelina," and did not like it. Old Johnson's applause shows what an old brute

* Afterwards Lord Taunton.          † The Canada Corn Bill.

he was.  Those parts which are really offensive, and like nothing that ever existed in this earth by way of manners, are those which his coarse appetite delighted in.  If the conversations really represent the manners of speech common among men and women of those days, we are altered much, and that, too, for the better ; but I never can believe that the picture is accurate.  " Cecilia" I have tried to read, but failed.  Strange reading, you will say, for a lawyer on circuit.

*April* 6, 1842.—This India news is very terrible *—nothing like it since the day on which a detachment of English troops surrendered themselves prisoners to Montcalm, in Canada, when the French Indians destroyed men, women, and children.

*April* 8.—So the foolish papers, for the want of something better to do, have been trying to take me in hand again.  The Whigs are plainly trying to turn the feeling of some of my friends at Bath to their own service, hoping, evidently, to frighten me into silence.  This they will not do, however.

From the papers I learn that there is a vacancy at Montrose, so I suppose Hume will soon be back in " Honorable House." I hope so, for his sake, as I really believe him to be exceedingly unhappy by his exclusion.  I am delighted with the journal. ——'s exploits and little words are far more pleasing to me than the story of much greater doings.  I drive off to the last the thing that is nearest my heart, for I dare hardly trust myself to think or speak of it.  Have you no letters from America for me ?

The next mail from Canada brought the news of his mother's death.

The approaches of the Houses of Parliament were, on the 2nd of May, 1842, filled with crowds, attracted by announcements that the Chartists of the metropolis intended to carry their "monster national petition" in procession to Westminster.  The demonstration began in Lincoln's Inn Fields, and, as it traversed the principal streets, was witnessed by large masses of citizens.  The petition, bearing 3,315,752 signatures, demanded the passing

* The retreat of the British army from Cabul after the treacherous murder of Sir W. Macnaghten, on December 23, 1841.

of "The People's Charter." The excitement attending these proceedings penetrated even into the precincts of the House as the great roll made its way to the doors; for it was so large that the truck upon which it was carried by sixteen bearers broke down on the way to the lobby, and a perfect avalanche of paper closed up the door for some minutes, barring all ingress to the House. The petition was subsequently carried up in separate packages and placed on the floor in front of the table. Mr. Thomas Duncombe moved that the petitioners should be heard by their counsel or agents at the Bar. On the debate that followed, Mr. Roebuck spoke for the motion. But its supporters were weighted by the disfavour aroused by the extreme propositions of the document, from the extravagant conditions of which they were compelled to dissociate themselves. Mr. Roebuck denounced these and their author, supposed to be Mr. Feargus O'Connor, in no measured terms. The petition had, he said, been drawn up by "a cowardly and malignant demagogue." His speech was described at the time as unquestionably the speech of the night, because of its masterly eloquence, the logical precision of its language, the breadth and clearness of its views, and the high moral courage which it displayed. But by insisting that the Charter, rather than the hearing of the petitioners, was the real issue, he helped the opponents, among whom were included Sir Robert Peel, Lord John Russell, and Mr. Macaulay, whose strongest weapons were supplied by the language of the petition itself. Only 49 members could be found to support the motion, against 286 drawn from both sides of the House, and including many of the most staunch Liberals.

Mr. Roebuck's most sensational achievement in this session, however, related to the corrupt agencies which had notoriously been at work in the constituencies during the General Election of the previous year. These were more rampant than at any time since the Reform Act. Numerous petitions alleging bribery and corruption were presented, only, however, to be withdrawn, under singularly suspicious circumstances.

It was openly said that progress was stayed on the undertaking of the sitting members, given personally or through their agents, to vacate their seats within a given time. Mr. Roebuck, ever alive to what might affect the honour of the House of Commons, at once resolved to test these allegations. The course taken was, as he described it himself, an extraordinary one, and it caused a great commotion in the House. On May the 6th he separately challenged in their places six or seven members, and called upon them categorically to say, then and there, whether the arrangements alleged to have been made in their names had their cognizance and approval. Several angrily declined to recognize the right to put them in the confessional, and refused to answer. Captain Plumridge, however, a blunt sailor, at once acknowledged that such an arrangement had been made by his lawyer without his knowledge, and he declared he did not like it. Captain Fitzroy, another of the challenged ones, said he would vote for a committee. Lord Palmerston objected to the inquiry altogether, on the ground that unless it was contemplated to bring in a Bill on the subject, it was useless to investigate. This begged the question, for if there was no evidence, there could be no Bill.

The excitement caused by these proceedings, both in Parliament and in the country, was immense. Mr. Roebuck was, for the time, the best-abused man in the kingdom. Mr. John Walter, as defeated candidate at Nottingham, was involved in the accusations, and this especially aroused the furious animosity of his journal, the *Times*, which accused Mr. Roebuck of having pursued its proprietor spitefully, from 1835 to September, 1841, when, unsuccessfully moving to condemn the *Times* for breach of privilege, he openly advised any one attacked in that journal to horse-whip its owner.* Sir John Cam Hobhouse had wrested from Mr. Walter the Nottingham seat; and in this, again, on the strength of Mr. Roebuck's earlier electoral fight against his brother, Mr. H. W. Hobhouse, was found evidence of personal enmity. Mr. Roebuck had, however, the consolation, amid storms of imputation and *tu quoques*, of receiving from all parts of the country expressions of gratitude from the advocates of electoral purity; and when, before his committee, the charges were fully proved, there arose such a universal outcry against the shameless corruption disclosed, as largely to silence the other side. The committee reported the existence of corruption at Nottingham, Reading, Harwich, and five other towns, justifying a suspension of the writs for new elections, and it recommended further inquiry with a view to the punishment of guilty persons. But the matter ended with the exposure, for Parliament declined to act upon the committee's report. When that was brought up, a stormy debate terminated in the rejection of the three resolutions founded by Mr. Roebuck upon it. These asked the House, firstly, to condemn the corrupt practices now laid bare; secondly, to declare these practices to be a breach of privilege; thirdly, to suspend the writs for the constituencies concerned. A caricature of "H. B." at this time represents a confessional, with the member for Bath sitting in it, listening horror-struck to the avowals of the member for Nottingham (Hobhouse) who kneels outside.

Mr. Roebuck took an active part with his colleague, Lord Duncan, in a great Anti-Corn-Law demonstration held at the Guildhall, Bath, on January 27, 1843, Mr. Cobden and Colonel Thompson being both present. The Chartists had now adopted the policy of opposing every

* Mr. Walter had, indeed, to be called to the Bar of the House before he would give evidence, as he had refused to attend before a committee of which the advocate of horse-whipping was the chairman.

agitation which could withdraw public attention from the necessity for electoral reform, and this action greatly detracted from the unanimity of the meeting. Though supporting the Anti-Corn-Law Leaguers on this occasion, Mr. Roebuck was largely out of sympathy with many of their methods, and a few months afterwards he attacked them in the House of Commons.

A fragment of Parliamentary journal, written by Mr. Roebuck, relates to this period—

*Thursday, February* 2, 1843.—Parliament opened by Commission. The chief topics—foreign affairs, China, Afghan, and America, sorrow for deficit, etc.

The agitation by the Anti-Corn-Law League had led people not conversant with the *internal* affairs of Parliament to believe that there would be a grand display in the debate of this evening by the gentlemen connected with the League ; but Mr. Cobden, the corypheus of the party, was absent (his child, an infant of ten months, having died on January 23), and Charles Villiers seemed not altogether willing (or able ?) to supply his place. When I expressed to C. V. my opinion that Cobden had made a mistake in staying away, his answer clearly proved that he (C. V.) did not look with complacency upon the manner in which Cobden had superseded him in the lead of the Corn question. " After his sails have been so filled with favouring winds (said C. V.) he (Cobden) ought surely to have come into port. The honours showered on him by the Scotch lately were not given without a purpose. He was expected to be here, and his friends out-of-doors will be grievously disappointed." The truth is that there is a great difference between talking to large public meetings composed of favourable auditors, who cheer every word you utter and speaking to the fastidious audience found in the House of Commons, the greater part of whom are bitter opponents and all critical listeners. Cobden's success out-of-doors will excite attention for him in the House ; but he will be required to reach a high standard to acquire the influence within the walls of Parliament which he has attained among the enemies of the Corn Laws.

The debate was dull and peculiarly uninteresting ; the only

incident worth remarking was the effective answer given by Lord Stanley to Lord J. Russell. Lord John's carping received a suitable rebuff.

Sir R. Peel gave notice of a motion of thanks to Lord Ellenborough and the Indian army, and I that I would move for a committee to inquire into the justice and policy of the Afghan war—both motions for February 16. I gave notice also respecting the [Quebec] Beauharnois Canal.

During the debate, Lord Palmerston declared that he would attack the Treaty with America on some future day. He showed himself extremely willing to be mischievous, but not very able. His speech was an impudent piece of spite. " He showed blunt teeth," said Lord B. [Brougham] to me next morning. The figure was apt. No amendment moved.

*Friday, February 3.*—On bringing up the report of the address, old Walter (the *Times*) made a set speech, in which he declared in favour of a fixed duty on corn—a poor display, much pretension, but poor performance. Villiers is to bring on the Corn question some early day, and Lord Howick is to move for a committee of the whole House on distress on Monday week. I gave notice of a motion for pardon to the Canadian convicts now in Van Diemen's Land for Tuesday next. I this morning breakfasted with B. [Brougham], and talked over and settled plans as to my Afghan motion.

*Monday, February 6.*—Almost a *dies non*, the only matter of interest being the statement of Sir R. P. that he intended to confine his vote of thanks entirely to the military operations, the policy of withdrawing the troops, and of the war originally, being a question completely reserved. It will, I think, nevertheless, be difficult to confine the debate to the mere military operations. If Peel blames the preceding operations, the whole question will be dragged into discussion. This I shall be sorry for, as I want the war itself to be thoroughly canvassed, which can only be properly done on such a motion as mine.

Sir R. P. recommended us to wait till we saw his papers, and the terms of his motion.

Mr. Roebuck's speech on the first Afghan War, its causes and its consequences, was long remembered by those who heard it, as the best that he had made in Parliament. It

sketched in a short and clear manner the events which led
to the interference of England in the troubled affairs of
Afghanistan, and condemned the mode of that interference
as most unjust and impolitic.

*Lord Brougham to J. A. Roebuck.*

*House of Lords, Friday.*—DEAR R., The impression has been
very great. I hear but one exception, viz. the strength of some
expressions as to Auckland supposed to have weakened effect.
Yours ever, H. BROUGHAM.

In the hot controversies aroused by Sir James Graham's
Factory and Educational Bill of 1843, Mr. Roebuck
anxiously advocated the imposition of obstacles to employing children of tender years.  He unsuccessfully asked
Parliament to affirm that in no place of education, maintained or enforced by the State, should any attempt be
made to inculcate peculiar religious opinions.   But his
refusal to join in general condemnation of Sir James
Graham's Bill brought him into strong conflict with an
influential section of his constituency.  Attending a meeting at Bath, called to oppose what were held to be the
objectionable clauses in this Bill, Mr. Roebuck had
to fight against some clamour raised by men who resented quotations from the report of the Commission on
Education, illustrating the dire ignorance on matters both
religious and secular, prevailing in the manufacturing
districts.   But more formidable was the elaborate and
powerful challenge offered to his views by the Rev. Dr.
Waddy, who became one of Mr. Roebuck's strongest
opponents in Bath, and afterwards in Sheffield.  Mr. Roebuck, while admitting that Graham's Bill was bad, and
full of objectionable clauses, vehemently declined to incur
the terrible responsibility of rejecting anything offering
the least amelioration of the horrible condition of the
children of the country.   He advocated, therefore, the
policy of endeavouring to make a bad Bill good by

amending it clause by clause; and he propounded his old views in favour of entirely separating education from religious teaching. Dr. Waddy, on the other hand, lengthily analyzed the Bill, to show that it was irretrievably bad; and he elaborately criticized Mr. Roebuck's views on education. The controversy was carried far into the night, and its echoes went rolling on until they had an appreciable effect in severing Mr. Roebuck's connection with Bath.

Speaking, in Parliament, on the Irish Arms (Coercion) Bill, Mr. Roebuck said—

The chief evil in that country was the rampant Church of Ireland. . . . If he had the power, he would disencumber that Church at once of anything like maintenance of power in Ireland. He would propose at once to take the revenues of the Church, and give them, if to any Church at all, to the Church of the majority . . . but he should prefer to apply them to temporal purposes. The Irish Church was the great mischief, grievance, and sore of that country. . . . If they wished to remove all ground for the cry of repeal, he entreated them to govern Ireland as they governed England.

The appeal was useless. There were: for the second reading, 270; against, 165.

The following letter touches on this ever-recurring Irish question:—

*J. A. Roebuck to Mrs. Roebuck.*

*York, July* 16, 1843.—As to O'Connell's plans, I cannot believe him to be so unwise as to convene any body of delegates in Dublin. The ruin of his party would certainly follow; they, not having any real power, would quarrel amongst themselves. They would not only commit themselves, but O'Connell also, and the Government would pounce upon him, and make him at length pay for all the annoyance he has given them. If he be quite quiet, he will succeed; if he steps ever so much beyond the law as to give the Government a fair opportunity, they will test his courage by bringing him to trial. If Peel had an ounce of courage, he must, by watching his opportunity. Risks must be run, and, were I in his place, I would run that risk, if O'Connell gave me a chance. The Church must go, or rents will; and then what will Irish landlords do?

The Government did "pounce." When Parliament met, in 1844, public attention was largely centred on the trial, then proceeding in Dublin, of Daniel O'Connell and his fellow Repealers.* The chronic discontents of Ireland were acuter than ever, and the subject was prominently referred to in the Queen's Speech. Early in the session, Lord John Russell moved for a committee of the whole House to inquire into the condition of Ireland. Mr. Roebuck's chief panacea was disestablishment of the Irish Church. He asked—

Would repeal of the Union relieve the present evils, bring peace, and remove discontent?

As far. as he could judge, it would only aggravate the mischief: He could not conceive any one mischief greater to Ireland than repeal, excepting the continuation of a military Government. . . . Peace could never be produced while the Irish Church remained as it was. . . . He was for pulling down the present system, for taking the proceeds into the hands of the Government, and applying them to the great purpose of educating the people. Why should a Church in Ireland be maintained, doing all that a Church ought not to do, causing animosity and discord throughout the land? Why should it not be put down, in order that peace might be at once restored? He would tell them. They feared that the principle, if applied to Ireland, would be hereafter applied to England.

* Mr. Roebuck went to Sir Thomas Wilde's (afterwards Lord Chancellor Truro) to look over, with Mr. Sheil, papers connected with the trial in Dublin. While so engaged, Lord Brougham was announced. He came, he said, to ask the Attorney-General's opinion regarding the safety of Count D'Orsay's dining with him on that day, and requested him (Sir Thomas Wilde) to send him an opinion before six o'clock on these points: Whether Count D'Orsay could dine in safety with him, an ex-Chancellor, the two Chief Justices (Denman and Tindall), and the ex-Attorney-General. Supposing a detainer put in, would it be valid on a Sunday?

*To Wm. Tait, Edinburgh.*

*March* 1, 1844.—I should much like to put upon paper a description of the great Irish debate. Would you like such a sketch ? As it would be a series of personal criticisms as well as general reflections on the state of Ireland, I should not like to be openly known as the author, though you need not fear any libellous matter at my hands. And, indeed, it is not that I should wish to write anything really disparaging of any that took part in the debate that makes me desire to be *incognito*. But the taking upon one's self openly the character of a critic on such an occasion, and in my position, would be presuming.

The debate itself was a very remarkable one, by far the best I ever heard. Throughout it was good, and the change of feeling and opinion it showed in the leading men of all parties, and in the parties themselves, was a good omen for the future. The person who appeared in the least favourable position was Lord John Russell. His party completely left him behind.

In the first days of the session there was some competition between Mr. Roebuck and Lord Ashley for priority in bringing before the House the controversies respecting Lord Ellenborough's annexation of Scinde, and his treatment of the Ameers. Lord Ashley, getting the first place, warmly espoused the cause of the Ameers. Condemnation of Lord Ellenborough involved condemnation of Sir Charles Napier, the chief executor of his policy, and raised questions as between Napier and Major (afterwards Sir James) Outram—for Napier, in superseding Outram, had rejected his methods and counsels. Roebuck, in moving an amendment to Lord Ashley's motion, in a speech of, for him, unusual length—heard, as the reports complain, with difficulty in the press gallery—devoted a large part of it to a championship of his old friend Napier. And, indeed, although the fact was not openly manifest in the debate, there was evidently behind the discussion very strong personal feeling between the partisans of Napier and Outram. As to Ellenborough, while disliking his treatment of the Ameers, in itself, Mr. Roebuck defended it as inevitably necessitated by the impolitic conduct of his predecessor, Lord Auckland. Lord Ashley's motion of censure was negatived by a large majority.

The Duke of Wellington told Lord Brougham, "Your friend Roebuck made a most excellent speech in the House last night." Lord Brougham : "Does he not always make excellent speeches ? " "Yes, yes, he does; but he never made so good a one as last night. I agree in every word of it. I agree in all he said about Lord Auckland." Sir James Graham said Mr. Roebuck's speech *saved* the Government. The House was ready to listen that evening, and the Whigs were quite ready to make an onslaught on Lord Ellenborough, and with him General C. Napier, which was put an end to by Roebuck's speech.

*Sir W. Napier to Mr. Roebuck.*

Your speech, though cruelly mauled by the papers, has given me as much pleasure as it has given pain to the Whigs, and that is not small.

A few days afterwards these controversies were again raised, on a motion of thanks to Sir Charles Napier * and his army, but in this debate, although Sir Robert Peel had given him early private warning, by his own hand, of the opposition to the motion, Mr. Roebuck did not speak. Only nine members voted against it—"The nine muses, graceless youths," Sir William Napier sarcastically dubbed them.

In connection with the ten hours clause in the Factories Bill of this session, Mr. Roebuck unsuccessfully divided the House on a motion directed against interference with the power of adult labourers (including women) to make contracts respecting the hours for which they shall be

* Sir Emerson Tennant told Roebuck that he was one of a deputation to offer the kingdom of Greece to General Sir Charles Napier, who was at that time in Cephalonia.

employed. His attitude at this time drew from Lord John
Russell some sarcasms on his tendency to arrogate to himself the possession of all the wisdom and purity of motive
of the House ; and the *Times,* losing no opportunity to disparage its fierce foe, followed this up with an article heavy
with lumbering irony. Commenting on this, a Welsh
newspaper, claiming to speak neither as friend nor foe, but
as a perfectly impartial spectator, said Mr. Roebuck's power
and influence were undeniable, and wrote :

Mr. Roebuck's position in Parliament is one he has good
grounds to be proud of. He has power, and he owes no patron
anything for it. Nor did he obtain it by rank, by luck of loins,
or any other luck. It is not the effect of any adventitious
circumstances. Such as it is, it is his own. His mind made it.
He has a good strong mind, and that alone, unaided and un-
friended, has made its possessor what he is.

It was somewhat remarkable that Sir James Graham,
while admitting Mr. Roebuck's arguments to be unanswerable, weakly excused himself from acting on them.
The *Times* called this a "confession that he felt with the
philosopher, though forced to act with fools."

*P. A. Taylor to J. A. Roebuck.*

*May* 7, 1844.—Will you allow me to plead the interest I feel
in the Factory question, and the steps I have taken through our
mutual friend, Dr. Black, in regard to it, in excuse of my expressing the obligations that I consider the opponents of that measure
are under to you for your very admirable speech in the House on
Friday ? If any evidence were necessary to show the effect it
must have produced, it is amply furnished by the vituperation it
and you have met with from the journals of the two factions, and
the soreness of the Whig leader, Lord John Russell. But in and
out of the House your arguments remain unanswered and untouched, and their truth will, I fear, be ultimately proved by those
consequences of which you have given warning, though unavail-
ingly.

Mr. Roebuck's share in the episode connected with Mr.

Ferrand's charges against Sir James Graham and Mr. Hogg, which occurred in this session, will be told in a chapter recording Mr. Roebuck's duelling experiences.[*]

The following record relates to the end of 1844 :—

For five days Mr. Roebuck has been engaged in a cause before the Privy Council relating to a dispute between the Lieut.-Governor (Napier) and the bailiff and jurats regarding the interpretation of the laws of the Island of Guernsey. On all hands Mr. Roebuck has been complimented for the very able manner of doing business. Baron Rolfe praised ; Lord-Chancellor Lyndhurst was very attentive and kind. General William Napier [†] writes word to-day, " I hear from Dampier, from Brotherton, from Cavendish Boyle, and from my brother Richard, who is rather a fastidious critic, that your talents, your knowledge of your subject, your sharpness of repartee, your self-possession and temper (this last from Dampier) were very remarkable."

* See *post*, chap. xvii. p. 196.
† Then Governor of the Island of Guernsey.

# CHAPTER XIV

IN 1845 Mr. Roebuck purchased Ashley Arnewood, a pleasant old manor-house with a delightful garden and about two hundred acres of land attached to it, situated six miles from Christchurch, on the edge of the New Forest. His idea was to farm this property, and he did so for some time ; but as his engagements increased in London, it was found impossible to carry on both London and country work at the same time. This necessitated the constant presence of Mrs. Roebuck at Ashley, where she undertook the study of practical farming, and eventually made it a success.

"I remember well," writes Miss Roebuck, "her pride in her beautiful herd of cows. My father used to come home on Saturday, returning to town the next Monday, but almost every day that he was absent he wrote to my mother, and sometimes twice a day. In the end of 1854, after my father recovered from his illness, the farm was given up, and we went to live at 19, Ashley Place."

In the spring of 1845 Mr. Roebuck engaged with Lord Duncan in a debate on the oft-battled question of the Window Tax. He renewed his protest against subjecting incomes derived from professions and trades to the same tax as incomes from property ; and he obtained the support of thirty-two members for a motion designed to extend the incidence of the Income Tax to Ireland. In

connection with Mr. T. Duncombe's attack on Sir James
Graham for post-office espionage, he denounced ministerial
tampering with letters in the post-office, and supported
Lord Howick's unsuccessful motion for a select committee
to inquire into the allegation that Mr. Duncombe's letters
had been detained and opened. It was in the debate on
the subject that Mr. Disraeli attacked Sir Robert Peel with
scathing vehemence, and originated the famous phrase,
"that, having caught the Whigs bathing, he had run off
with their clothes." On the question of the settlement of
New Zealand, Mr. Roebuck strongly insisted on unity of
administration, and sketched a plan for making the island
self-governing and self-supporting. But here he did not
refrain from indulging in an attack upon the missionaries.
By charging them with base and sordid motives, he gave
great offence, while his support of the Government proposal
to increase the Maynooth grant brought him into further
conflict with a section of his constituents.

*J. A. Roebuck to William Tait.*

*August* 26, 1845.—I have determined to write a history of the
Whig Administration from 1830 to 1841, and shall go by arrangement to Cannes * this winter, for the purpose of acquiring
information respecting certain parts thereof. In what way
should such a work be published? Money is not my chief
purpose; but while furthering my political views, I should not
object to making a penny. Pennies are not so plentiful with me
as to make me careless of them.

*September* 8, 1845.—Do not object to the somewhat exalted
tone of the paper. The tendency of things now is so prone to
a vulgar selfishness that we ought to do something to introduce
a more generous tone of morality. I smiled at the notion of
my living on the reputation of what I *might* do. The world is
not very willing to give me credit even for that which I have
done.

Towards the end of this year Mr. Roebuck undertook

* Where Lord Brougham was residing.

a private mission to Belgium in connection with the promotion of a railway enterprise. The following letters describe his experiences, and his impressions of the Court of Brussels and the people and politicians of Belgium :—

*To Mrs. Roebuck.*

*Hotel de Flandre, Brussels, November* 8, 1845.—I arrived at Brussels after a trying and most disagreeable journey, with six hours of constant illness. On arriving at Ostend, owing to being cramped in one position, I fell suddenly and completely lame. The king arrived from Paris to-day, and I have made arrangements for an audience. This lameness stops work ; but as you know how often it happens, I am never surprised at it. I am near the church, and was awakened this morning at five o'clock by the row of bells, which continued some hours, to the annoyance and discomfort of such mundane people as wished to sleep.

*November* 9, 1845 ; *Sunday, ten o'clock.*—I mark the day and hour, for without it you would not enter into the next part of my history. Just now is playing a very pretty march of Mozart's on the carillons, as a preliminary to the grand Mass. This to an English pietist must seem strange. I asked if there was to be any music to-day at the Mass, remembering that in 1830 I had heard some pretty music—a regular orchestra—at church on Sunday ; and I remember both mine and Graham's astonishment when we heard the music of the opera in the great church at Bruges. The answer to my inquiry was, " No, monsieur, there is nothing but the organ and singing. The archbishop has changed everything, and prohibited all profane music in the church." " To make it more grave," said I. " Yes, sir. Everything is changed since the time of the French," answered the *garçon.* " Ah ! I have seen sixteen revolutions, and every one has left us *pauvres gens* worse off than before." I now hear the drums in the distance ; the carillon is hushed, and a loud organ is playing. I can hear everything nearly as well as if I were in the church, in place of being in bed, where my lame leg still chains me.

*November* 10.—I have just returned from witnessing the opening of the Legislative Session, and was amazed by the farcical imitation of France and England. The form of the chamber

is semicircular, as in France, with tribunes all round up to the
ceiling, like a theatre.   The room is large, but not at all pretty
or imposing.   The thing that most struck—I may say shocked—
me, was the applause given, by the members clapping their hands
and shouting "La Reine!" or "Le Roi!"   Fancy the House of
Commons, with the Speaker in the chair, clapping their hands
and shouting like a mob at a theatre!   The king is growing old
and infirm.   His manners are sedate.

At one o'clock to-morrow, Van der Hagen writes me word,
that the king wishes to see me at Laken; and then I receive an
invitation to dine with their Majesties here in Brussels at six
o'clock.   Royal invitations are commands; so I go.   I also hope
to soon take wing.   My residence here has been anything but
amusing.   I have passed days bound to my bed in great pain, and
shall be glad to be free of my legs again.   The weather is
beautiful, and I am sitting at this moment with my windows
open; and, though it is nearly eight o'clock, they are singing
away in the Church as if it were morning.   This simple Church
music—the broad style—is the only thing which pleases me.
About an hour since, I hobbled into the church.   The singing
was not what it is now.   At the present moment it is simply
a part of the regular Church Service, and is the old music; but
when I was in the church, they sang what in style would have
suited well with the *Flauto Magico*, or any other popular
opera.   At one end of the church were three priests, evidently
suffering from bad colds, crossing themselves vehemently.   At
the other end was the director of the band, the leader, stick
in hand, leading with all the antics and placid fury of a regular
maestro.   Still, the singing was pretty, but nothing to the fine
masculine broad stuff that now compels me to listen.

*Friday, November* 14.—Yesterday was raining, after the
fashion of London, all day; and through the slosh I went to
Laken to wait on the king.   I found him extremely civil, talking
as if he had known me all my life, inquired after my lameness,
etc.   He has a fashion of shutting one eye, and of putting his
head on one side, that gives him a resemblance to a jackdaw
looking into a bone.

Well, I returned; and, as I was to dine, I sent for a crush-
hat.   Full tilt comes the hatter.   "Monsieur wants a hat to go
to the palace to-night?   Monsieur shall have one immediately—

with a feather, I suppose?" "A feather? The d—l!" I said. "What have I to do with such nonsense?" "Ah, monsieur! it is a *chapeau diplomatique.*" "*Diplomatique* or not, I want a plain, simple hat fit for a gentleman, not a mountebank; so get me one." The man seemed quite out of spirits, but did as he was bid. In due time I went to the palace, where I found the company arranged along the walls of the room—the women together, then the diplomatic body, then members of the Chambers, and lastly, the ministers. When the king and queen entered, he took the lead, and spoke to every person in succession. Her Majesty spoke French-English. "Is it of a long time, Mr. Roebuck, that you are here?" She condoled with me on my lameness, and said that the king had told her that I was a sufferer. After dinner, her Majesty sent Van de Weyer to me. She hoped I would sit, as she knew I was in pain, and was sorry to see me leaning. All this was very civil, and very considerate. On going into the dining-room, I took the first seat that offered, and soon addressed my next neighbour, whom I found to be a member of the Chamber, a Liberal, and thoroughly anti-Catholic. We talked for some time, and at last fell upon the forms of the Chamber. I spoke of the clapping of hands as to me new, and not altogether befitting, saying, "I have a sort of feeling of caste about it, being myself a member of a representative body. "What body?" "The House of Commons." "Ah! then you can tell me if a compatriot of yours is at this table, whom you can point out to me. It is Mr. Roebuck who is here, for the king told me so. Do you know him?" "Yes, indeed, for I am he!" We struck up an acquaintance; and afterwards I got Van de Weyer to formally introduce me. I was also introduced to a M. van Praet, who is in office here, and a man of some importance, but a regular coxcomb. He speaks English perfectly.

*November* 18.—Lord Arran took me over the house belonging to the Duc d'Aremberg—a fine specimen of a nobleman's house. There are some good Dutch pictures, and one thing above price, the head of the Laocoön—the real Greek head. Beside it they have a cast of Michael Angelo's restoration, and the inferiority of the great Italian is very remarkable. The Greek head is of a higher character: the pain felt is more intensely marked; and anything more wonderful than the mere handling of the

marble I never saw. You would declare it was flesh. This
was the only thing that excited and interested me in the house,
which, nevertheless, would have been a source of great delight
to you, as it was full of all sorts of inconceivable china. Arran,
who is bitten, like yourself, was in raptures with the vases, etc.
I find all the houses built on a Spanish plan of a square, with
an open centre and rooms on the sides of the quadrangle. They
have a grand air, but are not fit for the climate—dark and
dismal; for a hot climate delightful. What would be delicious
in Spain or Italy, appears wretched here. You want to court
light and heat in this cold nook of the world.

Yesterday I went to a distribution of musical prizes by the
Minister of the Interior, in the presence of the king and queen.
It was a pretty show, and took place in a vacant Protestant
church fitted up for the occasion. The music very good, the
people exceedingly well-dressed. The population, however, is
awfully ugly. To-day I am going to the debate on the King's
Speech, in the Chamber of Representatives, for which Van de Weyer
has just sent me a permanent ticket. They are all mighty civil.
I only wish they would settle my business and let me go.

*November* 20.—I have not brought affairs here to a close.
There is now a Ministerial crisis in this Barataria, and Van der
Hagen and his colleagues are now fighting for their lives in the
Chambers. Not being men of business, they can think of
nothing but their debate, and consequently all business, important
or not, is postponed to this personal strife. Fancy a debate,
which begins at half-past twelve, and ends at four p.m., occupying
the whole mind of a Ministry ! The members of the Chambers
take matters very coolly. When four o'clock comes, there is a
general cry of " Adjourn ; we must go to dinner ! "

The various *tables d'hôte* begin at half-past four, so delay
beyond the hour of four is a loss of a cheap dinner. So ends the
day's work. One need not wonder at English influence and success,
when such things occur. Sir Robert Peel and Sir James
Graham would repose on roses had they only a debate of three
or four hours to think of ; and such a debate ! The funniest
row you ever heard—interruptions of all sorts, cries, interpellations,
little speeches made sitting ; the President shouting, " Don't
interrupt ! " with his hammer like an auctioneer, and in desperate
cases ringing his bell like the postman ; five members on their

legs at once, gesticulating like madmen, and the tribunes full of people shouting, laughing, criticizing—make up a bedlam rather than a deliberative assembly. Arran and I had three days of it, and are sick of it. The ignorance, too, of what is going on around them is wonderful. There were constant appeals made to English Parliamentary usage, and as Van der Hagen is the head of the Opposition, we naturally talked over the debate. I gave him hints from our history, and described some of our rules. He did not know what was meant by the Leader of the House of Commons! He did not know that Peel was the present chief of the Tory party, knew nothing of Earl Grey, and as for Lord Althorp, he neither knew nor could pronounce his name. Notwithstanding all this, they all quoted English history and example with the utmost confidence, and one man went so far as boldly to assert that Peel had dissolved Parliament since last coming into office; and turning round with great self-complacency to an opponent at the same time, he requested him not to quote English history again without being better informed! So much for this nonsense. I am off for Ostend at three o'clock to-day.

While Mr. Roebuck was absent in Brussels, this country was face to face with that national disaster—the failure of the potato crop. This swept away the remaining vestige of Peel's cleavings to the Corn Laws, leading up to Ministerial dissensions and party revolt. When Mr. Roebuck paid a flying visit to London, he found the country eagerly watching the movements of ministers, and drawing the most ominous conclusions from those meetings of the Cabinet, at which Peel was fighting out his struggle with some of the most influential of his colleagues. The moment was seized by Lord John Russell to write his famous Edinburgh letter, declaring himself against the Corn Laws; and the excitement was increased by the announcement that Peel had decided on convening Parliament for the first days of January, to recommend a consideration of this impost preparatory to its total repeal. The day after this statement was made, Peel resigned, with assurances of his readiness to support measures in

M

accordance with the general principle of Lord John Russell's letter. By the time Mr. Roebuck had returned to Brussels, Lord John Russell had confessed his inability to form a Ministry, owing to Lord Grey's insistence that Palmerston should not be Foreign Secretary. Sir Robert Peel, with a reconstructed Cabinet, was, in consequence, reinstalled in office. The following letter, written on Mr. Roebuck's return to Belgium, gives a vivid account of the turmoil accompanying these events, of the mystery surrounding them, and also of the inability of politicians to divine their true outcome :—

*To Mrs. Roebuck.*

*Brussels, December* 29, 1845.— . . . On my arrival in town I found a letter from F. Mills, appointing a meeting at the Reform Club. I had a cold run to Dover. We went on board the steamer, some half-dozen persons, all men, more like criminals going to execution, than mere voyagers crossing the Channel. I remained on deck to see the plunge through the surf at the bar of the harbour. The sight was fine, and the gallant vessel seemed indeed instinct with life. Through it we dashed—right through all the seas, coming out on the other side in comparatively smooth water. The wind, luckily, was fair, and we drove before it like a mere flake of froth on the top of the waves. Our crossing was done in five hours and a half. The rain, when we reached Ostend, falling as if it was resolved to flood the country, which resolve— if such it made—is now fulfilled. Such a slop I never saw ! It was pitiable to see the fields of wheat lying in such a swash. Nothing would tempt me to live in a country of this description. Walking is out of the question, and if you drive, you can only go on a raised causeway with a deep ditch on each side, and sweltering fields all around, as far as the eye can reach.

As for London, I never saw it in such a hubbub ; everybody saying to his neighbour, "Well, what are Peel's plans ?" Answer : "I don't know." And still the question repeated. The quidnuncs of the Reform Club were a study. Rumours and stories of all sorts flying about, among them one I certainly do not believe, though I really wish it was true, viz. that Brougham is to be the President of the Council in Peel's Cabinet.

The sum of the news is, that nobody *knows* anything respecting Peel's plans, and everybody is guessing at them. My own opinion is, that he has none yet settled ; but I fear he will be driven from office, no matter what plan he takes. The boldest will be the safest ; but his character is not one to follow such a course.

As is well known, Sir Robert Peel did take the boldest course, for in the ensuing session he brought in his famous measure of Free Trade.

*To Mrs. Roebuck.*

*Brussels, January* 1, 1846.— . . . News I have none. I shall see the king in a few hours. The New Year's Day passes in paying visits. Everybody calls on everybody ; and the king and queen receive everybody. The poor king complained to me of "the love these people have for long speeches." "I hope they do not require of your Majesty long speeches in return ?" "Oh yes, they do. I make them all, and it is very fatiguing, I assure you," he replied.

*January* 7.—Yesterday I dined with an advocate here, quite *en famille*—a very pretty dinner, quiet, and well managed. They are what we should call well-bred people ; nothing distinguished, not marked with the peculiar stamp of *gentleman*, but still, I should say, of a better description than a common London lawyer's class. The lady is not Belgian, but French—clever, quick, well-bred, not *noble*. It is strange—in spite of the Revolution—of what importance this mark seems yet to be. They talk of *égalité* ; it does not exist—that is, social equality—and I, for my part, believe such a thing wholly impossible. The difference may rest upon a different foundation than it now does, but difference there always must be—social difference, that is. The conversation was chiefly respecting England and English habits, of which they necessarily have extremely imperfect and incoherent notions. They seemed surprised at my abstinence, not at all in accordance with their preconceived notions of Englishmen. Moreover, among advocates, I found myself alone dressed for dinner. These classes have, apparently, no medium between official costumes—uniform, in fact—and every-day dress. The higher classes do as we do, and imitate our dress. The ludicrous part of the matter is the funny imitation of the *varmint* man—the attempt at a dashing tilbury, dogs, horses, guns, hunting, top-boots, and leathers, etc.   The drollest thing I have seen is the supposed wig of the *cocher Anglais*.   I have half a fancy to buy one as a curiosity.   The *bif tek de mouton* is the only thing that equals it.

I went afterwards to the play.   The theatre pretty, and the *prima donna* said to be English.   She was pretty, but without a fine voice.   I was bored to death with the row-dow and the smell of gas.   Moreover, a *Belge* is not a Frenchman.   The mercurial Gaul is a much more amusing animal than these present supposed descendants of the ancient Belgi.

Yesterday morning, wanting to see the Minister of Public Works, I wrote him a note, simply asking him to see me some time after twelve o'clock.   I got for answer, that, as M. le Ministre did not understand English, I must have the goodness to wait until my note was translated.   Shortly after, the garçon of the hotel comes running into my room with an open note in his hand.   "It is you, monsieur, who wrote this *billet*, is it not?"   "My own note, by the Lord!" said I to myself.   "Yes. Well, what then?"   "Why, monsieur, they can understand it all at the *Ministère* except this word"—pointing to twelve.   "That is *deux*, is it not?"   "Not two, but twelve *midi*."   "Ah, par exemple!" said the garçon, and rushed out to explain to some one below the meaning of the mystic *twelve*.

The minister at length sent me an answer.   I saw him; and after we had talked over business, asked me very civilly to his ball last evening.   I went with the A——'s.   I speak by the card when I say that I did not see one pretty woman.   The Belgians are, to my fancy, universally hideous.   They were well-dressed, and the rooms were elegantly furnished—some peculiarities, indeed, to be seen : little places for birds, sham grottoes with squirting fountains, and gold-fish in a pan.   I left early. The weather detestable ; we have had snow, frost, rain, fog —everything that weather can bring.

The fools of Holland and Belgium, who seem by Providence chosen to rule over both countries, are trying to add their small modicum of dispute and quarrel to the mass which is fermenting throughout the world.   To spite each other, these two countries have begun a war of tariffs, and cannot understand that they are each respectively cutting off their own noses. Holland imports coal, having none, which coal Belgium provides cheap. Holland, in a fit of spite, puts a duty on coal; but this will fall of necessity only on the poor Dutchman, who will pay the tax in the shape of increased price. Hereupon, the *brave Belge* gets magnificently angry, and proposes to put a duty on coffee, sugar, and wood, all of which absolute necessaries Holland furnishes. So, because the Dutchman cuts off his own nose, the Flamand, in a passion, and to satisfy his own injured honour, does the same. Was ever there anything so absolutely mad?

*January* 15.—Well, yesterday I went to the ball [at the Palace]. The invitation came, as expected, but I learned the wisdom of Sancho Panza's rule, "Though your wife's advice be bad, if you do not take it you are mad." I left my Court toggery at home, and last night wanted it; so I went out and hired the Belgian Court dress—a sort of half civil, half military uniform. When the dancing had continued some time, the king rose, and went into one of the salons for the purpose of talking. I happened to be there, when the king came to me, and kept me half an hour in conversation. Being in Belgian costume, the English could not make out who I was. The king was very civil, and tried to pump me as to my views on the coming storm in the House of Commons. I said to him what I should have said to any one else, and he seemed well pleased.

Nobody (English) seems to know anybody but the nobles here; but they are a sad, vapid, and effete set, while the bourgeois, lawyers, etc., are men of ability. There must have been six hundred persons present last night. The only pretty English-woman was a Lady Bedingfield—very handsome, and, when young, must have been transcendent. I met Keppel [Lord Albemarle], who has now left. Seeing me, he cried, "Any commands for Ashley?" He is gone to try Lymington. This business keeps me a close prisoner in Brussels.

*January* 17.—Breakfasted this morning with the American minister here, Mr. Clemson. Had a long confab with his wife, a thoroughly (southern) American lady. She is a daughter of Calhoun. The conversation turned on the uses of Indian corn. I shall sow some for an experiment, as proposed by Clemson.

This experiment was tried, in the garden at Ashley

Arnewood. Well-manured mounds of earth being prepared, the corn was planted in American fashion, viz. three
corn seeds and one pumpkin (squash) to a mound. The
summer being unusually favourable, the success was
complete. The plants grew to six and seven feet high,
and the cobs ripened completely.

## CHAPTER XV.

### THE FALL OF PEEL. 1846–1847.

IT is unfortunate that there are but slight references in Mr. Roebuck's papers to the great events of the first half of 1846, when Peel, triumphant over the systematic obstruction with which Lord George Bentinck and Mr. Disraeli fought the battle of the Protectionists, was driven from office by his furious followers, who made the Irish Coercion Bill the medium for wreaking their vengeance. Writing to Mr. Tait, Edinburgh, on January 28, the day after Sir Robert Peel had explained his proposals for the reduction of import duties, both on manufactured articles and on food and corn, Mr. Roebuck exclaimed, "Well, Sir Robert is the best reformer, after all. We are really going ahead." The following was written on the same date :—

*To Mrs. Roebuck.*

*London, January* 28, 1846.— . . . Peel has certainly settled the question of corn protection, as you will see by the paper I send. You know I have always said, if he had courage to produce a new and good tariff, he might succeed. He has nearly done this. A new tariff, and, in certain matters, a good tariff, he has proposed to us, and it must be accepted. The landlords and the League will grumble ; but they must yield. The League will be angry because their game is up. The lecturers, the printers, the patriots, will cease to have a pretext for their union, their outcry, and *ergo*, for their pay, and thus an army of noisy people will be suddenly disbanded. This of itself will give rise to petty disturbances ; but they are done for. The landlords, poor fools, fancy themselves ruined, but they will find themselves happily deceived ; in a short time all will go right. The worst part of the tariff is the putting off the final settlement for three years, and the sugar duties. In fact, only one harvest really will be affected by the new Bill; and for the benefit, if any, of this protection, you have three years' uncertainty. The great measure is put off till Monday week, but I shall not be able to leave till Saturday. The Temple affairs require my presence.

*June* 23, 1846.—I wish to have Keene's *Bath Journal.* See if there is a letter signed "Gossip." It contains what is a correct version of the Montpensier business. The source of the information, the author, and the letter, you can easily guess.

Mr. Roebuck's Parliamentary attendance during the earlier portion of the session was lax. Professional business seems to have taken him away, but he flung himself, on occasion, into the Corn Law fray. With Mr. Disraeli then in the full swing of his terrible invectives against Peel, Mr. Roebuck repeatedly crossed swords. They were not mere fencing-bouts. Occasionally, indeed, Mr. Disraeli somewhat contemptuously parried, but at other times he retaliated with a vicious earnestness that left wounds.

*To Mrs. Roebuck.*

*June* 2, 1846.—Last night, as we were leaving the House, Mr. Sheil* addressed me.

*S.* "Do you not intend to vote with us against this Bill?" (Peel's Coercion Bill).

*R.* "That depends."

*S.* exclaimed upon this, "Why, surely you who have voted against all Coercion Bills will not support this? You will not agree to shut the people up all night?"

*R.* "But what answer will Lord John give me? Will he pledge himself and his friends not to bring in a Coercion Bill?"

*S.* "They cannot do it!"

*R.* "Aye, aye ; I hardly know what they can do. I must have some positive declaration to that effect, and, what is more, the country must have it, for it requires it."

* The Right Hon. Lalor Sheil, then M.P. for Dungarvon.

*S.* " That is impossible ! "

*R.* " No honest man—no man will deny that crime exists to a fearful extent in Ireland. If things remain as they are, the law must be strengthened, and I tell you what they ought to do, and probably will do—suspend the Habeas Corpus in certain localities, not in large towns, and not for political purposes. This being done, every rogue—for they are well known—can be taken up at once. For example, I myself, with that Mr. Cohen, whose name has been so often mentioned, would in a few hours be able to take up every rogue in Tipperary. At present the existing law is utterly paralyzed, and something must be done to protect the lives of the people."

Mr. Roebuck did, however, vote against the Bill, and thus helped to defeat the minister who had given Free Trade to England. This did not prevent him from adopting his customary attitude of contemptuous hostility to Lord John Russell and the new Whig Ministry, more especially on their policy as to Parliamentary reform and education.

Ireland, with its famine and its outrages, had the first place in the Queen's Speech opening the session of 1847. Having missed the golden opportunity presented by Lord Stanley's Bill of 1845, intended to give effect to the main recommendations of the Devon Commission, Parliament was destined to go on, talking and tinkering year after year, confronted by evils to the root of which, in face of the opposition of the land-holding peers, it had not the courage to go.

The following refers to a speech made in the debate on the Address. It counselled the extension of the existing Poor Law to Ireland, as well as the imposition of an Income Tax. It also described the real position of Irish landlords with regard to their tenants.

*To Mrs. Roebuck.*

*London, January* 21, 1847.— . . . I stirred up the landlords of Ireland after my fashion. The Irish are really furious ; but I spoke the opinions of nine-tenths of the people of England, and, as usual, the House paid me the compliment of profound attention. The hit was successful, and as Dizzy followed, and failed completely, the contrast was amusing. The *Times* has a fair report.

I breakfasted with Brougham. The Government are to bring forward their plans with a proposal to remit the present duty on corn, and to suspend the Navigation Laws. Molasses to be used in breweries and distilleries, and the price of barley to fall, *they say*. I say no. Famine threatens everywhere. The ministers are right glad to have me bear the brunt of the battle, as it affords them a means of parrying the constant attacks of these insatiate mendicants. The people of England are with me, and are delighted to have some one who will speak the truth amongst all this hurly-burly of cant, hypocrisy, and selfishness. The weather is frightful.

On the third day of the session Lord John Russell's proposal to suspend the Navigation Laws came on. Mr. Roebuck wished them to be altogether abolished; but this was resented by Mr. Disraeli and Lord George Bentinck, with the result that there was a "scrimmage."

### *To Mrs. Roebuck.*

*January 22.*—We had a scrimmage last night. I received from every quarter thanks and congratulations for my speech, and this morning Keppel * met me with open arms, and declared in most exaggerated terms that mine was one of the most eloquent speeches he had heard. Now, this is a phrase, and as a phrase goes for nothing. I could see from Lord John's manner, and that of all his understrappers, that they desire my assistance. I shall not be able to be at home to-morrow. On Monday the grand Irish row begins, and I shall have to meet all the rabid Irishmen who howl for sport.

*Saturday, January 23.*—My doings have certainly produced an effect. The people of Bath are in ecstasies, and the protection gentry are furious.

On January 25, Lord John Russell introduced the Govern-

* The late Lord Albemarle.

ment scheme for alleviating the present, and improving the future, condition of Ireland.

*To Mrs. Roebuck.*

*January* 27.—Next week will be a busy one, as then the Irish discussion will come on in earnest, and having already taken a prominent part in it, I must go on. Lord John's scheme is a foolish one. He spoke exceedingly well, and his concluding advice to Irishmen was really excellent. The introduction of an effective Poor Law into Ireland will also do much good ; but the attempt to buy waste lands, and lend money to landlords, will never do, and I am quite certain will not be permitted by the English. My conduct has been universally approved, and I receive letters from all quarters expressing a hope that I may continue to stand up for the English. I cannot understand why Lord John should have fathered such a scheme. I have a fancy that if I choose to meet the Ministry steadily this year, they will endeavour to make friends. I shall not deal in a hostile spirit with them, but shall certainly employ my power upon their doings, not upon them. It is strange how completely I have assumed my old position in the House. People fancied (and the Palmerites especially) that because I did nothing last year my vocation was gone. There is an infernal organ grinding away, and putting all my ideas into confusion.

*January* 30, 1847.—We had a meeting with Lord John yesterday. The deputation consisted of delegates from all the Metropolitan parishes, and they all declared they would vote for no one who did not support my motion to extend the Income and Property Tax to Ireland.

*Friday, February* 11.—We had a grand scrimmage last night, when I gave Lord George Bentinck an infliction such as he never got before. The House in ecstasies of applause, Whigs and all. As usual, the real scene is not, and could not be, given merely by giving the speeches, and consequently the newspapers are but a poor transcript of the proceedings. The Treasury benches are beginning to find that they need me, and are now civil. The Peelites very nearly took me round the neck. The debate begins to-night on the Irish Railway Bill,* but will not end.

* Lord George Bentinck's scheme for lending £16,000,000 to Irish railway companies. It was thrown out on second reading by 214 majority.

Lord John called his friends together yesterday—I, for the nonce, being one—and told them that he would resign if the Railway Bill was carried.   This upset the Irish, who are, without exception, the most consummate rascals that ever bore the name of gentlemen.   At one time the Whigs fancied that the union of the Protectionists and the Irish would give George Bentinck a majority ; now it is quite certain that the Ministry will have a good division—I believe a good majority.   The feeling out-of-doors against the Irish [members] grows apace, and I am overwhelmed with letters applauding my conduct.

On Wednesday I dined with Mackinnon and the literary men. . . . Mr. Douglas Jerrold is, I find, the cock of a little walk, the small leader of a small set who admire and praise him.

Napier * has written to me, sending extracts from Irish letters, confirming all I have said.   I am absolutely besieged by deputations of all sorts, and I was pestered yesterday by a parson, who wished me to present a petition to impeach Lord John Russell. I gave him to understand that I thought he had better take some cooling medicine.   He bounced out in great dudgeon.

*February* 13, 1847.—The debate † began last night, and, as I expected, was adjourned, and may last some days.   The plot thickens, and the whole burden of resistance is so completely thrown on myself that I see no chance of getting away.

The Irish Poor Law, as proposed by the Government, is a useless measure, and no one is prepared to make it efficient, and if I go away the money will be granted, and we shall have no security for the future maintenance of the poor Irish by the rich of that country.   In this state of things I am compelled to remain, and while the frost remains with us, no farming can go on, so, in fact, no harm happens beyond the annoyance of being here alone.

The "hubbub" mentioned in the following letter was caused by a renewal of the proposal on which Mr. Roebuck had long been harping : "That plans for the relief of the Irish poor would be unjust and impolitic unless accompanied by a system of taxation of property such as was

* Sir William P. Napier.
† On the second reading of Bentinck's Irish Railway Bill.

already in force in England." The motion was rejected by
121 to 26 votes.

*To Mrs. Roebuck.*

*March* 9, 1847.—Well, I did make a hubbub, and kept
" Hon'ble House " in a roar for an hour and a half by acting
several parts. The reports give no adequate idea of the scene—for
it was a scene. But the speech as reported will tell.

I breakfasted with Brougham. He was so full of his doings
in the Lords that he forgot to deliver me a message from Lord
Normanby, which Lady Malet, however, detailed at great
length, she and I being great friends. She seemed pleased at
having something pleasant to tell.

Lord John Russell's plan for the education of the
people, introduced on April 19, offended against some of
Mr. Roebuck's strongest principles. Roman Catholics
were, at present, to be excluded from a share in the grant
of £100,000, and the Prime Minister held that the proposal to make education secular was opposed to the opinion
of Parliament.

*To Mrs. Roebuck.*

*London, April* 22, 1847.—I spoke last night on the Education scheme, and against the Government. I will explain why
to-morrow.

On coming here I found a letter of a month old from my
Aunt Tickell, a lady who was very fond of me in days of old, but
treated one of my brothers ill, therefore we were unfriends. She
writes to ask me for my countenance to one of her nephews.
This is Nemesis again. I wrote her a note, yielding at once to
her wishes, and giving my reason—my unwillingness to be unkind
to a young man beginning life with but a few friends.

*House of Commons, April* 23, 1847.—The Government is
evidently going to the ——. Grey and Palmerston are, *on dit*,
quarrelling about Peel's doings respecting France. The Factory
Bill has divided the whole set, and the new Education scheme has
divided them all. Poor H. is in fits of funk; he is smarting
under E. Gibbon Wakefield's Colonization scheme, and says that
I am right about him. C. Buller and H. hardly as good friends

as before. Such a confused mass of disturbance and suspicion in the political world as at this moment I never knew before. All is topsy-turvy, and no one knows who is friend or foe.

*April 24, 1847.*—Last night * was a most triumphant night for me. I will send you the *Times*, which will give you a faint notion of what took place. The fact is, that the late negotiations of the Ministry with the Wesleyans, conducted by Ashley as a go-between, were, I sincerely believe, mainly intended as a means of ousting me from Bath. Ashley laid the scheme, and Lord John and Co. were nothing loath, and they fired the mine which has blown up themselves. Having, then, no reason to be very well pleased with the Ministry, I took the occasion of stripping off the disguise which they have assumed. Every blow told.

*May 19, 1847.*—In the evening I went to the House, and found Ferrand † in full roar against the Poor Law. Charles Villiers was sitting behind me, and carried a message from me to George Grey, who was taking notes to answer Ferrand. My message was, that if he would leave him to me, I would give Ferrand a dressing. The answer came, "Only too happy; pray proceed," and so indeed I did. The reports give but a pale, faint shadow of what was said and done.

*No date—about end of May, 1847.*— . . . Last night I repeated my infliction on Ferrand, carrying the House triumphantly with me, and obtained the warm cheers even of the Treasury Bench, with Lord John leading the band. I never made so successful a speech, giving them a slice of what I mean by eloquence, not overlaid balderdash, but an attempt, at least, at a masculine appeal to all that was generous and true in their spirit at the moment. The sensation was great. A speaker, like an actor, feels what his audience feel ; he is a species of thermometer, and my recording index marked blood-heat. I have seldom seen them more excited. Charles Villiers felt himself personally indebted to me, as I defended Lewis ‡ against the atrocious charges brought by Ferrand against him, that of *murder* being one.

* Fourth night of debate on Government plan of education.
† Member for Knaresborough.
‡ Mr. (afterwards Sir) George Cornewall Lewis (November 2, 1846) filed a criminal information against Mr. Ferrand for the publication of letters charging him with conspiracy and falsehood in connection with the Keighley Union inquiry in 1842.

## CHAPTER XVI.

### FINAL REJECTION AT BATH. 1847.

DISSOLUTION was already in the air, and Mr. Roebuck was destined to find that the "ecstasies" of the people of Bath were by no means so favourable to him as he had supposed. His antagonism to the Government Education Bill had brought him into open conflict with the Ministry, and Lord John Russell had, with considerable asperity, resented the attacks of one who, without producing any measure of his own, carped and cavilled at every proposal made by others. In May, Lord Duncan and Mr. Roebuck attended, in Bath, a preliminary meeting called to consider whether the sitting members should be supported by the joint efforts of their respective friends. Several of Mr. Roebuck's former supporters declared their determination not to vote for him again, and there was much plain speaking.

*To Mrs. Roebuck.*

*Bath, May* 28, 1847.—On my arrival here I found affairs in pretty much the state I expected. The Ministry are evidently at the bottom of the row. Duncan and I arrived, and met the Liberal Association; both of us declared we should stand jointly. Hereupon Murch began a laboured discourse against myself. He went over all the six years of the Parliament, and quoted from his notes all my evil deeds. This I answered so completely that I shook him. Wilson Brown also began from notes, but he let the cat out. I had been a censor of the Whig Administration, so he could not support me. So said Norman, who said he was always opposed to me! Well, the upshot was that the meeting resolved, without a dissentient voice, to support us both.  Murch is our treasurer.  I treated him with the most civil kindness, answered him without one bitter word, and with expressions of good will and respect.  This flattered and surprised him ; he sent me a message of thanks by Duncan, and expressing a wish to see me. I went.  This annihilates so much of the plot.

The following is a portion of the answer to the charges mentioned in the above letter :—

It is a long indictment running over six years. . . . The first instance of absence from the House of Commons adduced * was in February, 1842, and just at that time the Northern Circuit was in full play, and I was compelled to be present in it.  Every one of the instances objected to occurred at similar seasons.  My health, too, prevented my attendance on many occasions.  Those around me only knew what miserable sufferings I had to endure.† A continuation of terrible pains made me wish when the sun rose that it was time it had gone down, and when it was down that it was time to rise again.  He says I have an ungovernable temper.  Now, that is not so.  I can assure him I have my temper under control ; but if he knew in what kind of atmo- sphere one lives, he would then know the difficulty of making an impression without speaking out firmly and fully.  I will go to the present session (1847) to give you an account of what has been going on round about me, while I have been defending the indefeasible right of the poor.  While I was speaking upon the question of a Poor Law for Ireland, gentlemen around me were audible in their expressions, not only of taunts or of bitter hatred, but one was even heard to go so far as to threaten me with personal violence.  In such a state of things it was necessary to drive home, and because those gentlemen felt it, and created an uproar in consequence, the reverend gentleman [Rev. J. Murch] now says that I lost my temper.  Not so ; those gentlemen were noisy because I was not afraid of them.  That is the secret. . . .

I am much pained in having to refer to that great man, Mr. Daniel O'Connell, the news of whose death was brought by the same train by which I came.  I call him a great man, for,

---

\* Mr. Charles Villiers' annual motion on the Corn Laws.
† From neuralgia in the knee.

with all his faults, he was so, and it is with extreme and sincere regret that I should have to say anything which might wound the feelings of his already afflicted family ; and as Mr. O'Connell has left a great name which is public property, I think I may refer to it now, although it will be with great compunction.\*

I do, then, believe that Mr. O'Connell, Mr. Smith O'Brien, and the other leaders of the Repeal Party, used language calculated to mislead their ignorant and unhappy countrymen ; that they were continually endeavouring to create and foster differences, divisions, and animosities between Celts and Saxons,

---

\* Several years earlier, Mr. Roebuck, in a speech to his constituents, had made some interesting remarks as to his association with the great Irish demagogue. "I have stood by him with a few," he said, "when to be his friend was considered a political disgrace. On the first night of my speaking in the House of Commons, I raised my voice in behalf of Ireland, and after the close of the debate, on the floor of the House, Mr. O'Connell came up to me and said, ' Mr. Roebuck, I have not the honour of a personal acquaintance with you; but I would now address you as a friend of the Irish people.' When the Coercion Bill was passed, the small body of Radicals, which was then in the House, opposed it in all its stages. We fought against it by the side of Mr. O'Connell for three whole weeks. And yet he turns round on us now and calls us Tory Radicals. But we will tell Mr. O'Connell that the English Radicals are not to be bullied into any measure of which they do not approve."

Speaking at Galway (October, 1858), Mr. Roebuck said : "I began my political life as the friend of your great friend, Mr. O'Connell. It was my fate to enter Parliament as a very young man, an enthusiastic Englishman ; and I found myself side by side with the great friend of Ireland. I was a Radical then, and I am so still, and I found O'Connell was the friend of the Radicals, therefore we got side by side. But there was that in O'Connell which we seldom find in any member of Parliament—and I must say not in Irish members of Parliament—he was able to command the attention of the British House of Commons. He had that weight of eloquence which commands respect, that brilliant imagination which wins everybody's applause, and when he opened his lips, the listening Senate heard his words with admiration, if not with approbation. I was at once attached to O'Connell. I asked myself what was his object—what he desired to have for Ireland ? I found it was this : that Englishmen and Irishmen should, before the law, be entirely equal, that there should be no preference for a man on account of his country or creed. The first subject on which I voted—the first matter that occupied the attention of the Reformed Parliament—was the Irish Coercion Bill, and on that subject I voted side by side, as a humble militant, with O'Connell. I always voted against it, and so did he, and English statesmen have since learnt that the small minority which then opposed the measure was in the right." See also Roebuck's "Whig Ministry," vol. i. p. 78, *et seq.*

N

Catholics and Protestants, Englishmen and Irishmen ; and there was not anything which they could devise calculated to harass and distress the Administration which was not adopted by them.

When Mr. Smith O'Brien came to the House of Commons, making his professions of sincerity for Repeal,* I did express my condemnation that he should so deceive and mislead his country-men. I know they did not want Repeal of the Union, for now their cry for it is gone ; and we are to be blamed because, foreseeing what would be the issue of their conduct, and having a deep and anxious desire for the permanent welfare of Ireland, we en-deavoured to expose the fallacy we knew would lead to such dire conclusions. What has Conciliation Hall, and all the violent epithets and denunciations employed by its orators, done for the poor peasants of Ireland ? Has any other effect been produced than that of weakening their means of meeting a time of famine by extracting from their pockets money for the support of brawling agitators ? Seeing what was coming, was it strange that I should be somewhat warm in maintaining not only the right of our own countrymen, but the peace and comfort of the world— for it must be remembered that to such a pitch of excitement had the Irish people been worked up, that a spark from either of those I referred to, when speaking in the House of Commons, would have set Ireland in a flame, the probable results of which it is impossible to estimate. Shall I, then, be condemned because to some ears I used strong expressions towards those who were living upon the earnings of the starving poor ? †

If you could see me in the House of Commons, I should appear to you as cool and composed as I do now ; and yet, were the phrase now uttered to come to you unaccompanied by the connection in which it was used, you would probably say, "Here is another of Mr. Roebuck's violent statements." Mr. Murch has said the proceedings on the Irish Poor Law were like a boxing match ; I think the simile would have been more correct if he had said it was like one poor fellow being worried by twenty. Seeing the millions of English money about to be voted for Ireland, I said, as I shall say again, that the conduct of the Irish landlords had produced a great part of the mischief, to remedy which that money was required. No sooner had I sat down, than one Irish landlord after another got up and abused

* June 14, 1845.            † See *post*, p. 198, chap. xvii.

me as I was never before abused in my life. I then told them, " You are angry because I have told you the truth." Am I, then, to be blamed because those gentlemen did not like the truth, and chose to make the House of Commons a bear-garden ? I called on the Government to adopt such measures as should compel those gentlemen to do their duty, and secure the permanent welfare of the poor of Ireland. I stood almost alone in thus reminding the Irish landlords of their duty. Bushels would not hold the letters of thanks I have received from all parts of the country for the course I took on the Irish question.

In the case of Mr. Cobden, I am also charged with having held aloof from the Anti-Corn-Law League, from some private pique towards that gentleman. The real cause of my not taking an active part in the League was my unfitness for outdoor agitation. I may also mention that in one of the last conversations I held with Mr. Bright, Mr. Cobden's most particular friend, he said to me, " Can I do anything for you at Bath ? " I said, " I shall have a hard fight with Lord Ashley, probably ; " and he replied in a quick way, which some might perhaps term violent, for Mr. Bright, though a Friend, has a quick, startling manner, " Will you ? will you ? If you find it so, let me know, and we will do what we can for you, for we must have you in the House of Commons."

With respect to the Indian War, I was decidedly opposed to it ; and having read every paper of authority on the subject, I came to the conclusion that Lord Auckland was wrong, and that Lord Ellenborough was right.

*To Mrs. Roebuck.*

*June* 4, 1847.—Last night I saw Parkes, who spent a long time in discoursing upon the wisdom of my accepting some place, the present object being, as he fairly acknowledged, to make me consent to leave Parliament. The Whigs, he says, are so thoroughly afraid of me that they will not consent to give me anything which would keep me in the House, and render me either independent, or enable me to build up a further reputation. Parkes recommended me to fix upon some lucrative post out of Parliament, and to ask Lord John for it. He suggested an Indian judgeship. He professed great friendship, but I could not help believing that he was charged with a mission respecting myself. There is a growing feeling, and one very generally expressed, that I have been scurvily treated.

*June* 5, 1847.—After writing to you yesterday, I saw Hawes,[*] and learned what it is he wishes me to accept. It appears there is need of "a man of firm mind and clear head" at Guiana, in South America. A code has to be formed, a constitution and law to be established. The governor of this place is a poor old creature. They want me to take his place. Hawes spoke of the salary as large, and this, he thought, in a few years, would lead to independence. I positively declined. The climate is deadly, at least on the coast, and nothing would induce me to take you there. If I should be driven to accept, I should go alone, and trust to my luck to exist for five years. . . . Graham[†] scouts the idea.

*London, Friday, June* 11, 1847.—There never was such a life of hurry-scurry as mine ; not one moment have I, night or day, free from tormenting solicitations to take care of other people's affairs, the last request being from the citizens of Dublin to take O'Connell's place in a committee in order to protect their interests against jobbing and roguery. I was obliged to decline. The Bathwick Church occupies me all day, Railway Bills during the early hours of the evening, and public business the rest of the night. The debate on Portugal begins this evening, and will not finish, so that here I am kept.

Did I tell you that I had a formal offer of a judgeship in India ? I refused it. Every one not immediately connected with the Whig Government advises me strongly to keep where I am. The design of getting me away is plain, and John Mills[‡] said to me this morning, "They cannot, for fear of the law, cut your throat, which, as the shortest way of getting rid of you, would please them best, so they offer you an office, first in a deadly climate, and next try to bribe you by a show of making you independent." Frank Mills is really going to Bath to aid in my election.

The Tories are almost as anxious for my services as my old Radical friends. The two ends of the scale meet here. John Revans is working away to keep me in Parliament ; Frank Mills

* Under-Secretary for the Colonies.
† His lifelong friend, G. J. Graham.
‡ Of Bisterne, brother of Frank Mills.

and Lord Lonsdale are writing and aiding the same thing. "Suicide" is the word I most frequently hear when I speak of retiring. Brougham raves and denounces ; Napier warns me against trusting to the Whigs if they offer me anything abroad.

*Sunday (about June* 20), 1847.—The debate on Portugal still goes on, and I have had an opportunity of ruining the present Administration, but have preferred rendering them an important service. Tufnel came to me, asking what I intended to do, deprecating attack, and declaring his fears as to the result. The object was to prevent a division on Hume's motion,* and I undertook the office of endeavouring to persuade Hume not to divide. Failing, however, in this, I concocted with Duncombe an amendment, which he moved last night, and which I shall support to-night, and which will preserve the Ministry from defeat. Hume and a few others are angry at this ; but I am confident the course I have taken is the really prudent one. Had we rushed headlong into a division, we should, in fact, have given a triumph to the Bentinck party, and have gone to the elections ourselves divided and angry with one another. Such a state of things would undoubtedly have been very gratifying to the Tories, but to us it would have been fatal.

Lord Duncan had an interview with Lord John Russell yesterday, and was assured by Lord John that everything had been done—and should be done—to discourage Ashley. This I believe to be true ; but I am still more convinced than ever that Ashley was sent to Bath by the Whigs. Lord John said, "I am disappointed by Ashley's speech," and gave his disappointment as a reason for stoutly opposing him.

*London, June* 22, 1847.—Lord John is very angry with me. On Friday last I suggested that he might save public time by withdrawing at once, and without further discussion, the Health of Towns Bill and Strutt's Railway Bill. He was then very angry, and attempted to revile me into silence. I consequently smashed his Health of Towns Bill to atoms. Yesterday he withdrew it, and Strutt makes a two hours' speech, occupies a whole evening, and ends by withdrawing his Railway Bill. Whereupon I remarked upon the peculiarly undignified mode of proceeding, and urged the withdrawal of the Irish Railway Bill. Hereupon Johnny talks of my asperity, blusters as to how he is

* Censuring ministers for needlessly interfering with affairs of Portugal.

determined to proceed with that Bill.   The report of the *Times* speaks of my warmth.   Now, the fact was that I was so hoarse that I was unable to speak above a whisper, and one paper spoke of my indisposition.   I was not angry, but satisfied at the adoption, however late, of my last week's advice, and spoke without the least appearance of any emotion, except, perhaps, some contempt.

Lord Lincoln and Graham (Sir James) came to me, and expressed their entire concurrence with my opinion as to the wretched and imbecile conduct of the Ministry.   It brings not only themselves, but their office and Parliament, which permits them to retain office, into contempt.

*London, Saturday, June 26, 1847.*—I have just time to say that I have arrived here from Bath, where things are looking very well, and our people are again in heart by my going there.

I wish to be in the House on Monday respecting Irish railways ; Wednesday I dine with Lord John (Russell), and on Thursday go again to Bath. . . .

I met an old lady in Bath.   She sent for me—Mrs. Colonel Lisle.   She knew my mother, and was a passenger in the ship that brought my mother and her three children—myself among the number—home from Madras.

The old lady—eighty-four—remembered their names, and called Henry, Warrenne—as he was then called—and spoke of Ben *Riot*, and Johnny *Quiet*—two names that, as far as the world goes, have been somewhat reversed.

*London, July* 4, 1847.— . . . The Lords have in their wisdom thrown out the clause which we [the Commons] put into the Poor Law respecting aged couples above sixty being allowed to be together in the poor-house.   This would enable me again to shelter Lord John's Administration, but I suppose my hands are tied.   The devil tempts me, nevertheless ; and if George Bentinck was worth a farthing, one might lend a hand to give the existing men a lift.

There is a report (Marcus Hill was my informant) that Ashley went to Lord John and asked if the Government really supported me.   The answer of Lord John was, "Certainly ; we are all against you, Ashley.   We have great respect for you, but we must support with our whole strength Roebuck and Duncan."

*J. A. Roebuck to the Rev. D. Wassell (Bath).*

*White Hart, July 2,* 1847.—I beg to acknowledge the receipt of your letter addressed to Lord Duncan and myself, and proceed at once to answer the queries it contains as completely as I can in the confined space of this letter.

1. I have always resisted every attempt in the House of Commons to appropriate the public money in aid of any peculiar religious opinions, and have invariably endeavoured to render all men equal before the law, without any regard to the religious opinions they might entertain. It ought, however, to be recollected that the system and genius—if I may use the word—of our legislation has never been of this strict and undeviating description. In every quarter of the globe, English money and influence have been employed to disseminate Christian, and generally Church of England, doctrines; and in India, at this moment, we have taxation for the purpose, in some degree, of maintaining the priesthood and temples of the Hindoo and Mohammedan people under our sway.

In Ireland we have Maynooth and the Regium Donum, together with a regular Established Church. In England we have an Established Church; we have National and Foreign School Societies; we have money voted for the printing of the Scriptures; —in short, in a thousand forms, both at home and in the colonies, we have money voted for direct and indirect religious purposes; and I sincerely believe that a very large majority of the thinking men of our people would not consent to our pursuing strictly the rule which, in my conscience, nevertheless, I believe the most wise and beneficent. And I cannot help thinking that the sudden heat, and the general doctrines that have been promulgated of late on the part of certain of our Dissenting brethren, have their origin rather in a confined consideration of one particular event than in a careful and comprehensive view of all the many consequences fairly deducible from the principles which they have somewhat peremptorily enunciated. A purely secular system of legislation would not, in my opinion, find favour with the religious people of this country, and yet the complete non-interference suggested by your questions, and advocated by the Nonconformists, means a purely secular legislation.

2. On the subject of the State Church, my opinion has ever

been openly expressed. I do not consider such an establishment, in the present divided state of men's opinions, either just or politic. But I am not prepared at once, and without further ado, to propose the utter subversion of this Church as by law established. The majority of the people wish it to be maintained. That majority must be led, they cannot be coerced; and I am prepared, at all proper times and seasons, to support my principles by sober and temperate argument, and to endeavour, by all legitimate means, to win favour and support for my opinions; but I cannot unite with those whom I hear denouncing their opponents as infidels and enemies of religion because they happen to adopt an opinion differing from my own. I allude to a manifesto lately issued by the Nonconformist body, in which I was sorry to perceive what I believe to be a good and true principle much injured by what, in my humble judgment, appeared very like intolerance.

The complete sweep which you propose as regards the Established Church, you must perceive, is, in fact, nothing short of a very violent revolution in our whole political system; and I confess that the tranquillity of this great country, and with it the tranquillity of the whole world, is, in my judgment, of such paramount importance that I should tremble were I called upon to put it in hazard by that immediate and violent change which you contemplate. All that is really oppressive may, and I believe will, be soon reformed. The Church rates cannot last much longer; ecclesiastical dominion, as exercised by ecclesiastical courts, will soon, I hope, be put an end to; political and civil disabilities of every description, resulting from religious professions, must cease; and we shall then enjoy a real practical equality. And I do believe that no right-minded man need repine at the forms which may remain when all the substance of irregularity has been removed and destroyed.

One word as to education, and then I have answered, I believe, everything which your queries propound. I differ from those who think that the State has no concern, and ought to take no part, in the education of the people. On the contrary, I think the first, the chief duty of the State is to prevent evil; that punishment is but a rude and inefficacious means of attaining that end; but that education is the most legitimate and the most efficient of the means which human wisdom can employ to promote virtue and happiness. So believing, I shall certainly support every plan for the education of the people by the State, which does not interfere with the religious feelings and opinions of the parents and guardians of the children to be educated. If the State can—and I believe it can—instruct the people without offending or injuring them, it is, in my opinion, its bounden duty to do so. And every measure which legitimately attempts to attain this most worthy end shall have my most strenuous and hearty support.

### *To Mrs. Roebuck.*

*Early in July,* 1847.—I go to Bath to-morrow. The papers are full of my contest there. I travelled up with four women, and one, a very pretty girl, would tread upon my toes. How is it that these things happen when I am growing old, and, as the French say, *très sage ?*

The contest at Bath was characterized by all the fierceness and acrimony that had attended Mr. Roebuck's previous electoral struggles. Feeling on both sides was at fever heat, and all manner of accusations were freely bandied about. Lord Ashley and his supporters were openly charged with exercising various forms of terrorism, while the favourite cry of the Tories against Mr. Roebuck imputed to him infidelity, atheism, and contempt for religion. The bills circulated bearing these charges were so scandalous that, on the hustings at the nomination, Mr. Roebuck openly refused to shake hands with Lord Ashley. But more serious than the scurrilities of opponents was the alienation of many of Mr. Roebuck's former supporters. Departing from the rule he had laid down in his earlier contests to abjure personal canvassing, Mr. Roebuck made systematic visits to the electors, and the unfavourable reception he met with at the hands of the Rev. William Jay and other prominent Dissenters quickly became public property. To their dissatisfaction with much of his Parliamentary career was added remembrance of references disrespectful to Dr. Watts's "Second Catechism," made in the article on

Children's Books in *Tait's Magazine*, as far back as 1833. The Rev. Jerome Murch, Unitarian Minister, whose opposition, as we have seen, Mr. Roebuck thought he had effectually countered after the meeting in May, was so active an opponent that he, like Mr. Jay, was singled out for personal notice by Mr. Roebuck in the speech in which, after the result of the poll was known, he castigated his antagonists and shook the dust of Bath for ever from his feet.    For, notwithstanding the fact that throughout the campaign, and on the hustings, Mr. Roebuck had been the favourite of an enthusiastic populace, the poll had resulted thus : Lord Ashley, 1278 ; Lord Duncan, 1228 ; Mr. Roebuck, 1093.

Contrary to the advice of his friends, Mr. Roebuck insisted on addressing the excited crowds immediately after the voting had closed.    Accustomed at all times to say exactly what he thought in the most pungent language at his command, the emotions of this moment found expression in a very hearty scolding of the authors of his defeat.    At the nomination, all his denunciations had been poured upon Lord Ashley and the Tories.    Now the vials of his wrath were emptied on the heads of alienated friends. Rejecting a suggestion from the crowd that he had been defeated by bribery, he said, No, it was not bribery, it was bigotry.    The three persons who contributed to his defeat were a Whig (Mr. Norman), a Dissenter (the Rev. Jerome Murch), and a Waiter on Providence (Mr. Wilson Brown). He also singled out the Rev. William Jay for individual reference.    He continued—

And now, then, gentlemen, I bid you adieu.    Again I shall not appear here.    There are many constituencies that will ask, demand, require, such a representative as I am ; and they who, after fifteen years' service, have rejected me, in their hearts let there be the shame and the scandal which will be redeemed by others who will ask me to appear in the House of Commons. But, gentlemen, I have no ambition to be there.    I want not to appear in the House of Commons. My only hope is quiet ; my desire is literary ease ; my pleasure is my family ; my hope is content and quiet. If I would fight your battle, it is the battle of freedom that I would fight for you—for all of you to be secure at home ; to be in your families that which you would desire— fathers to guide, to direct, and to be the friends of that family without pain or suffering abroad. That I am not permitted to be. But I shall go a member of the Church of England—mind you, Dissenters, a member of the Church of England—remembering well that the Dissenters are not worthy of freedom. Now, as I never wish, as I never will, no matter what may tempt me, come down and behold that Abbey more, I care not what these men may say. I am here a free man, thank God, once again. No religious bigotry binds my tongue, no influence coerces my heart. The people of England are those of whom I think—self is annihilated in the balance. But when I behold religious intolerance, bound up with the selfishness of personal consideration, I will mark that with the finger of scorn ; and I tell you, once for all, your liberties as a town are beaten underfoot. And whom have we to thank ? The Dissenters of Bath. I have supported them on every occasion, and now, under the pretence of religious feeling, they have sought a sharp-seeking " consideration." * Well, then, it is for me—and you can well understand the sensation of my heart when I look around me—to say that word which is most painful to all, Farewell. As that sun shines and dazzles my eyes at this moment, no earthly consideration shall ever induce me again to solicit the votes of the people of Bath. When I have won for you the suffrage, my non-elector friends, then I will venture here. But the Dissenters of England, as represented by the Dissenters of Bath, are such cowards at heart that they are unworthy of an honest man as a representative unless supported by the non-electors of this town ; and when I have that body, I shall appeal to you, or any body of electors, and be sure of a triumphant return. Such pitiful, shameful, wretched, miserable humbug I never met with in my life. I have done with them for my life henceforth. Never again will I venture my boat upon the water to be blown about by the breath of Dissenters. Henceforth I am for the people, the unrepresented electors of England ; on them I will depend, and upon no section,

* This is the phrase in the newspaper report.

whatever that may be, will I, in any degree, base my fortune. This is the careful consideration of everything I have undergone for many years past. I hope for ease and peace in the bosom of my most cherished family. I wish not for political contention or party strife. I would rather see my wheat grow, even than see your faces. I would rather garner up the proceeds of the God of Nature, even than get your approval. The time may come that they who have now repudiated me may wish me here. They shall never have me, and I do say an eternal farewell.

In a written address, Mr. Roebuck took leave of his old constituents in more temperate terms, and his friends in Bath subsequently marked their appreciation of his fifteen years' service by presenting a testimonial to him. This consisted of £500, placed in an oak cabinet covered with carved emblems and figures, each one of which was executed by a separate workman. A pretty salver in silver was given by the wives and daughters of the Liberal electors of Lyncombe and Widcombe, and a work-box in inlaid woods—also a production of Bath—from the Ward of St. James, was given to his little daughter.

*To Mrs. Roebuck.*

*November* 6, 1847.—My reception at Bath was the most striking thing I ever witnessed, but this I must describe by word of mouth.

Lord Ashley, afterwards Lord Shaftesbury, the successful candidate in this election, years after, at Sheffield, said how much he regretted that he had ever opposed Mr. Roebuck at Bath.

# CHAPTER XVII.

## THE DYING DAYS OF DUELLING.

THE conflicts in which Mr. Roebuck's directness of attack and pungency of speech involved him were not by any means confined to words. At the commencement of his career duelling, though gradually dying out, was not yet dead, and Mr. Roebuck had in large measure that courage and readiness to appeal to muscular force which are not infrequently characteristic of men physically slight and even feeble. It has already been related how, after his first election, he resented impertinence by striking the offender, and he was a little apt to counsel a resort to blows, or to horse-whipping editors. Departing from the chronological arrangement otherwise observed in this book, it may be convenient to devote one chapter to an account of Mr. Roebuck's duelling experiences. The following narration is by Mr. John Temple Leader, who, describing the gatherings at his house at Putney Hill, writes—

*John Temple Leader to the Editor.*

One evening, as we were sitting in the library, enjoying the pleasant warmth of a cheerful wood fire, and talking of things in general, some one mentioned a scene in which Daniel O'Connell had used very strong language to a Tory M.P in the lobby of the House of Commons. Turning to Roebuck, he asked, " What would you have done in such a case ? " " I would have knocked him down," answered Roebuck, fiercely, and clenching his fist. This made us all laugh, considering the great physical difference between Roebuck, who was a small spare man, and O'Connell, who was a stalwart Irish giant.

In the third Pamphlet for the People (1835), Mr. Roebuck discussed " The Stamped Press and its Morality " with much directness of personal reference to the conductors of the *Times*, the *Morning Chronicle*, the *Examiner*, and the *Public Ledger*. This quickly resulted in visits from friends of Mr. Albany Fonblanque of the *Examiner*, and Mr. Sterling of the *Times*. They were commissioned to demand immediate withdrawal. Sir William Molesworth acted for Mr. Roebuck in both cases. Hostile meetings were averted by disavowals, retractions, and regrets, which Sir Francis Knowles for Mr. Fonblanque, and Col. Campbell for Mr. Sterling, accepted as satisfactory. The other editors, Mr. Black and Mr. J. L. Stevens, contented themselves with pen-and-ink rejoinders. With Mr. Black, however, Mr. Roebuck was destined, a few months later, to come into more warlike collision.

The *Morning Chronicle* had dragged into a controversy with Mr. N. Goldsmid a taunt that he was a Conservative Jew. Mr. Roebuck, in the Pamphlet for the People, issued on November 11, 1835, stigmatized this as brutal. To make the ignorant, the prejudiced, and the vulgar join in the cry against Goldsmid was, he wrote, base and utterly disgraceful, and, if Mr. Black had any shame left, was a proceeding of which he must heartily repent.

In discussing the remedies within Mr. Goldsmid's reach, Mr. Roebuck specified, among others, two. He could beat his assailant and drub him soundly, or he could call him out and endeavour to shoot him. These alternatives were dismissed with the remark—

It is evident that Mr. Goldsmid has little chance of saving anything by trying to beat the said John Black, he being a strong, lusty, hard-headed, and hard-fisted north-countryman, and Mr. Goldsmid being a slender and by no means strong person. In the second place, the said John Black is a philosopher, and

I feel confident that to fight duels for the *Chronicle* is not in his bond ; and I suspect the proprietor has not hired a regular fighting man for the concern.

Mr. Roebuck was undeceived as to Mr. Black's fighting propensities, for he received a letter, dated 232, Strand, November 13, 1835, in which, discovering an imputation of cowardice in the Pamphlet, and objecting to the epithets "base" and "utterly disgraceful," Mr. Black said—

I wish to know whether you are the author of the article containing these offensive epithets ; and if you are, I then call on you to retract them without qualification or reserve. My friend who delivers this will convey to me your answer.

As Mr. Roebuck was then staying at the seaside, near Christchurch, Mr. Simon McGillivray, one of the proprietors of the *Morning Chronicle,* the friend entrusted with this message, wrote, asking to be informed " when and where you can afford me the opportunity of delivering personally the communication with which I am intrusted."

*J. A. Roebuck to Mr. McGillivray.*

*Christchurch, Hants, November* 15, 1835.—I am now staying at Mudeford, near Christchurch, Hants. This letter will reach you to-morrow morning. You will probably leave London on Monday evening, and arrive here on Tuesday morning at twelve. I will at that time be at the Humby's Hotel, Christchurch. I make these arrangements, as I am desirous of so managing affairs as not to let any one have an idea of the purport of your visit, which I suppose, from your letter, to be a hostile one.

A narrative of the affair, subsequently published, says—

In compliance with the appointment, Mr. Black and Mr. McGillivray proceeded to Christchurch, where they arrived on Tuesday morning ; and at an interview at the King's Arms Hotel, Mr. McGillivray delivered Mr. Black's letter to Mr. Roebuck, who acknowledged himself to be the author of the article complained of, and refused to retract any part of it. He proposed also to write to London for a friend to act for him. Mr. McGillivray objected to this delay, and said that as Mr. Roebuck had recognized his letter to be a hostile one, he expected to have found him more prepared. Mr. Roebuck replied that the delay was Mr. McGillivray's own fault, in not having communicated more clearly the object of his mission ; and he declined either coming to London or appointing a friend on the spot, both of which plans had been suggested by Mr. McGillivray. In short, Mr. Roebuck refused any other alternative than to write to London for a friend, and to meet again at the same place on Thursday at noon ; and finally Mr. McGillivray acquiesced in this proposal. On Thursday, the 19th, Mr. Black and Mr. McGillivray accordingly returned to Christchurch, when Mr. Roebuck introduced Mr. S. Revans * to McGillivray as his friend, and after some discussion and preliminary arrangements, a meeting took place.

The seconds afterwards each published his own version of what had actually happened. They agreed that Mr. Revans, on behalf of Mr. Roebuck, admitted an error of detail in his Pamphlet, and disavowed any intention to impute cowardice to Mr. Black, as he really considered him a philosopher, and as such would, of course, not fight. But he absolutely refused to retract the words "base and utterly disgraceful." Upon that ground the gentlemen went into the field, to which Mr. Roebuck showed the way.

Mr. Roebuck received Mr. Black's fire, and fired, so Mr. Revans declared, in the air. Mr. McGillivray, though declining to confirm this, did not contradict it beyond saying that both shots were fired simultaneously.

After the first fire Mr. Roebuck repeated that he had no intention of imputing cowardice to Mr. Black, but he persisted in refusing to withdraw the terms "base and disgraceful," which he maintained the conduct objected to

---

* Mr. Revans was a barrister who, after emigrating with Mr. H. S. Chapman to Montreal in 1833, returned to London in 1837. He was secretary to the Wakefield scheme for settlement in New Zealand. He afterwards lived in New Zealand. See "Dictionary of National Biography." John Revans, his brother (p. 180), was connected with the English and Irish Poor Law Commissions.

deserved. Mr. McGillivray accordingly said the affair must go on. Shots were again exchanged without effect. An apology was again demanded, and again refused. Mr. Revans declared that they were there with their minds made up, and that, if Mr. McGillivray desired, the affair must continue. Then followed an altercation in which Mr. McGillivray, showing disposition to take the quarrel upon himself, was told that if he wanted to fight, he must fight with Mr. Revans, who was quite ready; and Mr. Roebuck declared that he was not to be driven from the right of stigmatizing the conduct of a public man as it deserved by threats of assassination. Thereupon Mr. McGillivray found it unnecessary to carry the matter any further. Upon which Mr. Roebuck "expressed his high respect for Mr. Black," though still asserting the right to speak of his acts as he had done.

Mr. Roebuck's precautions for keeping the matter from the knowledge of his family were not so successful as he had wished. Mrs. Roebuck once wrote—

I remember it but too well. We had been some weeks at the seaside near Christchurch, Hants. I missed Roebuck, and a short time after heard four shots. As persons were forbidden to shoot near the house, I remarked that they were two and two, and sounded differently and sharp, unlike a gun. The mystery was explained when our friend rushed in, saying, "Roebuck is safe." Explanation followed. Dr. Black had pointed his pistol at Roebuck and fired twice. Twice had Roebuck fired in the air.

Mrs. Roebuck was accustomed to tell how, when Mr. Black and Mr. McGillivray arrived at the inn at Christchurch, they paraded their pistol-case open on the table of the sitting-room. No magistrate lived at Christchurch, so, said she, they were not likely to be taken up, however much they wished it.

Mr. Roebuck's second duel was fought in 1839. His antagonist was Lord Powerscourt, who thought himself

o

aggrieved by expressions used by Mr. Roebuck respecting his conduct at the election of 1837. The Hon. Henry Fitzroy, M.P., was the bearer of Lord Powerscourt's challenge, which came at a very painful moment, the Rev. Dr. Falconer having died somewhat suddenly in the presence of his son-in-law only a few hours before.

After a necessary delay, and as Mr. Roebuck categorically reiterated his statements—which charged Lord Powerscourt with the hypocrisy of sanctioning accusations of irreligion against his opponent, while, at the same time, he was sanctioning the corruption of the electorate with drink—a meeting took place at Coombe Wood, near London. Mr. Roebuck, who had been supported by Sir William Napier's advice, had Mr. Edward Trelawny as his second. The following official account was published by him and Mr. Fitzroy:—

4, *Putney Hill, February* 28, 1839.—On the evening of the 28th, Lord Powerscourt, M.P., and Mr. Roebuck met by appointment at Coombe Wood, seven miles from Town; the former accompanied by the Hon. H. Fitzroy, M.P., and the latter by E. Trelawny, Esq. On the ground, efforts were renewed to avert the necessity of proceeding to extremities. Lord Powerscourt's friend insisting on Mr. Roebuck retracting or apologizing for the words complained of in the correspondence, and the opposite party declining to do so, the ground was then measured and the principals placed at twelve paces. On Mr. Roebuck receiving his adversary's fire, he discharged his pistol into the air, and, advancing to Lord Powerscourt, said, "Now, my lord, I am ready to make any apology your lordship may suggest, for certainly in my speech at Bath I did not mean to imply anything personally offensive." All parties being entirely satisfied by this frank procedure of Mr. Roebuck, returned to Town.

After this, two memorials from his Tory constituents were sent to Lord Powerscourt, rebuking him for the part he had taken. One was from the clergy of the city of Bath. His lordship, who had undoubtedly been egged on by others against his own better judgment, pleaded his deficiency in "that exalted moral courage which could alone have enabled him to despise the scoffs of the world and the sneers of his associates" if he had not vindicated himself.

It is but just to the memory of Lord Powerscourt to record that he heartily regretted the part he had taken in this affair; and years afterwards, when on his death-bed, he sent Lord Jocelyn to ask for Mr. Roebuck's pardon and forgiveness.

While ever quite prepared to vindicate his conduct, Mr. Roebuck always showed himself watchfully jealous against all attempts—then of frequent occurrence—to supplement the rules of the House of Commons for ensuring decency of debate, by calling upon members to justify outside, at the mouth of a pistol, expressions used within. Although things had largely changed since 1798, when the Speaker, instead of intervening to prevent a duel between Mr. Pitt and Mr. Tierney, went down to Putney to see it fought, challenges from member to member were rife. Mr. Roebuck was largely instrumental in arousing the House to a sense of the gravity of this breach of privilege. Even so great a Parliamentarian as Sir Robert Peel had shown himself not superior to the pervading disposition to reply to inside words by outside threats. When he wrote to Mr. Hume, calling him to account for language used in debate, as impugning his honour, it was Mr. Roebuck who read the minister's letter in the House, and proposed to move that it was a breach of privilege for the Chancellor of the Exchequer to call out the member for Middlesex.

In May, 1842, "The National Convention" sitting in Bolt Court, Fleet Street, had sent a deputation to Mr. Roebuck in the lobby, demanding to know whether in his assertion that the National Petition "had been drawn up by a cowardly and malignant demagogue" he referred to

Mr. Feargus O'Connor?   Mr. Roebuck replied that he made it a rule never to give any explanation of words used by him in the House of Commons.   Nor did an attempt to get an explanation in the House meet with more success. It was recorded that Mr. O'Connor, resolved upon deeds of blood, lay in wait for Mr. Roebuck, " with a view of provoking that satisfaction which one gentleman expects of another."   But not meeting with him, the affair ended in nothing worse than valorous vauntings.

There was an episode in Parliament, in 1844, with almost whimsical developments as to Mr. Roebuck.   The well-known Mr. Ferrand (Knaresborough),* in his violent opposition to Sir James Graham's Factory legislation, had, at a meeting at Leeds, charged the Home Secretary with having used his power as a minister to induce an assistant poor-law commissioner to make a false report for the purpose of crushing him (Mr. Ferrand).   Sir James Graham, treating the matter with just contempt, took no steps, but Mr. Roebuck brought Mr. Ferrand's charge under the notice of the House.†   He peremptorily called upon that honourable member to state distinctly to the House to what minister and to what member he referred.   This was the introduction to a series of not very edifying scenes, in which much time was taken up at several sittings in mutual recriminations.

" The beginning of strife is as when one letteth out water."   For when, goaded by Mr. Roebuck, Mr. Ferrand not only refused to retract the charges he had made outside, but deliberately repeated them in the House, Sir James Graham could no longer hold aloof.   And then

---

* See *ante*, chap. xv. p. 174.

† Interventions of this kind, and in such matters as the corrupt withdrawal of petitions in 1842; the Crimean War, 1855; and Mr. Butt's case, 1858; gave rise to the feeling, expressed in Kinglake's sneer ("Invasion of the Crimea," vol. vi. p. 358), that Roebuck "appointed himself to the office of public accuser."   But they do not justify Kinglake's exaggeration that he " clung so fondly to his chosen task as to be rarely engaged in any other."

another member, Mr. Hogg, of Beverley, was dragged in. For, following up Mr. Roebuck, Mr. Hume and Mr. H. G. Ward volunteered information that Mr. Ferrand had further charged the Home Secretary with having corruptly influenced Mr. Hogg, who had sat as chairman of the Nottingham election committee, to make a false report for the purpose of unseating Mr. John Walter, through resentment at his attitude towards the new Poor Law.

The House could not overlook this, and steps were taken for bringing Mr. Ferrand to book. He found defenders in Mr. Disraeli and Lord John Manners, both of whom not obscurely urged that the dispute was a private quarrel which ought to have been matter for "gentlemanly arrangement" outside. By these and others strong attacks were made upon Mr. Roebuck for what was called his mischief-making in interfering in an affair which did not concern him. The member for Canterbury, Mr. Smythe,* especially attacked Mr. Roebuck with great bitterness. He declared—

From an intimate observation and study of the hon. and learned gentleman's (Mr. Roebuck's) political career . . . I am not to be deceived by the mock severities of spurious patriotism; that assentation (*sic*) which masks itself beneath the guise of cynicism, assailing all men but sparing one man; aspersing all men, but fawning upon one man; continually inferring that were one not the Diogenes of Bath, one would wish to be the Alexander of Tamworth. . . . The honourable and learned member for Bath presents a remarkable antithesis in his own person, being at once the rebels' agent and the Queen's counsel—the champion of M. Papineau, and the defender of a Secretary of State.

It is difficult to find in the rejoinder this provoked anything very wounding to Mr. Smythe's honour. Mr. Roebuck, professing himself ingenuously surprised at the invectives hurled at him, and at the attempt to force him into the position of an offender put upon his defence, said

* Afterwards Lord Strangford.

the accusations made against him must come from a more formidable quarter before he would answer them.   And he added—

> When the honourable member for Canterbury speaks of being rewarded by one's enemies, may I ask, Has he forgot what it is to be disappointed by one's friends?   Disappointment may have poisoned the arrows shot against friends ; it cannot have poisoned those shot against enemies.

The sting of this allusion lay in the fact that Mr. Smythe had, in the previous year, found it necessary, in explaining to his constituents some vote, to assert that, never having asked any favour of Sir Robert Peel's Government, he was acting on conviction, not through disappointment, in voting against it. Mr. Smythe immediately construed Mr. Roebuck's remark as a charge of violating honour and integrity by voting, under disappointment, contrary to his convictions.   And, not content with an emphatic denial of the imputation immediately it was made, he acted on the counsel given by Mr. Disraeli and Lord John Manners to Mr. Ferrand (for which "direful and barbarous" advice they were severely taken to task by Mr. Roebuck).   The member for Bath accordingly found himself waited on by one Captain Darrell, bearing a defiant cartel.   Mr. Roebuck forthwith proceeded to the House, and brought the challenge under its notice.   Mr. Smythe's letter was read by the clerk at the table.   The member for Canterbury, after some wriggling, was compelled to make a full and unreserved apology to the House, and to give assurance that the matter should proceed no further.

When, in January, 1845, the friends of Mr. William Smith O'Brien sought to stop freedom of speech in Parliament by means of the absurd custom of requiring a man to stand up and be shot at for what he had said in debate, Mr. Roebuck took the best means of discouraging further similar proceedings by bringing before the House, as a breach of privilege, a challenge he had received from Mr. Somers, member for Sligo. The matter ended by Mr. Somers unequivocally apologizing both to the House and to Mr. Roebuck.

In 1849, after a violent scene with a group of Irish members, Mr. Roebuck was the recipient of a hostile message from Mr. Fox, member for Longford; but by the judicious intervention of Captain Berkeley, the resort to pistols was averted.*

* See *post*, p. 228.

## CHAPTER XVIII.

### THE WEST RIDING.  1848.

EXCLUDED from Parliament, Mr. Roebuck retired to his farm and his books—to the literary quiet and the domestic ease for which he had yearned.  It appears that he had contemplated writing a " History of the Reformation."  The work was, indeed, announced, and partly printed but never published.  He completed and brought out "The Colonies of England," but his thoughts chiefly turned to the fulfilment of his long-cherished desire of writing a " History of the Whig Ministry of the Reform Era."  Upon his historic labours, however, vacant constituencies constantly intruded, and it is evident that, notwithstanding his farewell words to the electors of Bath, and though he tried to persuade himself to the contrary, his heart was still in the House of Commons, clamorous to be back in the turmoil of politics.  Mrs. Roebuck, at least, was under no delusion on this point—

*Mrs. Roebuck to Dr. R. Black.*

*Ashley Arnewood, November,* 1847.—I hope Roebuck may be in Parliament when the dearly beloved Ministry become well aware of the loss they have sustained in R.  A more sensible set of men would have *petted* him.  Roebuck tries hard to persuade himself that he *likes* farming.  I doubt ; he really likes politics best.  Success is of more value to his health than *air*. He is really *spiritual*, and could I only see him in Parliament, and in office, I should die happy.

### *J. A. Roebuck to Dr. R. Black.*

*Ashley Arnewood, November* 24, 1847.— . . . I cannot, must not, spend money. Debt frightens me. I would starve, and be all my life out of Parliament in preference to putting myself into the slavery of constant debt. I am now really working hard to put this place into paying order, which I shall accomplish. But Parliamentary expenses I cannot provide for just now ; and if Finsbury cannot be won without my spending money, I will not attempt to win it. The labourer is worthy of his hire, and I have laboured long enough for the public. They know what I am good for ; if they want me, they must elect me for nothing. . . .

At the beginning of 1848, Mr. Roebuck was back in Brussels, engaged again, on behalf of Mr. Francis Mills and others, in forwarding such projects as had taken him there in 1845–46. In addition to these matters, there are in his letters references to that scheme for cutting a canal through the Isthmus of Panama, which M. de Lesseps afterwards took up with disastrous results. This design greatly attracted the fancy of King Leopold; and Lord Palmerston, when the matter was brought before him by Mr. Roebuck, seems to have given it an encouragement which he systematically refused to the Suez Canal enterprise.

### *To Mrs. Roebuck.*

*Brussels, January* 17, 1848.—A dream of politics, which has long haunted me, may be made indeed a reality. . . . You can easily guess to what the scheme relates, when I tell you it is the one great scheme of which I have often talked, by which to give England the command of the two great seas of the earth— *Panama.*

*January* 18.—I suspect you laughed at my mysterious epistle of yesterday, and so do I to-day. The truth is, that the scheme is really a great one, and I am sure might be, and one day will be, executed ; but whether by England remains to be seen. The scheme for Panama I shall show to Palmerston. The scheme was communicated to the King of the Belgians, who liked the plan much, and said, "Ah, Mr. Roebuck, if I was a *positive* monarch, the thing might be done."

Anything more *triste* than this town, you never knew. The Court is in mourning for Madame Adelaide, and the Chamber has been adjourned till to-day, so that even the ordinary gaiety and interest are wanting. It has never ceased to freeze since I have been here. The snow has covered the ground the whole time, and a cold fog obscures everything; yet the people here constantly talk of our miserable climate, and evidently give me no credence when I declare that England, as I know it, is a far better climate than theirs. I am miserably tired of this idle life, and long for to-morrow evening, when I leave this place.

*London, January* 31, 1848.—I saw Palmerston yesterday, and found him ready to do all I wished. My plans coincided with his own. Whether Mills [Francis Mills] can now get monied men to join the scheme remains to be seen. My part is successfully brought up to the point at which he must begin to act; but though the project is a great one, yet, in these times of panic, everything is regarded with dread. Still, the inherent goodness of the proposal may induce some far-seeing men to act; and, a beginning made, I have no fear of the result.

*January* 31, 1848.— . . . Fearon and company are somewhat of mere *professors*. I was told that they were about to be very complimentary and grateful. Not one word, however, has yet been sent, and I shall leave London without knowing anything of their estimation of my proceedings. The completion of the business they will find difficult. You recollect the Dender Valley affair. They sent £40,000 to Belgium as caution-money, got themselves into a scrape, and came to me. I so arranged their affairs as to make it quite possible to carry out their scheme, but being obliged to return to England, could not actually finish the negotiation. When I came here they grumbled and tried to shirk paying me, not because they had any reason to complain of what I had done—they had expressed their warmest thanks—but they grudged a few pounds. I told Murray that they would rue their parsimony, and so they have. Not one step did they make beyond the point to which I had brought them, and to this hour their £40,000 lie in the hands of the Government. The railway has not in any way proceeded, and thus the whole scheme has been blown up, and their money confiscated. So much for this instance of niggardliness. I suspect the present will be like that case. Everything now appears so smiling and smooth that they will fancy my services no longer needed. I shall hear no more, and the whole of the negotiations will linger, and be at length a mass of confusion, and end in nothing. In the mean time, I hope my oats will be sown, my barley in the ground, and my mangel-wurzel in fine order. What a month I have passed! I ought to be well paid.

### To Dr. R. Black.

*Ashley Arnewood, April 16, 1848.*— . . . Just now I am busy with my sowing—I have no time. My days are passed in the field, my nights, writing steadily my history; * and sleep I have hardly any, but feel well, though somewhat fatigued. Still, I shall go, and get, on. The Chartists have made a pretty hash of it. F. O'Connor is a rogue, a liar, and a coward—a precious compound! Hume tells me that the M.P.'s are to meet. You will see that the suffrage question is put back, and off. The working men who have some discretion ought to work on, however, and abstain from idle threats. I know, you know, they know, and *the Duke of Wellington* knows, they cannot, dare not fight. It is all braggart talk.

### To Dr. R. Black.

*Ashley Arnewood, Milton, Hants.*—I have received a printed paper signed by Lovett and others about their plans.† If I can do anything to assist, I shall be glad, and really believe the present not merely a good opportunity for stirring, but one which imposes on the true friends of good government the duty of making some attempt to rescue the working classes from the dangers to which they are now exposed. The late doings of the Chartists have been seized by the Whigs with delight, as they have afforded them a pretext for expense, and given them a means of retaining office. They will now effect a junction with a large section of the Tories, and we shall have a dead-set made at the persons who endeavour to change the representation in

* " The Whig Ministry of 1830."

† This probably refers to a Chartist address on universal suffrage from " The Radical Reformers of England, Scotland, and Wales to the Irish people."

this country.   I have a strong feeling in my mind about all this ;
so grave do I deem the present crisis, that I feel greatly tempted
to step forward and take the lead in a movement for the purpose
of effecting a real Parliamentary reform.   My political econo-
mical notions run so thoroughly counter to the vain visions of
many of the working men, that they would look upon me with
distrust.   I am sure that wages cannot be raised or kept down by
Act of Parliament, and that any scheme for giving to every man
a fixed sum, without regard to the value of his labour, without
regard to his skill, industry, or honesty, is the most mischievous
delusion ever practised on the people.   Moreover, I am not at
all ready to allow the operatives to call themselves *par excellence*
the people, the working classes, and the real producers of wealth.
I consider myself just as much one of the people—one of the
working classes, one of the producers of wealth—as a weaver
of ribbons, as a spinner of yarn, or a digger of coal.   I have
no schemes for employing the people—no lottery—no farm for
them to live on.   I want none of their money, and won't flatter
them, so I suppose they will with difficulty be brought to listen.
Still, it might be done.*

### To Thomas Falconer.

*June* 29, 1848.—I carried your note at once to Brougham,
and he is to see Morpeth about it. . . . The weather has changed
to hot and dry, and I am really beginning to be very anxious
about my turnips.   Things here are in a pitiable condition.
The government is in truth below all feeling—even that of
contempt.   There never was such a spectacle exhibited.   I see
now war in the distance.   Austria, as I always prophesied, will
beat the Italians, and France will interfere.   A general war will
follow—no care can prevent this.   If we keep out of the fray we
shall be fortunate, and certainly our people will profit by other
nations' disasters.   My notion is that Russia will step in, take the
part of Austria, and *order*.   France will have to seek for allies
in Germany and *England*.   What a pill for the French !

### To Mrs. Roebuck.

*Penrith, Tuesday, October 3,* 1848.—Brougham has promised
to answer all my queries with regard to the history, and I steadily
* See *ante*, p. 118, and *post*, pp. 354-5.

occupy my time in preparing and arranging all the matter. . . . There are two little girls here, but I miss my own very much, and long to be back again with you both. Home is the only place in which I do not feel weary.

*October* 11.—In the midst of the turmoil yesterday I missed writing. Miss Burdett-Coutts and Co. so occupied the house, and created such confusion, that I escaped out-of-doors. Miss B.-C. is tall and thin, unaffected in manner, on the whole rather pleasing, a quiet retired sort of person ; but the two doctors and one wife are too much for human endurance.

My drive to the hills was really beautiful, but the whole beauty is so changeable, and the lights and shadows vary so rapidly, and give so little outline, that sketch there is none to be taken. Besides, it is too cold for sitting abroad. The general character of the country can only be depicted by colour. The flitting lights and shadows, the bright autumn tints, the rolling mists, and the mass of hills, make the beauty of the scene. The black lead pencil gives none of these, and I have no colours here. Still, it is all in my memory, and I shall see what can be done to put it on paper when at home.

*London, November,* 1848.—I saw, some time since, in the library here (Reform Club), a very little man. ——, with him, came to me and asked, "Would you like to be introduced to M. Louis Blanc ? " " By all means," I replied. On which the said little man and I were introduced in due form. He is very small, *I* can say that. He has a brown skin, sharp brown eyes, with the whites of a brown hue, a retiring forehead, and an eastern nose. He was very anxious to make himself out a friend of order, a partisan of democracy, universal suffrage, and to make me believe that he was ready to submit to the majority. This, however, I do not believe. I am to meet him at dinner on Monday.

*Tuesday, November* 14, 1848.—Well, I dined with M. Louis Blanc. A more complete charlatan I never saw. A thoroughly poor creature, dealing in phrases, and fancying himself a dis-coverer, because he has revived doctrines that have been exploded a quarter of a century since. Opposite to me sat a Doctor Ashburnham, who brought himself to my recollection as an opponent of mine twenty years ago, he supporting Robert Owen's views of social economy, and I opposing them. I could not help exclaiming to him while Louis Blanc was indulging in a regular French *tirade*, "Why, we have gone over the whole of this rubbish twenty years since!" He could not help assenting, and owning that the mare's-nest had been found and taken in those days.

By Lord Morpeth succeeding to the Earldom of Carlisle, a vacancy was caused in the representation of the West Riding of Yorkshire. Mr. Roebuck's name was brought prominently before the electors and the Liberal Election Committee. The Hon. Charles Fitzwilliam, who had first come forward, failed to obtain general support to his candidature on the part of the Liberals. The county electors of Sheffield urged the adoption of Mr. Roebuck, and instructed the delegates they sent to the central conference at Normanton to promote his nomination. They failed, however, to carry the point—Sir Culling E. Eardley being chosen as the Liberal Candidate. Mr. Fitzwilliam retired, and then ensued a memorable contest between Sir Culling Eardley and Mr. Edmund Beckett Denison. The split created in the Liberal Party by disagreements as to the candidate, resulted in the seat being captured by the Tories.

*To Mrs. Roebuck.*

*London, November* 16, 1848.—The idea of my going to the West Riding made a sensation here, as it has evidently frightened the Whigs; but the bigotry of the Dissenters would be a great annoyance to me. I must bide my time.

*November* 17.—At last the West Riding people have sent to me, and Fairbairn * is the ambassador. He has persuaded me to go to Leeds to-morrow afternoon, as on a visit to him, for I am unwilling to appear in the matter publicly till I see my way.

*London, November* 19.—The telegraph has just brought an earnest request to go to Leeds, so I start to-night at nine. I go not in the slightest degree compromised to any course. I shall listen to what the Liberal party will say, and, before I

* Mr., afterwards Sir Peter, Fairbairn, of Woodsley.

consent to be a candidate, I shall require a strong requisition, and a distinct written understanding for them to bear all the expenses. The expenses of the polling places alone amount to nearly £800, so the mere standing is a thing I could not undertake, even if sure of success. . . . To fight this battle with a fair chance and to be defeated will not tell against me. The case is not an ordinary one, and to be asked to stand by a great party for the West Riding of Yorkshire is a feather in any man's cap.

*Leeds, November 22, 1848.*— . . . There is a meeting of delegates at Normanton at midday, and at four o'clock I shall learn their decision. On coming here I found Baines * was in reality the only difficulty, and he took up the old quarrel of the Dissenters—but they are in a fix. If, however, it should appear that I am not cordially called upon, and not to be loyally dealt with, I shall refuse the invitation. The great difficulty is, in fact, the money, and in these times of commercial pressure money is not very rife with the merchants, who are, in fact, fighting this battle. Yesterday young Fitzwilliam began his public proceedings by appearing in the Cloth Hall here. I did not hear his speech, as he spoke only for a few minutes. Fairbairn and I walked into the crowd, and listened to what was going on. Some persons found out that I was there, and, as matters proceeded, the cry was raised that I was present, and demands for me to appear upon the platform and address the meeting. At length the meeting almost unanimously called for me, and I was forced, *literally* forced to appear. I refused, however, to appear as a candidate, and abstained from any exposition of my own opinions. Had I wished, the temper of the meeting—a very large one—was so completely with me that I could have taken it at the flood, and forced myself into the position of a candidate. This, however, would not have been wise. The responsibility of choosing or refusing would then have been taken away from the delegates, and assumed by myself. The shufflers would have taken advantage of this, and I should have found myself saddled with the expense and odium of a contest. I leave the rest of the page for the statement of the delegates' decision ; and when I think of the turmoil and strife into which I am about possibly to plunge, I shall hardly be disappointed if I find myself in the railroad carriage on my way

* Mr., afterwards Sir Edward, Baines, of the *Leeds Mercury*.

home. Every day makes me love the quiet of our present privacy more and more.

*London, Thursday.*—The decision of the delegates did not reach me until late in the evening, and as I felt sure that it was against me, I came back at once. Personally I do not regret the decision. I sincerely believe, however, that it is a public evil, because it shows how strong the bigotry of the people still is. My opinions on education and want of sympathy with the Anti-Catholic outcry, was the cause of the enmity and opposition of Baines. I believe now the Tory candidate, Beckett Denison, will succeed.

*November* 23.—The *Times* of to-day has an article speaking in very handsome terms of myself, and blowing up the bigots. Lord Melbourne is, if not actually dead, so near it that he may be said to be extinct. Brougham's letter shows that he knows nothing of what is going on here. The times he speaks of are past, and cannot return, and he is really half crazed about the mob. I do not like the mob one whit more than he does, but it is useless to kick against the pricks. The people will have a hand in the affairs which interest them, and all we can do is to make them wise enough to be able to decide correctly.

### To Thomas North (Bath).

*Reform Club, November* 24, 1848.—You will see by the papers what has been the decision of your Dissenting friends. *I* have never proposed to stand without a requisition being previously sent to me, as without such an invitation I should have been saddled with the expense, and have, therefore, never allowed any one to speak of me as a candidate. What the people of Yorkshire have done has been their own voluntary proceeding. They have preferred Sir Culling Eardley simply because he is a bigot in religion. He opposed the Reform Bill, voted for General Gascoigne's motion to turn out Lord Grey's Government, and was a violent enemy of any enlargement of the suffrage ; but he is a violent hater of papists, and that is enough to please Mr. Baines of the *Leeds Mercury.* So you see, I am free from the trouble of this election. I am, however, pretty well assured that, if I had been selected, I should have had no contest—all parties would have been pretty well content.

In a letter to Mr. Peter Fairbairn, declaring his determination, in the interests of party unity, not to offer
himself as a candidate, Mr. Roebuck repeated his warning
lest an exchange of the old watchwords of civil and
religious liberty for a narrower feeling of religious antipathy, should lead to the permanent disruption of the
Liberal party.  He wrote—

My great object, during the whole of my political life, has
been the steady advancement of rational freedom.  From the
pursuit of that object, no temporary expediency, no personal
ambition, no party or sectarian passion, has made me swerve;
and now I wish so to *improve* the present incident as to make it
subservient to this great end of all my endeavours, by healing
all differences between those who have long been friends, and
uniting them again into that bond of fellowship which has, in
past times, produced glorious results, and which will, if it be
maintained, lead to others not less worthy of admiration and
gratitude.  To be among my friends during the present contest—
to state my political opinions before the great constituency of
the West Riding—would, indeed, be of itself a subject of gratulation and honourable pride; to have been able to place this great
contest on the broad ground of national interests; in this hour
of the world's dismay and almost universal confusion, to have
made manifest to the world that my countrymen were still
self-possessed, and ardent as ever in the pursuit of freedom—that
they were neither frightened from their purpose by the follies
of other nations, nor excited to wild hopes by theories and
experiments not yet tested by experience; to have given them
the opportunity of proving themselves what they really are,
cautious, yet ardent, tolerant to others, while vindicating their
own rights, and loving and seeking freedom and security,
political, social, religious, not for themselves alone, but for
mankind;—to have been able to fairly do all this would have
been a reward for a long life of labour.  But this I willingly
forego—any expectation of success I cheerfully relinquish—in
the hope that by so doing I contribute to reunite the friends
of civil and religious freedom; that I afford an opportunity
to old friends to forget present differences, and to join heart

P

and hand in the great work before them—a work not yet half accomplished—viz. the giving to the people of this great country, in fact, and not merely in name, THE GOVERNMENT OF THEMSELVES.

### *To Mrs. Roebuck.*

*November* 29, 1848.—Charles Buller is dead—he died this morning at six. Two days since I saw Fleming, and from his manner concluded that Buller was in danger.

H. [Hawes] again attacked me, saying he had been speaking of me to his chiefs, and again asked if I would take an Indian judgeship. My answer was fiercely, "No." Out of England I do not go but for the purpose of returning—for me—rich.

*November* 30.—The West Riding election *might* have been carried by a *coup de main*—and might be so now, but I am very fearful of getting into debt, and finding myself hampered through the rest of my life.

I asked Fairbairn for an introduction to Richardson, the artist—the real successor to Copley Fielding. His style is to me a fascination. I dined with Lady Duff Gordon. She told me her father was demented in favour of small farms, and something very like Communism; her mother ditto. What has come to all these clever people?

### *To Thomas North (Bath).*

*Milton, Hampshire, December* 23, 1848.—I have received your letters and the enclosures. I was quite certain that the rumour about Manchester was an idle one; besides, that place and its people are not the right sort for me. As you might learn, even from the letters you received, neither the one nor the other of those persons would have supported me. The Manchester bourgeoisie is in many things like that of Paris; but, fortunately for it, has a stout soldiery to protect it. It dreads the people—that is, the working classes—and is Liberal only so far as it believes Liberality, *i.e.* free trade, to be profitable. I write in great haste, and great alarm and trouble. Mrs. Roebuck has been very dangerously ill—is still in bed, and far from safe. I sometimes fancy I am half mad from anxiety.

*To Mrs. Roebuck.*

*December*, 1848.—  ——  has gone to Liskeard [vacant by the death of Charles Buller], but I have no great faith in him.  T. S. wished to put Macaulay in my way there, but he (M.) at once most handsomely refused.*

*Leeds*, *December* 30, 1848.—Fairbairn went over to Bury, and got from me a promise to come here, where I have been treated with every possible kindness. In Bury they treated me like a prince; and, indeed, the luxury and wealth everywhere exhibited absolutely astounds me. The landed people can show nothing like it. The only drawback is that all is *new;* but so magnificent and really good that no one can turn up his nose. I have been so *fêted* that I am almost ill. My frugality of eating surprises and, I fear, annoys my hosts. Had I forty parson-power, I should be more popular.

* Macaulay records in his diary, November 29 and 30, 1848: "I was shocked to learn the death of poor Charles Buller. I could almost cry for him. . . . Tufnell [Treasury Whip] sent for me, and proposed Liskeard to me. I hesitated; and went home leaving the matter doubtful. Roebuck called at near seven to ask about my intentions, as he had also been thought of. This at once decided me; and I said I would not stand, and wrote to Tufnell, telling him so. Roebuck has on more than one occasion behaved to me with great kindness and generosity; and I did not choose to stand in his way (Trevelyan's "Life of Macaulay," ii. p. 245). Mr. R. Buddon Crowder, afterwards a judge, was elected for Liskeard without opposition. In former years Roebuck's estimate of Macaulay's power as a Parliamentary orator, as expressed in his "Diary of an M.P.," in *Tait's Magazine*, had not been a flattering one.

## CHAPTER XIX.

IN the early days of January, 1849, Mr. Roebuck was
entertained by the Reformers of Bradford, Wiltshire, and
presented with a piece of "drake's-head green cloth," the
manufacture of the place, on which an inscription was
worked in silk recording that it was intended as a token
of respect for his manly conduct in the House of Commons.
Mr. Roebuck took the opportunity of discussing the condition of the people and the state of the nation.  The recent
defeat of Sir Culling Eardley, in the West Riding of Yorkshire, enabled him to point the moral of what he considered
the "spiritual pride" of the Dissenters, and, as he regarded
it, their sacrifice of civil rights for theological dogmas and
religious intolerance.

*J. A. Roebuck to Francis Place.*

*Milton, Lymington, Hants, January* 17, 1849.—I am hard at
work writing a history of our friends, the Whigs.  Can you let
me see any collections or MSS. of yours relating to the Reform
Bill and subsequent events ?   The state of the popular mind in
1830–33 is a point of great interest, about which you have,
I know, collected much evidence. . . . I am writing and working
very assiduously, as I want the work off my hands before returning to Parliament, which I may or may not be asked to do,
though the probability is in favour of my being asked.

### To Thomas North (Bath.)

*Milton, Hants, January* 22, 1849.—As respects myself, all things seem to work very well; whether any result worth having will follow, I cannot say. If certain parties can keep me out, they will do so; it remains to be seen what their power is. The *Times* certainly is, for it, very complimentary. The only persons besides mere Whigs who are opposed to me are the Wesleyans and some other members of Dissenting bodies. The *Leeds Mercury* was furious against me for what I said at Bradford, but all my friends in Yorkshire entreated me to give him no reply, which indeed I never thought of doing.

### To Mrs. Roebuck.

*January*, 1849.—I dined with Wortley. Hallam I found deeply wounded by Macaulay's great success, though perhaps to careless observers no evidence of such a feeling exists. As for news, all the world is expecting what Parliament will bring, and nothing occurs. In Paris they are endeavouring to get up a row, and will not succeed. The Ministers have anticipated Cobden by declaring that they intend to economize. We want men, or rather a *man*, in India. Had Napier been in Gough's place this check would never have happened.

Mr. Roebuck looked forward to the coming of a new Conservative party.

A great Conservative party must soon be formed, one which will govern England for some years. Not a feudal party, but a compound of persons quite willing to advance, introducing all sorts of administrative reforms willingly and *proprio motu*, yielding in respect to political changes to the widely expressed and strongly felt wish of the people regarding them. They will follow the public mind freely, fairly, cordially, but they will not in political affairs lead it. On the one side, they will have a bigoted party, and on the other, the fanatical political one, and should steer a middle course between these extremes.

### To Mrs. Roebuck.

*February*, 1849.—. . . I find Frank Mills vehement against my leaving England. One other person to whom I mentioned it is furious.

*To Francis Place.*

*Milton, March* 1, 1849.—When I am somewhat further advanced,* I should like you to look over my labours, if you can give your time to it. I am afraid that I shall offend some of my friends by saying what I think. This, however, cannot be helped. I am very much attached to these friends, but I must not sacrifice what I think the truth, because that truth is disagreeable. This difficulty was a reason indeed for not writing the book, but to that I am now pledged. You will not be offended, but you would tell me plainly what you thought in- . correct as statements of facts. As far as opinions are concerned, we should, I think, not differ much.

I was surprised to find in your MS. that you considered the going by the king, on November 9, 1830, to the Guildhall was *dangerous.*† The Whigs all sneered at the idea of danger to the king. They said to the duke, "Stay you away and no harm can happen." You don't seem to think this true. You say that the blackguards would have made a row, whether the duke was away or not. The thing is not very important now, though at the time it created a great noise.

*To Francis Place.*

*Milton, March* 4, 1849.—I send you the first chapter of my "History." You will see it is merely a general *résumé* of affairs from 1815 to 1827, written with a view of bringing the Whigs on the stage. I proceed step by step to make the history more particular and the conduct of the Whigs more apparent. Remember my "History" is that of the *Whig Administration.* What illustrates that is suitable for my purpose ; anything beyond I do not want. As I go on my "History" will be that of the Empire at large, as affected by the Whig Administration. At present I have not yet expanded to that extent. I am now treating of the great Reform question, and I am just bringing the Whigs on the stage as an administration. While writing the truth, I wish to make my relation a striking history.

Some of the statements made, even in this summary, are

* With the " History of the Whig Ministry of 1830."

† Walpole's " History," vol. iii. p. 185, *et. seq.* and Roebuck's " Whig Ministry," vol. i. p. 411.

curious. The one respecting the Whigs' refusal to take office if the Ministry should be dismissed on the queen's business,* Lord Brougham has insisted on my inserting as true. If true, it is highly honourable to the party of which he was then the most important member.

I will send from time to time the MS. I am writing hard and writing really without regard to my health ; still, it must be done. I have debts to pay, and, if I die in the struggle, that must be done. I believe that a great game is before me if my health hold, but of that I am not sure. Still, I go on. So let me know when you have gone through the first page of my " History " and I will send you another.

*To Mrs. Roebuck.*

*March* 17, 1849.—Mrs. Buller [mother of Charles Buller, M.P.] is dead. She went out ; died asleep almost. Now one day well, another ill, but every day sank more and more, till at last she fell into a sleep which came to that last long one called the end. This thing called life—how poor it is after all ! Here she dies a broken-hearted old woman, whose youth was happy, gay, sparkling with pleasure—the bright Queen of the Ganges. Glorying in her two boys, and fixing her happiness on the one's success—she is left alone. Her husband dead, her son dies, the other abroad—she dies in a stranger's house. This is but a poor close after all. The sun seems to go down in clouds and rain—we die in sorrow, wishing the day ended. The old story : one pegs the other out—Lady Duff Gordon had a son and heir last night. She is very happy, and very well. I have seen a sun picture of Lord Brougham that is inimitable. The day for taking it must not be very sunny, but a clear sky with flying clouds. There is no exaggeration of parts ; everything is in right perspective and harmonious. I shall go myself, and bring with me my own reflection, and you shall judge. If it is as like as Lord B.'s, then I shall see my own likeness, which I fancy I never have done.

*March* 19.—Well, I have been to the sun, and I have had my picture, such a queer thing. I shall try to get Brougham. I should like to have C. J. Napier. F. Mills has heard some passages from my " History," and is greatly pleased with it.

* " History of the Whig Ministry," vol. i. p. 9.

*To Francis Place.*

*March* 26, 1849.—Thanks for your suggestions. . . . When
I began my work I was quite aware of the very *nice* difficulty
I should have to avoid about B. [Brougham.]  I hoped, nevertheless, to be able to tell the truth and fairly state my own
opinions without giving him offence ; but, as I proceed, I fear
more and more lest I shall inevitably wound him.  To avoid
this will, I am afraid, be impossible.  I shall not use any harsh
words.  My very sincere and warm attachment to him personally
will prevent this, even were there any disposition on my part,
which there is not, to employ harsh epithets.  But I cannot take
his views of men.  He now lives with the Tory party, and his
kind nature forces him not merely to like the people with whom
he is in daily intercourse, but also to approve of their conduct
and to adopt their political views.*  This I cannot do, and my
opinions I must express.  These he will find so completely opposed
to his own that he will, I fear, be hurt.  Now, I cannot avoid
this.  Do not decide, then, upon isolated passages, but judge by
the whole.  You will find that my decision on his acts is so often
unfavourable that one or two expressions of kind feeling towards
him will hardly be enough to make people think me his echo.
I confess that when I find him right I am not unwilling to say
so rather strongly, and when I find him ill-treated, to speak of
those who so treat him with some indignation.

Now for your criticism as to my having treated the years from
1817–22 with greater brevity, and having made them less
important than the years from 1822–27.  My " History " properly

---

* In an article in *Tait's Magazine*, December, 1833, p. 325, Roebuck,
speaking of Brougham, then on the woolsack, had said : " He has obtained a
vast renown upon a very slender foundation.  His failures—and they have
been many—have proceeded from two causes.  He has pretended to too much,
and he wants moral courage.  By attempting everything, he is unable to
deal with any subject effectually.  He knows nothing to the bottom.  His
incessant activity surprises the fools, but has ruined his own mind. . . .
Present approbation is the very breath of his nostrils.  To obtain this approbation he will sacrifice anything and everything."  And then, contrasting
Brougham's boldness on the platform of a public meeting with his demeanour
in the Lords, he says : " In the latter he bends to their influence, cringes to
their prejudices.  He has not the courage to face their frowns or to despise
their scorn.  He has no hardiness of spirit."  See also Roebuck's " History,"
*passim,* and especially Appendix A., vol i.

begins at 1830, but I was obliged to go back some years in order to bring forward my *dramatis personæ* and place them fairly on the stage at the real rising of the curtain in 1830. All that goes before is merely an introduction. The stream of history beginning at 1815 gradually expands, becomes larger and larger, till it comes in full tide at 1830. And thus it happens that the years nearer to 1830 are more minutely treated than the earlier ones. But I must not convey wrong impressions while doing this ; and, as I think with you the *Parliamentary* proceedings from 1817–22 were of more importance than the *Parliamentary* proceedings from 1822–27, I must use some expressions to show my value of these two periods. But it is only the *Parliamentary* proceedings that I deem of this superior importance. The working of the public mind, the political and economic literature of the latter period, were of very great importance. The effect of that literature on the popular mind during the latter period was much greater than during the preceding years ; in fact, from 1820–30 I believe the most wonderful period in our history, if we look merely at the importance of the people's *opinions*. The writings of Bentham produced a silent revolution in the *mode* of treating all political and moral subjects. The habits of thought were entirely new, and the whole body of political writers, without (for the most part) knowing whence the inspiration came, were full of a new spirit, and submitted all acts to a new test. Utility (I mean the true meaning of that much-abused term), and not mere unmeaning sentiment, was this test. In this sense, then, I think this ten years deserving of great attention. To discuss the changes that occurred is very difficult. It is not a history of battles and murders, or great party conflicts, but of wonderful mental changes in a whole people. To give anything like a true conception of this I find very difficult. Having lived through that time an observant and very sanguine enthusiastic spectator, I wish to make others who shall come after us feel as I feel about these times, but to do so is almost impossible.

I am now finishing the general election in 1830, and have described briefly the Middlesex and Yorkshire elections. These were two remarkable events, the *symptoms*, not the causes, of change.

The decrease of the Duke of Wellington's popularity from the passing of the Emancipation Act to the commencement of the

General Election, is a very curious political phenomenon, for which I have found it not easy to account. I can see a number of separate circumstances, by themselves not very important apparently, but which, taken altogether, produced that great change. He really *did* nothing to make himself unpopular, but the world *guessed* that he was opposed to Parliamentary reform, and they were right. The doings of the French Ministers were evidently the most influential circumstances as causing a change of the public feeling. They (the people) assumed that Wellington, like Polignac, was ready to be the minister of despotism, and I fancy they were not far wrong as to the Duke at that time. He grew wiser in after years. . . . I was in town disturbed by a matter connected with Parliament. I shall be there, I fancy, soon. In the mean time I go on working hard.

### *Francis Place to J. A. Roebuck.*

*March*, 1849.—[After explaining that ill-health prevents him from looking up authorities as he would like]. Mind, I have no quarrel with Brougham, neither do I wish you to take my words as for more than a caution on your own account solely. I never will have a quarrel with him. With other men under similar circumstances it would be otherwise. But the good he has done so greatly over-balances the evil, that I have on several occasions defended him from his enemies. Between ourselves, however, I think it my duty to caution you to go with the utmost circum- spection, lest you should commit yourself in a way which may subject you to the imputation of having been misled by him to the damage of your own reputation.* I fear there is ambiguity, or rather an actual misleading in the note, page 9, of your first chapter, and in chapter ii. where you speak as if Brougham were considered as having been duly appointed leader of the House of Commons on the popular side, which he certainly was not. In 1817 his conduct respecting both the press and the people was very bad. It was said at the time that the countenance he gave to the proceedings of Lord Castlereagh encouraged him to con- tinue those proceedings to the extent they were carried. There

---

* A shrewd forecast, for see article "Brougham" in "Dictionary of Universal Biography," which warns readers that Roebuck's "History" was "largely inspired by Brougham, and for that and other reasons must not be implicitly trusted."

was certainly much unbecoming conduct on Brougham's part in the House of Commons, in respect to his being returned for Westminster, for which he was rebuked with not undue severity.

In March, 1849, Mr. H. G. Ward, one of the members for Sheffield, was appointed Lord High Commissioner of the Ionian Islands. In looking for a successor the eyes of the Liberals in the constituency at once turned, with singular unanimity, towards Mr. Roebuck. The occasion was regarded as favourable for healing the differences which the recent contest for the West Riding had caused. The most influential member of the party was himself in favour of bringing forward Mr. Macaulay, who had been rejected by Edinburgh, but he yielded to the views of the others. Mr. Roebuck at once accepted the invitation of the Sheffield electors. He pointed to his past life as a pledge of what his future career would be. He was recognized as a thorough-going Radical, and while that did not alienate from him the support of more moderate Liberals—who thought that he went too far in the matter of the franchise—it disarmed a threatened Chartist opposition, based on Mr. Roebuck's refusal to support a universal suffrage that should not except rogues, thieves, and vagabonds. The extension of the franchise sketched by Mr. Roebuck as worthy of support was practically household suffrage. A Mr. T. Clark did, indeed, offer himself as a candidate in the Chartist interest, in opposition to Mr. Roebuck, but after an interview between the two candidates, Mr. Clark withdrew, finding that on the subject of the suffrage there was no material difference. "Our great bond of union as Chartists," he wrote, "is the suffrage; and whatever Mr. Roebuck's opinions may be upon other subjects, on that of franchise he approximates so closely to us, that opposition to him would, I think, be both unwise and unseemly."

The choice was very generally applauded throughout

the country, even Mr. Roebuck's old foeman, the *Times*, remarking that Sheffield would do itself honour by reinstating Mr. Roebuck in his natural and proper position. " Mr. Roebuck out of Parliament, and Parliament without Mr. Roebuck," were, it said, " equally imperfect. How many times," it exclaimed, "since last November twelvemonth, have the public missed the vigorous eloquence, the honest indignation, the home truths, the mother-wit,' the sterling good sense—albeit clothed sometimes in a stoical if not a cynical garb, for which the member for Bath stood unrivalled and alone."

### *To Mrs. Roebuck.*

*March* 17, 1849.—I shall remain till Monday, and, if Ward accepts, I shall start at once for Sheffield and hoist my standard there.   I have no fear of the result.

*Monday, March* 18, 1849.—Ward has accepted, so Sheffield will be vacant.   I am making arrangements, but it will not be declared till Easter.

### *To William Fisher, Sheffield.*

*April* 13, 1849.—I hope to be of service by promoting good feelings between working-men and their employers.   If I commenced with difference between the Chartists and myself, my chance of peace-making would be very much diminished. Besides, I own that I have strong feelings of sympathy with the working-men.   There are admirable traits in their character which have always excited my regard—a sterling manliness which I could wish all classes to share.   A quarrel with the men themselves would really give me pain.

### *To Mrs. Roebuck.*

*Sheffield, May* 1, 1849.— . . . Well, it is really to be a walkover for the first time in my life.   We had a large open-air meeting last night.   The weather was beautiful, and everything passed off well.   The extraordinary nonsense of the workingmen's ideas would startle you.   I met everything with a perfectly fearless answer, and therefore, in some cases, I was met by loud groans. I quickly conquered the meeting, but carefully abstained from all appearance of suiting my words so as to please them.

I found that Ward had not deceived the people by his acts, that his deeds and his words squared, but his *manner* had evidently misled the men, and they complained of his *soft sawder*, a commodity which I bluntly told them they would not receive from me. On the new Poor Law, abolishing the House of Lords, Socialistic theories, I brought out my refusals to agree with them, with a steady peremptory roughness. The mode told, and they grumbled assent to my election. On Thursday the nomination or election will take place. George Edwards [his late Chairman of Committee at Bath] is coming, with others, to the nomination ; what right-hearted fellows !

*Sheffield, May 2, 1849.*—All goes well, and I suppose by to-morrow I shall be M.P. for Sheffield. So soon as I am really returned I will send you a line. . . . A Mr. Fenton, a reverend curate of Norton, came to claim cousinship with me ; his father, Colonel Fenton, having married Miss Roebuck, the daughter of Benjamin Roebuck, of Meersbrook. He told me that I had a family vault in the parish church here, if I was at all particular as to my lying when the time comes. I thanked him for his information, but said I was careless of the whereabouts when that time did come. I am a sort of bulwark here by which the masters hope to be defended : the men fear while they are compelled to elect me. Altogether my position is new and curious.

On May 3 Mr. Roebuck was elected as member for Sheffield without opposition.

### To Mrs. Roebuck.

*May 4, 1849.*—I have lying before me a note directed with the old addition of M.P., and so I am, having walked over the course. The events of the election have been peculiar only in their quietness. I have been the means of healing differences, and uniting the Liberal party.

*May 6.*—I have taken my seat ; the congratulations without end, but, just as I was leaving the House, I found myself quite lame, so that I was for the present *hors de combat*.

*May 9, 1849.*—The Cobden party are horribly annoyed by my

quiet statements at Sheffield. They feel themselves put down. I could not help this. Common sense required my statement, which I made without reference to their peculiar views and feelings, but this was from the nature of things, not from my desire.

F. Mills is full of my doings, and is so kind that I am absolutely overpowered. In truth, the world within a few days has borne an aspect so different from that of former times, that I am touched and melted. My course has required courage, but it is now clear it was a wise as well as an honest one. At present I am watching events, in order fairly to take advantage of wind and tide, which are now in my favour. Certainly such a position ought not to be sacrificed after the long labours by which it has been won.

My book [" The Colonies of England "] is now being printed.

# CHAPTER XX.

### To Mrs. Roebuck.

*May,* 9, 1849.—I have not yet seen Palmerston, but shall do so in order to learn what his feelings are respecting my motion as to the debts due by foreign governments to our Government and British subjects.   Cobden's anger at this notice was curious.   He is under the control of Bright, who, being a Quaker, chooses to be really warlike in favour of peace.   Cobden is overborne by the pugnacious peace-talking Friend.   His bugbear is war ; his one idea, saving.

Last night was about as dull an affair as possible, and the majority in the Lords giving 49 as majority to ministers, has destroyed every hope of the Protectionist party.*   To-night will finish the business in the Commons.   It is all cry and little wool. I find everybody exceedingly kind, rather more than commonly so.

The ministers are on Monday to bring in a Constitution for Australia.   This rather anticipates the Colonial Society.

*May* 14.—They have appointed me on the committee to inquire about £7000 being paid to M.P.'s.†   They have come to me to take up the whole case of the Bankruptcy Laws, and the public and private debts of foreign governments to us.   This is enough for one pair of hands.

*May* 15.—I did make a speech ; and the Irish, as usual, set

---

* The proposed repeal of the old Navigation Laws was made the rallying ground of the Protectionists.   The Bill, practically giving free trade to shipping, was fought stoutly in both Houses.   The majority in the Lords on the second reading was carried, not by 49, as stated above, but by 10, and that only by the Government having more proxies than the Opposition.

† There was a large sum unaccounted for in connection with the Parliamentary promotion expenses of the Eastern Counties Railway.

up a howl. Lord John Russell was compelled to enter into a defence of his policy. He was very civil, but was at first desirous of escaping me by a jocose reply. This did not suit my purpose, and I compelled him to deal gravely with the subject. The mere violent abuse and vulgar epithets of the Irish I turned from with one fling of contempt, to which the House heartily responded. Sir James Graham exclaimed to me, " Well, you have done good service in putting your hand in that nest of hornets ! We have all-along much wanted you." The universal observation being, " You may judge how your blow told by their anger." This band of hungry, noisy, unscrupulous Irishmen has absolutely disgusted the House into silence. The Government is worried to death by their clamorous impertinences, and nobody likes to encounter their abuse. They have hitherto ridden roughshod over the House.*

There is a row in Montreal. Lord Elgin has been mobbed. They have burned the Parliament House, and really become rebels. These are the loyal English party.†

*May* 16.—The imbecility of the Government was curiously manifested last night. The Canadian riot has excited great attention here. The Government shuffle, and will say nothing, entreating us to wait till more information is obtained. There is no need of this ; we know everything that need be known, and have the power of at once forming a right decision. They know this ; but yet, for the purpose of gaining a delay of a few hours, they shuffle and put off the day. They are all casting about for a means

---

* The subject was the Land Improvement and Drainage of Ireland Bill. Mr. Roebuck denounced the scramble of Irishmen for English money. They wished, he said, to acquire without work, and the English taxpayers were asked to provide for those—not the Irish poor, but the Irish proprietors—who would not provide for themselves. The Government had destroyed self-help by lavishing English money on the country. The " vulgar abuse " with which these remarks were resented may be judged by Mr. John O'Connell's opening sentences : " The thunderbolt has fallen, and we are not crushed. The storm has come with all its fury upon us, and enforced with the grimaces of the mountebank and the spite of the viper." On July 9 Mr. Roebuck made similar protest against the expenditure of the hard-earned money of the people of this country on an advance for railways and distressed unions in Ireland.

† The outbreak was caused by resentment at Lord Elgin, the Governor, giving assent to a Bill granting indemnities to those whose property suffered in the insurrection of 1837–38, without excepting such as might themselves have been rebels.

of throwing off responsibility from their own shoulders upon that of the Canadian Ministry. To-day I have again asked the Government about Canada.* Again they have shrunk, and everybody out-of-doors is allowed to talk, form opinions—aye, theories —all without answer, simply because these people are unfit to govern.

*May* 17.—The Canadian news has startled everybody here. They are now beginning to see that I was right when I said that separation would come from the English party.

On Thursday next I hope to have an opportunity of bringing forward my Colonial scheme. The Ballot is on for that night, but may not occupy the whole time. Hawes † has read the book, but I have not yet learned whether the Government will allow me to bring in a Bill.

Mr. Roebuck, on May 24, asked leave to bring in a Bill for " the better government of our colonies." The speech that sketched the outline and purport of the measure, was described by the speakers who followed in the debate, as one showing great ability and knowledge. The leave was opposed by the Government on the plea that a Bill on the same subject was to be introduced next day, an announcement which drew from Mr. Chisholm Anstey the remark that most probably such a Government measure would never have been heard of, except for Mr. Roebuck's book and present motion.

*To Thomas Falconer.*

*Terrace, Spring Gardens, May* 17, 1849.—You will have by to-day's post a copy of my book. I am so harassed by projects of every sort that I do not know how to turn. For the moment I am employed in my colonial scheme—foreign debts, railway exposures, and bankruptcy. You may see here a pretty large bill of fare. Besides this, the letters I receive keep me almost completely employed. Every applicant fancies himself insulted if not

---

* Had the Government sanctioned the Canada Indemnity Bill, for surely Lord Elgin must have received instructions from the Colonial Office? Lord John Russell declined to answer.

† Under-Secretary for the Colonies. The book referred to is Roebuck's " Colonies of England."

Q

answered, even though the matter of his letter interests no human being but himself. . . . A pretty kettle of fish in Canada ! They are beginning to find out that we were right when we warned them against the English party. I have to-day a letter from Sir George Sinclair, in which he confesses that in 1837 I was right.

*To Mrs. Roebuck.*

*May* 20.—We are just now endeavouring by a committee to discern the truth of certain charges respecting Hudson * and the railways. It will come in this case to nothing, but the scene is a most remarkable one. The rascality now brought to light is astounding.

*London, June* 4, 1849.—The last news just received is, that there is another insurrection in Paris, regular fighting and barricades, and, sooth to say, the men who revolt have right on their side—that is, they are right in the matter of their complaint against the Government ; but that does not justify revolt. The French fancy they have shown that the Government is in error. They have no notion of yielding to a majority, but immediately turn to fight. Everything now will be confusion and misery.

The potato blight has appeared in Ireland, and I find the same statement made here in England.

*June* 15, 1849.—I was in time for the motion about the Jews,† and gave them a speech much applauded. "Dizzy" complimented me, saying the speech had greatly advanced the cause, which was "the best praise a speech could receive." This he said himself, coming over and shaking hands. The day was, on the whole, a curious one. Graham (Sir James) walked across, sat down by me, and said, " I owe you great amusement and instruction. I took your book with me on my holidays, and read it with the greatest interest. It is a most instructive as well as a most amusing book." This is very civil, and from Graham I like it. He is clever, and knows what he is about. I have a beautiful lithograph of Charles Napier, sent by Lady (William) Napier.

---

\* The charges were made by shareholders in the Eastern Counties Railway against Hudson, the chairman of the company.

† The Parliamentary Oaths Bill. Third reading carried by a majority of 66.

On a proposal in committee to vote a grant to defray the expense of militia and volunteers in Canada, amendment was made, praying for the Royal Assent to be withheld from the Canada Indemnity Bill until assurance was given that no person who engaged in or aided or abetted "that unnatural rebellion" should participate. In seconding that, Mr. Baillie Cochrane trumped up the old charge against Roebuck of having defended rebels at the bar of the House. Indignation at this brought Mr. Roebuck perilously near to launching a challenge. "Had that assertion," he said, "not been uttered in the House of Commons; had it been uttered by any man not clothed with the protection of the House——" The remainder of the sentence was drowned in cries of "Oh, oh!" As he proceeded with his argument against the amendment he calmed down, and, before resuming his seat, apologized for the somewhat excited state in which he began. Thereupon Mr. Cochrane disavowed any intention of casting imputations on Mr. Roebuck.

*June* 15.—We had a stormy night. In the midst of the Canada debate, Mr. Baillie Cochrane thought fit to make a vulgar attack upon me. I answered, and gave him a scarification. I shall have another set-to with him this evening. Gladstone moved in the matter, and has got himself into a scrape. The Ministry last night asked me to speak. The Attorney-General was the man sent to me.

*June* 16.—The result of the Canada debate will tell well in Canada. The majority was two to one, pretty nearly. Gladstone and Sidney Herbert acted foolishly. Sir James Graham came to me for information, and voted with me. Lord John [Russell] also came to me, and they made me, in fact, their authority. Dizzy's speech was very poor, bad in argument, expression, and delivery. My answer to Baillie Cochrane has gained me great applause. It is now past four p.m., and I have been up since eight, having gone to bed at three. No night except Wednesday have I been in bed before two. At this moment, I am so sleepy

that I can hardly see, and for my sins I am going to dine with
M. D. H.

In consequence of doubts expressed as to the power of
the Crown to exercise the prerogative of mercy in the case
of Smith O'Brien, Meagher, and others convicted of high
treason, a bill was introduced, placing the matter beyond
dispute. The Irish State prisoners, however, demanded
that, instead of being transported for life, they should
either be set at liberty or executed according to the original
sentence, and they petitioned to be heard by counsel
against the Transportation for Treason (Ireland) Bill. In
the debate on this question, the Irish members set off in
full cry on Mr. Roebuck's track. He had declared that
he would hang the prisoners to-morrow rather than they
should escape by a quibble, contending that if this Bill
were defeated, the capital sentence ought to be carried out.
The scene that ensued was extraordinarily heated. Mr.
R. M. Fox (Longford), Mr. Reynolds (Dublin), Mr. R. D.
Browne (Mayo), Mr. Lawless (Clonmel), and Mr. J.
O'Connell, all in succession assailed Mr. Roebuck, who
replied in kind, and the air was thick with recriminations
and with appeals to the Speaker. Mr. Roebuck was
accused of charging one member with falsehood, another
with being drunk, and a third with insolence. The Speaker
was conveniently deaf, and Captain Berkeley interposed
with the remark that the interruptions of the Irish
members were so contrary to the rules of the House, that
he did not wonder at the violence with which Mr. Roebuck
resented them. Mr. Roebuck's own account of the affair
is given in the following letters :—

*June* 19.—I have been all day busy with an Irish row. They
have made a run upon me, in the hopes of running me down.
However, Captain Berkeley (Grantley's brother) has stood by me,
and now everything is right, and not only right, but nothing could
be better, and I have in my favour the opinion of every gentleman I have been able to meet. A Mr. Fox, of Longford, Ireland,

thought fit to call me the "hired advocate of rebels." I at once said he had asserted a *falsehood*. The Speaker for the first time in my life called me to order. I retracted the word as regarded the House, *but not the member, Mr. Fox!* Therefore he sends me a message. I refer him to Berkeley, who thinks me quite right, and makes the man retract his assertion, and there the matter rests. I have the letters. The ministers behaved like cowards, as they are, but I shall gain with the people, my best friends, as I find every minute.

*June* 20, 1849.—I find everybody of one mind respecting these Irish ruffians, and the conspiracy being so plain, everybody thanks me for resisting them. I get letters from every part of the country saying this. I dined here yesterday with Lord Malmesbury, an exceedingly agreeable good-natured person. He offered me his grandfather's papers for my "History." This is really valuable. Alfred Montgomery will let me see Lord Wellesley's, so I get materials. To-morrow I shall bring forward the subject of Rome. The introduction of the French * is diabolical.

*London, June* 22.—To-day brought me letters from Sheffield full of thanks and praise for my opposition to the Irish. I am just going to bring on the Roman business. . . . The French conduct excites great disgust, and I am determined to give expression to the general feeling. To-day is so fine that I feel in a state of misery at being a prisoner here. I dined yesterday with Bickham Escott,† and met Cross the philosopher, and made him talk on his subject. He says if you put a sheet of lead on one side a pail, and a sheet of copper on the other, and connect them by a slip of copper or lead, and fill the pail with water, you may put a piece of meat therein, and it will keep sweet for months, but will lose its taste in four days. He says he is making experiments in this line of inquiry, and is expecting great results. The conversation was amusing.

*London, June* 23, 1849.—My Roman question has made a sensation. Peel, during the whole time of my speaking, was

---

* The expeditionary force which attacked Rome in support of the Pope. Roebuck asked whether England had expressed disapprobation? Lord Palmerston would not say more than that the British Government had seen the action of the French with great regret.

† M.P. for 'Winchester 1841–47. He unsuccessfully contested West Somerset, Westminster, Cheltenham, and Plymouth. See p. 106.

ostentatiously noisy in his cheers. He sat forward so as to bring himself out from the row of persons on each side of him, and vehemently cheered me from the beginning. If the papers omit to mention this, they will pass over one really marked incident of the scene.

*London, July* 12, 1849.—We had a dinner last night at Sir Joshua Walmsley's, with the leading Radicals . . . Hume, Milner Gibson, Charles Villiers (a fish out of water), Cobden, Bright, Rev. W. J. Fox, and a Colonel Salwey. The object was to see if any combined system of action could be devised, and it soon became plain that, amongst these men, a leader or a system was impossible. Villiers came there to prevent any such result, ditto Milner Gibson. Cobden is a poor creature, with one idea—the making of county voters. He is daunted by the county squires, and hopes to conquer them by means of these votes. Little Fox . . . was about as much fit for a political chief as I am for a ballet dancer. The only man of metal and pluck was Bright, the pugnacious Quaker. Walmsley himself is a well-intentioned, hard-headed manufacturer.

Lord Grey * has sent to me to talk with him on his colonial legislation. I shall ask him if his father left any papers he could let me see for my "History." . . .

*July* 13, 1849.— . . . For the first time this year I went to the Opera to see Grisi in the *Ugonotti*, a most magnificent piece of acting. This was, however, after a piece of acting, most successful, too, of my own in " Hon. House." †

I saw Lord Grey yesterday, who made it a favour not to oppose his Australian Bill. A word from me would have put an end to it.

I *will* be home next week. Everybody is fleeing, and I shall run away also.

Mr. Roebuck did not, however, " run away " so soon as he had intended, for he was in his place up to within a day or two of the prorogation, taking active part in the debates. Thus, in cordially supporting a motion of Mr. Drummond's on the taxation and large expenditure of the

---

* Secretary of State for the Colonies.

† On Mr. Anstey's motion on illegal ordinances, or acts of Council for the taxation of the people of Van Diemen's Land, and charges against the Governor (Sir W. Denison) of attempting to intimidate the judges.

country, and for inquiry into places, salaries, and establishments, he said he would gladly support a Government that had vigour enough to carry out its own intentions ; but he could not give his support to those paltry, hesitating fears, that shrinking trouble, that self-deceit which, like the wild ostrich in the bush, concealed its head, and thought it concealed its body. If he could force out such a Government and force in a strong one, he would willingly do so. He opposed a motion by Mr. Herries for a fixed duty on corn, and in a debate on the Russian invasion of Hungary, he vigorously attacked both Russia and France. He expressed approval of Lord Palmerston's conduct at the Foreign Office, but insisted that the moral power of England should be used to settle the dispute. War, he said, was a dreadful calamity, but there were calamities more dreadful.

*To Mrs. Roebuck.*

*January* 27, 1850.—The Tories, had they been wise, would have dropped Protection, taken the Colonies up, and have driven out the Whigs at a blow.*

*January* 31.—The affair † went off very well, though the getting there was a disagreeable journey.

*February* 2.— . . . A fit of illness, brought on, Elliotson said, by cold ; Arnott, who was in the Temple with me, by an overwrought mind. Perhaps both. It lasted all day.

*February* 4.—The colonial affair is put off in the Commons till Friday. The *on dit*, according to the *Times*, is an adoption of my plan.

*February* 9. — The Government explanation ‡ about the colonies was made last night. Lord J. Russell spoke of the

---

* A Protectionist amendment to the Address was negatived in the Lords by 152 to 103, and in the Commons by 311 to 192.

† His first lecture at Salisbury.

‡ On proposals for the better government of the Australian Colonies, and authorizing them to levy customs duties. Roebuck (Feb. 18) objected to giving them power to make constitutions for themselves. He wanted the House not to devolve its authority, but to send out a matured plan which would at once place liberal institutions there.

consolation he derived from the fact of members in that House having paid attention to that subject, and then mentioned Molesworth and myself. Molesworth made an elaborate speech with oranges and handkerchiefs. . . . Long after, I followed with a very short statement, that at once excited the House, and made a debate. Sir James Graham paid me compliments privately, Gladstone publicly, so did the speakers who followed me.

1, *Spring Gardens, February* 13, 1850.— . . . I am going to dine with Admiral Berkeley and Lady Charlotte to-night. I like him; he was very staunch and friendly to me last year during the Irish row, and is really a good fellow. Peel's cheers to-day on my statement * were peculiar—marked, and even vociferous; and I feel that my last speech on the Ceylon affair has produced an effect. The canters of the Bright set will not like it; but the common-sense of the country is with me. Edward Ellice met me yesterday while he was walking with his daughter-in-law, and, after paying me all sorts of compliments, said, "Strange that these people" (we were in Downing Street) "could not do the thing, and should be indebted to you for doing what they ought, as a Government, to have done." I shall be glad to get into Chambers, as I shall be really able to work there, which I am not in my present state.

*February* 14.—We had yesterday a brush in the House, and I took the opportunity of doing what I thought justice to the Colonial Office in the case of Ceylon.† Joseph Hume was at his wits' end because I objected to the nonsense he and others talk respecting our Government in the East. He accused me of being tyrannical, and made a most amusing scene. The Government had good reason to be greatly obliged to me. This, however, was not my object. All I desired was to see justice done.

*February* 28.—Molesworth has just started a crotchet—the strangest possible, viz. that the Crown cannot form a Colonial Government without representative constitutions—this in the teeth of all the Colonial Charters which have just been re-published.‡

---

* In refutation of certain unfounded allegations which sought to attribute to Mr. Roebuck's relatives a share in the Canadian rebellion.

† The debate was on February 11. Mr. Roebuck deprecated inquiry and interference.

‡ Sir William Molesworth's view is more accurately stated in the Rev.

*March* 4.—I have been all the early part of the day endeavouring to make Rothschild come to the struggle in the House of Commons to-morrow. What happens to-morrow depends chiefly on Mr. Speaker.

When, in June, 1849, the Lords, according to their wont, threw out the Jewish Disabilities Bill, Baron Leopold de Rothschild resigned his seat, and appealed to his constituents of the City of London. They sent him back by an immense majority over Lord John Manners, his opponent. Roebuck pressed Rothschild to present himself at the table, and bring the question of the oath to an issue, but the baron delayed, believing that the Government would take some action. It was not until July, 1850, that, ministers still procrastinating, Baron de Rothschild went down and claimed to take his seat. At first the officials declined to swear him on the Old Testament, and a few days afterwards, having reconsidered this decision, his refusal to take the oath "on the true faith of a Christian" excluded him from the House. The long struggle for removing this disability continued until July, 1858, when, eleven years after his first election, Baron de Rothschild at length took his seat. The long antagonism of the Lords had been overcome by a compromise. On the occasion of the third reading, Mr. Roebuck had a final fling at the Lords. "They had," he said, "written themselves down asses; after stating that a Jew was morally unfit to sit in Parliament, they had sent down a Bill by which Jews might be admitted. The Lords were always doing the same thing" (see their conduct on the Trent Corporation Act, Catholic Emancipation, English and Irish Municipal Corporations, the Corn Laws, and so forth). "They had done a good thing in a foolish manner, and had cut a remarkable antic on this occasion. In attempting

W. N. Molesworth's "History of England," vol. ii. p. 359. On this night Roebuck supported Hume's motion in favour of Household Suffrage and the Ballot. It was defeated by 242 to 96.

to maintain its own dignity, the House of Lords had covered itself with dirt."

*March* 5, 1850.—I have been all the morning with Lord Grey, at his invitation, talking over his Australian Bill. I was all last evening fighting the Irish Bill,* and I am now most popular with the Irish. They came to shake me by the hand with true Irish fervour, because of my advocacy, and I certainly forced Lord John to change his course in their favour during the night. He, as usual, got angry, and wanted to bounce, but he could not. The debate was a curious scene.

Lord Grey spoke of my going Circuit, and *strongly advised* it. This was curious. Everybody seems of one mind on it, and all appear to take an interest in my favour. How different this from the old times long gone by !

*March* 6.—I have been busy all day, and finished by making a speech in the House,† for which I have been rapturously applauded, David Dundas saying it was the best speech made this year; Compton of Lyndhurst, the best he ever heard in the House; and many others to the same effect. Take all this for what it is worth. It means that I have placed their wishes and opinions before the world in a way exceedingly gratifying to them. I hear men now wishing that I was of their party, and intimating that if I was, I could lead. So I know I could ; but that is not possible.

*York, March* 7.—I cannot help laughing when I think of the effect my speech of yesterday produced. To see all the old gravities of the House flocking round me, to thank and praise me, to hear Mr. Speaker profuse in compliments, was quite a new thing, and amused me vastly.

Cobden, I understand, answered me ; but I had left the House, having paired, and being obliged to prepare for my journey. He never told me that he was to reply. I have no idea of what he said or how he met my arguments. The House was thin when I spoke ; had the speech been made towards the end of the debate, when the House was full, I sincerely believe it would

---

* Parliamentary Voters (Ireland) Bill. Roebuck struggled, in committee, to lower the franchise.

† Against Marriages (Deceased Wife's Sister) Bill, which, " if passed, would plant a thorn in the side of almost every family."

have affected the division.* As Trelawny was opposed to my view, you will hear all that is against me from ——, but you may trust me, the effect was remarkable, and by no means to my injury. I feel I am right.

*March* 13, 1850.—I shall take up my quarters at 2, Cloisters. I shall also see Dundas, and discuss with him, who is really my friend, my views and prospects. From long consideration of my own prospects I feel that I should prove an acquisition to the Ministry, if they choose to accept me frankly. The only difficulty lies in their aristocratic desire to destroy all who are not of them by blood ; and if they took me into their ranks they would wish to *compel* me to be an underling. This I will not submit to. But, looking to the condition of politics now, I could accept office with them, and make their Government the object of my support and defence. Heaven only knows whether they look at me with these eyes. The Hawes, Ward, and Hayter tribe I cannot submit to join ; but if they will take me as one of themselves, I will join— and a powerful supporter in the House would be of use to them, if they knew their own interests.

*York, March* 15, 1850.—I hear from Frank Mills that the state of France is becoming alarming. The late Socialist returns for Paris have frightened the timid and moderate in England, as well as in France.

*Woodsley, Leeds, March* 19, 1850.—As Lord Ashley is renewing his work as to the factories, I thought this a good opportunity for learning what the manufacturing world think of the matter, and applied to some friends here for information. . . . Mr. Heaton has a passion for farming (he is partner in a large woollen house), and took me to Mr. Eddison, who won the pig prizes last year for the large Yorkshire breed. He, Eddison, is a solicitor, and an admirer of mine. He gave me up the whole of yesterday, and so soon as I joined him in the morning began talking of my having resumed the circuit, stating how glad he was, and how glad his brethren were, and begged of me not to be disappointed, for that success was certain. (Well, we shall see.) We then went to various mills, and finished by meeting a party of the leading men at the Town Hall. Thence we took carriage, lunched at

* The Bill was in the charge of Mr. James Stuart Wortley. The second reading was carried by 182 to 130. The third reading was subsequently carried by 144 to 134.

Mr. Eddison's, were joined by Mrs. Eddison, and drove out to
their newly acquired farm, and there I saw the pigs. They
are the large breed. I measured the boar with my stick; he
was exactly twice as long as it, and is by name Emperor!
We then looked at a trip * of a week old, and beautiful they
are. Eddison says he will select the two best for me. From
Mr. Heaton I got a beautiful boar of the small breed, and will
keep it till the others are ready. Depend upon it, they are the
perfection of the pig tribe, and I do not mean to be talked out
of, my conceit. When they arrive, in about two months' time, we
must try to make S. take an interest and pride in them. When
they are a year and a half old, they will make the Hampshire lads
open their eyes.

*Leeds, March* 20, 1850.—I have to-day received another letter
from Walmsley, who has certainly stirred up his friends, and they,
being men of business, set to work in the right way, and in
earnest. I was never more struck with the difference between the
habits of men of business and those of other men than now.
The business man brings the habits of his working life into his
friendships, while our people, doing the same, think, wish, ponder,
hesitate, prophesy, and discourage—do everything, in short, but
*act.* But acting is just the very thing wanted.

*Liverpool, April* 3, 1850.—The results of last night as far as
regards myself were ludicrous enough. I was asked to speak
after Lord Sefton and Cardwell,† and I went to dine with the
Sandbachs, Mrs. Sandbach being one patroness of the ball and
Lady Sefton the other. . . . The dinner was pleasant. We
laughed and talked, but the inexorable time had to be kept. We
took carriage, and drove into town, four miles. On arriving at
the Town Hall, we found Lord and Lady Sefton alone, nobody
having arrived. The speaking was to be between eight and ten,
and then the dancing was to begin. Cardwell, I found, was in an
awful *funk,* professedly because of the strange medley of politics
in the town, and the consequent chances of giving offence. I
said, " Why not put an end to the difficulty by beginning the
ball at once ? Take Lady Sefton, and let Lord Sefton, who
doubtless knows how to dance, lead out Mrs. Sandbach ; bring
the military band upstairs and begin." This bold mode of

* A litter of pigs (Hampshire dialect).
† The late Lord Cardwell, then M.P. for Liverpool.

proceeding frightened him ; but he kept looking at his watch, exclaiming, " Well, the time is going fast, and nobody is here." Sure enough nobody came. The two patronesses were seated to receive the young Liverpudlians, who came by ones, twos, and threes, absolutely boys and girls, some very nicely dressed, and some very queer figures. I whispered to Cardwell, " I think the best thing for me to do is simply to bolt." He said, " I wish to God you would,". . . and, having made my adieux, off I went ; and to this hour I do not know what occurred after. Mrs. Sandbach told me that they possessed two statues by Gibson, which she wished me to see, and I am going to-day, for I have heard of these works, an " Aurora " and a " Hunter."

*Temple, April* 18, 1850.—Yesterday I was so occupied all day that I did not get home till after post time, so you had no history of that day. But the *Times* will show you what I was doing— a long speech on the Education Bill,\* of which speech I hear this morning very loud praises. I hope they are deserved.

The affair of the Indian offices I take to have been a *feeler*. They are not vacant, and even if one of them was promised on the vacancy occurring, there would be no certainty, for the very existence of the Ministry is not worth three months' purchase. They evidently hope to silence me, and place their gaudy flies before me, in the hope that I may bite, and, living in hope I shall live also in silence—or giving them support. This won't do.

*April* 19, 1850.—We had a great fight in the House last night,† and at length I roused Peel from his lethargy, and we beat the Government, who supported Sir John Pakington in his attempt to give two justices of the peace the power in Petty Sessions to sentence men of sixteen to be flogged. We conquered at last, though the row was immense. To-night, very possibly, the House will reject Lord Grey's scheme for the Australian Colonies, that is, they may throw out the one chamber part of it.‡ I shall speak against that part of the scheme, though

---

\* Brought in by Mr. W. J. Fox, M.P. for Oldham, to promote secular education. On the previous evening Roebuck had spoken in favour of Mr. Milner Gibson's motion for the repeal of the paper duty.

† On the Larceny Jurisdiction Bill.

‡ Three plans were discussed—(1) a single chamber, one-third consisting of nominees of the Crown; or (2) two chambers, one elective ; or (3) two chambers, both elective. Molesworth and Roebuck were in favour of the third.

without any asperity, and I shall endeavour to oppose the sort of running down of Lord Grey which seems the fashion. I think him mistaken as to the difficulties in his way, but he means well, and there is much to say in support of the scheme.

The combination of parties is strange. First, there is Molesworth and Co.; Gladstone and his friends; Adderley and that clique; Dizzy and the Protectionists—and myself. I fancy Sir James Graham also with us. Upon Peel much will depend. If he declares in favour of the second chamber, the Ministry will be in a minority; and as they have brought this scheme forward, they stand pledged to it. A defeat will, I suppose, break up the Administration. Still, there is such a feeling of the impossibility of making another government—why this feeling is entertained I cannot tell—that many will support Government who do not agree with them.

*April* 20, 1850.—As I supposed, Peel saved the Government last night, but he did it after a shabby fashion; he paired off in their favour. This was known to his followers, yet his son voted with us. The report of the debate is a very poor one, as always happens when a debate occurs in committee. I sincerely believe the speech I made was the best I ever made in the House, and certainly the most effective. It was well received on both sides. Keogh said to me, " I intended to follow you, but I was *daunted*, for I did not dare rise after a speech which had produced such an effect upon the House." Dizzy threw to me a complimentary note as soon as I sat down. Molesworth even came to me eagerly to state that I had made an admirable speech.

Of the fight of the night before, I have not met a man who has not praised; all say that my opposition caused the defeat of the flogging scheme.

The long conversation I have had with Dizzy has evidently worked on his mind. He feels his own false position, and he sees that we feel it.

*Tuesday, April* 24, 1850.—Yesterday slipped away before I thought of the time. You will see more in the papers than I can describe, though they give but a very imperfect conception of what occurs. Last night the discussion on the Australian Bill came on again, and very nearly all my suggestions were attended to, Sir James Graham standing up manfully for one of them, *i.e.* my plan of defined and narrow limits for each colony. One curious thing occurred. Evelyn Denison asked me to speak on the subject of waste lands; my plan alone referred to waste lands. Well, Sir James Graham adopts, praises, and presses my view. Thereupon E. Denison speaks of it as the plan and proposal of the Right Hon. Baronet, leaving me out altogether. This was the old Whig fashion, but now it will not do. Lord John was obliged to be civil, and attend to me, because the House stands by me. The reign of insolence, as far as I am concerned, is over. Lord John yielded to my suggestions, and said, as far as he could judge, that my statement was fair and wise, and if I would consent, he would see my suggestions embodied in words to be brought up in the report.*

*April* 27, 1850.—There seem to be many intrigues and endeavours to soften and to silence me in the House, but they have not yet taken the right way.

2, *Cloisters, Temple, May* 3, 1850.—Last night we had a grand scene of confusion in the House, the attorneys and barristers being concerned.† I said my say, and I almost fear to go into Westminster Hall, as my brethren are very angry when they hear the truth. The confusion was the result of the position of the Ministry. They are too weak to manage the House.

*May* 3.—Lord Brougham says he will not leave Paris before to-morrow, because he insists that there will be a revolution—why, he does not say. I do not think that his expectations will be realized. There is no cause for a disturbance, unless the small clique of people who wish exclusively to govern France determine to create a row in order to get rid of a popular chamber. Unfortunately, there are not many persons in France who know what is intended by, "Government."

---

* Throughout the proceedings in committee, Mr. Roebuck was ceaseless in his endeavours to alter the details of the Bill; and even on the motion for the third reading, he seconded an amendment of Mr. Gladstone's in favour of withholding further sanction until the colonies should have had opportunities of considering the measure, because of the numerous provisions requiring the interference of the authorities at home, and the desirability of reducing occasions for interference. Mr. Gladstone and Mr. Roebuck acted as tellers, and they were defeated by a majority of 98. When the Bill came back from the Lords (August 1) with amendments, Mr. Roebuck entered his final "most solemn and earnest protest" against it.

† The County Courts Extension Bill. Mr. Roebuck, resisting strong professional pressure, protested against abuses of the fee system.

*May* 6.—I have been all day at work on my proposed report on Turton. It grows under my hand; it may be interesting, and show something of the actual law of Bengal.

*May* 28, 1850.—Everything is in a most prosperous state. The Navigation Laws repealed, and such freights as never were seen. Corn Laws repealed, and an overflowing exchequer. Protection is done for.

*Wednesday, June* 19, 1850.—We are in a regular row. On arriving here on Monday, I learned from Frank Mills that the Stanley party were resolved to attack Palmerston in the Lords,* and that they were sure of a majority. The Government people did not *quite* believe this, and, as the night wore on, the doubt became every moment greater. What would be the result no one knew. I found Graham and the young Peelites in the gallery of the Lords, all excited. This proved that the Peelite party were no longer willing to support the Government. I went away, tired of the debate, and found next morning 37 majority against Ministers.

. Up to four o'clock p.m. they [the Ministry] have not resolved on their line of conduct. I gave notice this morning that I should ask to-morrow what line of conduct they intend to pursue, and I have offered them to move an approbation of Palmerston. If they shirk from this, they must go out; for it is quite impossible for them to remain with this slap in the face. They are reduced to nonentities in Europe by it; so, if they are not willing to try the House of Commons, I will compel them. I think they will accept my offer. I am going to a public dinner at which young Stanley presides. This is funny enough.

*Thursday, June* 20, 1850.—I am to ask Lord John my question [What course the Ministry intend to pursue] this evening, and he will answer it. . . . I then give notice that to-morrow I move an approbation of Palmerston's policy. This will bring the matter before the House of Commons. If the Administration have not a good majority, which is very doubtful, out they must go.

Lord John Russell's answer was that the Ministry intended to do nothing at all—virtually to ignore the adverse

* Motion by Lord Stanley, censuring the Government for undue interference in the affairs of Greece.

vote in the Lords. Thereupon Mr. Roebuck gave notice of this motion : "That the principles which have hitherto regulated the foreign policy of her Majesty's Government are such as were required to preserve untarnished the honour and dignity of this country, and in time of un- exampled difficulty, the best qualified to maintain peace between England and the various nations of the world."

*June* 21.—The papers will tell you what has happened, and the plan adopted. Next Monday I may possibly have enacted the part of the ministers' saviour. But there is a great division of opinion among all parties. The peace gentry—Cobden and Bright—blame Palmerston's warlike proceedings. The Peelites do not know what to be at. Who would have supposed that I should ever stand in this relation to the Whigs !

To-morrow I shall not be able to write, according to the new plan of post-office proceedings,* which are beginning to succeed admirably ! The humbugs have been regularly bitten.

*Tuesday, June* 25, 1850.—I could tell you nothing yesterday, for I spoke from five to half-past seven. The post was gone. I received on all sides great compliments, and I enclose Delane's † few words, which, as he is a violent partisan, speak volumes. Many men said it was the best speech they had heard me make. The attention of the House never flagged, and for two hours I had them completely in hand. The respect shown by all parties is the marked and peculiar feature of their conduct towards me. Thoroughly have I conquered insolence and prejudice in that House. There are many errors in the report—many side hits, and all the acting necessarily left out. The result is very doubtful. I may have a majority, but to be of any use it must be a large one. If they (the ministers) go out, a combination so-called Liberal Ministry will come in ; and Graham, who made a most powerful attack, is evidently playing for the leadership, for which, with all his ability, I fancy him unfit.

*Wednesday, June,* 1850.—Last night Palmerston made his defence, speaking four hours and a half. The speech was by

---

* Stopping Sunday collections and deliveries of letters.

† The Editor of the *Times.* The speech referred to was that in which Mr. Roebuck moved his resolution approving of the foreign policy of the Government.

far the finest effort of oratory I have ever heard in that House. He spoke without a note, quoting dates throughout with perfect accuracy, reading only one or two papers, preserving his temper, using not one hard word, saying no one thing that any man could complain of—keeping the attention of all unbroken from the first moment to the last, and at times rising to the very height of a reasoning and impassioned oratory. In short, it was a great speech.

*Thursday, June 27.*— . . . No news to-day. The eyes of every one are directed to the House of Commons, and the only question now heard is, What will the division be ? The House and country only wish to hear Peel, Lord John, and Dizzy ; all others are only bores. The facts are all now known, and the result is impatiently desired. . . . I find myself taking a front rank in the House, and acknowledged by all to deserve that position.

*Friday, June 28.*—A stupid debate occupied the whole of last night. I shall leave this to-morrow for home ; I am tired, and not well.

*June 28.*—The queen was attacked and *struck* yesterday.[*] You will see the accounts. I am exceedingly grieved for this. The horrible insecurity which might be created in her mind by these dastardly and cruel brutalities may do her harm. Simply looking at her as a young mother, my blood boils when I behold such things. Brougham is talking about going to America this autumn. The sight of him among the Yankees would be worth seeing.

The Pacifico debate ended in a majority for the Government of 46 in a House of 574 on the morning of June 29. As the sun was rising, Mr. Roebuck and Sir David Dundas walked away together towards the Temple. In front of them was Sir Robert Peel, and Sir David, looking at him, said, "I consider that man to be the happiest in England at this moment, for he has just voted with his party, and yet also in accordance with his own feelings and opinions." A few hours after, Sir Robert Peel was thrown from his

---

[*] By Robert Pate, late lieutenant in the 10th Hussars. He was sentenced to seven years' penal servitude.

horse on Constitution Hill, receiving injuries from which he died on July 2.

Mr. Roebuck, having left town for Hampshire early that same morning, did not learn what had happened until two days later; and when the *Times* containing the news arrived, he brought it to Mrs. Roebuck, who was in the garden, saying to her, " I have some very bad news, which you will be sorry to hear. Sir Robert Peel has met with an accident which, I fear, will kill him." He then read the account, and was much distressed at the tragic occurrence.

In the garden at this moment a swarm of bees was about to be hived, or, locally, " potted." This was still in the days of straw skeps. A short time afterwards, Mrs. Roebuck remarked to Turner—the man who hived the bees—that the last swarm did not prosper, owing probably to its being a very late one. The answer was, " No, ma'am ; I never did think those bees would thrive, for just as I was going to pot them, master came into the garden and read some bad news about that gentleman, who died after-wards of the accident."

*To Mrs. Roebuck.*

*Wednesday, July* 10, 1850.—I find it very difficult to preserve what you call a *rational* course. Last night, or rather this morn-ing, I did not get to bed till four o'clock, and was awake by half-past seven, breakfasted with Frank Mills by nine, was with John Abel Smith at ten in Belgrave Square. At three, I am to meet Sir John Dodson in consultation. In the mean time I have to indite a letter to Palmerston. At six I dine with Mills, and at nine I start for York. Now, what say you to rationality ?

I gave the House last night a piece of my mind anent the post-office. The report is but a faint shadow of what was said, and what occurred. The House cheered to the echo, and, in fact, rescinded the former resolution [stopping the Sunday delivery of letters]. Lord John played false, and regularly sold poor Locke. . . . All this disgusts his party ; and so fatal is the effect of such conduct, that, were this the beginning instead of the end of the session, the Ministry would not last a month. Dizzy and Gladstone see office dancing before their eyes, and are like two kings of Brentford. Dizzy wins, I bet.

The world here is out of joint. Peel's death has put all things wrong; and the ministers are hurrying to a close, in the dread of such a defeat as will drive them to resign.

The rescinded resolution was one for the presentation of an Address to her Majesty, praying that the collection and delivery of letters in all parts of the kingdom might cease entirely on Sundays. This motion was proposed and carried against the Government in the House of Commons by 93 to 68 votes on May 30, 1850, by Lord Ashley. On June 10 her Majesty assented to the request of the Address, and the post-office directed that no inland letters nor foreign correspondence should be carried on Sundays; but the inconvenience suffered by the public was so great that in a month's time the matter was again brought before the House of Commons, with the result that the Sunday delivery was at once resumed.

*To the Rev. J. Maclean.*

*Milton, Christchurch, Hants, April*, 1850.—Your letter of the 15th ult. I have only read to-day, as, during my absence on circuit, none of my London letters were sent to me. I hope you will be so kind as to excuse what has been only an apparent and not a real neglect of your letter. I am sorry to say that I cannot accede to your request. I do not believe that communication by post during Sunday is at all mischievous. None appreciates more highly than I do the advantages to be derived from the rest of the Christian Sunday, which, in my mind, bears no relation whatever to the Jewish Sabbath. As a Christian, I treat the Sunday as a feast day, in the true and proper appreciation of the word; and by judicious application of labour on that day, we render it what it was intended to be—a day of quiet, rest, peace, and happiness; and I can imagine a thousand cases in which much labour, care, anxiety, and misery would be saved—and in fact, are saved—by letters being delivered on the Sunday. And because I believe this, I cannot consent, with my present lights and opinions, to adopt your view of the subject.

### To Mrs. Roebuck.

*Gilling Castle, November* 1, 1850.—I am somewhat better, though still not well. We went yesterday to see Castle Howard, and the cold of the empty house chilled me into absolute discomfort and illness. The pictures are poor—one celebrated, the Marys by Carracci—a collection of red-eyed, red-nosed, ugly old women. The castle is a stupid, heavy-looking thing by Vanburgh; not a good room in it. The woods and the park beautiful. Nature when left alone has done great things.

*Temple, November* 13, 1850.—I really hope that my case will come on to-morrow, but am far from sure. In the mean time I go on steadily with my book,* and have the great assistance of a file of the *Times* in our—the Temple—library, in which—the *Times*, I mean—I find some curious things. From the Parliamentary debates, I was led to suspect that there were intrigues with Brougham while chancellor, during the very heat of the Reform fight, and that the anti-Reform party hoped that he would desert Lord Grey, and join their party; and I find in the *Times* a broad assertion that the king distinctly asked Brougham to remain chancellor when Lord Grey resigned in May, 1832. I should like to know if the king *did* make such a request; I will ask B., but unless I can get letters and papers written at the time, I cannot trust his memory. I shall endeavour to obtain a sight of Peel's papers, but Cardwell will, I fear, not aid me.

* "History of the Whig Ministry."

## CHAPTER XXI.

RE-ELECTION FOR SHEFFIELD.    1850–1853.

THE "Papal Aggression"—the popular name given to the Pope's action in establishing a Romish hierarchy in England—set the country in a blaze in the closing months of 1850. Lord John Russell's famous missive to the Bishop of Durham drew from Mr. Roebuck an angry letter of protest, directed against what he regarded an unwise and unstatesmanlike favouring of "detestable intolerance," all the more censurable as violating those principles of civil and religious liberty for which Lord John and the party he led had aforetime fought.

*To Mrs. Roebuck.*

*December 6, 1850.*—I find that I cannot get away to-morrow. I have to-day one of my headaches, and I believe in this case it is attributable to a horrible fog, as yellow as ochre, and as thick as mud. My letter [to Lord John Russell] has created a sensation. The papers are furious, and yet feeble. Fisher,* my proposer at Sheffield, one of the most respected men in the town, sent me a letter of eager, hearty thanks. Phinn met me to-day, saying, We all think with you, though we have not yet the courage to say so openly.

The session of 1851 was largely occupied by struggles over the Ecclesiastical Titles Bill, diversified by a Ministerial crisis consequent on the resignation of the Russell

---

* Mr. William Fisher, the father of Mr. Roebuck's subsequent election chairman. Both father and son were tried and true friends.

Ministry on Mr. Locke King's County Franchise Bill, following the narrow majority by which a Protectionist motion of Mr. Disraeli's had been defeated. But, other combinations failing, Lord John Russell and his colleagues resumed office. Mr. Roebuck's * records of this year, as Mrs. Roebuck was in or near London the greater part of the summer, are exceedingly scanty. In the debates on the Address, and on the various stages of the Ecclesiastical Titles Bill, he reiterated his censures on Lord John Russell for "lending the sanction of his great name to the puritanical bigotry of England." He took no part in the divisions on the first and second readings, but he sedulously fought the Bill in its progress through committee.

*To Mrs. Roebuck.*

*Temple, March* [18], 1851.—After I wrote yesterday we had a little *scrimmage,* in which I rolled Dizzy over, quite to my own satisfaction.† I am to see Edward Ellice this afternoon about Lord Grey's letters, and I understand that they want to know if I would take a Master in Chancery's place. Again, they want to get me out of the House, and, sooth to say, I am not quite sure that I should say no, if the thing were offered, so changed am I, so completely conquered. I cannot bear this horrible isolation. Were I twenty years younger, I should feel differently, but I cannot keep myself at work when away from you.‡

*Temple, March* 22, 1851.—Lord Grey endeavours to intimidate me by threatening an injunction to prohibit my book.§ He claims a property in his father's letters, and as he is going himself to publish them,‖ wishes to prevent my giving to the world Lord Grey's opinion of Brougham. . . . I said also that the Whigs were the most consummate detractors that ever existed.

---

* While at Bushey, in Hertfordshire, Mr. Roebuck had a short but sharp attack of illness, from which he recovered slowly.

† On proposed censure on Lord Torrington's Ceylon Administration.

‡ At this time Mrs. Roebuck had to remain at Ashley Arnewood to watch over affairs there.

§ "The Whig Ministry of 1830," which was published early in 1852.

‖ "Correspondence of Earl Grey with King William IV." London: John Murray, 1867.

That their ability in whispering away a character was wonderful, and that now that I had an opportunity of exhibiting the utter falsehood of many things said by them with respect to Brougham, nothing should deter me from making use of it. He repeated his threat of an injunction, which I told him I was quite prepared to meet, and would myself argue it before the Lord Chancellor.

In a debate on our treatment of the Kaffirs, Mr. Roebuck enunciated views on the annihilation of aborigines which, often reiterated, exposed him to frequent animadversion. The extirpation of the coloured man by the white was, he held, the inevitable consequence of colonial expansion. He defended Lord Torrington's policy in Ceylon against Mr. Baillie's proposition that the punishment inflicted during the disturbances was excessive and uncalled for. His old attacks on electoral corruption were renewed in connection with occurrences at St. Albans and Falkirk burghs, and he supported Mr. Cobden's motion directed towards arranging with France a policy of reduced armaments. A Sunday Trading Prevention Bill was the signal for a renewal of his accustomed assaults on Sabbatarians. Throughout the session he lost no opportunity of girding at Lord John Russell's Ministry for its impotence, and for the fashion in which, without power, it clung to office. In May, Mr. Hume had carried against the Government a motion limiting the operation of the property tax to one year, and, a few days after, a resolution by Lord Maas on home-made spirits in bond was carried against them by the casting vote of the Speaker. On this Mr. Roebuck taunted Lord John Russell with having submitted to defeat four times—Mr. Locke King's County Franchise motion, and a question relating to the Management of Woods and Forests, making, with those just mentioned, the quartette. He wanted to know what the Government intended to do, and how much longer Lord John Russell meant to submit to such a state of things? The Liberal leader made a spirited reply—as, indeed, was his wont when subjected to Mr. Roebuck's frequent plain speaking. From the 8th of July to the end of the session (8th of August) the Parliamentary chronicles give no trace of Mr. Roebuck's attendance. Although he spoke on a minor question on the former date, he took part neither in the debate nor in the division on Mr. Berkeley's motion in advocacy of the ballot. It would appear from the following letter that Mr. Roebuck was partly at Ashley Arnewood and partly on circuit.

*Thomas Dunn (Sheffield) to J. A. Roebuck.*

*Richmond Hill (Sheffield), August* 17, 1851.—I have not heard from you since you left York, but hope sincerely you are pretty well over the awkward accident you had with your dogs. Few persons are more fond of dogs than I am, but I confess I should not like to be bitten even by one of my own dogs.\* I think in the last note I had from you, you rather hinted that you should be at Liverpool at the Assize. That will be, I suppose, some time this week. Now, you will, I dare say, have got an invitation to the annual dinner of the Cutlers' Company on September 4, which I hope you will be able to attend, and the more so as you were not there last year, and 'tis possible, I suppose, if not probable, that before the dinner comes round again we may have a general election, and I am sure I need not tell you that corporate bodies are very sensitive on these little matters. So I hope very sincerely you will be able to accept the invitation.

Mr. Roebuck did accordingly attend the Cutlers' feast.

*To Mrs. Roebuck.*

*Tuesday, January* 27, 1852.—I had an amusing journey up with the Mackinnons. He was on his way to town to publish his notes on America. He is very full of the Yankees, and swears that they will in ten years ride over us and everybody. This is too short a term, I *guess.* Among other advantages

\* It was not his own dog, but a Newfoundland belonging to Mr. G. J. Graham, which, while playing round Mr. Roebuck, accidentally caught his hand and slightly bit it.

resulting from his journey to America, is the sharpening of the wits of his boys. This effect he attributes chiefly to the clearness and dryness of the atmosphere !

### *To Mrs. Roebuck.*

*Thursday.*—I dined yesterday with the Rothschilds, and went thence to Lady John Russell's—mighty civil all of them—and to-day I find a card from Lady Granville for Wednesday next. My book will, I hope, be ready on Monday.

Some days later, he encloses a review of the " Whig Ministry " with the comment, " I am certain that whoever wrote this article, never read the book."

Years after, this judgment was confirmed by Mr. Shirley Brooks, the author of the article in question. He described to Mr. Roebuck how, on coming home late from some dinner, he found awaiting him the two volumes of the " History," with an urgent note requesting an immediate review. " I was tired and was very cross at having to write instead of going to sleep. I read the first chapter and but little more. I cannot say that I really read the book at all."

### *To Mrs. Roebuck.*

*February* 19, 1852.— . . . I have seen all sorts of people. Edward Ellice asked me on Tuesday to dine and meet J. Romilly. The others, Thiers and Duvergier de Hauranne, Grenfell, M.P., and Byng, made the party agreeable, and we had some good talk, especially with Keppel—Lord Albemarle, I mean—who in his manner to me was quite affectionate ; there is no other word to describe it. The next morning I breakfasted with Monckton Milnes, where Thiers was, and Van de Weyer, Cardwell, and others—pleasant people, very good conversation. Thiers' voice the strangest ; it is a sort of wheeze, like the sighing of wind through a keyhole. Van de Weyer was more amusing. The two appeared like the French and Belgian Thiers.

Last night I went to Lady Granville's, and saw—whom did I not see ! I met Sir James Graham, who came to me with, " Oh, the historian," and thereupon expressed his great admiration, saying, " You have in a very difficult matter steered with great judgment and firmness." Edward Ellice says that Brougham goes about saying the "History" is not correct, and not given with his authority. Whereupon Ellice said to some one standing by, when Brougham was gone, " Now, Brougham really thinks he is telling the truth ; but Roebuck is right, and he has related what Brougham has told him ! "

To-night I dine with ——, and go afterwards to Lady Truro's. There will, however, be a sharp brush in the House about Clarendon, whom I shall support.

On February 20 Lord Palmerston, who had retired from the Foreign Office in the previous December, in consequence of the disapproval of his independent methods by the queen and Prince Albert, gave Lord John Russell his " tit for tat " by carrying an amendment against the Government's Militia Bill; and the Ministry at once resigned.

*To Mrs. Roebuck.*

*Saturday, February* 21, 1852.—Well, they are out. Palmerston has had an early revenge. As for myself, I was dining with ——, and on my return, found the House up and the business done, so I personally had no hand in the killing. Nevertheless, I am glad my prophecy has proved true. Lord Derby will now take the Government ; we shall have realities to deal with, and great principles really discussed. In addition, an immediate election I fancy inevitable ; and I find there is to be a contest for Sheffield, in which I wish to take but a small part, and expense to any extent I will not bear. If I find my chance small, I will not stand, but accept the offer of the Tower Hamlets. I find Dunn * in alarm for Parker. . .

I cannot very well quit town to-day, as Monday afternoon will be important, and I want to-night to see all the world at Lady Palmerston's.

*February* 23.—I write early in the day, not knowing what the bustle of the afternoon may be. To-night Lord John formally

* Chairman of Mr. Roebuck's election committee. Mr. John Parker was Roebuck's colleague in the representation of Sheffield.

announces his resignation, and you will see by the papers that Lord Derby is in. He (Lord Derby) has long since had his Cabinet ready, and he is to propose a five-shilling duty on corn—the very thing which I desire of him, as this will make our opposition clear, and a matter easily to be understood. Nothing can be done for a week or more. The new writs must be moved, and the returns made, so that if nothing especial happens I shall leave town for home to-morrow. The crush at Lady Palmerston's was enormous. I nearly fainted from the stifling heat and my giddiness, which has returned.

*Leeds, March* 3.—I am now doing well, and gaining strength rapidly. What of late I have suffered most from is an extraordinary nervous uncomfortableness in my hands and feet. This at times during the night has been almost beyond endurance; however, this is diminishing, and all day long I have been free from it.

We know nothing as yet about what is to be done about a Ministry. For my own part, I cannot see the difficulty, *if Lord John was put on one side ;* but Lord John Russell's carriage stops the way, and his tenacious hold of power makes all the difficulty.

*London, March* 14, 1852.—You will see by the papers what occurred yesterday. The meeting * was Whig, and the object of it plainly to bring back the late Administration ; but, in spite of the supposed unanimity, this scheme will not succeed. Nothing will be done till Monday, when Lord John will begin his game of opposition ; and I, for one, do not intend to follow him as a leader, or aid in bringing back the late imbecile Administration. The scene was a very curious one in Chesham Place, and to one accustomed to Whig policy, very significant. I think, however, a very little more will checkmate Lord John.

*March*, 1852.—Last night I was asked to stand for Glasgow, with promises of certain success ; but this is impossible, and I do not believe that any place will be safer, or more comfortable, than Sheffield. I suppose that I am doomed to be opposed always.

A few days after this Mr. Roebuck spoke in support of a motion of Mr. Hume's in favour of manhood suffrage and

---

* Of Liberals, at Lord John Russell's house in Chesham Place, where it was resolved to compel the new Government to make a full declaration of its policy. Russell he held to be "weak, narrow-minded, obstinate and vindictive."

the ballot, and in the following month, in one of the discussions on the Militia Bill, he caused some sensation by bluntly calling it a measure of defence necessitated by the jealousy of the French people—jealousy of which a bad man might take advantage, and a bad man (President Napoleon) was in power.

In a debate relative to the Kaffir War he reiterated, with sundry hits at "Exeter Hall," his belief in the law that the black man must disappear before the white, and he insisted that England must choose between a recognition of this fact and the abandonment of her colonies.

*To Wm. Fisher (Sheffield).*

*April* 1, 1852.—I feel confident that when you have seen and heard me, and are not dependent upon report, you will come to the conclusion that hard words are not employed by me, and that the petulance and acerbity so freely attributed to me are creatures of the imagination of those who wish to find fault with me.

The work of the coming election began a few days after this. At a large open-air meeting in Sheffield, Mr. Roebuck was shown to be the more popular of the two members, the vote for Mr. Parker indicating that, although Mr. George Hadfield had been brought into the field ostensibly against Mr. Roebuck, it was Mr. Parker's seat which was in the greater danger. The Conservatives sought to take advantage of the Liberal split by running Mr. William Overend, Q.C.

*To Mrs. Roebuck.*

*Friday, May* 5.—I had resolved to go to Sheffield next Monday, Dunn sending for us ; but I find that on that day we are to have a grand battle with the Government, on the question of what to do with the seats vacant by the disfranchisement of St. Albans and Sudbury. The Peelites oppose Dizzy's proposal,* and there is to be a grand field day.

---

* To assign the four seats for Sudbury and St. Albans to the West Riding of Yorkshire and the Southern Division of Lancashire. The proposal was negatived by 234 to 148, Mr. Gladstone leading the attack.

I have seen the Amateur Water Colours. Miss Blake I think quite equal to any of the professionals ; Mrs. Bridgman Simpson very excellent, and also Miss Kennion. In fact, I was very much surprised by the excellence of the exhibition. I went to the Royal Academy, and liked one or two things among a multitude of daubs. Winterhalter has sent a picture painted for the queen, which is very beautiful, and some of Stansfield's are excellent ; Roberts' interiors finer than any I ever saw ; Maclise simply detestable.

*Tuesday, May* 9, 1852.—On Sunday I was at Bushey, and passed a pleasant, chatty day with William [Falconer, his brother-in-law].

The Government were beaten last night, but the division was called for so suddenly that no speaking was possible, and I was dining with Fairbairn, intending to run back and have my say. I sought no pair. The dissolution now must occur immediately.

I went to see the Water Colours. The exhibition is not a good one, and Richardson's great drawing (Fairbairn's) does not please me so much as I thought it would. The trick of cutting the paper, and substituting one sort for another, and thus making a mark right across the picture, is mere quackery, and does not, in my opinion, aid the effect of the drawing.

In May the fight at Sheffield was in full swing, all the candidates addressing numerous meetings. Mr. Roebuck, although feeble and in bad health, had a hard week, delivering sometimes three speeches a day.

### To Mrs. Roebuck.

*Sheffield, May* 18, 1852.—My week's work is nearly at an end. Our meetings have gone off well, and I am told that the canvass places me at the head of the poll. . . . I dined yesterday with one of my most staunch supporters, and found a pretty, neat house, well appointed in every way, and a very excellent dinner, over which good taste presided ; the hostess, a quiet, rather pretty woman, at her ease. There being an absence of all affectation or pretension, and a strong dose of sound common sense manifest throughout, the affair was agreeable. The smoke is the great enemy of comfort, but the house I was in yesterday is nearly free from that evil ; and really that quarter is pretty and clean.

After this labour Mr. Roebuck returned to his home in Hampshire in a very exhausted condition. Even then rest was denied him, for two days after his arrival a message came from London, asking for his presence and advice concerning Baron Lionel Rothschild's election address to the City of London. He went immediately to town, to Mrs. Roebuck's distress, and returned the same evening ill, a slight attack of paralysis having come on during the journey home. The mischief was not great, and might soon have been overcome, had not the old-fashioned prescription of leeches to the head been applied before Dr. R. W. Falconer could arrive to prevent it. He was greatly annoyed at this barbarous proceeding. The result was that the nerve powers were lowered still more, and double vision ensued.

The dissolution of Parliament did not take place until July. During the closing weeks of the session Mr. Roebuck was unable to be in his place. And although he took no further part in the active work of his own fight, he attended the final scene of the Sheffield election, when he was returned at the head of the poll by a majority of 239. But he lost his old colleague, Mr. John Parker, who, after holding the seat for twenty years, was defeated by Mr. Hadfield by 273 votes.

The rest of the summer was passed at Ashley Arnewood, where the pure air and quiet did much towards restoration of health; but the double vision continued, and put an end for ever to the favourite pursuit of water-colour drawings. This was a great privation, but however deeply felt, no complaint was ever heard, for though anxious and eager for improvement in health, it was a rule of life with Mr. Roebuck never to indulge in useless repining over what could not be altered or removed. To this rule he owed much tranquillity of mind, never more needed than at this period of his life, when illness came seriously to hinder progress and success in his public career.

The return of health being slow, he became wishful for London advice. Unfortunately, there his case was utterly mistaken. The wise and gentle treatment of over-taxed powers was not so widely understood then as it is now, and lowering processes were applied, the result being that he returned to Hampshire worse than he had left it. A Sheffield friend now suggested that the water cure might be tried with advantage. Mr. Roebuck proceeded to Malvern, and there pursued that treatment under the advice of Dr. Gully, who at once began a process of " building up." This was afterwards continued at home during the next summer and winter, with the happiest results.

During this time his constituents at Sheffield generously excused him from any attendance in Parliament "until he felt perfectly well and able to return there." He had been unequal to attendance at the autumn session of the new Parliament (November 4 to December 31), which was fatal to the Derby government; and throughout the whole of the session of 1853, when Lord Aberdeen had come into power, he was absent. In the autumn of that year he visited Sheffield. On the way down the Great Northern express ran into a coal train at Hornsey. Several passengers were injured, Mr. Roebuck receiving a severe cut on the forehead. Unlike the Lord Mayor and others who were with him, Mr. Roebuck continued his journey, and resolutely appeared at the Cutlers' feast, although so feeble as to be obliged to sit in the reception room and compelled to plead that the few sentiments he uttered in his short speech " had shaken him with emotion." The theme of that speech was that England to be respected, and to maintain peace, must be feared. He described the naval review that he had lately witnessed at Spithead, " as a great peace meeting," where he had seen magnificent vessels marching against wind and tide, without the semblance of motion save their progress onward. In the poet's phrase, each one seemed to " walk the waters like a thing of life," to dare the elements to stop them. That steam fleet was a great curator of the peace of Europe, and more efficient for the purpose than any meeting that could be collected of persons professing to be the promoters of peace; and he held it to be no wise economy to attempt to cut down these our means of defence.

While Mr. Roebuck was still seeking a restoration to health in the repose of Milton, he was subjected to some annoyance by a newspaper proclamation that he intended, as soon as Parliament met in 1854, to demand from ministers a categorical explanation of rumours, freely circulated, of undue interference by the Prince Consort in affairs of State. Mr. Roebuck warmly resented the "unwarrantable liberty" thus taken with the name of one leading " so quiet and retired a life." He had no intention of taking any such step. He was, indeed, not only without any evidence as to the prince's conduct, but was actually unaware that any charge had been seriously made against him.

## CHAPTER XXII.

### THE CRIMEAN AND CHINA WARS.   1854–1857.

IN the spring of 1854 Mr. Roebuck returned to Parliamentary work; but he only spoke once—on Mr. Layard's motion concerning Russia and the Porte—when he had to ask the indulgence of the House on account of his recent illness.   It was a warlike speech, advocating an immediate resort to the sword, and including a tribute to the "loyalty and honesty of purpose" exhibited by that Emperor of France who, when President, he had denounced as a bad man.   This was on February 17.   On March 27 war was declared against Russia.   Although weakness prevented him from taking any large share in Parliamentary debates, and compelling, indeed, protracted absences, Mr. Roebuck watched the course of events with constant anxiety.   When the terrible histories of cold, hunger, and utter misery, suffered by the English army in the Crimea came to light, he was deeply moved; and, feeling that such events cried aloud for investigation, he quietly resolved, although hardly recovered from his long illness, to find means for an inquiry of some kind to be made.

One evening in January, 1855, he returned home early from the House, and startled the members of his family by saying, "I have just given notice that I shall move for an inquiry into the state of the army in the Crimea!" This was on the 22nd.

An eye-witness thus describes the scene when Mr. Roebuck gave his notice—

The House was tolerably full at the moment that Mr. Roebuck rose to speak. There was a momentary hush, deepening into solemnity, during which no sound was heard save the sharp ring of the member for Sheffield's voice. It was a flash of forked lightning cleaving the darkness, a clear significant utterance of purpose. There was a gravity on the Treasury Bench amounting to dismay. There was a gasp of surprise everywhere—that kind of sensitive shrinking with which men might witness the uplifting of a weapon to lay a victim prostrate.

On the 23rd, in consequence of that notice, Lord John Russell resigned, and, on the 27th Mr. Roebuck moved, "That a Select Committee be appointed to inquire into the condition of our army before Sebastopol, and into the conduct of those departments of the Government whose duty it has been to minister to the wants of that army." Twice during his speech Mr. Roebuck was unable to proceed through physical weakness, and, notwithstanding a gallant attempt to go on, he was compelled to stop, after having scarcely opened his case, and without any elaboration of his indictment.

The Ministry fought hard against the motion, but in vain; and it was carried by a majority of 157, in a House of 453 members.

The resignation of the Aberdeen Ministry followed immediately. Lord Palmerston formed a new Government, with little change in its *personnel.*

The work of constituting the Sebastopol Investigation Committee took some time, its composition being the source of much contention. But at last, on February 27, it met for business. Mr. Roebuck was then elected its chairman, after an attempt on the part of Lord Seymour to propose himself for that post.

Sir John Pakington, with a view to collecting evidence with greater certainty and ease, proposed that the committee should be a secret one, and this proposal was reluctantly laid before the House by Mr. Roebuck. The general sense being strongly against secrecy, the motion was withdrawn.*

A vast mass of evidence as to the actual state of things in the Crimea was soon gathered from eye-witnesses from the Duke of Cambridge downwards; but the causes of the confusion and disorganization that had prevailed were more difficult of elucidation. In several instances, when witnesses were sent for, they did not appear, or were not to be found. Mr. Roebuck often afterwards said, "I felt corruption round about me, but I could not lay my hand upon it." †

The report of the committee was published in June, 1855. The original draft of it, drawn up by the chairman, is interesting, as showing what was the impression made upon his mind by the collected evidence. On July 17 Mr. Roebuck moved the following resolution, founded upon the report of the committee :—"That this House, deeply lamenting the sufferings of our army during the winter campaign in the Crimea, and coinciding with the resolution of the committee that the conduct of the

---

* Mr. Kinglake's account of the proceedings in connection with the Sebastopol Committee is written in a tone wholly unfriendly to Mr. Roebuck. His reference to the above proposal is unfair and inaccurate. Roebuck, in making the motion, was not, as Kinglake implies ("Invasion of the Crimea," vol. vi. p. 362), carrying out his own project; he was simply fulfilling the wishes of the majority of the committee. The members were, indeed, unanimous in the opinion that secrecy was required; the only difference of opinion was as to the extent of secrecy. The majority were in favour of this being complete. Lord Seymour, the report of whose speech does not contain the word "foolish" attributed to him by Mr. Kinglake, simply urged that the exclusion of the public should not extend to members of Parliament.

† Mr. Roebuck moved the Duke of Newcastle to indignant anger by telling him, "that the conviction upon the minds of the committee was daily gaining strength . . . that the key to many mysteries could only be found at head-quarters, and that in a high quarter (Prince Albert) there had been a determination that the expedition should not succeed." Prince Albert's memorandum recording the Duke of Newcastle's report of this conversation, with his own scornful comments, is given in Martin's "Life of the Prince Consort," vol. iii. p. 219.

Administration was the first and chief cause of the calamities which befell that army, do hereby visit with severe reprehension every member of that Cabinet which led to such disastrous results." The debate occupied two nights, on the second of which two petitions, one from Birmingham and the other from Bradford, praying that the ministers might be impeached, were presented by the originator of the debate. The previous question being moved and carried by 298, as against 182, the motion was lost.

The town of Sheffield, by its mayor, W. Fisher, sent thanks for services rendered to the country in the Crimean Committee. Bath, also, did not forget her late member, for a large meeting voted thanks to be sent through Mr. G. Norman, an old supporter; and numerous letters testified to the interest felt all over the country. The public sense of Mr. Roebuck's services on this question led to a subscription among his constituents for a testimonial. It was not presented till September in the following year, when it amounted to eleven hundred guineas, and a portrait by Mr. Richard Smith, which hangs in the Sheffield Council Hall.

Mr. Roebuck helped to swell the storm of disapproval, raised on imperfect knowledge of the facts, with which Lord John Russell's conduct in connection with the Vienna Protocols was met—a storm before which, as culminating in Sir E. B. Lytton's threatened motion of censure, Lord John was driven from office for no less than four years.

The noble lord (said Mr. Roebuck) held, or acquiesced in, language at the Conferences of Vienna which was unworthy of any English minister. I say that no English minister, especially the author of reform in Parliament, ought to have put his hand to that protocol, the object of which was to take from an independent people (Servia and the Principalities) the power of self-government. English interests are the interests of the world—her interests are the interests of civilization and self-government; but in this case the noble lord. Sided with the despots of the

world, who would crush an independent people, and deprive
them of the right of managing their own concerns.

This was uttered in a speech delivered in the debate
on the continued prosecution of the war, when Mr. Roebuck emphasized the general suspicion of half-heartedness
in the Ministry, and of the presence in the Cabinet of
men more anxious to conclude peace than to carry on the
war with thoroughness.

Mr. Roebuck took his full share in public work throughout the session of 1856, speaking frequently on subjects
involving a wide range of foreign and domestic interests.
He opposed the appointment of a board of general officers
to inquire into the allegations of the report of the M'Neill-
Tulloch Commission to the Crimea; but he declined to divide
the House with the characteristic remark that he was, as
he usually found himself, in a palpable minority.  On
Lord John Russell's resolutions for enlarging the system
of National Education, and supplying deficiencies in school
accommodation from the rates, he repeated his often-
expressed views in favour of secular teaching, including
instruction in those universal moral truths which are above
sectarianism, and the basis of all religion, whether Jewish
or Gentile, Roman Catholic or Protestant, Unitarian or
Trinitarian.  He watched carefully, and endeavoured to
amend many projects of legal reform; but he was chiefly
occupied, towards the end of the session, in strenuously
opposing, through all its stages, a Bill for the retirement
of the Bishops of London and Durham.  He denounced
this as a corrupt contract, an offence against the ecclesiastical law, and a great scandal.  These bishops, he
exclaimed, were seeking to avail themselves of an Act
of Parliament in order to perpetrate a breach of the law.
Impotent from disease and age, they said to Parliament,
"If you will buy us off, having enjoyed two of the richest
bishoprics in England for many years, we are willing to

go." And, his opposition to the Bill as a whole being unavailing, Mr. Roebuck fought it clause by clause in committee, seeking especially to reduce the sums payable as pensions to the prelates on retirement. Another ecclesiastical matter which excited his indignation, was the attempt, when New Zealand refused to pay a bishop conferred upon it by Lord John Russell, to impose the salary on the British taxpayer.

In February, 1857, the Hudson's Bay Company asked for a renewal of their licence to trade over that north-west territory adjoining the two Canadas, which extends from the Rocky Mountains to the Pacific, including Vancouver's Island. The Colonial Secretary, Mr. Labouchere (afterwards Lord Taunton), brought this request before the House of Commons, and asked for a select committee to consider the matter, as his desire was to see at least a portion of this vast territory colonized. Mr. Roebuck agreed heartily with this wish, pointing out that the interests of a fur company dependent upon solitudes where wild animals abounded, were antagonistic to colonization. He had taken the same line in 1849, when a former representative of the Colonial Office (Mr. Hawes) had ridiculed the idea of colonizing the "dreary territory" and "barren tracts" of the Hudson's Bay Company.

The rivers running into Hudson's Bay, passed, Roebuck said, through the most fertile territories belonging to the Crown, and if England did her duty, she would make that country the Germany of North America, and form a vast confederation in Canada. A great nation might be created there. The creation of such a nation was a duty which England ought to perform, and the interests of a small company should not be allowed to stand in the way of the great interests of humanity.

The expulsion from Parliament of Mr. James Sadleir, member for Tipperary, in February, 1857, enabled Mr. Roebuck to claim this as a further illustration of the fact that what he thought to-day Parliament thought to-morrow. For, true to his custom of watching over the dignity and morals of the House, he had advocated this vindicatory step in the previous July. " I am always too soon," he remarked at finding his rejected counsels followed six months later. A year afterwards, the instincts of Parliamentary policeman being still strong within him, Mr. Roebuck obtained a committee to inquire into allegations that Mr. Isaac Butt had corruptly received money from an Indian ameer, to advocate in the House of Commons his claims for the recovery of territories. That Mr. Butt had received money from the ameer was proved; but as these payments were not in reference to proceedings in Parliament, he was exonerated.

The English hostilities with China in this year did not meet with the approbation of the House of Commons, and after a sharp and protracted debate on a condemnatory motion by Mr. Cobden, which Mr. Roebuck supported in a speech delivered on the fourth night, a division took place, in which the Government was defeated. The combination of various sections arrayed against the administration is indicated by the fact that Mr. Gladstone and Mr. Disraeli, Lord John Russell and Mr. Roebuck, Mr. A. H. Layard and Mr. H. A. Bruce, were found in the same lobby, voting for Mr. Cobden's motion.* Lord Palmerston immediately advised a dissolution of Parliament. His conduct was so popular in the country, that in the elections his opponents were utterly routed. Both Mr. Roebuck and his colleague, Mr. Hadfield, had voted against him, and Mr. William Overend, the defeated Tory candidate at Sheffield in 1852, seized the opportunity to offer himself, claiming to be a supporter of Lord Palmerston. There was another

---

* About 1857 to 1859 there sat together, on the front Opposition bench below the gangway, Lord John Russell, Mr. Roebuck, and Lord Robert Cecil, the present Lord Salisbury—a remarkable company mentioned by *Punch* in a paragraph which describes Mr. Roebuck as a dog fancier, and Lord Robert Cecil as a vinegar merchant.

difficulty on the side of the old members, due to the split
of the Liberals, owing to the great indignation felt by the
moderate party on account of the means used in 1852 to
defeat Mr. John Parker.    In 1857, therefore, the local
Liberals had to perform a double operation of extreme
delicacy.    They had to heal their split, and also to condone
the vote of Messrs. Roebuck and Hadfield against Lord
Palmerston, who was as popular in Sheffield as in any other
part of the country.

*To A. Booth (Sheffield).*

19, *Ashley Place, S.W., March* 7, 1857.—I thank you for
your letter, but I do not at all share in your sanguine view of my
prospects at Sheffield.  I find the feeling of disapprobation so
strong among my friends that I am very much inclined at once to
say that I shall not present myself to the constituency at the
coming elections.   I am surprised—I will not add what my other
feelings are—at the opinions I hear expressed on the subject of
the atrocities of which we have been guilty in China.

Mr. Roebuck's belief that " the honour of England had
been desecrated by the proceedings at Canton," brought
him into unwonted co-operation with Mr. Cobden, for he
presided over a public meeting of protest at the Freemasons'
Hall, at which Mr. Cobden and Mr. Layard were the chief
speakers.  He seemed conscious that this conjunction with
Mr. Cobden might occasion remark, for he was at pains,
while referring to "the glorious success Mr. Cobden had
achieved, and which would live and be remembered when
he and all around him were dead and forgotten "—to declare
that he was no follower of Mr. Cobden's, or indeed of any
man.  He had opposed him when he thought him wrong,
and he followed him now because he thought him right.*

---

* He had supported motions by Mr. Cobden advocating arbitration in
international disputes (June, 1849), and in favour of a general reduction in the
armaments of the Great Powers.

*Wm. Fisher, Junr. (Sheffield) to Mr. Roebuck.*

[*Sheffield*] *March* 26, 1857.—I have observed from reports of [election] meetings that you have several times remarked upon the absence of some familiar faces. I may flatter myself in supposing that you perhaps have missed me, but I cannot bear the pain of feeling that you may believe me to be away from indifference or inconstancy. The fact is I have as grave objections to Mr. Hadfield as I had when he first came to Sheffield. It is not merely that he disturbed the Liberal party, but that he never gives a vote or makes a speech on any subject connected with the education of the people, or with the management of our foreign affairs, which does not annoy or disappoint me, and I consider him also very narrow on the Sunday question. For these reasons I cannot divide my vote on this occasion, nor ask any of those with whom I have influence to do so. Mr. Overend is as objectionable to me as Mr. Hadfield—not more so. It does not seem to me fair for me to go to the joint-committee, unless I could vote and work for both. I beg, however, that you will not believe that I feel any diminution of gratitude to, or regard for you, or that I am not working for you.

*To Mr. William Fisher.*

*April* 1, 1857.—No one is more ignorant than I of the internal condition of things in Sheffield, so that I know nothing of the history of individuals or of parties in the town. My mind is engrossed by the affairs of the nation, and I fancy I do wisely by keeping myself as much aloof as possible from all merely local politics.

The local difficulties, by a wise and self-sacrificing party loyalty, were overcome. The elections elsewhere ran strongly against Lord Palmerston's opponents, and especially against "the Manchester School," including Mr. Cobden and Mr. Bright; but in Sheffield the result was the triumph of the old members.

When the new Parliament met, Mr. Roebuck, in the debate on the address, congratulated the House on a pledge given by Lord Palmerston, to introduce a measure of

Parliamentary reform during the session. The pledge was not fulfilled.

On the motion (May 21, 1857) to grant to the Princess Royal, on her marriage with Prince Frederick William of Prussia, £40,000, and an annual sum of £8000 as an annuity for life, Mr. Roebuck urged that, as combining generosity to the sovereign with justice to the people, it would be better to grant a round sum as dowry, as was done in the case of a former Princess Royal, the daughter of George III. " Do not," he said, " hamper this country or yourselves by an annuity paid every year. Let her Royal Highness have everything that her necessities and her happiness require ; let it be done generously, but let it be done once and for ever."

In July Mr. Roebuck brought forward a motion declaring the authority of the House of Commons weakened by the Government entering upon a war with Persia without laying papers before Parliament, and expressing strong reprobation of this proceeding. This was rejected after two nights' discussion by a majority of 352 against 38.

There were two subjects that always ruffled the temper of Lord Palmerston—the Suez Canal and the Empire of Brazil. It was Mr. Roebuck's fate to approach both of these at times while Palmerston was leader of the House of Commons. In the case of the Suez Canal, the member for Sheffield foresaw the immense advantage that would accrue to this country if that project were carried out, and he urged that it would be wise for England at least to look favourably upon it.

Palmerston would have nothing to do with it, and on June 1, 1858, Mr. Roebuck brought forward a motion censuring opposition to the scheme. This was rejected by 290 to 62.

The abolition of the office of Lord-Lieutenant of Ireland had long been advocated by Mr. Roebuck. In 1850 he had spoken in support of a Bill introduced by Lord John Russell for that purpose.   In July, 1857, he himself brought forward a motion, and one of the main arguments against it being founded on the fact that there was no proposal to substitute anything for the abolished viceroyalty, in the following year he repeated the proposition, including in it the creation of an Irish Secretary of State.   But the Irish members themselves were the strongest protestors against the change. Mr. H. Grattan (Meath) had opposed the Government Bill in 1850, and Mr. McCullagh Torrens carried the previous question against Mr. Roebuck's motions by large majorities.

# CHAPTER XXIII.

## "TEAR 'EM." 1857–1859.

AFTER the General Election of 1857, Lord Palmerston seemed
to be secure of an indefinite lease of power. But the Orsini
conspiracy had the result of entirely upsetting this anticipation, and in February, 1858, the English Ministry was
swept away by the tide of indignation caused by what
Mr. Roebuck called "the degradation and humiliation"
of Lord Palmerston's proposal—in presence of irritating
braggadocio of the French colonels, and the threats and
dictations of the French emperor, who allowed the *Moniteur*
to call this country a den of assassins—to enact that a
conspiracy in England to commit murder abroad should be
punishable like a conspiracy to commit murder at home.*

---

\* "Roebuck is himself again. Of course he looks older than he did before
his illness. His hair is thinned and grey, his features are sharper and his
shoulders are rounder; but all this may be traced to age, for he is fifty-seven.
The sickness under which the honourable member so long languished appears
to be entirely gone. He walks now without support; his voice rings through
the House as it used to do when he was the pet Radical member for Bath,
and his action is just as dramatic as it was a dozen years ago. . . . Amongst
the circumlocutionist trash, which is now the fashion of the House, it is
refreshing occasionally to listen to the direct, manly, vigorous denunciations
of the olden time. He hits hard—no doubt harder than is necessary,—and
his asperity of language, intensified into an appearance of malignity by the
tones of his voice, his scornful looks, and his emphatic action, we could sometimes wish to be a little softened down; but he tells plain truths which need
to be told, and is the able organ in the House of feelings and opinions held
by a large portion of the community which ought to have utterance. The
conduct of Louis Napoleon . . . was a fine theme for Mr. Roebuck, and it
was capital fun to hear him in his unadorned, but biting eloquence, denounce

The Earl of Derby thereupon entered upon a brief tenure of office.

The session was, indeed, one in which foreign affairs were prominent. There was the excitement caused by the capture of the *Cagliari* by Neapolitan cruisers, and the imprisonment of the English engineers. Mr. Roebuck "would have sent a three-decker to Naples within cannon-shot of the royal palace." There was Mr. Gladstone's motion in championship of the national claims of the people of Wallachia and Moldavia, which Mr. Roebuck supported;* and there were hot debates on the expediency of discontinuing the practice of authorizing the British squadron for suppressing the slave trade, to visit and search vessels under foreign flags. The fall of Palmerston's government had put an end to their Bill for transferring India from the Company to the Crown, and a new measure, introduced by Mr. Disraeli, met with so little favour that procedure by resolutions was resorted to, and on these yet a third Bill was framed. This ultimately became law. Mr. Roebuck was throughout resolute in his resistance to the proposal to set up and irresponsible council to aid an advise the Secretary of State. Acknowledging on one occasion the certainty that there would be an immense majority against him on this point, he said—

But that to me is no new thing. I have brought forward many propositions which were at first rejected, but afterwards became the creed of the House. Some years ago I contended for a particular course being followed in our colonial policy, and I was always out-voted, but the time came when that which had been

the quondam refugee, and to see the dismay on the faces of ministers." ("The Inner Life of the House of Commons," by William White, vol. i. pp. 38, 39.)

* Mr. Roebuck was constantly consulted during the negotiations for forming the two Danubian Principalities into the State of Roumania, the intermediary being M. Demetrius Bratiano, brother of one of the new state's first ministers. An early act by Roumania was to confer citizenship upon Mr. Roebuck and Mr. Gladstone, in graceful recognition of their efforts for her welfare. Lord Brougham also took great interest in the same subject.

so often rejected, almost with scorn, became the creed of the Colonial Minister.

Mr. Gladstone himself made handsome acknowledgment of Mr. Roebuck's services in this respect. In a speech on a motion of Mr. Roebuck's against a renewal of the expiring privileges of the Hudson's Bay Company, he referred to the member for Sheffield as a veteran in these matters. "It is a fact," he said, "upon which he has a right to reflect with gratification, that upon this subject and other questions relating to our policy in British North America, he has frequently been the expositor of truths at an early date which, although not at once acknowledged, have subsequently obtained complete recognition."

The eloquence and lofty standard of national morality proclaimed in the speech in which Mr. Roebuck ranged himself on the side of the Government in defeating the attack on Lord Ellenborough for his censure of Lord Canning's proclamation in connection with the confiscation of Oude (May 17, 1858), elicited the warm admiration of M. de Montalembert. In a spirited description of the debate, the eminent Frenchman attributed the collapse of the Opposition in a large measure to Mr. Roebuck, who, he said, "lifted himself far above the vulgar preoccupations of personal and national politics." Up to the time when Roebuck spoke, "no one had as yet entered upon the question with so much frankness; no one had as yet marked so clearly the importance of the question, the sacred character of the principles involved, and the danger of subordinating these to the interest of party." Mr. Roebuck had said—

It is for us now to decide whether this immense Empire shall be governed according to the principles of honour and virtue, or with the sole end of increasing the power of England. I am an Englishman, but there are things which to me are more sacred and greater than the greatness of England, and among these things are the progress of mankind in instruction and in the practice of virtue and honour. . . . There is a way of making our Empire lawful, and there is only one—it is to labour for the happiness of the people we govern ; and the first condition of this happiness is to be indulgent and merciful.

Mr. Roebuck ended the session by stoutly opposing, and fighting sedulously in committee, the Corrupt Practices Act Continuation Bill. A more mischievous Bill he had never seen, for it struck a deadly blow at all purity of election by making return to that House a mere matter of personal ambition, and placing individual aggrandisement before public duty. By permitting the conveyance of voters to the poll at the candidate's expense, and by similar provisions, it was made a Bill for the admission of the rich and the exclusion of the poor.

In this year Mr. Roebuck obtained for himself the name of " Tear 'em," which, taking greatly the public fancy, as hitting the nail exactly on the head, and equally lending itself to use whether in praise or in blame, stuck to him through life. It was at the Sheffield Cutlers' feast in September that Mr. Roebuck applied to himself the designation of the faithful watchdog in " Guy Mannering." He had been visiting the fortifications at Cherbourg, and he came back full of warnings about the national danger caused by the " standing menace " in " the waters of a despot."

In the same autumn Mr. Roebuck visited Ireland in connection with a scheme for developing Galway into a great harbour as the head-quarters of a line of trans-Atlantic packets. In a speech at a Galway banquet, Mr. Roebuck, after some eulogistic references to Daniel O'Connell, said his own object had ever been to complete the union between the two peoples. The people of England deserved well of, because they meant well to, the people of Ireland. He continued—

I believe, from the bottom of my heart, that if there be anything disagreeable to Ireland, you have only to make your statements of grievance to the English House of Commons, in order to be attended to. Let the clergy employ their power for the union of the two countries, to make Irishmen men of the United Kingdom. There can be no hope for England or Ireland without the perfect union of the two countries. If you wish for justice, send us men as your representatives who can tell what you desire. Send such men as we can listen to, and who can command respect and attention, and I promise you that every word they utter in your name will find a ready response in the English House of Commons. From my knowledge of that House I can say with truth that the people of Ireland have no better friends than the members of the English House of Commons, who all wish you well.

### To Mrs. Roebuck.

*Dublin, Wednesday, October,* 1858.—I met last Sunday with Whiteside,* who wanted me to stay some days with him here. I consented, and shall stay till Monday. We had grand doings at Galway, where my speech caused an excitement, and raised the ire of an Irish Yankee. I dined on Sunday with Lord Naas.† To-day I meet Walpole. Lord Eglinton invited me to dinner on Tuesday, but as that was our great day at Galway, I was obliged to decline. I have many things to tell you, but you know from experience I am not a good gossip, and cannot write a letter of news. Galway is but a mean place, but I intend that in our time it shall rival Liverpool. One of the most interesting persons I have met is "the ubiquitous Father Daly"—a priest very unlike a priest, who made friends at once with me. Everybody is exceedingly kind.

### The Dean of Elphin to Mr. Roebuck.

*Deanery, Elphin, Ireland, October* 15, 1858.—As a minister of the gospel, as an Irishman, a British subject and a Christian, I beg to thank you for your speech at Galway, and to express the pleasure with which I read the report of it. Let Englishmen of ability, of enlarged views, of philanthropic spirit, continue to come among us and to preach "peace and good will" from their country to ours. Let them stimulate us to industry, self-reliance, and progress, and exhort us to charity, and you may rest assured their labour of love will not be in vain. . . . Let us have a

* Right Hon. James Whiteside, M.P. for Dublin University.
† Sixth Lord Mayo.

T

united Empire, abolish all institutions which are symbols of separation ; let us have good government in Ireland, free from the oscillations caused by Castle intrigue or clique influence, and we shall soon cease to "give to party what was meant for man." Ireland will arise to a real freedom from the thraldom in which centuries of misrule have bound her. A brighter day has dawned, and statesmen of all parties seem to have opened their eyes to the truth that no union can be secure or lasting which is not based on community of interests, and a similarity of object and pursuit. Pardon me, sir, for troubling you with the accompanying paper. I wish, in trespassing on you with these observations, to prove to you that I am no convert to the views I profess. It is true that persons in my profession who have uniformly endeavoured to carry these principles into effect have had, hitherto, little to encourage them, except the consciousness of rectitude, and the progress of their principles towards ultimate, and I trust not distant, triumph. The favour of the State, whether Lord Palmerston or Lord Derby rules, is reserved for the repenting political sinner.—I am, etc., WILLIAM WARBURTON, Dean of Elphin.

*The same to the same.*

*November* 7, 1858.—. . . If the legislature will only continue its encouragements to education, and increase them, the want of progress will be stimulated. . . . I believe that if members of Parliament were deprived of all patronage, it would be better for them as well as for the public, and they would retain a greater number of friends and make fewer enemies than they do at present. . . . I believe that a great acceleration of progress has been gained during the last session, and I am persuaded that public opinion in England is irresistible, and that, rightly directed, it will carry all parties forward in the direction of reform and improvement, and that in a few years more good will have been effected than the most sanguine reformers a few years since could have hoped for in their days.—Yours very faithfully, WILLIAM WARBURTON.

Mr. Roebuck's reception, when next he went down to address his constituents, is described in the following letter. As to Reform, he devoted himself to establishing its necessity and defining its limits, explaining the methods of extension and redistribution which he thought wise and practicable. But the remarkable part of his speech was his warning that domestic policy was in danger of being postponed by foreign complications, and a renewal of his keen denunciation of the Emperor of the French. The jealousy of despotic and tyrannical Europe was, he protested, a danger to isolated England. Her alliances ought to be with freedom, not with despotism.

I have no faith in a man who is perjured to his lips. I recollect, when at Cherbourg, seeing the Emperor of the French visit the Queen of England ; . . . but when I saw his perjured lips upon her hallowed cheek, my blood rushed back to my heart to think of that holy and good creature being defiled by the lips of a perjured despot. . . . Depend upon it, no alliance with foulness can be made without foulness attaching to the ally ; and I say at once that, rather than be the ally of a despot like Louis Napoleon, I would at once break with him and be England alone. For, so being, we can withstand all his anger and all his power ; but you must support your Government in that great move. If you do that we need not fear, though the world stand in arms against us.

### To Mrs. Roebuck.

*Sheffield, January* 14, 1859.—I write simply to say that I am very well, and that to-morrow I go to Leeds. I have not seen the *Times*, so I don't know whether you have learned the history of our doings yesterday. The true story of those doings will, however, never be known. We had a meeting at the Town Hall, and, just as I began to speak, a cry was raised of " Adjourn to the Surrey Music Hall " !—the fact being that Y[oudan] the proprietor, having got into a great scrape, wished to get some popularity by having us at his room. The adjournment was opposed by an overwhelming majority of the meeting. Still, the twenty or thirty persons who raised the cry, and whom I believe to have been hired for the purpose, kept up such a riot as to render it impossible to go on with the meeting, and I took up my hat and departed. This step startled the meeting. The mayor, who presided, dissolved the meeting, and there seemed an end of the whole affair. Our committee, however, met at the Royal Hotel opposite, and it was resolved to go at once to the Temperance Hall, thus defeating the object of the rioters. So we went, and found a crowded room and a very well-disposed audience. Our meeting eventually went off very well, though the row-dow drove out of my head many things which I wished to say. Still, I think my say will do good.

*Leeds, January* 17, 1859.—I am amused by the various criticisms upon my speech at Sheffield. Apparently the world generally has been taken by surprise. I heard that the Harewood family expressed themselves as entirely agreeing with me, especially in what I said about Louis Napoleon. This acquiescence seems general, but the newspaper people are all afraid of saying aye to me on that score, though the *Times* does so in reality. It complains under its breath of my hard language, seeming to forget that it has said things quite as strong. A Manchester paper is particularly hurt by my allusion to the queen, "though we all thought and felt as Mr. R. describes; but, then," etc. The thoughts I gave expression to were new, but to me old, and the argument was of such a sort that they cannot answer it; so they throw all attempt to answer overboard, and simply criticize myself. But on this head they are rather complimentary than otherwise.

The transactions in connection with Parliamentary Reform, opening with the fancy Franchise Bill, introduced by Mr. Disraeli on behalf of the Derby Ministry, on February 28, 1859, led Mr. Roebuck into attitudes which began a strain upon his relations with his chief supporters in Sheffield, destined, ten years after, to reach the breaking-point. Mr. Roebuck's opposition to the Government proposals was, at first, uncompromising and emphatic. In the following memorandum, he records the effect upon himself of Mr. Disraeli's statement, and his communications with Lord John Russell on the subject :—

"What do you intend to do?" said Lord John Russell to me, when Mr. Disraeli had finished his exposition of the reform measure proposed by Lord Derby's cabinet. "Oppose the measure at once," I answered. "The move is not one in advance, it is retrograde, and the measure must at once be destroyed. I shall denounce it directly." "Then I will do so," said the noble lord; and thereupon he rose, and in strong, good set phrase declared against the measure. I did the same.* The second reading was appointed for that day three weeks. This was on Monday. On the next Wednesday I dined with Lord John. After dinner, I said to Baron Rothschild, who sat next me, "I wish you would ask Lord John what he intends to do respecting the proposed measure of reform." Rothschild, addressing Lord John, said, "Roebuck wants to know what you are going to do respecting the proposed reform." I observed, "This was not the mode in which I wished you would ask the question. But since you have put it in my name, I will plainly state to Lord John what I think upon the subject, and submit to him a course of conduct for him to pursue, which I believe will meet the approbation of the great majority of the Liberal party. Lord John and the world know my opinion of the proposed measure. Further, I believe that the proper mode for us to pursue is at once to meet the measure by a direct negative; and therefore, if Lord John will move that it be . read a second time that day six months, I am sure he will be followed by the whole Liberal party, for we consider him not merely the father, but the grandfather of reform." It was therefore agreed that Lord John should make the motion, and that, on the coming Monday week, the Liberal party should be called together by Lord John, at the Thatched House Tavern, in order that they might be told what he intended to do. Soon after this was all definitely arranged, we separated. Days went past, but no circulars appeared calling us together. Rumours were afloat that Lord John had changed his mind, and the papers reported that he had consulted the leading members of the Palmerston party as to the course he should pursue, and that, by their advice, he had determined his line of conduct. I spoke to Mr. Forster, member for Walsall, asking him if he knew anything of the matter. His answer was, "Oh yes; the arrangement we made at Lord John's has been

---

* The Bill, said Mr. Roebuck, would not give one iota of power to the working classes. It was a measure of disfranchisement, not of enfranchisement. Its object was to enhance the power of the landed interest in Parliament. "We have given the Government a generous support," he exclaimed; "and this is the reward."

entirely changed.  He has consulted Charles Wood, and George Grey, and Sir James Graham, and he will give notice of a resolution to be moved by him on the second reading." Learning this, I determined to speak to Lord John, thinking the whole proceeding very much after his old insolent style.  I went into the House, and so soon as he seated himself, I said to him, "Lord John, is it true, as stated by the papers, that you have taken counsel with Charles Wood, George Grey, and Labouchere, as to what you are to do with respect to the Government reform measure ? Before you answer me, however, I would assure you that, if you are to receive your inspirations from that bench "—pointing to the Opposition bench—"you may give up all hopes of leading the men below the gangway.  I can only speak of others, as believing what they will do.  I do not presume to speak in anybody's name, but I can speak for myself ; and I beg frankly to state to you, that I never intend to allow those gentlemen to act as my leaders again."  "Why, you would not," said he, "throw them all overboard ?"  "There is one, and only one, under whom I would act, and that is George Lewis.  As for all the rest, they are false and imbecile."  His only answer was a short laugh of surprise—" Eh, eh ! "

Mr. Roebuck's dissatisfaction with Lord John Russell's conduct in putting on the books a resolution which would, he contended, be fatal to any chance of passing a Reform Bill that year, instead of moving resolutions on which a bill could be framed, was expressed in the House.  While, on the motion for second reading, renewing his declaration that the Government measure would give no satisfaction to the working classes, whom it failed to enfranchise, he expressed the view that it was hopeless to look for reform at the hands of Palmerston and Russell.  More, he declared, could be got from a weak Tory Government, in touch with the House of Lords, than from the Liberals.  But his antagonism to the bill as brought in remained unabated. The Government appealed to the country, and Mr. Roebuck appeared before his constituents for re-election with the remark : " We are here because we would not give our sanction to a sham." He and his colleague, Mr. Hadfield, were returned without opposition. This was at the end of April (1859). In May he attended a meeting at Milford Haven to advocate that Galway Packet Scheme already mentioned, to which the Derby Government, aiming to secure Irish support, had granted a subsidy. This was openly called "The Galway Job." It was then that Mr. Roebuck first gave token of a new influence. That Reform Bill which had been "retrograde" in February and "a sham" in April, was found in May to indicate a true reforming spirit on the part of its authors. In his speech at Milford he said—

On June 7, the House of Commons would have to choose whether the country should have Lord Derby or Lord Palmerston for Prime Minister. In what camp should he be ? In the camp of the people of England, and that camp, he sincerely believed, would be opposed to Lord Palmerston. It was a miserable contingency—whichever side was uppermost, mischief must come, but he believed that as the greater mischief would accrue from changing the administration, Parliament would prevent such a change. As an independent member his consideration was for England, and for England's sake he said, don't choose Lord Palmerston, who is false and hollow, and the great enemy of the Liberal party. Lord Palmerston's appearance as First Minister would be throughout the continent as a torch of war.

And in the same speech, Mr. Roebuck sowed the seeds of future trouble by speaking of Italy's struggle for liberty as likely, at best, to result in a change of masters, and by putting himself in antagonism to the public enthusiasm aroused for Kossuth.

Again, in June, when a meeting was held at Willis's Rooms to reunite the Liberal party in view of the Parliamentary campaign, Mr. Roebuck startled his auditors by asking " how, if the Government would promise a thorough Reform Bill, the Liberals could oppose them ? " He could not, he said, support Lord Palmerston, who had truckled to France and dragged the country through the mire; and could only form a feeble and divided administration. When Parliament met, Lord Hartington proposed a vote of " no-confidence " on the Address; and Mr. Roebuck spoke and voted against that change of Government which he had before described as the first duty of the new Parliament. He said the effect would be to let in a Government in which he should have less confidence; that to keep Lord Derby's Ministry in office would make them Reformers in spite of themselves, and would be the way to get a Reform Bill. And in this confidence that the Tories would be more sincere Reformers than the Liberals, Mr. Roebuck gave his vote with the minority that vainly endeavoured to keep them in office.

*To William Fisher (Sheffield).*

*June* 10, 1859.—If what I said at Milford were new, if the expressions I then used were used by me for the first time, I could understand the surprise and anger expressed; but the language I held on that occasion I have often held before, and my opinion of Lord Palmerston has been openly and constantly avowed. No man has rendered Lord Palmerston greater service than I, and this, too, in spite of having spoken very strongly against him. I thought that my first judgment respecting him was rendered incorrect by his subsequent conduct; but further experience only confirmed my first opinion, and now I believe that his advent to power would be a great calamity to England. Now, am I, holding this opinion, so far to forget my duty to my country as not to act on this opinion, because certain hungry people may be kept out of office in consequence of my acts? I should indeed be base and unworthy did I yield, and run contrary to my own judgment. The hired press accuses me of corruption. What have I gained through life? What will this conduct bring me? Obloquy, the disapprobation of my dearest friends, and no personal advantage whatever. I live retired. I keep aloof from many associations that would give me great pleasure, in order that I may maintain my own proud independence. And yet with all this, having dwelt in the very midst of every temptation for a quarter of a century; having borne as much suffering as has fallen to the lot of most men, and having never turned to the right hand or to the left, I am now, when age and hard work have told on me, when I have spent my best years and my strength in the service of my country, I am foully accused of corruption, and the Whig organs are hounded on to abuse and vilify me. And it is required of me that I should hold my peace and bow my head, as if I acknowledged the justice of this vituperation; but they little know me, who expect that this is the course that I shall pursue. They shall find that they have hunted a tiger when they believed they were chasing a hare; and to my country I appeal with confidence. A short time and my judgment will be confirmed. This will not be the first time that to my opinion the world has come, having at the outset deemed me so wrong as to think me mad. If my constituents think me utterly wrong, and unworthy to be their representative, let them say so; to their judgment I am prepared at once to bow; the time will be short which will suffice for them to learn how right were my judgments, how wrong their own. . . . I am now not acting under the influence of strange personal prejudices. I have carefully watched Lord Palmerston for thirty years, and I feel certain that he is utterly unfit to be the leader of England.

### To an American Correspondent.

*Yarmouth, Isle of Wight, September* 9, 1859.— . . . I should have liked much to talk over with you the relations that do, and those that ought to, exist between the United States and England. There is much required to be done to make the reciprocal feelings on both sides of the Atlantic such as they ought to be. But do not suppose that there exists in England any prejudice against the United States. There may be some fools and bigoted people who still retain the feelings that many of our forefathers felt. But all the enlightened men, and the educated classes generally, have very kindly feelings towards those whom we always call our brethren on the other side of the water. These kind feelings I believe to be returned by the genuine Americans. You have, however, a very active class, whom the injustice of England has sent among you—I mean the Irish and their descendants—who hate the very name of England. These men are in possession very generally of the press in America; they are active and they are noisy, and they give a tone to your periodical press that misleads English people. I hope, however, the growing intercourse between the two peoples, and their growing intelligence, are daily rubbing down asperities, and that we shall be, what we ought to be as the only free people on the earth, united heart and hand against despotism and bad government, wherever found.

# CHAPTER XXIV

AT the close of 1859, and in the opening days of 1860, we
find Mr. Roebuck among his old constituents at Bath, and
addressing the Mechanics' Institutes of Middlesborough
and Sheffield on his favourite theme of the education of
the working classes.  In Parliament, Mr. Roebuck's con-
tribution to the discussions on the commercial treaty with
France was a protest against truckling to Napoleon III.,
by agreeing to that treaty without having previously
expressed condemnation of the dishonourable conduct of
the Emperor in regard to the annexation of Savoy.

On a Bill regulating Bleaching and Dye Works, Mr.
Roebuck delivered a speech which made a profound impression.  Admitting that the fears under which he formerly
opposed Lord Ashley's factory legislation, had been shown
by the working of the Acts to be unfounded, he pleaded
powerfully for the suppression of evils inflicted on women
and children, which, as recorded before a Parliamentary
committee, made his blood creep.  "Think," he said, after
quoting from the evidence—

Think of the poor child, and compare her work with ours.
We complain of the labours which we undergo, but as compared
with our life here, it is the life of the damned. . . . I ask you, the
gentlemen of England, if you will bear this ?  I hear great talk

of humanity—lip humanity—about the American slave.   No
man can view with more indignation than I do the horrible condition of the black in America ; but I cannot help regarding with
at least equal indignation the condition of the white slave in
England. . . . Any one of our daughters might have been a
factory girl ; and is there any man present with any feeling for
his child who could think of her working, almost without cessa-
tion, for thirty-seven hours ?   Think of her tender years ; think
of her delicate little hands.   I have it in this book that children's
hands are often blistered, and the skin torn off their feet, and
yet they are thus obliged to work, the persons who overlook
them being sometimes forced to keep them awake by beating on
the table with large boards.   For God's sake, then, I say, don't
let us listen to the honourable gentleman !   I appeal to you as
men ; I appeal to you as fathers ; I appeal to you as brothers ; and
I ask you, for God's sake, not to be participants in this horrible
cruelty.   The weak and the miserable appeal to you now for
compassion and for aid ; and I, their humble advocate, also appeal
to you in perfect confidence that you will listen to their prayer,
and will pass this measure for their relief.

It is recorded that the House was deeply moved by
what was described as one of the most marvellous triumphs
of rhetoric ever achieved within those walls.

If oratory is to be judged by the effect it produces in moving
men's hearts and minds, this speech must ever be remembered as
the most wonderful piece of oratory of modern times.   Mr. Roebuck was under an inspiration ; and though there was still the
old mannerism which we know so well—still the same short and
vigorous sentences, and the same tones, yet on this occasion they
were inspired with a life of passion and feeling that ran through
the House from heart to heart and mind to mind like an electric
current, until all the members were moved as trees of the wood
are moved by the wind.   There was little cheering of the rapturous
sort ; for when the House is deeply moved it does not break out
into vociferous cheers.   Every man's eyes were riveted on the
speaker ; and when, in suppressed tones and with impressive
action, he described these poor people as living the life of "the
damned," there was a silence as of the grave, broken at the end

of the sentence by what the reporters call "cheers," but which were more like deep sighs than cheers. Almost immediately after Roebuck sat down the House divided ; and to the astonishment of the poor bleachers and the dismay of the masters, there were, for the second reading of the Bill, 236 ; against it, only 39.

*The Earl of Shaftesbury to J. A. Roebuck.*

24, *Grosvenor Square, March* 22, 1860.—It is impossible that I should refrain from thanking you for your heart-stirring speech of last night. The wretched girls and women of the bleach works will owe you, and will pay, a deep debt of gratitude. God grant that the issue of this movement may be (and who can doubt it ?) as happy and successful as that on behalf of the factory population. Thousands of these females, who would otherwise have been mere specimens of degradation and suffer- ing, are now fulfilling the duties, the honours, and the joys of exemplary daughters, wives, and mothers. And who have been injured ? The trade has increased tenfold ; the profits of the mill-owners. approach to the fabulous ; wages are raised ; educa- tion is extended ; the people are satisfied ; the masters admit the moral, physical, and financial improvement of all classes ; and a good understanding (the object I ever had in view) prevails between employers and employed. Once more let me say that eloquence and feeling were never better applied than in your speech yesterday.

Mr. Roebuck's letter in reply is published in Mr. Hodder's "Life of the Earl of Shaftesbury," vol. ii. p. 205. But Lord Shaftesbury's biographer is scarcely justified in calling Mr. Roebuck's speech a "recantation." For, while deprecating interference with adult labour, as long ago as 1843, he had earnestly advocated placing restrictions on the employment of children of tender years.[*]

In the autumn of 1860, Mr. Roebuck visited Austria, where changes in the direction of giving a constitutional and representative Government to a hitherto despotic Empire, were in progress. The spectacle, on the one hand, of a courageous and liberal-minded Emperor advancing his

* *Ante,* p. 148, chap. xiii.

people in freedom; on the other, of the people rising to the use of that freedom, through many difficulties, in a quiet and practical manner, greatly interested the old political Reformer.

He exerted himself in strenuous advocacy of an Anglo-Austrian Alliance, which, in his view, would be irresistible in Europe, while immensely promoting the mutual advantage of the two countries. He urged this upon Count Apponyi in the following elaborate paper :—

*J. A. Roebuck to Count Apponyi.*

According to my promise, I put upon paper the substance of what I stated to you during our conversation of last Monday. The subjects upon which I spoke to you were—

1. The conduct which Austria should pursue, with respect to the Zol-Verein, and her foreign commerce generally ; and

2. On the navigation of the Elbe.

I stated that what I was going to say, was in the character of a European statesman, and not as an Englishman merely. I assumed, however, that the interests of Europe and England were identical ; that what tended to the benefit of England, tended to the benefit of the world ; and that what was for the advantage of mankind was also beneficial to England. A large assumption, I allowed, but I believed a correct one.

Before speaking of the conduct to be pursued by Austria, I described what I conceived to be the position and policy of Prussia. At the present moment Prussia, it appeared to me, had two opposing purposes in view. The one was to constitute herself the head of Germany, the *head* of the state—in fact, wishing to be, in place of King of Prussia, Emperor of Germany ; the other was to relax her present protective provisions respecting Foreign Trade ; and for that purpose to enter into a commercial treaty with France. In order to attain the first of these objects she has allied herself with those states who have united to form the Zol-Verein and adopted their protective policy. By this means, she hoped to persuade these states that she was intensely German—thus to acquire power over them, and induce them eventually to grant her the headship of the German people. But as to relax her trade provisions is to run counter to the feelings of these states, she dares not enter into a commercial treaty with France; and when the time comes for renewing the compact of the Zol-Verein in 1865, she will adhere to that compact, and will not enter into any commercial treaty hostile or opposed to the wishes of the Zol-Verein. But the states of the Zol-Verein wish for, and hope to obtain, the adhesion of Austria to their compact. Prussia, indeed, does not wish this adhesion. The power rival to herself in Germany is Austria, and she desires to constitute herself the one German leader. Now, in these circumstances, would it be the wisest course for Austria to pursue, to unite with the Zol-Verein, and thus combat directly with Prussia, and struggle with her openly for the German headship? My answer to this question is decidedly in the negative, because I believe a far more effective proceeding lies open before her; one which will not merely make her the leading power in Germany, but raise her greatly in the opinion of the world at large, and place her firmly amongst the first and most powerful nations of Europe.

I assume that Austria has frankly and honestly entered upon a constitutional career; that the constitution granted by the Emperor is a real constitution; that the solemn promise he has made, he will loyally and with all honour maintain. If the people generally of the Austrian Empire can be induced to believe this, Austria will be a united Empire, and, being united, will exercise a most important influence in Europe, both politically and morally. Now, in order to lead to this most desirable result, England and England's opinion may be made a most efficient instrument. Once make the people of England believe that Austria, instead of being the leader of the despotic powers of Europe, was now really a constitutional power, that her people were a free people, governing themselves, and ruled by law, and not by one man's will,—and then the friendship and warm sympathy of the people of England would be enlisted on the side of Austria. It is felt here that Austria has no interests hostile to England. We have seen her acting with us loyally in times of great danger and difficulty; and we hold her existence and prosperity to be requisite as a counterpoise to the other powers which are not friendly, whatever may be the smoothness of their professions. If once the undoubting good will and good opinion of England could be gained for Austria, her internal difficulties would quickly cease. The

discontent of the so-called Liberal party among her people, now
fostered and maintained by the noisy press of England, would no
longer receive support, and would soon die out; the sentimental
talk now so prevalent among us would be laughed at, and put
an end to by scorn and contempt, and Austria and England,
shoulder to shoulder, would govern the opinions and the policy of
Europe.    And this brings me to the practical conclusion from this
long preamble.    What can Austria do to convince the people of
England that she is earnest?    I know not whether you have
remarked that, though we exercise a mighty, and I will say a
beneficial influence upon all the affairs of Europe, there is a marked
hate of everything English in the minds of most of the rulers of
Europe.    Nowhere is this more shown, in spite of all alliances,
than in Prussia.    This dislike, this hate, is caused by two things—
our freedom, and our success.    Our success is also twofold; we
have been successful in war, but we have been and are successful
in commerce.    Now, despotic governors hate our freedom; and
the people of Europe under the influence of despotism and
ignorance hate our commercial success.    In no country has this
feeling been more manifest than in Germany.    The legislation of
the Zol-Verein has been more hostile, and directly hostile, to
England than has been that of France, and an Englishman is
treated with far more courtesy in France than he is in Germany.
The adhesion of Austria to the Zol-Verein would lead England to
believe that she participated in those feelings which distinguish
that body, and our belief that [they were] caused by our commercial success and our freedom would be invincible.    And this
being so, to hope that our people would forget the past history of
Austria, and believe that she had begun a new career of freedom,
would indeed be idle and illusory.    But if Austria would free
herself from commercial, as she has done from political, despotism;
if she would throw her ports and country open to English
commerce; if she would benefit her own people by allowing our
manufacturers and merchants to have free access to them, she
would do much to conciliate our good will, and convince us that
she was really free, and really bent upon making her people
happy, and furthering good will and peace among mankind.
Here, then, comes my practical conclusion—one to which I would
invite the serious attention of the statesmen of your country.    It
is not to the petty clerks, not to the narrow-minded men of

office, that I address myself. These men have too long swayed the destinies of mankind, but now I hope a new era has begun. I hope that men of true intelligence are henceforth to govern among you ; that your leaders will raise their minds to the height of their position ; and that we shall have large and benevolent principles guiding their conduct, instead of wretched rules framed by narrow ignorance. The practical conclusion to which I come is : Instead of joining the Zol-Verein, let Austria enter into a liberal commercial treaty with England. Let her make Trieste the rival of Marseilles. Let her attract commerce up the Adriatic, and let her vast resources find an outlet by means of English enterprise and capital. Let it be sent to every quarter of the globe, and let her take her true position among the nations of the world ; and let her be, as she ought by her capabilities to be, the great leading, guiding continental power.

It unluckily happened that Mr. Roebuck's visit to Vienna was contemporaneous with efforts on the part of the Lever group to obtain certain shipping, or banking, or railway concessions from the Austrian Government. An inquiry before a Parliamentary committee, and actions in the law courts, had thrown much light on the devious ways of the Galway Packet Company. So far as Mr. Roebuck was concerned, the facts only redounded to his honour. Attracted by the advantages accruing to Ireland through establishing direct steam communication between Galway and the United States, he had thrown himself warmly into the scheme of Mr. John Orrell Lever and Father Daly, and had allowed himself to be made a provisional Director of the Galway Company. But speedily finding that this brought him into association with men whose ways were not his ways, and who were actuated by motives far different from his own, he washed his hands of the whole transaction. The promoters had reserved £10,000 in paid-up shares for distribution among themselves. Mr. Roebuck not only refused to receive the proportion offered to him, but he retired from the provisional Board, and never became a Director of the Company as

U

finally constituted. He had, however, been so perilously near the flame that, until his upright conduct was fully and authoritatively vindicated, he for a time suffered somewhat in popular estimation by the association of his name with a venture that speedily got into ill favour; and his companionship with Mr. Lever, at Galway, and Milford, and Bolton, and Vienna, gave colour to suspicion, more or less openly expressed, both in Parliament and outside. It was further unfortunate that, through Lever's influence, Mr. Roebuck became connected with various ill-starred banking enterprises which, throughout some years, brought upon him much anxiety and annoyance.

His expressed admiration for Austria exposed him to misapprehension of another kind. It was not his encouragement of Austrian reachings towards constitutional government that alarmed Liberals. What aroused their disapprobation was the fact that this sympathy led him into a defence of Austria's retention of her Italian possessions. For it has to be remembered that at this time the struggle for Italian unity was exciting the intense sympathy of the English people. With pained disfavour they had watched the cession of Savoy and Nice to France, but this shock had been largely forgotten in the enthusiasm caused by Garibaldi's overthrow of the Neapolitan Government, and the assumption by Victor Emmanuel of the title of King of Italy. Austria's occupation of Venetia stood menacingly opposed to "Italy for the Italians;" and when Mr. Roebuck, in the House of Commons, boldly declared it to be England's duty to prevent the expulsion of Austria, he ran counter to national opinion, and scandalized many of his most loyal admirers. It is easy to see now that, amid the excitements of the moment, the sentences in which Mr. Roebuck advocated the retention by Austria of her Italian possessions, stood out in such relief as to rivet public attention, and to blind men's eyes to the broad argument of which they were the mere setting. That argument was based upon the distrust, so long preached by Mr. Roebuck, of France and its Emperor. French troops were in occupation of Rome, and thus, even if Austria were out of the way, Mr. Roebuck maintained that France rendered Italian unity impossible. The presence of Austria in Venetia was, he insisted, an essential counterpoise to France, Austria presenting a valuable obstacle to the aggrandizing designs of Napoleon—an obstacle all the more formidable because of the growth of enlightenment and constitutional government under Francis Joseph. By the public at large, however, this contention that Austria was necessary as a counterpoise to prevent the Italian people becoming the vassals of France, was overlooked or derided. What fired the popular indignation was the spectacle of Mr. Roebuck warning the English Government of the danger of the course they were pursuing in endeavouring to exclude Austria from her dominion in Venetia. There was the fact. They would not listen to reasons. " Considering both the interests of England and Italy, I say it is our duty to prevent the expulsion of Austria from Venetia at present." On that sentence, friends and foes alike fastened in angry protest.

Immediately there arose a general cry of remonstrance, nowhere louder than in Mr. Roebuck's own constituency. Although a demand that he should go down to Sheffield to explain a speech which had caused " widespread surprise and regret," proceeded only from a small knot of self-constituted nobodies, calling themselves " the friends of Italian liberty," Mr. Roebuck at once asked the Mayor to convene a public meeting.

*J. A. Roebuck to R. J. Gainsford (Sheffield).*

*March* 28, 1861.—I believe that the outcry raised against me has, in the first place, originated in selfish interest, and next, from ignorance ; and I hope that a plain tale, and what I deem unanswerable arguments, will at once put an end to bare

imputations and to foolish mistakes.   The questions on which I
had to decide were grave, were momentous questions.   I brought
to their decision such abilities as God has given me, and perfect
disinterestedness.   All this I shall be able plainly to show,
and I only ask for a patient hearing.   I think all right-seeing
men will agree with me, and I am sure that all honest men
will acquit me of dishonesty ; for with dishonesty I have been
charged after thirty years of completely gratuitous labour for
the public.

The first meeting, owing to the clamour of those
excluded, and to the crowded discomfort of those admitted,
was broken up in confusion ; but on the following day, in
a larger hall, Mr. Roebuck won a respectful hearing.   It
was a triumph of combined pluck and skill.   The spectacle
of the dauntless veteran, shattered in health, and physically
fragile, unflinchingly facing his accusers, scornfully defying
detraction, and vindicating his integrity before an audience
watchfully unsympathetic, was one that appealed strongly
to Yorkshire hearts.   It may be safely said that the whole
assembly felt pride in the bearing of the old man at bay,
and an almost personal relief in the completeness with which
he brushed away every breath of suspicion on his integrity.
But in endeavouring to make palatable to Italian sympathizers his defence of Austria's continued presence in Italy,
he had a task beyond even his great powers.

The meeting heard him patiently—and retained its
own opinion.   It declared itself perfectly satisfied with
Mr. Roebuck's explanation in reply to the attacks on his
uprightness, asserting its complete confidence in his personal
worth and political integrity.   As to Austria, however, a
resolution was passed which adroitly glossed over the points
of difference, and emphasized those on which both sides
were agreed.   But there was a grimly significant hint in
its expression of " ardent sympathy with the efforts of the
Italians to free their country from internal tyrants and
external domination," and in its hope "that before long

Venetia and Rome may be peacefully united to the Italian kingdom."

Mr. Roebuck's visions, founded on the beginning of Austrian constitutionalism, were subsequently dimmed by the establishment of the dual government of Austria-Hungary. He looked upon this as a source of future weakness, as he held that an empire to be really strong should not have its governing and executive powers divided. His objections to Irish Home Rule were largely based on the same reasons.

*To R. J. Gainsford (Sheffield).*

*October* 30, 1861.—I shall read with much attention, and I have no doubt with instruction also, your article on Hungary. I fear, however, the people of this country are so wilfully blind, that nothing will enlighten them but time and actual experience. That they will be taught their error, I am convinced. In the mean time all I have to do is to bear abuse as best I may.

# CHAPTER XXV.

### FIGHTING WITH WILD BEASTS.  1862–1865.

ALTHOUGH Mr. Roebuck had triumphed over his detractors as to the suspicions excited by the Galway contract, and had beaten down the hostility raised by his tolerance of Austrian dominion in Italy, it would be erroneous to suppose that the old terms of cordiality between himself and influential sections of his constituents had been re-established.  The resolution passed on his Austrian policy was, read between the lines, practically a verdict of "Not guilty—but don't do it again."  The rift within the lute had been temporarily stopped, not permanently healed, and Mr. Roebuck, instead of taking pains to prevent it from widening, seemed rather to seek opportunities for discordantly playing on the cherished convictions of his supporters.  Thus, in one of the many lectures on education, delivered by him at mechanics' and other institutions in different parts of the country, he contrived to introduce words which, rightly or wrongly, were immediately interpreted as a dire insult to the working classes of Sheffield.  This was at Salisbury, on January 16, 1862.  He was contrasting the modes of life and the home surroundings of different classes of society—of the educated man, the mercantile clerk, the agricultural labourer, and the artisan.  And, speaking of the large wages earned by iron-workers, he asked—

How is the life of the man in the north passed, who earns wages of that high character ?  He gets up in the morning and

goes to work.  He comes home, and the first thing he usually
does is to swear at his wife.  Perhaps he beats his children, and
then he caresses his dog.  His whole life is passed in mere
sensual enjoyment ; getting drunk is his chief business in life ;
and when he has got drunk, his next business is to get sober.

A few sentences earlier Mr. Roebuck had said that he was
speaking of that which he had known, and was "thinking
of his constituents in the north," when he described the
working classes as herding together more like animals of
the brute creation than men and women.  In the offence
given by thus speaking of the faults of the worst as if
typical of the whole class, the excellent incitements to
education which Mr. Roebuck's address supplied were forgotten, and hot indignation at the picture thus drawn for
the benefit of the Wiltshire people, of the workmen of
Sheffield, obliterated all other considerations.  Again,
attempts at temperance legislation, such as the Permissive
Bill and Mr. Somes's Sunday Sale of Beer Bill, evoked Mr.
Roebuck's fiercest denunciation.  It was when asking the
House to refuse leave to introduce the latter measure (May
6, 1864) that Mr. Roebuck spoke of Sabbatarians and
teetotallers as "two muddy streams," which, after running
side by side for some time, "had at last united their waters,
and now they formed one foaming, muddy river, which it
was difficult to stem, and very disagreeable to see and to
smell."  "If," he said, "the promoters of the Bill were anything more than canting hypocrites, they would propose a
law for the rich as well as the poor."  He "spat" at a Bill
which was "canting legislation" intended to turn the
nation into a sour, ascetic, hypocritical people.

Of still wider importance, because tending to embroil
England in the great struggle then being waged between
the Northern and Southern States of the Union, was Mr.
Roebuck's attitude towards America, and the language he
used of her.  In August, 1862, he took advantage of a
visit paid by Lord Palmerston to Sheffield to urge on his

lordship immediate recognition of Southern independence. He stigmatized the attempt to reunite the states of America as an immoral proceeding, totally incapable of success. They could, he declared, never be united.   The conduct of the people of the North to this country he described as "insolent and overbearing."   A divided America, he protested, would be a benefit to England.   And an additional sting was given to the following words by the fact of their being uttered in Lord Palmerston's presence—indeed, almost addressed to him personally: "The North will never be our friends.   Of the South you can make friends. They are Englishmen.   They are not the scum and refuse of Europe."   It was reported that Lord Palmerston said of one of Mr. Roebuck's speeches on the recognition of the Confederate States, that it was "a devilish good speech," and just his opinion, but he could not officially say so.

Mr. Roebuck lost no opportunity of using all his influence on the side of the South.   He advocated its cause at meetings of his constituents; in Parliament he moved an address to the Crown praying her Majesty to enter into negotiations with the great Powers of Europe to obtain their co-operation in recognizing the Confederates.   This motion had been preceded by, and was indeed largely based upon, a remarkable transaction.   Mr. Lindsay, member for Sunderland, who had the *entrée* of the Tuileries by reason of having been consulted on navigation matters, accompanied by Mr. Roebuck, had proceeded to Paris, with endeavour to stimulate Napoleon to take active steps towards acknowledging the South.   They were accorded an audience.   The inevitable result of amateur diplomacy followed.   None of the parties to the interview agreed as to what actually took place.   The Emperor disavowed, or declined to be bound by the version Mr. Roebuck gave to the House of Commons of the conversation.   The amazement and amusement with which this mission to the "perjured despot" of a few years ago was received by the general public, was expressed in very pungent sarcasms by speakers like Lord Robert Montagu and Mr. Bright. Lord Palmerston pointed out the embarrassments inevitable upon communicating to the House of Commons matters that had passed between private members and the sovereign of a foreign country; and on his strong representations, Mr. Roebuck reluctantly abandoned his motion.

In 1863 there was a movement in Sheffield to bring into the field a local candidate for the representation of the Borough—Sir John Brown. He had twice filled the office of mayor, and his large share in promoting the industries of the town encouraged those anxious for a change in the representation to put him forward " on commercial grounds only, and not as a political movement." It was, however, pretty well understood that the candidature was directed against Mr. Roebuck. It was with reference to this threatened opposition, and the manner in which it was met by his supporters, that Mr. Roebuck wrote the following letter—

*J. A. Roebuck to Robert Leader (Sheffield).*

*Swanage, September* 21, 1863.—MY DEAR SIR,—I have read both your articles with great pleasure, and much admire the frank and straightforward manner in which you speak of all parties. The amount of knowledge of men and things which is really required to furnish forth an effective and competent politician is very little thought of, or known. In a country like England, and in an assembly like the House of Commons, every act of one who is a portion of the Sovereignty is attended by a terrible responsibility, because it may be fraught with terrible consequences. It may seem a strange thing for me to say; but truly I never speak in the House of Commons without dread and without hesitation. It is not that I am not self-possessed—it is not of myself I am thinking when fear comes upon me. But when I know that every word uttered there resounds throughout the world, and may bring suffering to thousands, then it is that I tremble, and pray for wisdom and sagacity. Looking thus upon the office of a representative of the people before I proposed to assume it, I went through a careful and severe training. I spent my youth in study, and went carefully over the vast fields of political science. And I own that I view with wonder the audacity and rashness of those men who come from other walks of life, without training, without even thought, and take upon themselves the performance of the most arduous duties that a man can assume. After having given hours and days, nay, years, of patient thought and careful inquiry to the formation of an opinion, I find men, upon the mere impulse of the moment, or the suggestions of some passing interest, suddenly forming and vehemently maintaining opinions hostile to mine, and at once branding me as a fool and a knave, because I differ from them. Heaven knows I do not pretend that I am always right—but I do assume that there is a greater chance of my being right than a man who, without pains or study, has formed a conclusion ; and I assume also that the conduct of my life ought to protect me from imputations of baseness or folly—imputations which flippant insolence so easily makes, and which inherent unworthiness so readily suggests. But I fear you will deem me egotistical. Bear with me, however. You hardly know what obloquy he encounters who, as a politician, seeks to serve his country.

*To Mrs. Roebuck.*

*Munich, November* 21, 1863.—You will be surprised at the date, that is as regards the place. —— takes as much care of me as if I were a woman, and determined to remain here to-day, and start to-morrow. I have been again to the picture-galleries, and have come to the conclusion that the pictures are nothing wonderful. We, after the picture-galleries, went to call on Lord Augustus Loftus. We talked politics, and he was very curious to know what I thought of the Emperor N. after my interview with him, and then gave me his thoughts on the present state of things, wanting me to try to influence Austrian politics with respect to Prussia. He said that Austria was greatly in my debt, and that she ought to listen to me. But my belief is that nothing can be done in the sense he wished. From Lord A. L. we went to the Sculpture-Gallery, and to the Dominican Church— the marbles poor, the church tawdry. At Paris we alighted at the Grand Hotel. The first person I met was Gudin, whom I used to see at the house of Frank Mills. He, G., was then a great friend of the Orleans family. Now, he said, " I wish you could stay to see my grand picture of the Emperor Napoleon."

Thus runs the world away.

Although Mr. Roebuck declined (July, 1864) to vote for Mr. Disraeli's motion attacking the Government for its policy on the Schleswig-Holstein question, he impartially indulged in severe criticism at the expense of the leaders of both parties, and strongly assailed Prussia, describing it as a compound of pedagogue, drill-sergeant, and highway-man. His old distrust of Lord Palmerston was changed almost into confidence by contrast with his inveterate dis-belief in Earl Russell, for condemnation of whose foreign policy he could find no words too strong. Lord Palmerston, he said, would have done very differently if rid of his Foreign Secretary. And in the next month, at Sheffield, Mr. Roebuck made a very unusual confession. He acknow-ledged Lord Palmerston's superior wisdom in not acting as he would have had him act towards America and Denmark.

*To William Ibbitt (Sheffield).*

*April* 26, 1864.—I do not think that giving the suffrage to all men of thirty years of age would be any real protection against unworthy persons. If precaution be necessary, something more effective than restriction as to age ought to be found. The more I consider the matter, the more puzzled I become. In order to make the interests of the representatives co-extensive with those of the represented, something very near to universal suffrage is necessary ; but we cannot shut our eyes to the danger resulting from power being placed in the hands of the ignorant. That danger can, I believe, be avoided only by careful and slow proceed-ings. We ought, in my opinion, to take every safe opportunity offered for enlarging the suffrage, and we ought in every way to promote the education of the people. I have great faith in my countrymen ; but the experience of America frightens me. I am not ashamed to use the word *frightened*. During my whole life I have looked to that country as about to solve the great problem of self-government, and now, in my old age, the hopes of my youth and manhood are destroyed, and I am left to reconstruct my political philosophy, and doubt and hesitation beset me on every point. I don't know how you, as an old reformer, feel ; but I must acknowledge that I am very uncomfortable.

At this period Mr. Roebuck further disappointed that section of his constituents which had resented his pro-Austrian sympathies by throwing the cold water of prudence on the heroic measures they wished to see taken in aid of the struggles of the Poles for freedom. As to Ireland, he denied the existence of any troubles that were not self-made and self-curable; and in connection with disturbances in New Zealand, he reiterated with unmitigated harshness his often-proclaimed views on the inevitable law that the price of civilized colonization is the extermination of aborigines. The sooner, he said, the Maoris were destroyed, the better.*

All these things united many sections of Mr. Roebuck's constituents in strong disapprobation of their member. It was not only that they differed from his views. They were, indeed, fairly well accustomed to his habit of putting his truths in exaggerated and paradoxical forms. "Roebuck," it was remarked, "is always saying something which is lying at the bottom of other people's minds, but which other people do not say. They keep it for examination and modification before it is allowed to come into free thought or open words. Roebuck digs it up, and puts it before us, and makes us look it full in the face at once. Sometimes we do not thank him for the office"—and assuredly he was not thanked by those who had been vivisected as a warning to the rest. These were wounded by his aggressive ways, and by biting epigrams whose rankling pain caused angry indifference to the substance of the arguments they were intended to enforce. He had

---

* He had no sentimental illusions regarding the North American Red Indian, whom he has somewhere described as a " melancholy man," and as such destined to fade before a more vigorous race.

thus secured for himself an exceedingly hot reception when, on the dissolution of Parliament in the summer of 1865, he went down to Sheffield for re-election. Mr. Roebuck boldly defied his critics at a great open-air meeting. There, on an extemporized rival platform, were gathered in fierce array temperance men, bent on avenging the "muddy stream" and "canting hypocrite" epithets, and the Bill that had been "spat" upon. There were the sympathizers with the North, angry at the "scum and refuse of Europe" speeches; and the friends of Italy and Poland, and the humanitarians shocked at the doctrine of exterminating the black man. To these were added others unreasonably, but all the more furiously, discontented on a local water question. Mr. Roebuck was unfairly charged with having espoused the cause of the water company against the town, in matters arising out of the calamity of the bursting of the Bradfield reservoir, and the sins imputed to him on this matter out-weighed even the opprobrious description he had given at Salisbury of the working man. There had been various attempts to modify, or explain away, the many offending sarcasms. In the House of Commons, Roebuck himself, replying to Mr. Bright, had said that "the scum of Europe" was applied to the armies, not to the people of the North. He sought to limit the description of drunken working men who beat their wives and caress their dogs, as applied to individual instances, not to a whole class; and as to the "canting hypocrites," he wrote—

*J. A. Roebuck to Robert Leader.*

The words "canting hypocrites" were not used at Sheffield, but in the House of Commons. They must be taken in the context, and I should then hope that Mr. Barber will not deem them applicable to himself. The subject on which I was speaking was not the Permissive, but the Sunday Closing Bill. I had given notice that, if this latter Bill were carried, I would in committee move a clause compelling the close of all the clubs in London at the same time that the public-houses were to be closed ; and I said that any one who voted for closing the public-house of the poor man, and would not vote for closing the club of the rich, was a canting hypocrite. I said this then, and I say it now ; but I cannot believe that any honest man would take offence at such a statement, and put the cap upon his own head. This is my answer, and all that I can say.

But these offences were too rank to be glossed over by explanations. There was only one course open, and it was entirely in consonance with Mr. Roebuck's temper and inborn pugnacity to take it. This was bold and open defiance. Speaking at the excited open-air meeting, he said—

I leave my fate in your hands. I am not afraid of the result. I believe that I have done my duty honestly. I know I have done it fearlessly. I don't fear you. I don't fear anybody. What I think right I say. What I think right I do ; and that is the only promise I make you. . . . Now, gentlemen (turning to the medley crowd of his opponents), what have you got to say ?

The *Times* wrote—

When Roebuck made his parting salutation, several inglorious carcases were dragged away. Indeed, if there be a teetotaller now left in Sheffield, he must be in a very mangled state. Roebuck's fight with the wild beasts of Sheffield might have entitled him to be member for Ephesus. . . . It used to be a favourite doctrine with the last generation of bull-baiters that the bull liked the baiting quite as much as the dogs or the spectators. Roebuck evidently took an intense joy in his baiting. No one came within reach of his horn but he went high in air and came down howling. . . . The meeting voted him back to his seat by a majority of ten to one. Mr. Roebuck was reminded by his audience that he has been member for Sheffield for sixteen years, and this is the style in which he has always treated them. He is as safe with the men of Sheffield as the Lord of the Manor of Boroughbridge used to be when he was returned by the votes of his butler and his bailiff. It is very creditable both to the representative and to the town. We do not often agree with Mr.

Roebuck, and we are sometimes obliged to say hard things of him, but it is highly to the honour of a great constituency like that of Sheffield that they can abide faithfully by a man who, when it pleases him, votes against their public opinions and their local interests, and abide by him from sheer admiration of his pluck and honesty of purpose. It is refreshing to see a friendship like this between a man with a strong will and a constituency with a tolerant appreciation for a sturdy, though often mistaken, love of truth. Of the electors of Sheffield who make Mr. Roebuck's place in the House of Commons so secure, there is probably not one who approves much more than half what he says and does. Yet the vast majority accept him for what they like, and tolerate in him what they dislike ; and they protect him against the enemies he makes by the unmeasured scorn he pours upon all that is mean, or sectional, or socially tyrannical ; and they seem to like him the better the more he scolds them. It is a piece of our electioneering system that deserves to be noted and applauded.

Mr. Roebuck's seat was, however, by no means so safe as the *Times* supposed. A very significant sign was that Mr. Dunn, the last man to be moved by effusive clamour, or to lose sight of substance in phrases, retired from the chairmanship of his election committee. But Mr. Roebuck received undesigned help from his opponents themselves. At first a Mr. Probyn, a most respectable moderate Liberal, had been brought out. It was soon manifest, however, that his candidature would be a greater danger to Mr. Hadfield than to Mr. Roebuck ; so he withdrew. Mr. Campbell Foster, a barrister with loud declamatory powers, was then selected, but the violence of his attack defeated itself, for its virulence rallied many semi-alienated waverers to Mr. Roebuck's side, and convinced reasonable men that Mr. Foster, with all his professions, would be an ill exchange for Mr. Roebuck, with all his faults.

One summer evening, at the commencement of the election contest, there was a very striking scene in Paradise Square, where Sheffield's great open-air meetings are held.

Mr. Campbell Foster's brief seemed to consist of the words, "No case, abuse the other side." In a ferocious attack he injudiciously taunted Mr. Roebuck with not having dared to be present. The prompt reply was the appearance, amid intense excitement and enthusiasm, of Mr. Roebuck and Mr. Hadfield in a carriage. They were accompanied by a brewer's dray filled with their supporters. These vehicles, forced through the crowd, were drawn up at the foot of the steps whence Mr. Foster spoke, and throughout the remainder of the speech Mr. Roebuck sat impassively listening to a crudely lurid picture of himself, sketched by his assailant. There was an animated wordy warfare between the partisans of the two sides, but the confusion was too great to enable Mr. Roebuck to make his voice heard above the clamour. Both sides claimed the vote, so that it was a drawn battle; but the dramatic episode is still famous in local annals. With a beginning like this, the electoral proceedings were characterized by no lack of animation. But although there was a fourth candidate in the field to abstract votes (the Hon. F. Wortley, who, dissociating himself from the Tory politics of his family, solicited election as a moderate—very moderate—Liberal), the result was the return of the old members: Roebuck, 3410; Hadfield, 3348; Wortley, 2626; Foster, 1576.

The following letters relate to this period :—

### To William Fisher (Sheffield).

*May* 12, 1865.—I said [in reply to an intimation that the coming election would be very severe and expensive] that I was not prepared for any great expense, and that if I was told that great expense would be entailed on me, I should make my bow and retire ; that if the people of Sheffield were not satisfied with me as their representative they had only to say so, and that I would at once relieve them of all difficulty, so far as I was concerned, by withdrawing at once ; that if I, after three and thirty years of service, was to be called upon to pay largely for the honour of representing Sheffield, I was not prepared to accept the representation on those terms, and that I was quite prepared for the quiet and obscurity of private life.

### To William Fisher.

*May* 15, 1865.—Do not fancy that I shall take a verdict from any but a public meeting. I intend to see my constituents face to face ; to meet those who find fault with me before the great body of the people. I never yet quailed before any opposition ; and I am not yet so old as to have lost my head or my heart. My cause, I know, is a good one, and I rather fancy I know how to deal with my fellow-countrymen in public meeting assembled.

### To Mrs. Roebuck.

*Sheffield, July* 7, 1865.—Well, we had our turn last night at a large meeting in the Temperance Hall, at which the opposing party did all they could to prevent my being heard, but as our friends were twenty to one, silence was at length compelled by turning one noisy fellow out of the meeting more hastily than ceremony or courtesy required. I then had my say, and warmed the people completely, and we carried our motion triumphantly, showing that at the poll, the result will be as already predicted. We called on the Browns ; he is ill in bed, and poor Mrs. Brown said she had not slept for a week. Everybody is very kind ; and the Fishers really seem as if they could not do enough to show their friendship. The Southern (West-Riding) Division election seems getting on well—and all our friends are busy and fully on the alert. There is no doubt of the result.

*Sheffield, July* 10, 1865.—I have really no news ; things are going on, in their actual train, and everything, so far as I can judge, promises an easy victory. The vulgar abuse of Mr. Foster does no harm to anybody but himself, and if the feeling shown at the public meetings be any guide, the matter is really decided. Should the result be different from what I now expect, it would indeed be a great surprise—I suppose it is my being older that makes me feel the trouble more now than formerly—and, indeed, the disgust that comes over me at times is so great, that I am inclined to say, "Let it go to the devil. I will not stir in the business more." This does not arise because I am doubtful, but because of the shock to my dignity, and to the respect that I feel is my due. If ever a man passed a life of purity and

x

disinterestedness, I have done so, and yet that every venal, vulgar blackguard may raise up his foul voice against me, is to me a cause of shame as well as of disgust. However, this way of talk is idle; I am in for it, and must abide the result. As to Mill's election, I am in the dark, though my instinct tells me that it will be Mill and Smith. P.S.—I have just come from a meeting of working men, and have nearly had my arm pulled off shaking hands.

Mr. Roebuck had taken an active interest in the election of his old friend, John Stuart Mill, for Westminster. In April, when the Liberals were considering the rival claims of Mr. Mill and Mr. Coningham, late M.P. for Brighton, he had warmly championed Mr. Mill's cause. One speech, in which he pronounced an eloquent eulogium on Mr. Mill's fitness, contained some interesting reminiscences as to their early association.

He and I were young men together, and he, in fact, though the younger of the two, was the leader. He taught me pretty much all I know upon politics and philosophy. He was my guide. I followed him, and I owe him a greater debt of gratitude than I owe to any man, living or dead. I cannot help thinking of those days and those hours we spent together in the investigation of great subjects—

> "For we spent them not in toys, or lust, or wine,
> But search of deep philosophy,
> Wit, eloquence, and poetry—
> Arts which I loved; for they, my friend, were thine."

The House of Commons ought to contain some man whose mind is of such an order that he should represent the thought, the philosophy, the great powers of the thinking people of England. Where is such a man to be. found? I look to my early friend, and there comes over me a melancholy as well as a pleasurable thought—melancholy to think I have not equalled the anticipations that he had formed of me; pleasurable that he has more than equalled every hope and aspiration that I formed of him. That man does not come to the House of Commons unprepared. His mind has been trained and he has studied legislation as a science. He has given proof of his fitness to every man who can read a book.

Mr. Mill, as we all know, was elected, defeating Mr. W. H. Smith. But Mr. Roebuck afterwards shared the general feeling that Mr. Mill, in the House of Commons, had not fulfilled the expectations formed when he entered it. This appears from the following letter, found among his papers and endorsed, " A letter to John Mill that probably will never be sent, and indeed, probably will never be finished " :—

*J. A. Roebuck to John Stuart Mill.*

*April* 13, 1868.—DEAR MILL,—After some deliberation I have determined to write to you. The time of our youth comes back to me, and I call to mind all that I mentally owe to you. Our early friendship—the break in that friendship—and the long estrangement that followed, all pass before me, and I ask myself what can I hope from this present, this late appeal to the mind, maybe to the affection, of my old friend ? The answer, I know not what ; no harm can follow, some good may. After many years of separation, we have found ourselves members of the same House of Commons. The time is a remarkable one. The whole frame of the constitution of England is in a state of change—and whether that change shall be for good or evil, depends much upon the men who preside over and direct that change. Now, I have lived my life in the House of Commons, and while you have been giving lessons of wisdom to the world through books, I have been fighting what I have believed the good fight in the great legislative assembly of which I have for so many years been a member. I did what I could to assist in bringing you into Parliament—what little influence I had, I gave to that end, and I believe that my efforts were not wholly without effect. I did this because I believed that your mind and thought, imported into our debates, would really be a new era in the history of the House of Commons ; that your clear and masculine English style would induce men to listen to the teachings of a wise philosophy, and that you would bring to bear upon our debates, that which they much wanted, a large and liberal spirit of generalization—a tone of thought and feeling above that which appeared in party strife ; in short, I hoped that you would be a philosopher acting as a legislator—that you would enlighten and guide us. I fancied that I had not lived for nothing. I believed that I had learned something of human dealings in my long Parliamentary career. I had studied, and studied carefully the writings of your father, of Bentham, and yourself, and I believed I saw mistakes that a very little know-ledge of the actual business of life would have corrected ; but I felt certain that the great intellectual power which enabled them to write such works as those by which they were im-mortalized, would, had it been permitted, have enabled them, with very slight experience, to efface and rub off those small blemishes or mistakes which I fancied my large experience enabled me to detect. Full of this idea, and strongly under the influence of this feeling, I hailed with something like rapture your election for Westminster. I watched, I cannot say with anxiety, but with great interest your first steps as a member of Parliament. The estrangement of which I have spoken, I found rendered it impossible for me to offer you any advice, or to enable you to profit by the lessons which time had taught me, so that I was a passive spectator of what was taking place. I soon found that there are things which the most powerful minds cannot learn in their closets, shut out from commerce with their fellows. The temper of the House of Commons is peculiar, and of that I quickly saw you were profoundly ignorant, and you had so long accustomed yourself to look with something like contempt upon the intellect of the House of Commons, that you were unwilling or unable to assume a port and bearing, or to take steps that would alone enable you to guide and instruct that very remarkable assembly. It is, believe me, a very perspicacious assembly. It takes the gauge of men instantly, and for the most part correctly. It judges, it is true, from its own point of view—but from that point of view, its judgment can usually be depended upon. . . .

Mr. Mill, like Mr. Roebuck, was rejected at the General Election a few months after this letter was written, and the House of Commons knew him no more. How Mr. Roebuck lost his seat remains to be told.

# CHAPTER XXVI.

### REJECTED BY SHEFFIELD.  1865–1868.

AT the Cutlers' Feast of 1865, Mr. Roebuck again showed how changed was his estimate of the French Emperor's policy. "We," he said, "have had our old enemy, now our ally—the French—meeting us in friendly concourse and friendly emulation on the waters of Portsmouth. It is a fact significant of this, that, while England and France hold together, the world must be at peace. The Emperor of France employs that power which he has, and so well exercises, for the benefit of mankind."

Parliament met in February, 1866, under an administration of which Earl Russell, consequent upon the death of Lord Palmerston in the preceding October, was the head. The promise of a Reform Bill was the *pièce de résistance* in the Queen's Speech, but that document contained also an ominous reference to the disturbed state of Ireland, where the Fenian conspiracy had developed itself. The discussions on both these subjects were destined to lead to action on the part of Mr. Roebuck which finally broke down the allegiance of the Liberal party in his constituency. The result was an entire revolution in his relations to the two great political parties. Every step of alienation from the Liberals drew him nearer into alliance with the Conservatives, and ultimately flung him into their arms.

This transition was, of course, gradual. At first it appeared as if Mr. Roebuck would be found supporting the

Ministerial proposals. Speaking, in spite of illness, at Sheffield, in April, he declared the measure, brought in by Mr. Gladstone, to be honest. "I cannot," he said, "understand the meaning of what is said about dishonesty in this Bill." It proposed not merely to enlarge the franchise, but to do away with the ratepaying clauses, to get rid of which, he had, he said, been fighting for thirty-three years. "Fairly and candidly will I deal with this Bill. I will steadily support it, and, by the grace of God, we shall carry it." Mr. Roebuck, who was seriously ill, was unable to attend the exciting debates which led to the overthrow of the Russell Government, by an adverse majority of eleven, on Lord Dunkellin's amendment fixing a rating, not a rental, qualification. The change of government put off the question of reform until the following year, Mr. Disraeli refusing, indeed, to give any pledge to deal with it even then, and Lord Derby hinting that much would depend on the possibility of arriving at an effectual agreement between the two sides.

*To William Fisher (Sheffield).*

*June* 7, 1866.—At this moment I cannot give any precise or definite information about myself, as I am in the very process of learning my exact condition, and of determining what steps I am to take. I went yesterday to Sir James Paget, the eminent surgeon, and his advice is that the best and safest course will be at once to submit to an operation, which he declares to be without pain or danger. On receiving his advice I wrote to Gully, asking him to come up to see me, and to give me his advice, by which I shall be guided. When I have consulted Gully, in order yet further to satisfy myself, I shall see Sir William Fergusson, who takes a great interest in me, and whose mind runs in the same groove as that of Paget. Gully is, of course, a different character. . . . When Gully comes I shall make my decision. I am, as you may suppose, anxious ; but believe me, I am not afraid. I am ready for the worst, and, as far as I am myself concerned, to die will not be terrible, or indeed unwelcome. I have done pretty

*Right Hon.<sup>ble</sup> J. A. Roebuck.*

much all I can hope to do, and though my career has been less distinguished than I had hoped, yet I have won for myself a good name, and I think my countrymen respect me. There are those who will be deeply grieved to lose me. But to part at some time is inevitable, and the only touch of selfishness I find in myself is that I had rather that the parting came by my taking precedence than by following after. These are gloomy thoughts and sad forebodings that may not now come to pass, but I write so that you may not be taken unawares. My dear wife and daughter are not aware of the desponding view I take of my case, and I do not wish them to know. If my anticipations prove correct, they will soon enough have cause for sorrow. If I be wrong—why, they will have escaped the misery that I think threatens.

*To William Fisher.*

*July* 11, 1866.—Sir William Fergusson has just left me, saying that I am now well. This, no doubt, is true, surgically speaking ; but I am yet very weak and very nervous, and totally unfit for work.

*To the same.*

*Rectory, Bushey, near Watford, Herts, July* 20, 1866.—I am here at the quiet parsonage of my brother, Mr. Falconer, getting strength daily from the fresh air and the calm and the sunshine. I am very much stronger than I was a week since, and all goes merrily with me as a marriage bell.

Some quiet and cheerful weeks passed at Endcliffe Hall, Sheffield, with Sir John and Lady Brown, whose unfailing kindness did much to bring about complete restoration to health. In September, Mr. Roebuck's attitude towards Reform legislation was far different from that he had taken up in the spring. He had, he said, supported the defunct Liberal Bill because he could not help supporting it. But by separating extension of the suffrage from redistribution of seats, the battle of the late administration was fought on a wrong point. Mr. Gladstone had endeavoured first of all to cajole the House of Commons, and, that failing, to bully it. To cajole the House would be very difficult, to bully it was impossible; so that Government fell. So far as he was concerned, the new administration should have a fair trial. The result would, he believed, be that the two great parties of the State would be united into one.

There is really no difference between the two, except some small rags of bigotry and intolerance that stick unwillingly to them. Let them get rid of these—let the Tories throw overboard the talk about the Church rates, the talk about the Universities—and they will do it—and even the Liberal, the moderate Liberal party, will join them, and form such a strong Ministerial party in England as will enable us to maintain the power of England throughout the world; as will make her feared by her enemies and loved by her friends, and be the protecting power of the people. I am sure that will take place. I am sure that Lord Derby will disappear. I hope that Lord Russell will disappear, and that other men will rise up in their places representing the united feeling of the people of England; and that then we shall be enabled to preserve the people of England from the control of ignorance and vice with which we are now threatened; and, in spite of all the demagogues in the world, the people of England will ride triumphant.

In the next session (1867), Mr. Roebuck, reverting to his often-proclaimed opinion, that a better Reform Bill could be wrested from a weak Conservative Government than any it was possible for Liberal ministers to carry, gave his support to that Derby-Disraeli scheme which was designed to "dish the Whigs." His speech in favour of the second reading was barbed with sneers at Mr. Glad-stone. When helping the Government to defeat that statesman's crucial amendment, dispensing with the personal payment of rates by the householder as a con-dition of the franchise, he again applied the epithet "pettifogging" to Mr. Gladstone's speech. By this time, too, Mr. Roebuck had changed his thirty-three years' views as to ratepaying. He now declared that he never heard any one object to the condition of the ratepaying clauses except the Radicals. "Of these," he said, "I was one, but I have seen the error of my ways."

*To William Fisher (Sheffield).*

*June* 7, 1867.—How completely my policy has succeeded! We have now a more Liberal Bill than has ever been proposed, and that Bill will be carried. I always said the Whigs never could or would carry any reform, and this statement which I made in 1859 has proved true to the letter.

After the Bill, turned inside out by Liberal effort, and presenting as an Act scarcely any possible resemblance to its original shape, had established household suffrage, Mr. Roebuck, at Sheffield, further explained and justified his course by saying—

I made a resolution with myself that, having got Lord Derby into power, we would, if it were possible, screw out of him a real reform of Parliament. It always appeared to me that the Whigs never could carry a second Reform Bill. I stated so in 1859. I was hooted and yelled at in this very town because I so stated. . . . Then came Lord Derby again, and then I recollected my old determination. "If ever a Reform Bill is carried," I said to myself, "it will be by those men, and so sure as they bring it in, I will support them." I was among the first who did so, and I was again received with a yell of disapprobation. Oh, how I was lectured! . . . Poor man! it was thought having lived so long I did not know what I was doing. Well, time went on, and I was called upon to resign my seat. Certain people here in this town, calling themselves Reformers—wretched people to teach me—these men called upon me to resign the great trust imposed on me by the people of Sheffield. I treated them with the contempt they merited. I steadily supported that Bill, and what has been the result? We have got a more Liberal Bill than ever Whig proposed. We have got a Bill that has frightened, I believe, the very persons who proposed it. It has not frightened me. I believe we shall find now what the people of England really mean. I have great confidence in the right-heartedness of my own countrymen. I have no dread of the future. . . . We have

got a great deal more good out of the Tory administration than out
of anybody else.   This Reform Bill is before us.   We have now to
work it. . . . I am quite sure there can be no harm to England
while we have a free press, a free people ; but with that press and
constant intercommunication of thought, it will render the passing
of the Reform Bill one of the greatest boons ever conferred upon
the people of this country.

Mr. Roebuck, throughout these Reform discussions, had,
as was said at the time, been true to his usual practice ot
so emphasizing by his strong expressions individual bricks,
as to concentrate attention on them, and divert it from the
entire edifice.   He had exposed himself to much adverse
comment in his constituency by opposing Mr. Laing's
proposal to make the six largest cities three-cornered
constituencies.   For, although he subsequently advocated
the claims of Sheffield to inclusion in the list, there was a
prevalent impression that this was a case of being zealous
to lock the stable door after the horse had been stolen.
Mr. Roebuck explained his course in the following letter :—

*To a Constituent.*

19, *Ashley Place, S.W., July* 19, 1868.—The story of the
three members' constituencies is a simple one, and can soon be
told.   Many attempts to stop and destroy the Reform Bill were
made under the guise of liberality.   The project respecting the
three members was one of them.   It was thought that Mr. Disraeli
had got to the length of his tether, that his party would go no
further, and that if they at this time could be induced to recal-
citrate, the Liberals who had hitherto supported the Government
must vote with the real enemies of the Bill, that the Government would be put into a minority, must go out, and that the
Bill would then be defeated.   Mr. Disraeli said in the debate that
the Government could not accede to the proposal, and that the
defeat of the Government on the motion would seriously endanger
the Bill.   We knew what this meant—viz. that his party could
not be induced to go further in the way of concession.   Seeing
this, we said, "We will not throw away the good we have attained,
for the purpose of adding six members to large constituencies, and

taking away six from small ones. This benefit, if it should be desired, can easily be obtained from the new Parliament when it meets. In the mean time we will insure the Bill." We voted for the Government, put them into a majority, and saved the Bill. But Mr. Disraeli, upon consulting his party again, found that they deemed the trouble of the contest a greater evil than yielding the point, and they yielded so far as four members were concerned. I complained of this, and strove for Sheffield ; but I was told that the party of Mr. Disraeli would go no further than four members, and so, according to my own expression, Sheffield was left out in the cold. This is the plain history of the case. It is a story that could be told of many other similar attempts to defeat the Bill, which attempts were defeated by our steady determination to carry the Bill, spite of calumny, spite of threats, spite of abuse. The Bill is now law, and is law because a number of Liberals were more far-sighted, ay, and more disinterested, than those who called themselves leaders of the Liberal party.

There were other subjects on which Mr. Roebuck's opinions and action were antagonistic to those of many of his Sheffield supporters.

Early in 1868, in a lecture on Capital and Labour, he affronted Trades Union feeling by dwelling on the sins of Labour without touching on the correlative errors of Capital. The meeting heard him patiently, but resented what it considered the one-sidedness of the lecture. The usual motion of thanks was rejected, because there was injudiciously linked with it an implied approval of the lecture, and a commendation of Mr. Roebuck's "usual dauntless advocacy of the commercial interests of this country." Subsequently the Trades Unionists called his action "indecent and unfair," as coming from one who was sitting on the Royal Commission at that time investigating, under the presidency of Sir William Erle, the constitution, character, and proceedings of the Trades Unions throughout the kingdom, and certain outrages which had occurred at Sheffield. The commission had delegated three examiners, who were armed with special powers conferred by Act of Parliament, to prosecute the local inquiry, and this brought home to agents of the unions a series of terrible acts of vengeance and violence. The Sheffield examiners reported in August, 1867, but the larger commission, of which it was a branch, continued its wider inquiries until the following year. Mr. Roebuck justified himself in the following letter :—

*To J. England (Sheffield).*

*February* 8, 1868.— . . . My great offence, then, or mistake, was that I abruptly terminated my lecture, or speech, without treating on the duties of Capital.

For a moment consider the circumstances in which I was speaking. The audience was one of working men of a town in which there had lately been horrid disclosures of murder and cruelty committed by men of the very class which I was addressing. These men had lately had an opportunity of bringing charges, and, if possible, of substantiating them against the possessors of capital. No such charge was preferred, and my belief is that none such, if made, could have been substantiated. My mind was, by the nature of things, directed to the subject occupying all men's minds, viz. the wrong views entertained respecting the nature of labour and capital. When I had explained what the errors were, I had really done all, as I conceived, that I was expected to do, and illustrated the principles I had laid down by one striking instance. I stated broadly what I thought ought to be the aim of the Legislature in any future legislation, and there I left the matter.

What is the conclusion drawn from this, to you, hasty termination ? Why, that my confidence in, and sympathy with, the working man has, if not totally disappeared, greatly diminished. Let me for a moment consider this conclusion. The real meaning of it I take to be this : that Capital and Labour are antagonists ; that having discoursed upon the mistakes upon the one part, I ought to have set forth the errors of the other. But, under the circumstances, was this needed ? I had endeavoured to show, and, I think, had shown, that labour and capital were equally necessary for production. There was before the world of Sheffield no proof of any glaring mistake on the part of the capitalist, and I had combined my views of labour and capital so that one exposition exhausted both subjects. My legislative life had been passed in supporting such legislation as prevents any improper influence which capital gives from being employed to the detriment of the labourer ; and because I did not descant on what might be the shortcomings of the capitalist, my past life was forgotten. I was hooted at as an enemy, though the whole vigour of my mind and body had for six and thirty years been steadfastly and disinterestedly devoted to protecting and watching over the interests of my fellow-countrymen of every class and degree.

You compel me to talk of myself. I reluctantly yield to the necessity. I ask you, then, to look at my career as a politician. Is there anything in it which has been caused or brought about by consideration of self ? Have I ever flattered or attempted to cajole the people ? When I have thought them wrong, have I not said so ? When I thought them right, have I not, at every risk, boldly supported and defended them ? But you say that "more constant intercourse with the rich and influential may have weaned your sympathies from the hardy sons of toil." At what time do you state this supposition ? Just when I have given the strongest evidence of my confidence in, and sympathy with, those hardy sons of toil. My influence has been strenuously employed in inducing the House of Commons to give those "hardy sons of toil" more power in the Government of the country than they ever yet enjoyed. And there are not few who will tell you that that influence was not wholly powerless in bringing about the passing of the last Reform Bill. But your supposition in its foundation is incorrect. My intercourse with the rich and influential has not been more constant of late years than through my whole life. My sympathy with the working man was not the result of associating with them, but arose from careful study and industrious investigation. My habits have been through life the same ; my fortunes have not changed ; experience, I hope, has corrected errors ; age has not chilled my sympathies ; and the temptations which failed to influence the young man will not now make me swerve from what I believe the path of duty, now that my career is coming to its end.

In a conversation on June 27, 1868, Mr. Walpole, the

Home Secretary, told Mr. Roebuck that if in his life he had never done anything else but *get at* the Sheffield outrages, he would have deserved well of his country.   Said he—

"I well remember your coming with the request of the masters, and then of the men.   I took the two petitions for inquiry to the Cabinet Council, and on my requesting their leave to grant the inquiry, they, with one accord, lifted up their hands and eyes, and point-blank refused.   I then said this was a serious matter to refuse inquiry to people so accused.   I said some other things, and that it was an opportunity not to be lost, it might never happen again, and so on.   They then told me they agreed to leave the matter in my hands, and to do as I liked ; and, as you know, I appointed the Commission.   How does it work, as I hear no two agree ? "   " I do not find that," said Roebuck. " Harrison * does not like it, but he has wonderfully changed since we first began."   Mr. Walpole added, " You fought the inquiry through the House, and not a soul of them helped you. It was *yours*."

In 1870, Sir William Erle, who had been Chairman of the Commission, said to Mr. Roebuck, " I shall always remember the two years passed in the Trades Union Commission, two of the happiest years of my life."   Sir Roundell Palmer joined the group with " Yes, an inquiry most nobly conducted, and most nobly ended; but it had one bad result, it terminated your Parliamentary career, and deprived the country of the services of a great statesman."

But what finally split up the Liberals of Sheffield, and completed the alienation of the majority of them from Mr. Roebuck, was the attitude he assumed towards the disestablishment of the Irish Church.   In former years, Mr. Roebuck had dwelt with vehemence on the wrongs done to the Irish by what he called " the greatest enormity in Europe "—an alien Church.   Mr. Gladstone, in 1868, addressed himself to the removal of this evil, coupling with it that equally great question of the Irish tenantry,

* Mr. Frederic Harrison.

which Sir Robert Peel, in the height of his power, had approached, but left untouched. To the general astonishment, Mr. Roebuck took up the old Tory plea for the Irish establishment, that it maintained an educated gentleman in every parish, who, with his family, spent more money than he received, and conferred the greatest benefit upon the locality. In Mr. Roebuck's opinion, that man was no statesman who would disestablish the Church. His favourite theme at this time was an insistence that the Irish had no grievance of which to complain, all their troubles being self-made. It was in April that Mr. Gladstone moved his resolutions, declaring that the Irish Church must cease to exist as an establishment, and providing that, pending the action of Parliament, no new life interest should be created.

### To Mrs. Roebuck.

*April* 4, 1868.—Last night Gladstone referred twice to me in his reply on the great debate on the Irish Church. The *Times* imperfectly reports both references. The first was a short allusion. Gladstone was explaining a change in his own opinion respecting the presence of bishops in the House. He said, as near as I can recollect, "I thought then, sir, that it would be wise to retain more Irish bishops in the House of Lords, and this, in spite of the sneer of my honourable and learned friend, the member for Sheffield, respecting churchmen and legislators—not that I mean to blame that sneer. No—it was perfectly true!"

The second was more marked, and the omission of the *Times* more significant. The words of Gladstone were to this effect—"And here I must answer a question put to me by my honourable friend, the member for Sheffield. He asked me in a marked and solemn manner, a pertinent and solemn question—one which he was perfectly justified in asking, and one which I am prepared to answer. It was whether I was prepared to pursue to the end the object of these resolutions. He said that the expectations of the people of Ireland had been often raised to be often disappointed. I admit this."

Gladstone then proceeded as is reported in the *Times*, and in a manner which induces me to think that he *foresees many difficulties* in giving effect to his resolutions, and that he was even then preparing for what might be another case of Irish disappointment.

A town's meeting in Sheffield sent up petitions in favour of Mr. Gladstone's policy, and in reply to a letter forwarding these, Mr. Roebuck wrote—

*To Robert Leader (Sheffield).*

*April* 2, 1868.—I will present the petition of the public meeting to-night. Mr. Gladstone's resolutions I shall support, and, I suspect, upon a more thorough-going principle than will be adopted by most of those who will vote for them. About the mover, I see that you and I differ. He holds so commanding a position, and is so eminently gifted, that his errors, if he commit errors, are far more mischievous than those of ordinary men, and I believe it to be my duty to speak plainly my opinion upon so important a subject. My country has a right to demand from me my real views, and I should be unworthy of the post I hold if I shrunk from this my duty, even from fear of offending many who certainly have not my experience, though they may be far more endowed with ability than myself. I write this because your hint, though short, was significant and somewhat imperative.

Mr. Roebuck did, accordingly, vote for the resolutions, but in his speech he hurled bitter taunts at the minister, and imputed that he was actuated by a desire for personal aggrandisement.

This speech, his colleague, Mr. Hadfield, reported, " was silently received." It was the last straw which broke the back of the long-suffering Sheffield Liberal camel. The local newspaper which hitherto had held staunchly to Mr. Roebuck, making the best of the many strains he put upon its loyalty, at length declared that the time had arrived when the honourable member's supporters owed it to themselves and the country to come to some definite understanding as to the relations they were in future to bear to him and to the Liberal party at large. And Mr. Hadfield recommended that the Liberal committee should meet and consider the position of the friends of progress and reform in Sheffield. "The constituents," he said, "must consider the duty they owe to themselves and to the country, regardless of the present members, except so far as they represent the best interests of the nation."

The details of what followed are of local, rather than of general interest. Towards the end of June a meeting of the committee of Messrs. Roebuck and Hadfield was held. This Mr. Roebuck unexpectedly attended to "have it out" with his friends. And there ensued an exceedingly frank and outspoken exchange of opinions, both sides sticking manfully to their guns. Mr. Roebuck treated the indictment against him as including these main counts: his action on reform, his attacks on Mr. Gladstone, his attitude towards trades unions—especially as shown by his treatment of witnesses before the Royal Commission—and his antagonism to restrictions on the sale of liquors. On the last he had yet once again, in this session, poured his contemptuous scorn. In the committee neither side convinced the other, and from that moment, all chance of harmony being at an end, the sword was drawn from the scabbard, and some of Mr. Roebuck's most influential friends, finding what they deemed loyalty to the interests of Liberalism incompatible with his retention of the seat, explained publicly why they could no longer support him, and why they threw the whole weight of their influence into the cause of Mr. Mundella, who had been brought forward as a candidate. If, said the newspaper which expressed their views, the electors were not prepared to let Mr. Roebuck ride them with whip and spur into the Tory camp, and make them fall into line behind Mr. Disraeli, they must unhorse him.

At the succeeding Cutlers' Feast, in September, Mr. Roebuck gave fresh offence by references to the United States, made in the presence of Mr. Reverdy Johnson, then

minister representing the Republic in England.　There
had, he said, been poured into America a tide of corruption,
"a feculent torrent" of almost all the vice and turbulence
of Europe.　"We see," he continued, "the wild Irishman, the
fiery Frenchman, the assassinating Italian, and the dumb-
founded Spaniard, all going out in one mass, and wishing
to fulfil their expectations in the mind of America."　The
*Times* having "most unreservedly condemned the out-
rageous indecency of this language, as unfounded in fact
as it was offensive under the circumstances in which it
was uttered," Mr. Roebuck protested against this "misconception of the purpose and effect of the speech."

### To the Editor of the Times.

You seem to assume that I intended to disparage the United
States, and that I did insult her minister by the remarks I made.
Now, to notice first the matter last mentioned.　I have the best
authority for saying that Mr. Johnson did not so conceive my
observations.　He knew full well that I had been active in preparing for him a warm welcome to Sheffield ; that I had put upon
record in words as strong as our language afforded the pleasure
that we felt upon the occasion of his visit ; and that, in one of
the addresses that were to be presented to him, I had most
earnestly spoken of the blessing that peace and goodwill between
the two nations would confer on mankind.　In fact, he has given
me every assurance that he felt greatly pleased by all that had
happened since his arrival here, and to myself personally he used
expressions of kindness and friendship which touched me very
nearly, which I shall ever remember, but which I need not repeat.
So much for the insult which you suppose I intended to fling, and
which you say I did fling, at the American Minister.

But that you should have fallen into this error is not surprising when one considers the strange construction you put upon
the words and arguments I used.　You seem to imagine that I
deliberately spoke ill of the United States, and that I said things
of her institutions that must necessarily have been offensive to the
gentleman who represented her.　Now, what was my purpose, my
reasoning, and what were the words I used ?　I was speaking of the

great change that had been lately made in our representation, and my purpose was to relieve the minds of my hearers of any alarms they might entertain in consequence of that change. To aid this my purpose I brought in America as an illustration. I said that there were two nations, and two only, who had really confided the government of their respective countries to the great body of their people. America had done so under conditions less favourable for success than England; and the argument was that, seeing how successful America has been, we need have no fear of England. I explained the differing conditions under which the two nations acted. America had one favourable condition that we had not—viz. unoccupied land to an almost fabulous extent; but I said that there was an element in her politics highly mischievous, and from which we were free—this was an emigration from Europe of persons of the worst and most dangerous character. Is not this assertion true, and is it not daily made in the United States in speeches in Congress, in the daily papers, and in every sort of publication?—made in words far stronger than mine; made, too, by the most thoughtful and patriotic Americans? That the course of American policy has been disturbed by this mischievous emigration no one who knows America will, I think, deny; that I may have overrated its mischievous influence may be true. I do not think so, and I know that my opinion is shared by many eminent Americans. In describing a bad thing you do not use words of eulogy; the epithets I chose may not have been happy, but as regards the thing described they are true. While speaking of this torrent of bad emigration, I did not include or allude to that vast body of virtuous and worthy persons who go to America in order to find a new and more favourable field for their industry and talent than their own country affords. That inestimable benefit has been conferred on the United States by such an emigration I well know. The same class of men have created our flourishing colonies over the world, and I hope I am not so foolish or so prejudiced as to confound things so essentially dissimilar as the two classes of emigrants that I speak of. That the bad element exists I am sure, that it has affected in an evil manner the politics of America I believe, in common with many of her most distinguished sons. To mention this fact, even before an American Minister, I cannot consider an offence against good taste and good manners; that no offence was taken I know.

I mentioned also one other thing, which is also notorious in America, and against which I warned my fellow countrymen—that was the almost universal withdrawal of rich and educated Americans from the business of politics, and the consequent advantage taken of their absence by mere political adventurers. Is this not also true ? And where was the harm of mentioning a fact which is notorious, when the mentioning of it might be a beneficial warning to my own countrymen, and perhaps might also be useful in its influence upon the minds of Americans ?

I will only add a passing remark upon the hard words you use when speaking of myself. I rather fancy that my experience in political life is greater than that of the gentleman who wrote the article of which I am now speaking, and I should have hoped that it might have suggested itself to him while inditing his diatribe, that the veteran politician might be right and he himself in the wrong.

In the turmoil of the election which followed, Mr. Roebuck maintained his sturdy independence, and showed that time had not withered his old powers of spirited attack, or lessened the joys which fierce combat brought. In his election address he expressed the hope that as he had grown older he had grown wiser, that age had made him more tolerant, more patient, more ready to believe that men opposed to him and his views were deserving of respect and toleration; but his toleration seemed to be extended rather to the traditional opponents of "those great doctrines of intellectual and moral and civil freedom, of which he had ever been an ardent and faithful supporter," than to those who had worked, and were prepared to continue to work, in the same cause.

Two extracts from speeches he delivered during the election are given here :—

I am a man of peace, but I have been taught, and unhappily it is true teaching, that to preserve the peace you should be able to protect yourselves. In the wide world of ambition, and the search after glory, we may have things threatened and done if we are not able to hold up our hands and to defend ourselves.

Therefore I say that England must be defended ; she must be protected from insult ; she must be protected from injury. Her sons are over the globe. They go to Asia, to Africa, to America, and all over Europe. They are upon every sea ; every fishery is vexed by them, as Burke said ; so she ought to be able to protect her sons as well abroad as at home. But all this costs money ; and therefore it is a very poor economy to say you won't protect your children abroad. That is my view with regard to peace and war. No aggressive wars for me, neither in Europe nor in India. I am against all aggression ; but defensive war is justifiable, and England ought to be prepared to defend herself.

Again—

My object has been through life to make the working-man as exalted and civilized a creature as I could make him. I wanted to place before his mind a picture of civilized life such as I see it in my own life, and I ask him, as my friend and my brother, to meet me in that career. My life has been passed with a partner whom I am delighted to think of. She is gentle, kind, civilized. I wanted him to have a partner of the same description. My household has been a civilized household. It has been a house-hold in which thought, high and elevated ideas of literature, and grace and beauty, have always found everything that could recommend them ; and when I came home from my intellectual conflicts in the world, I found there a resort, and the pillow on which I could lay my head. There was everything there that could recommend man to his Creator. I wanted to make the working-man like me. His house might be made the abode of culture, the abode of everything that is civilized and humanizing. I wanted no drink, no dog, no wretched and degrading things to interrupt life and happiness. I wanted him to be like me, a civilized human being, cultivating my mind, thinking only of whatever would elevate me and make me that which I ought to be, a representative of my race.

The result of the election came upon Mr. Roebuck as a painful surprise. It was: Hadfield, 14,797 ; Mundella, 12,212 ; Roebuck, 9571 ; Price, 5272.

The current and sedulously encouraged opinion outside Sheffield was that Mr. Roebuck had fallen a victim to the anger of that worst section of Trades Union opinion, which was in sympathy with the crimes of violence associated with the name of Broadhead. This, however, was a superficial theory, untenable by those really acquainted with all the facts of the case and the ramifications of public feeling. But it largely increased the widespread regret with which Mr. Roebuck's exclusion from Parliament was everywhere received—a regret which was not altogether unshared even by those who, compelled to sunder long ties of friendship, and to sacrifice personal feeling and admiration on the altar of loyalty to principle, and in obedience to a stern sense of duty, had brought it about. And in this respect they had, at any rate, the sanction of Mr. Roebuck's own teaching, for, in reference to objections to his plain speaking and unsparing attitude, he was accustomed to say, " I don't care who the truth injures : I cannot help it. It is like the surgeon's knife, cutting through a sore and bad place. He cuts it off, gives pain, but does good." Mr. Roebuck's farewell address to his late constituents was dignified and temperate. After thanks to his supporters and to his executive committee, he said—

We must all accept the decision of the electors as the faithful expression of the present opinions of the majority of the electors. It cannot be expected that we should acquiesce in the wisdom or the justice of this decision. Whether time is to reverse this decree time must show ; for me it is a final one. I am too old to wait for the decisions of time, though I am confident that, when calm reflection takes the place of excitement and prejudice, it will be acknowledged that I have been always a faithful servant, and that my services deserved a different return. I make no complaint ; I make no accusations. The future must decide between me and the newly-made constituency of Sheffield.

# CHAPTER XXVII.

As when, in 1847, Mr. Roebuck was rejected by Bath he turned his freedom from Parliamentary duties to the compilation of his " History of the Whig Ministry," so now he seems quickly to have reverted to literary projects. There is in existence a memorandum in which he wrote—

My intention is, if possible, to write a faithful history of the House of Commons, which was constituted by the Reform Act of 1832.  The first House of Commons, chosen under the provisions of this Act, met in the spring of the year 1833.  The last House elected under the same authority was dissolved in the autumn of 1868.  The existence of this great legislative assembly was confined within those two periods ; and I desire to lay before my countrymen a record of the deeds done by it in that space of time. If I be not greatly mistaken, this record will exhibit a picture unparalleled in the legislative history of mankind—a picture of wise reforms wisely executed ; of a great revolution, gradually, peacefully, and effectively accomplished ; of the greatest solicitude shown for all existing interests ; of a resolute determination to exterminate abuse, to improve all the institutions of the State ; of calmness and justice presiding on the occasion of every change effected ; of courage attended by wisdom, by truth, and by honour.  In short, there will be pourtrayed a picture of a legislature proving itself worthy of ruling the destinies of one of the greatest people that ever played a part in the history of mankind.

This design, unfortunately, was never carried out.

*To an unnamed Correspondent.*

19, *Ashley Place, S.W., February* 15, 1869.—There is one subject to which I will call your attention, in order to suggest it to you as a matter for consideration. The subject is the Pulpit. What is its power at present as a means of instruction ? When the Christian pulpit was first used as a means of power and influence, it stood out as possessed of peculiar, nay, singular, advantages. An educated man, having the power of addressing frequently the same body of persons with great and over-whelming authority, aided by all the terrors which religion wields and superstition intensifies, would necessarily exercise a tyrannical influence. But this condition of things has been greatly changed by printing, and the spread of information which printing has brought about. The newspaper comes every day, is at hand at all hours, touches upon every subject that interests humanity, suits itself to every taste, and supersedes, as a moral teacher and general instructor, every other class of teacher. The pulpit now, and he who fills it, take a very secondary place as respects importance in the ranks of the guides and instructors of mankind. Then comes the question, Is the parson of no use to the community ? is he to be considered as a useless official, an idle appendage to an old and worn-out system ? My answer is, By no means. I consider the mere fact of an educated, and, for the most part, virtuous, man being placed in every parish in England, a most happy circumstance as regards her welfare and good living. But the means by which that man is to lead and guide his people are changed from what they were in times past. It is not now by the sway of mere intellect that he is to govern. His power over what people are to believe has almost entirely gone. His chief means of teaching is example. His duty is to be a pattern to his flock. He should teach men what to do, and leave to other instructors the teaching of what they are to believe. This will, I have no doubt, appear to you a wild phantasy of mine, but I believe, if you will calmly and patiently consider the whole matter, you will feel that there is a good deal of truth in my statements.

In March, 1869, Mr. Roebuck met at Sheffield his old antagonist at the Bath election of 1847—the Earl of

Shaftesbury. His lordship, who had gone down to lay the foundation-stone of some alms-houses, privately expressed regret that he had been the means of ejecting Mr. Roebuck from his first constituency. Mr. Roebuck somewhat prematurely spoke of his own presence on this occasion as the closing act of his political life.

On March 15, 1869, he was presented by his friends and admirers with £3000, invested in Consols in the name of his daughter. In the speech in which he acknowledged the gift some touches of real pathos were mingled with characteristic references to the consistency of his career.

I feel myself now as if, in going along the journey of life—and I apprehend it is pretty near to its end—I have arrived at the hill-top from which, turning round, I may look backward. To every man this sort of prospect is a bitter thing—hopes disappointed, wishes unfulfilled, motives misinterpreted, calumny used. All these things one looks back upon and sees in the career which we have passed through. But still, in every desert they say there is an oasis, and I, looking back, see one bright spot in my career, and that is my connection with Sheffield.

Speaking of his life, he said—

I set out in political life attached to no political party in the State—allied to neither. I saw before me a straight line of conduct to pursue. I saw contending powers—on one side the great body of the Tory party ; on the other the great body of the Whig party. I truckled to neither, and I incurred the hate of both. . . . My life, I say, has been dedicated to my country. I have gained nothing for myself, but I hope I have won a name. But what is in a name ? In a few short years I shall disappear, and the chances are my name will be forgotten. In this rush and hurry of the world, in the great mass of people who come before the world's eyes, there are ten thousand chances to one that I shall be forgotten. But until I do die I shall have the cheering spirit within me that throughout my life I have done my duty ; and, doing my duty, I have won the applause, and I believe the support, of the best thinking of my countrymen.

He predicted that those who had ejected him from Sheffield would find they had made a mistake. The time would come when they would say, "The old man was not so bad a fellow as we thought him."

At a banquet the same evening Mr. Roebuck delivered what he called his "political testament." It was comprehended in these three points: "Beware of trades unions; beware of Ireland; beware of America." The warnings addressed to the capitalists in this speech, to the effect that if they yielded to the demands of labour they were ruined for ever, exposed Mr. Roebuck to renewed criticism and animadversion by the representatives of the working-men.

*To William Fisher (Sheffield).*

*May* 25, 1869.—I always fancied that you considered my interests as a legacy left you by your father, and in all my correspondence with you, whether personal or written, I have ever felt as if he were present, watching over and, as it were, sanctifying our friendship. I dare say you will think this somewhat strange language to be held by so matter-of-fact a person as myself. But I have, as I find at times, a stratum of sentiment in the hard composition of my spirit, and the untiring kindness of yourself and Mrs. Fisher has softened what the world calls my stony heart.

In the August of the same year (1869), Mr. Roebuck attended a banquet given to the Duke of Norfolk on the occasion of his coming of age. He spoke very appreciatively of honours, power, and wealth, and the aristocracy, though, curiously enough, describing himself as well known to be "a thorough-going Radical." At the succeeding Cutlers' Feast, in giving the toast of the Army and Navy, Mr. Roebuck complained that statesmen were met with "a pitiful talk about economy," though we had "around us jealous nations of every sort, from the despot to the free republic." In these years he frequently delivered addresses on Education—at Dewsbury, Nottingham, Meltham (near

Huddersfield), and elsewhere.  In these he was accustomed to claim that he had not swerved from the plan of education submitted by him to the House of Commons in 1833, and seeing in Mr. Forster's Bill a substantial realization of the principles he had long preached, that measure met with his cordial approval.  From time to time opportunities were given to Mr. Roebuck to keep in touch with his old constituency, many of his supporters cleaving tenaciously to the hope that he would yet regain his seat. Some approaches had been made to Mr. Roebuck by a section of the electors of Marylebone.  The exchange of views led to the publication of the following letter :—

*To the Editor of the Times.*

19, *Ashley Place, May* 27, 1869.—In your paper of to-day you have a statement that I received a deputation from persons residing in the borough of Marylebone, and that I made to them certain statements.  Among other statements it is said that I declared to them that I was opposed to Mr. Gladstone's Irish Church Bill, because I believed it to be a robbery and a spoliation. As I never said anything like this, I wish now to say what I did say, and the circumstances in which I spoke.  Certain gentlemen wrote to me asking if I would receive a deputation of persons connected with the borough of Marylebone on the subject of the probable vacancy in that borough.  I wrote to them, saying that I should be happy to receive them, but I asked them to decide whether our meeting should be considered public or private. Because, I said, if it is to be public, though the principles which I shall enunciate will be the same as those I should put forth in a private meeting, yet the words I shall use may be different.  A prudent reserve in the one case may not be my guide in the other. I was told by letter that the meeting was to be strictly private, and that the deputation would consider themselves bound in honour to deem everything that passed strictly private.  When the deputation came they asked me in general terms what were my views as to Mr. Gladstone's Irish Church Bill.  My answer was that in my view Mr. Gladstone's Bill was impolitic and dishonest ; but I wished them to understand that in my view an

Established Church was a bad instrument for the propagation of religion ; that therefore I was on that ground opposed to the Irish Church.   Still, I could not but acknowledge that the Irish Church had done much good, and though upon the whole I did not consider it an institution that I should have established, yet, being established, I was bound to acknowledge, as an Englishman, it had rendered great benefits to the State ; that under these circumstances I was asked to disestablish it.   My answer was that I believed the proposal to disestablish it was (1) impolitic, and next, (2) dishonest.   It was impolitic because it would not satisfy that class of the Irish people it sought to conciliate, and that it was put forth under false pretences.   I endeavoured to prove both these propositions, but I said nothing as to the robbery or spoliation, holding as I do that the property of the Irish Church is the property of the people, and that they may do with it as they please.   My belief that Mr. Gladstone's Bill is impolitic and dishonest is wholly different from the statement that it is a spoliation and a robbery.   A spoliation and a robbery I do not believe it to be, but that it is impolitic and dishonest every hour proves ; and the future will show that I am right in denouncing the minister who thus recklessly proposes so dangerous a measure.

After the work of the Royal Commission on Trades Unions terminated, towards the end of 1869, Mr. Roebuck was appointed on another, an inquiry into the Labour Laws, of which the head was the Chief Justice, Sir Alexander Cockburn.

The never-failing love of reading stood him in good stead.   He brightened up his Latin, and apparently with some relief he would put aside the turmoil of present day politics and turn to the comparative calm of the old Roman writers, scarcely one of whom he passed over; but Cicero, Valerius Paterculus, Horace, and Virgil were his chief favourites.   Of Virgil, indeed, he never wearied.   One day it was said to him, " You never seem to tire of Virgil ? " " Ah," he replied, with a little twist of his shoulders, " there is a devil in him "—alluding to the ancient notion that an especial demon inspired a poet.

In the early part of 1870 it was found that cataract in both eyes had formed; and when one eye had become quite darkened the cataract was removed with perfect success. From his always abstemious ways, but little change of habit was necessary, beyond remaining in a darkened room, and not using the eyes at all.

At this moment the Franco-Prussian war broke out, and he followed the course of events with the keenest anxiety. Every morning came the question, "Are the French moving on? have they crossed the frontier?" Then as days went on, it was, "Ah, if the French lose their first *élan*, if they do not continue to move rapidly onwards, they will be beaten."

At last, one Sunday in August, the newsboys were heard shouting the *Observer* in the street. The newspaper was brought in, and was found to contain the news of the battle of Wörth, the first serious reverse of the French army.

Some days later, among other incidents of the time that were told to Mr. Roebuck, was an exploit by Achille Murat, who was then on the staff of the French Emperor. Finding that the French were defeated, he asked leave, and went at once to Paris, to his wife, a Montenegrin princess, whom he instantly brought away to England, with her three-weeks'-old baby and her mother. A man asleep at a London hotel was awakened early one morning, to find standing by his bedside a French officer, whose uniform was torn to shreds by bullets. This was Achille Murat, who had just arrived in London with his family. His English friend, on hearing the state of affairs, told him to take his family to his country house, giving him the key of the cellar, with the injunction to make the ladies feel at home for as long as was necessary. Murat did so, and then returned to the Emperor, whom he never left until the captivity at Wilhelmshöhe.

Mr. Roebuck's recovery of sight was steady, and though he could again see, his family would not, for nearly three months, let him read or write. He followed the daily history of the war with the greatest interest, until at last the accounts became so terrible that he could no longer bear to hear them read. At this time he was at Usk, in Monmouthshire, and passed much time in the open air. One beautiful afternoon in early September he was sitting with his wife and daughter under a mulberry tree on the grass facing the river Usk, when his brother-in-law, Thomas Falconer, came hastily into the garden with a telegram in his hand, saying, " There has been a battle at Sedan; the French army has surrendered, and the Emperor is a prisoner."

The contrast between this terrible tale and the peaceful and secure surroundings in which it was told, made a deep impression on those present not lightly to be forgotten.

In the following November there was a very remarkable display of the Aurora Borealis. The awestruck Monmouthshire villagers declared that the war was shown in the sky.

To an elector of Sheffield Mr. Roebuck, some months later, made the fishing remark, " I fear that my good word has not much power nowadays in Sheffield." In answer to this his correspondent had assured him " that in almost every public room in Sheffield expressions of regret have been made that we have not a John Arthur Roebuck in Parliament, but the mere links of a chain the Premier can rattle at his will." This elicited the following letter :—

### To a Sheffield Elector.

*January* 3, 1871.—I have seen in my time so many instances of short memories on the part of the people, that I felt that two years' absence was quite enough to wipe me out of men's recollections. I can easily fancy, however, that the want of a plain, bold speaker, with some political knowledge, may be felt at the present hour, when England's interests are trembling in the balance. I sit and chafe, knowing that I can do nothing, and seeing that weakness and imbecile vanity rule and guide our councils in this important crisis. The next year will place in jeopardy the honour, the power—aye, the very existence—of our country, and all we can do is to sit by with folded hands, and accept quietly what fate shall bring. But this language is useless. We must submit. As for myself, I am very well, and mentally I believe myself to be as vigorous as ever. My blindness, thanks to modern art, has been greatly relieved, and I can read and write as usual. I am writing to you by the aid of what I call my *new eye*, and the result lies before you—no very bad specimen of renovated sight. Years are stealing on ; I know not what I may be capable of when the time for action comes. But if then I shall be as I am now, I shall be willing, if called on, to fight my old fight in favour of truth and freedom, and to do battle against noisy humbug and vulgar hypocrisy.

*To William Fisher (Sheffield).*

*February* 21, 1871.—Is there any chance for me, if I stand again for Sheffield ? Now, I want you to answer me this question frankly. Do not fear that I shall shut my ears to the voice of a true friend like you. If you say that there is no fair chance, and that my coming forward would be a tax upon my friends, which they would consider a disagreeable burthen, I should at once abstain from putting myself forward, and consider myself as politically dead—a circumstance which would give me no great pain, certainly none equal to what I should feel if I believed that my friends looked upon my candidature as an unnecessary trouble, a thing not desirable, and upon me as a pestilent bore.

The answer to this inquiry may be judged from the fact that in March, 1871, Mr. Roebuck lectured in Sheffield on the events which had occurred since the General Election. The Irish Church Act and the Irish Land Act were both " unwise, unstatesmanlike, and fraught with danger." Nor were there wanting in his address scornful references to " those gentle cousins of ours " across the Atlantic. As to the Franco-German War, Lord Granville ought to have told both despots that before God and man their conduct deserved the reprobation of mankind. Another speech, on current political topics, appointed for December 14, 1871, had been deferred because, just when it should have been delivered, the Prince of Wales was hovering between life and death, and in the painful national anxiety public attention was riveted on the bulletins from his sick-bed.

*To an unnamed Correspondent.*

*December 2, 1871.*—I am alarmed, too, by the language of the bulletins, which is always in royal cases studiously guarded, but I fancy one can generally read through the lines, and find a meaning at the back. Following that plan now, I can, I believe, see that the prince has been far worse than the world is told. Besides the royal family, the person who suffers the greatest distress must be Lord Londesborough, whose house was the scene of the disaster, and whose care, by flushing the drains, called the poison into action. The same thing has so often happened, that I am astonished that a thing so well known to be dangerous should have been done. May it please God to avert any further calamity. The queen, poor lady, is in no fit state to bear up against any great grief. But gloomy anticipations are unwise.

*To the same.*

*December 9, 1871.*—If the Prince of Wales should die before the 14th, or if he continues in the same precarious state, it will be impossible for me, as a gentleman, to deliver my speech on the 14th. I know this will be the cause of annoyance, but I cannot help it. At this time to show disrespect to the queen and the Princess of Wales would not suit my feelings, and would certainly be thoroughly impolitic—would, in fact, be the height of folly. The state of the public mind here in London is such as has not been seen since the day of the death of Princess Charlotte; and I see throughout the country meetings of all kinds are being postponed. Under these circumstances, I beg of you to coincide with me in thinking that our meeting should be indefinitely postponed. A favourable and quiet time will come when what I shall utter, if there be anything of worth in it, will receive due attention, and my warnings, if worthy, will have their due weight.

*To the same.*

*January* 15, 1872.—My appearance at Sheffield this time has no personal object. I go simply because I was asked, not because I wished to appear, nor because I hoped from so doing I should reap any personal advantage. I have long since given up all expectation of re-election. I feel that my course is run, and that others think so. I think I was weak in yielding to Dodworth's request; but the bolt is shot, and the result cannot be very mischievous to my body. . . . I am not surprised that you should think old friends drop from me. 'Tis the nature of things—I am old; have been long, too long, before the world. Young faces and new hopes excite vivid emotions. I feel no pain at this and make no complaint. Old services are forgotten amid the rush of fresh expectations. And all this makes the passing away of life less of a regret.

The postponed meeting was held on January 17, 1872. Mr. Roebuck was careful to repeat that he had no personal object to serve in attending. He was there simply to gratify those friends who wished to hear opinions on the present condition of the country from one who, "cast, as it were, ashore, as on the bank of some rushing river, might look on that river with calmness and equanimity, and could regard affairs with a more tranquil, and calm, and assured, and penetrating eye, than if mixed up in the turmoil." The speech was largely an attack on Mr. Gladstone. He described him and Mr. Disraeli as bidding against each other, Mr. Gladstone overtrumping the card of Household Suffrage with Irish Disestablishment. He saw in every act the resolute determination of Mr. Gladstone to obtain personal power and domination, even at the expense of the State and the Constitution. He spoke of him as a man gifted with many great powers, but at the same time gifted with many great weaknesses.

He is a great speaker, but to my mind no orator. He has great powers of what is called eloquence, and he certainly has

z

the command of resource in the business of deception. Besides, he has that sort of feminine vindictiveness that always runs with weak-minded men, and you will see that everybody who, in any portion of his career, crossed his path, is punished by a crushing power. This is brought to bear in many and curious ways. He cannot maintain his own counsel, but out it comes ; what is within him he must declare. . . . If you allow the domination of Mr. Gladstone to proceed onward as it has been proceeding, you will be a very foolish people, deserving of every species of degradation to which people can be subjected.

This speech was remarkable as containing one of Mr. Roebuck's rare admissions of mistake in policy, or change in opinion. In an earlier part of this book we saw with what vehemence he assailed the House of Lords, and how impatiently he denounced Lord John Russell's acceptance of the peers' emasculation of the Municipal Corporations Bill. Instead of concessions, he had said, "Let us re-enact every one of our original measures, saying that such was the pleasure of the people—let those who dare resist it." And he had insisted that "unmixed is the evil which the House of Lords inflicts upon the nation, whether we view them as legislators, as judges, or simply as an aristocracy."

But now, after forty years, he found a long string of reasons in vindication of the House of Lords, and justifying its recent action in throwing out the Ballot Bill. "I have lived long enough," he said, "to find out that I have made blunders in life, and I have acquired the courage to proclaim the blunders I have made. . . . I recollect perfectly well in my youth having written a paper headed 'Of what Use is the House of Lords?' but I must say I made a great mistake."

He repeated this confession at the Cutlers' Feast in the next autumn. "I answered that question very much to my own satisfaction then, but very much to my own disapprobation now. I could not at that time see the great advantage which I now think arises from the existence of that assembly."

A year later (March, 1873), Mr. Roebuck, speaking at a Foresters' banquet, bade the working-men beware of "miserable" demagogues, "mischief makers," who, "like a serpent, come to bite and instil venom." This advice was not well received by those to whom it was addressed. In the same month the sound of the coming electoral battle was heard in the appointment of a committee to get up a requisition asking Mr. Roebuck to come forward for the representation of Sheffield at the next election.

It was, in fact, manifest that an appeal to the country could not long be deferred, and as it was deemed certain that the age of Mr. Hadfield would prevent him from seeking re-election, the Liberals of Sheffield were anxious to be provided with a suitable candidate, as a colleague for Mr. Mundella. But there were many causes of dissension, making agreement impossible. The natural result was that, when the end of the year came, two suggested Liberal candidates for Mr. Hadfield's seat were in the field—Mr. Alfred Allott, a local aspirant, and Mr. Joseph Chamberlain, then Mayor of Birmingham. Mr. Chamberlain's presence at a mass meeting, where he was enthusiastically adopted, filled the Conservatives with apprehension, and compelled Mr. Roebuck to make up his mind decisively whether he would stand or not.

*To John Lawton (Sheffield).*

*January*, 1874.—One great object in all I do and say is to meet the wishes of my friends and justify their kindness and friendship. Now, you must be well aware that amongst those friends there are often conflicting views and opinions, and that I must often be in a difficulty when endeavouring to meet the wishes of all that wish me well. I am in that position at this present time. Some of my heartiest supporters desire that I should hold a public meeting in January and address the electors. Other friends, equally hearty, believe that such a proceeding would be exceedingly unwise and out of time, and I must own that I believe this latter opinion to be correct.

Further consideration confirmed him in the opinion that it was inexpedient for him at that time to address the electors, and although this was based on the plea of the undesirability of prematurely involving the borough in the turmoil of a contested election, his followers despaired of having him as a candidate, and in public put forth reasons, based on " pride, and principle, and policy," why he should neither appear to court the suffrages of the electors, nor care to go back to the House of Commons. They made up their minds, indeed, that Mr. Chamberlain would fill the vacant seat. But when, on the sudden dissolution of Parliament a week or two after, it was found that Liberal opinion was acutely divided between Mr. Allott and Mr. Chamberlain, the chance was too good to be lost, and bolder counsels prevailed. Mr. Roebuck's hesitations were thrown to the winds. Telegram after telegram poured in, praying him to go down, and at last Mr. and Mrs. Roebuck went to Sheffield to stay with Mr. Thomas Jessop, a very staunch and hearty friend.

The Tories, avoiding the mistake of putting one of their own party in the field, united with the Roebuckites, and exerted all their strength to return one who, though still calling himself "a thorough-going Radical," systematically supported the Tories, and opposed the Liberals far more effectually than any Conservative could have done. The rival claims of Mr. Chamberlain and Mr. Allott were, indeed, submitted to a mass meeting in Paradise Square, and, in obedience to the verdict, Mr. Allott retired. But it was too late. The short time that intervened between the dissolution and the completion of the election, was eminently favourable to Mr. Roebuck and unfavourable to Mr. Chamberlain. It enabled Mr. Roebuck's friends to dispense with more than a single appearance of their candidate in public, and it gave Mr. Chamberlain very few

opportunities to make himself known to the electors—
a misfortune that was enhanced by the death of his father,
which compelled his absence from Sheffield for two or
three days.

Mr. Roebuck's one election speech was prefaced by his
customary bit of autobiography—

Something very near to fifty years ago, I determined within
myself to be a public man upon the public stage of England, and
I thought when I regarded the state of party in this country,
and the form of government under which we live, that there
required something more than there had hitherto been seen,
something more than the clashing battles of Tory and Whig, of
Conservative and Liberal ; that there ought to be a body of men
neither of one party nor the other, but simply of the party of the
country itself. I determined within myself to be one of that
party. I hoped that by showing an example others might follow
in my steps ; but I determined that everything—place, profit, distinction, honour—all should be sacrificed to the one great object
that I desired, namely, to bring before my countrymen a body of
independent members, who should follow only the interests of the
country. Now that has been my object through life, and so
steadily have I pursued it that although often place, power, and
profit have been within my grasp, I forfeited them all because I
wished to continue onward in the course which I had begun,
namely, an independent member of Parliament. That I have been.
From the beginning to the hour in which you withdrew your
confidence from me, I was emphatically an independent member
of Parliament. Neither Whig nor Tory could count upon me, and
the " whipper in " dared not approach me with his whip. It has
been invariably said—aye, I speak it with proud confidence—
" It is not worth while to ask for Roebuck's vote. You don't
know which way he will vote ; he votes as he thinks proper."
Now, that was the guide and rule of my conduct when I entered
Parliament.

Mr. Roebuck, aforetime, had been a resolute champion
of secular education. The exclusion from the model school
he founded in Bath of all religious instruction beyond a
reading from the Bible by the Master, proved a not

inconsiderable factor in his defeat at Bath in 1837.  Speaking now of religious teaching in our schools, he defined the Bible as "the great well of English undefiled," and in a few sentences afterwards he continued—

It is not one book, it is many books.  It is literature, it is history, it is law, it is proverbs, it is poetry, it is essays, it is all, it is everything, it is the Bible.  He is an ignorant man who wishes to shut the Bible out from the young of this country.

By a device, attributed to the other side, Mr. Allott, in spite of his protests, was nominated, and the mayor refused to allow his name to be withdrawn.  In the result, Mr. Roebuck polled 14,193 votes, Mr. Mundella 12,858, Mr. Chamberlain 11,053, and Mr. Allott 621.  The winners were jubilant, and from all parts of the country there were expressions of satisfaction, for not even Liberals were proof against the piquancy of the prospect of the House of Commons once more enjoying " Tear 'em's " pungent oratory.

Of course there were the inevitable banquets in Sheffield. At the first of these, in February, Mr. Roebuck said—

The work at the poll, and the emotion expressed this evening, are not the result of a mere passing feeling.  They are the reward of a life of service.  You tell me my life has been spent in a way that you approve, and when I think from whom that approval comes, that you represent, and represent fairly, the great bulk of the people of England, who are my countrymen, have I not a right to be proud, and shall I be accused of egotism because on this occasion I speak for myself and in obedience to your approval ?

He attributed the Liberal reverses to the feeling of insecurity created in the country by " a reckless, hasty, petulant course of action."

And here, again, there was another softening of old beliefs—

I say to my Liberal friends, you, in your younger days, believed that the Church of England was an institution that was very injurious to the people of England. I answer, as one of these, I did believe so, but time has gone on, and the Church of England has improved, and with her improvement my opinions have changed. I believe the Liberal party has changed. I ask the Liberal party if they would now have Disestablishment? I say no, I do not believe they would.

If I might presume to give any advice to the great men who may hereafter govern this country, I would say to them, "Make a new party; forget on the one side what is called Liberal, and on the other what is called Conservative, and make a National party. Let England be your concern, and not party considerations."

A "Working-men's banquet" followed a month or two later. Referring to some outside criticisms on his attitude on the Trades Union Commission, Mr. Roebuck remarked—

These are things that I regard not. I answer them by my life. I say to any man who has spoken in covert slander, "Look at what I have done, and why I have done it, and for what I have done it?" I have never been a paid agitator. I have never lived upon the hard earnings of my fellow working-men; I have never gone forward to spread discontent amongst working-men against masters whom they ought to respect. I have done none of these things, and perhaps, therefore, you dislike me. I am known unto you. My life has been dedicated to my country. Such as it is, governed by the intelligence which God has given me, it has been employed, I think honestly, fearlessly, on behalf of my fellow countrymen. I have not asked whether they be rich, or whether they be poor. Whether they be great men, or whether they be little men, I have expected nothing from them. I told them what I thought of them. If I thought well of them, I said that good of them; if I thought ill of them, I told them what I thought. And shall it now be said that I am sent to that Labour Commission to represent the masters?

He explained that when asked to serve on that Commission he accepted the position in obedience to the dictates of duty, although knowing it would cost him his seat in Parliament. He counselled Englishmen against leaving their country at the instigation of those who would have them emigrate, advising them to remain at home and make her great. "And I hold him to be a dastard Englishman who drives Englishmen from England. . . . There are many here that flit across the country like a bad miasma—or like the light that leads you into a bog."

The peroration was simple, but very effective :—

I remember what has been stated as to the allotted life of man. I have passed that. Many years are not allotted to me now, but those years, whatever they may be, shall be dedicated to my countrymen ; and I feel that in a community like the one I see before me I am doing good in my generation, and in my latter days paving the way for the good that comes when between Englishmen and Englishmen, rank and rank, men shall be brothers, and we shall fight the war of life against the whole world, shoulder to shoulder, Englishmen all, all brothers, all deserving before the law to be cherished and recognized, doing their duty, and doing it honoured amongst men.

# CHAPTER XXVIII.

MR. ROEBUCK did not take any prominent part in the debates in the first Session of the new Parliament. The expansion of the constituencies by household suffrage had given rise to a demand for an extension of the hours of polling, that the more industrious portion of the artisans might be able to vote in the evening, without leaving their employment during working hours.   Mr. Roebuck declared himself against the change, alleging that no working-man had complained to him.   In June he was found opposing, as usual, Sir Wilfrid Lawson's Permissive Bill.

In July, Mr. Butt brought forward a proposal for Home Rule, in the form of a motion " That this House will immediately resolve itself into a committee to consider the present Parliamentary relations between Great Britain and Ireland."   For some years past Mr. Roebuck had preached the doctrine that Ireland had no substantial grievances— her miseries, he insisted, were caused by her own weaknesses, prejudices, narrowness, mutual hostility, and improvidence.   The Irish members came to Parliament eternally whining like mendicants, and the Roman Catholic clergy had, he said, preached sedition, and had taught the Irish people to hate the English rule.   Ireland was not fit for Home Rule.   The result of it would be that civil war would break out before the power of England had been withdrawn a single hour.   The north would rise against the south and would put it down. Let Irishmen, he counselled, learn how much their true happiness is promoted by the union with England.

On the 2nd of July, Mr. Roebuck, with apologies for his feebleness, rose to enforce these views, to insist upon self-help and self-reliance as the one thing needed by Ireland, and to maintain how fatal separation from England would be. His voice was so low that he was called upon to speak up. On this, for a few sentences, he raised his voice to a pitch of clearness and emphasis reminiscent of his vigorous days. But almost immediately afterwards he stopped abruptly in the midst of an unfinished sentence.

The House gave him an encouraging cheer. He indicated his appreciation of its kindness, but he could not recover the thread of his argument. Extending his arms, with his hands open, and remarking, " My forces fail me ; I cannot go on," he resumed his seat, with the assistance of members near him. A minute before, it seemed as if he were possessed of his old energy, and would deliver an effective and vigorous speech. He sat down among many indications of the generous and warm-hearted sympathy which in the House of Commons rises superior to all political considerations. He did not, however, leave the House, but sat out the rest of the debate, and voted in the Division.

The state of health thus indicated compelled Mr. Roebuck to make his attendances in the House of Commons both brief and rare. Thus he took no part in the animated discussions on the attempt made in the Public Worship Regulation Bill to curb Ritualism in the Church of England. But his opinion on this much-controverted measure was expressed in a letter to a Sheffield clergyman, in which he described himself as deeply grieved at the strife raging in the Church. He could hardly fancy, he said, that the two Archbishops, and the present and past Lord Chancellors, promoted that Bill as part of a plan for pulling down the

Church. So far as he could see, the only object of the Bill was to put a stop to the silly and dangerous doings of men who were carried away by fanatical notions as to the importance of dress, posture, and genuflections—men whose great purpose seemed to be to make figures of themselves, to be stared at by young girls and silly women. He was prepared to aid in the endeavour to repress these follies.

In another letter, of somewhat earlier date, touching on the same subject, he had written—

I have a great contempt for the trumpery and puerility of what is called Ritualism, and, as being contrary to the feelings of the large majority of the members of the Church of England, I am prepared to insist that it be not manifested in the churches which are public. If a man build a church and continue it private property, he may be permitted to play in it what foolish pranks he pleases ; but he ought not to have the sanction of the State to what might be considered private or particular folly. As to the Ecclesiastical Courts, I am prepared to support any well-devised scheme for their reform or reconstruction. But the reform of a legal system is a far more difficult matter than unlearned persons suppose. The reform ought to be complete and systematic ; piecemeal reforms are mischievous. The thing ought to be completely done, or not attempted. I am not prepared to point out any known man competent to the task of framing a new and better system. There must, however, be such men to be found if properly sought for. Honesty, knowledge, courage, ought to be the chief qualities in the character of the ecclesiastical reformer.

There is nothing remarkable to record in Mr. Roebuck's Parliamentary work in 1875. He earnestly advocated the passing of the Burials Bill, and, speaking on yet another of the perpetually recurring Irish Coercion Bills, he repeated his old contention that, admitting the bad Government to which Ireland had been subjected in the past, since the Reform Act the House of Commons had honestly and successfully striven to do justice to Ireland. At that moment, he insisted, the people of Ireland were as well governed as those of England. He paid various visits to his constituents, and showed his old interest in education by attending the re-opening of the Manchester Athenæum by Lord Chief Justice Coleridge. In this year he received a very graceful compliment from his colleague in the representation of Sheffield. Mr. Mundella had been so fortunate as to acquire portraits of Mr. Roebuck and Lord Brougham, painted when they were in the prime of life, by Mr. Pickersgill, R.A., and he presented these to the local museum. The conjunction was especially appropriate, because of the relations of intimacy subsisting between Brougham and Roebuck. On the occasion of Brougham's death, in 1868, Mr. Roebuck had pronounced a eulogy upon him as "a wise, a great, and a good man," when urging upon the Government the suitability of erecting a monument to his memory.

Mr. Roebuck supported (1876) the proposal of the Government to add to the Royal style and title of her Majesty the appellation, "Empress of India." "I like," he said, "the word 'Queen' better than 'Empress,' but what I have to consider is the position which England holds on this question." He answered the questions, Was it wise to make any alteration at all? and, Was it wise to make the alteration which the Ministry proposed?—in the affirmative, although acknowledging that it would be well to localize the title and keep it strictly for use with regard to India.

*To Mrs. Roebuck.*

19, *Ashley Place, May* 8, 1876.— . . . On Saturday the Duke of Wellington called. He immediately began about the Titles Bill. In the course of the conversation he told me this story.

"My father was Prince of Waterloo, but he never called himself so. He had too many titles to mention them all on all occasions, but he had once to pay dear for them. He told a man to order dinner for him at a particular hotel. The man did so, mentioning all the Duke's titles. The Duke came, waited a short time, 'Is the dinner not coming?' he said. 'Why don't you bring the dinner?' The waiter answered, 'We are waiting for the rest of the party.' They had prepared dinner for about twenty people—and which cost £20."

Now, here is a letter of gossip for you!

The old dislike to coercive measures of sobriety cropped out once more on the Irish Sunday Closing Bill (1877). Mr. Roebuck admitted that, at first, under the impression that the people of Ireland wanted this measure, and that drunkenness was exceptionally rampant on Sundays, he was disposed to support it; but subsequently convinced of the inaccuracy of these beliefs, he strongly opposed provisions which, he argued, would increase rather than diminish Sunday drinking, and he urged that the proper plan was to provide rational amusement by opening museums.

When the disquiet that had prevailed in the Turkish provinces of Eastern Europe culminated in the Bulgarian massacres, Mr. Roebuck gave his support to the policy of Lord Beaconsfield's Government, maintaining that it was in harmony with the past history of this country, and that it was calculated to maintain the prestige and good name of England throughout the world. True to his antipathy to Mr. Gladstone and his methods, he aimed his invectives less at the Turkish crimes than at the great Liberal's fervid denunciation of them. This he described as a disgraceful clamour—"a row" made for party purposes without consideration of consequences, weakening the hands of the Government and endangering a war productive of far greater evils. Mr. Gladstone was, in his view, "a bastard philanthropist," and "no statesman." Roebuck was strongly in favour of sustaining the Turkish Empire; and while he denounced Russia for cruelty, falseness, and cowardice, he championed the Turk as "an honest kind of good fellow," and "the gentleman" amongst nationalities. But while the Turk was a man for whom he had the greatest possible respect, he hated and detested the Turkish Government as heartily as he abhorred that of Russia. The war he believed to have been entered upon simply for dynastic purposes, and the policy for England was to maintain peace, as far as it was consistent with English interests—which was only another way of saying with the interests of the world. With these views, uttered at the Sheffield Cutlers' Feast of 1877, were mingled scoffs at Mr. Gladstone's enthusiasm, passion, vanity, and self-sufficiency. " He may be a very good chopper, but, depend upon it, he is not an English statesman."

Being, at the commencement of 1878, unequal to the physical effort of addressing his constituents on this Eastern question, Mr. Roebuck complied with a request for a statement of his views, in the following letter :—

### To a Constituent.

19, *Ashley Place, January* 7, 1878.—It is with great difficulty that I bring myself to the task of answering your letter. I am oppressed by a great sorrow, and my mind is bowed down and darkened by a cloud which now hangs over me. The oldest and dearest of my friends * has died suddenly, and the blow has shaken me heavily. Excuse me, then, if my answer is short and general. You seem surprised that I have not publicly expressed my views on what is called the Eastern Question. I have been silent because I believed I could do no good by speaking, and might do harm. The evidence before the world is necessarily very incomplete, so that the means of forming a judgment is imperfect. Besides, I believed that the Government intended to do what was required by the honour and interests of England. I knew them to be men of ability, and furthermore, I believed them to be honest. They have before them the best evidence the case affords, and their judgments would not, I conceived, be aided by any suggestions of mine. Moreover, I knew that there was great danger of misconception abroad. Foreigners seldom understand us, and are always prone to judge all that we say with prejudice, and to draw conclusions from our words that were never intended

* G. J. Graham.

Seeing, then, that there was no necessity for my speaking, I held my tongue. I find no fault with those who take a different view. I suppose them to believe that they are doing their duty by giving expression to what I think crude and unsupported opinions—opinions which, if spoken by myself, with my views, would have been, in my judgment, simply mischievous impertinence. Well, then, you may ask, have you no opinions concerning the present state of things? My answer is, I certainly have opinions on the matter, and very strong ones, which I shall deem it my duty to set forth in my place in Parliament, but which would do no good if *officiously* stated at the present time and under present circumstances.

As my chief great aim is the maintenance of peace, and the preservation of the interests and honour of England, and as I believe that to be the aim of the Administration, I hold that the safest course for any one like myself, having no official position, is to abstain from interference in matters which are at present veiled from our view. I deem it unjust and dangerous to attribute intentions to our Government which no one can prove them to entertain, and which they altogether disdain. By so doing we weaken their influence abroad, and render more difficult the task which lies before them, and take away from the power for good which our country ought to possess. The discordant clamour of contending parties here in England does infinite mischief, as it leads foreign nations to believe that there is no stability in our councils, and that, for anything we can do in the great troubles of Europe, England may be left out of consideration. If, on the other hand, we were to exhibit to the world the spectacle of a nation steadily supporting our Government, the word of that Government would have weight with all parties interested in the conflict going on, and our endeavour to procure peace and an honourable settlement of the present discords would be successful.

The war, in my mind, is a thoroughly unjust proceeding on the part of Russia. The pretences she puts forth are, in my mind, mere figments. She is no less barbarous than Turkey ; she is far more dishonest. I have no admiration for the Turkish Government ; but I do not believe that the substitution of Russia for Turkey would be a benefit to the wretched people who are made the pretext for the present invasion.

In this state of things it is very difficult to choose a safe and honest course for England. To support either would be to support bad government. If we were to support Russia, in addition to bad government we should aid national dishonesty. Then, on the other hand, if we stand still and allow Russia to possess herself of all European Turkey, we should fatally injure the interests of England, and the cause of liberty in Europe. In this state, what are we to do ? Withhold aid from both parties, but give Russia plainly to understand that we shall make *territorial aggrandisement* a *casus belli*. Russia would not dare to go to war with England. We need no armies. A fleet in the Baltic and one in the Mediterranean would paralyze Russia ; and we may rest assured that Austria, France, Germany, and the lesser States of the East and South of Europe, look with no friendly eyes upon Russia. We have no interests that cross those of these countries. Peace with the world is our policy ; and, if we presented to the world the spectacle of a united people, we should have weight in the councils of Europe. But, quarrelling with one another, and tearing each other to pieces, the world believes us to be paralyzed by our discords, laughs at and scorns us. Would that we could put aside party feuds and act as brethren should act, and thus our course would be plain, and our policy safe and easy. In my present state of mind, I cannot write more ; but I hope the time is not far distant when I shall be able to explain myself fully upon this important matter, and support that policy which the true interests of our country require. ·

During the month that followed, Mr. Roebuck was compelled by serious indisposition to absent himself much from Parliament; but in May the opportunity which he had desired of exposing his views on the Eastern Question in Parliament, was afforded to him. In connection with this, there occurred an incident which gave rise to much feeling and misconception. The House was debating the action of the Government in bringing Indian troops to Malta, and Mr. Roebuck, on the evening of May 23, made a speech in support of this step, and in condemnation of the course pursued by the Opposition, in bringing forward Lord Hartington's hostile motion. From his place among the Liberals, leaning on his stick, he bitterly denounced them with scathing epigrams. An eye-witness of the scene wrote—

At first he spoke in so low a tone as to be hardly audible. The silence, however, speedily became so intense that every word could be heard, and, so encouraged, the hon. gentleman made an effort to revive his old style. In the middle of his speech a curious little incident occurred, which brought out the sympathy of the House. The stillness of the chamber had for a moment been broken by the movements of a clumsy member, and there was a cry of "Order." The interruption, which was unintelligible to the veteran, attracted his attention, and for a moment he paused to ascertain what it meant. Leaning forward on his stick, and turning round with evident difficulty, he inquired whether it was meant that he was out of order, and, by way of explaining his request, added the words, "I did not hear, and I cannot see." Out of consideration for the age and antecedents of the hon. member, the Liberals refrained from demonstrations of all kinds throughout his speech, while, for a similar cause, the Tories were all the louder in their applause, the loudest cheers being evoked by what was nothing more nor less than a covert attack on the sincerity of Mr. Gladstone. When Mr. Roebuck ended, he left the House amid a general exodus of members.

Later in the night, Mr. Roebuck was answered by Sir Henry James, who worked up the House to an intense pitch of excitement by quoting a passage from one of Mr. Roebuck's old Pamphlets. In this he had abused the Tories with even more vigour than that with which to-night he had vilified the Liberals. Sir Henry James, who was exceedingly animated, spoke amid continual interruptions from the Tory benches. When he quoted the declaration that the Tories were persons who only wanted to "fleece the people," there was quite an uproar in the House; and Sir Henry Drummond Wolff, amid loud cries, rose to inquire whether the quotation was in order. The Speaker, to the delight of the Opposition, ruled in favour of Sir Henry James, who, having with difficulty, and amid shouts of "Date," "Question," and other cries,

2 A

finished reading the extract, ended by dramatically tearing up the manuscript, flinging the pieces on the table, and inviting Mr. Roebuck to take his seat among his political allies.

Sir Henry James was still speaking to a crowded House when Mr. Roebuck made his appearance and moved slowly up the floor to his usual seat, the first below the gangway on the Opposition side.   Mr. Dillwyn, who claimed the seat, though conceding it by courtesy to Mr. Roebuck when advised of his intention to be present, showed no disposition to give way, nor did Mr. Walter or Sir Charles Dilke, who occupied the next places, make an effort to incommode themselves for Mr. Roebuck's convenience.   Some, on the other side, cried " Oh," and broke out into cheers when Mr. Gorst and Mr. R. Yorke ostentatiously crossed the floor and offered the hon. member a seat among the ultra Tories.   For a moment or two there seemed some hesitation in the mind of the honourable member.   In the result he accepted the invitation, and took the proffered seat amid the prolonged cheers of the Ministerialists.   Several around said to him, " Now you are here, why not stay with us ? "   His answer was a shake of the head, " That I *cannot* do.   It will not do."

About this period the " interviewer " for a London newspaper attributed to the " little man," whom he found in a shawl dressing-gown in Ashley Place, the statement that he had a very high opinion of a large proportion of the working class, but little sympathy with their leaders. He was represented as saying that he had often thought that, had he chosen to sacrifice his self-respect, he might have become a leader of working men himself.*   They liked, as soldiers do, to be led by gentlemen.   They had no distrust of their social superiors; on the contrary, trusting them far more than their own brethren.

---

* See *ante*, pp. 118 and 204.

They think a gentleman has nothing to gain, and they give him credit for perfect disinterestedness. In the main they are quite right. Sometimes I regret that I did not take them in hand. I feel certain I could have helped them, for I know their wants and feelings, their faults and failings, thoroughly, and I like and esteem them—that is, those who work instead of talking. I am perfectly frank in telling them of their faults, and they like me none the worse for doing so.

## CHAPTER XXIX.

### THE LAST YEAR—DEATH IN HARNESS.   1878–1879.

ALREADY, in the spring of 1878, politicians and constituencies were beginning to look forward to the time when the country would be called upon to pronounce a verdict on the doings of the Beaconsfield administration. The problems of the future exercised both Mr. Roebuck's friends and his opponents in Sheffield.

*To William Fisher (Sheffield).*

*April* 19, 1878.—My own wish is to retire ; the fatigues of Parliament pressing now heavily upon me.   But I feel this to be a great crisis when opinions are of vital importance.   I have been greatly pained by much of the talk that has been going on, while our country, its greatness, and even safety, are greatly threatened. In this state of things, to shrink from the strife, and for one's own ease to retire from the struggle, would be paltry cowardice. In this case, then, I wish to know the wishes of my old friends. Do they desire to retain my services such as they are and will be ? Do they think that I should be useful, with all the failings which decaying nature brings ?   Do they believe that, weak veteran that I am, my figure in the front of the battle would be an aid to the cause of our common beloved country ?   If they think and say, "Yes," then I am ready to undertake the struggle, and do my utmost in this hour of need and danger.   My life has been one continued strife in favour of great principles, and whenever I may retire I shall feel that most of the objects at which I have aimed have been won.   I should be proud, even when this is the case, to continue my labours for the purpose of upholding the honour and safety of England. To die in harness in such a cause would be a glory and a triumph.

In June the local Liberals threw down the gage of battle by adopting Mr. S. D. Waddy as Mr. Mundella's colleague when the next contest should come, and the challenge was taken up. Mr. Roebuck presented himself as a candidate for re-election, and delivered a speech which showed that he had lost none of his old habit of hard hitting. The meeting was notable as the first public acknowledgment of an alliance between him and the Conservative party. Those present pledged themselves to support Mr. Roebuck at the next election, " and whatever other candidate may be chosen by the committee of his Liberal and Conservative friends."

The last occasion on which Mr. Roebuck addressed the House of Commons was in the debate on the memorable resolutions of Lord Hartington (August, 1878), condemning the protocols of the Berlin Congress. He began with an apology. " I feel myself weak," he said, " and almost unable to appear before this House, and I beg therefore its indulgence on the present occasion." That indulgence was readily accorded to him, and he proceeded to express the opinion that the Government, with respect to the Eastern Question, had pursued the right course, " bravely, sagaciously, successfully."

At the end of the year, the declaration of war against Afghanistan compelled the Ministry to summon Parliament for a short session. Mr. Roebuck had intended to take part in the debate on Mr. Whitbread's motion condemning the policy which led to the war, but the death of a brother-in-law prevented him. This was unfortunate. Remembering the prominent part Mr. Roebuck took in the Afghan debates of 1843, his attitude, when history repeated itself, would have been interesting. The fact that he voted with the Government indicates the line he would have taken. He had come, by this time, to be regarded by the whips of

the Tory party as one of their flock.   There is in existence
a letter from Sir W. Hart Dyke regretting inability to
find "a pair" for Mr. Roebuck for the division of December
13, but offering to him the accommodation of his private
room during the hours of waiting for the debate to end.
Thus had Mr. Roebuck at last succumbed to that crack of
the "whip," which he so scornfully resented during the
election of 1874, when he said that neither Whig nor Tory
could count upon his vote, and that no "whipper-in" dared
approach him.

In 1878, Mr. Roebuck was, on the recommendation of
his antagonist of old days, then Mr. Disraeli, now Lord
Beaconsfield, sworn in a member of the Queen's Most
Honourable Privy Council.  He committed to paper, in
compliance with the wishes of his family, the following
"Story of my being made a Privy Councillor":—

Sir John Brown, at the end of July, 1878, wrote asking me
to request Lord Beaconsfield to be a guest at the next Cutlers'
feast.   I went, by appointment, to Downing Street, and after
our talk on this matter was over, Lord Beaconsfield said, "I had
intended, before I received your letter, to ask you to come and
see me, as there is a matter upon which I desire to speak to you.
Some time before I went to Berlin, the Queen wrote to me a
letter in which she spoke of you.  The paragraph was a very
pretty one, and I had resolved to show it to you; but in the
bustle of my departure the letter was mislaid, but I can tell you
the substance.  Her Majesty said that she thought that some
mark of her appreciation of your conduct should be conferred
upon you.  That conduct, she said, 'was that of a true patriot.'
These were her words, and she applied to me to suggest the mode.
I then proposed that the office of Privy Councillor would be an
appropriate distinction.  It would show that the distinction came
from her Majesty herself, and in this case would not be official
but simply personal; the result of her Majesty's own approval,
and not the appendage of any office.  Would this suit your views
and wishes?"

I answered, "Yes, certainly.  I had long thought that such
a distinction would be an honour, and one which, while it was

really an honour, could not be deemed by any one unworthy as the corrupt reward of corrupt conduct." "There is only one thing," said Lord Beaconsfield, "and that is to save you the trouble of a long journey to Osborne. I hope that the Court may go to Windsor, and that you may be sworn in there."

On the morning of the 14th of August Zippy saw me to Victoria Station, where I found that the Lord Chancellor, the Duke of Richmond and Gordon, the Duke of Northumberland, and Mr. Peel, Clerk of the Privy Council, were to be my fellow-travellers. There was pleasant chat on the way, the Duke of Richmond most completely fulfilling his promise to take care of me. He insisted on giving me his arm, and helping me in and out of the railway carriage, the steamers, and the carriages into which we had to get before we arrived at Osborne.

On the way down I said to Mr. Peel, on finding that I had to kneel to kiss her Majesty's hand, "By the Lord, I shall be like Gibbon if I go on my knees; it will require somebody to help me up. Seriously, it will be very difficult and painful." Whereupon the Duke of Richmond said that he would arrange it, and so he did; for after our arrival at Osborne he told me that the Queen had been so good as to dispense with my going on my knees, and that I should be permitted to kiss hands standing.

In due time I was called into the presence. Having made my bow, I found Prince Leopold sitting in a chair; next to him the Duke of Richmond; then the Lord Chancellor and the Duke of Northumberland, myself the last in the row, all standing. I was then called upon to take the oath of allegiance, then the long oath of a Privy Councillor; then I kissed hands, and was, as one of the Council, present at the business which was then done.

Before I was admitted to the presence Sir John Powell asked me to see him. I went, and found him with two books before him. He said that the Queen wished to have my autograph in those books on the date of my birth.

After I had come from the audience, I was informed that her Majesty desired to see me, and would send for me.

After some short time, the Duke of Richmond giving me his arm, we were ushered into the presence of her Majesty. We found the Queen standing near the door with Prince Leopold on her right hand. She advanced and said, as nearly as I can recollect the words, " I have sent for you, Mr. Roebuck, so that I might be able to express to you personally my high appreciation of what you have said and done upon the late trying occasions. I consider your conduct to have been that of a true patriot, and I am glad to have this opportunity of expressing to yourself my approbation and thanks."

I, upon this, expressed my sincere and warm thanks for her Majesty's goodness, saying that I was amply rewarded for all that I suffered, and I had suffered, because of what I had done, and which had won her Majesty's approval.

Her Majesty then beckoned to Prince Leopold, who shook hands with me. Then the Duke and myself retired.

To his own family Mr. Roebuck expressed himself as much touched by the handsome manner in which her Majesty spoke to him on this occasion.

At the Cutlers' feast of 1878 Mr. Roebuck was in his old form. Flattered by the uproarious welcome accorded to him, he flew at his opponents with glimpses of his accustomed vigour, tauntingly ridiculing those who suggested that he was "an old dog," toothless, and effete, and bound to retire. He reasserted his unchanging integrity, and defended his public career, avowing that he had never bowed his neck to any party yoke. What he had bowed it to was the yoke of duty to England. That was what had guided him through life—the interests of his country. " I have not," he said, " sought in party politics my line of conduct, but I have looked forward and asked myself this question — Does this conduce to the honour and happiness of England? England," he continued, " has been the sun by which I have guided my course." He saw at the head of affairs a gentleman, well worthy to guide the interests of the country, who, against all opposition and against mighty feelings of dislike and jealousy, would win the highest honour of the State. True, Lord Beaconsfield was a Conservative, but was he on that account to stand apart, bark at him, sneer at him, and write articles against him ? No; he put the consideration aside. It mattered not to him that Lord Beaconsfield was at the head of the State; if he did rightly he would support him; if he did wrongly, he would oppose him. "When," he declared, "I follow the interests of England, I follow the interests of the whole human race." The action of Russia in Turkey, ostensibly for the deliverance of the Christian, he treated in terms of scorn, exclaiming:

The poor Christian! I want to know how Russia treated the poor Catholic? Was the Catholic not a Christian in her mind? She whipped the Catholic into the Greek church, and that she called Christianity. Now this was the Power that I was abused for not supporting. I always said that I believed Russia was arrogant, unfair, unjust, and encroaching upon everybody—that she sought her own interests and her own interests alone—that she was utterly unworthy of trust ; and that I thought him void of wisdom who trusted her, if there were not behind some private interests which made the man declare in favour of Russia, when he had passed his life in opposing her—some private interest which induced him to blow the trumpet in her favour when no man of ability, except under such circumstances, would trust her.

He concluded by repeating that he thought only of his country. He was determined to lend the Administration all the powers he had, and they would meet the world with a united front.

*To a Sheffield Correspondent.*

19, *Ashley Place, April* 23, 1879.—I think you are anxious without cause. Public opinion will be governed by the result, not by the flourishes of wordy rhetoricians. You see that this morning's news proves the Government to have acted wisely and with energy ; and so you will find with respect to the Afghans and our policy in the East of Europe. My experience has taught me that it is unwise to trouble the constituency before an election, and you must remember that an election is not at hand. The Parliament will be kept alive as long the law allows, and addressing the people only harasses them, troubles them, and puts them,

in the result, out of humour with those who disturb them.
I pray you, think this over, and do not allow yourself to be
made anxious when there is no need for anxiety.  If fortune
favours the Government, if our arms are successful, if the
position of England be prosperous when the General Election
comes, the result will be in their favour ; if disaster happens,
nothing can save them (that is, the present Government).  So,
I say, it all depends on the result.  Such being my view, my
advice is to be quiet, and let our opponents talk themselves
hoarse.  When the General Election is imminent, then let us
act—not before.

Mr. Roebuck paid his last visit to Sheffield in July,
1879, when he opened the new asylum buildings of the
local licensed victuallers' association.  His extreme feebleness excited general remark, his voice being so weak that
it was with difficulty he could be heard a few paces off.
He alluded to the change that had taken place in public
opinion during his career—

I find myself now in company with persons allied in opinions
to me, who I recollect, in the days of my youth, used to make
a separate seat between me and them when we sat together in
the House of Commons.  But time, which conquers all things,
has brought truth to the foremost, and these opinions which I,
as a young man, upheld and boldly set forth in the House of
Commons—very much to the scandal of many there—I find these
opinions governing the country, and myself believed to be rather
behindhand.  People whom I recollect to be old-fashioned Tories
now look upon me as something not altogether Radical.  I am
told that I am changed ; but I am not now other than I was
before.  It is not I who have changed ; it is they.  Now, when
we meet upon equal terms and upon equal beliefs, it is not I,
surely, who should blush.  My belief is the one now predominant.
Theirs has gone—God knows where.

That was Mr. Roebuck's creed to the last.  From it he
never swerved.  It was his honest and conscientious belief
that while much around him had changed and altered, the

aims, the methods, and the principles of John Arthur Roebuck had, from first to last, been consistent in themselves—harmonious parts of the scheme with which he started public life. And not even his severest critics were disposed to deprive him of that great consolation of his declining years.

Mr. Roebuck's latest public utterance was a letter, dated November 21, 1879, to the Lord Mayor of London, read at the Mansion House, apologizing for absence from a meeting to promote a memorial to Sir Rowland Hill. He wrote :

I take a great interest in your efforts to mark the gratitude of the country to the late Sir Rowland Hill. He was a very old and much-esteemed friend of mine, and I believe few men have done so much as he for the good of his nation and his race. With his great scheme I was early made acquainted. Indeed, I have a letter somewhere in which his scheme is explained, with a request that I would not speak of it, as he was not ready to make it public "just yet." I say all this because my physical condition is such as to make me very unfit and very unwilling to attend a great public meeting. I hope, therefore, you will excuse my absence. I deem myself greatly honoured by your invitation, and nothing but absolute necessity keeps me away.

Although, as has been seen, Mr. Roebuck was inclined, in the summer of 1878, when a dissolution was anticipated after Lord Beaconsfield's return from Berlin, to contemplate again offering himself for re-election at Sheffield, increasing infirmity led him, in the following year, to relinquish any such idea.

Recognition of the necessity of retiring from public life seems, indeed, to have been forced upon him in January (1879). For in that month he wrote to his chairman, Mr. William Fisher, showing himself anxious to secure a successor in the representation of Sheffield, who would follow a course similar to his own. He described the kind of man that, in his opinion, the future member for Sheffield

should be. " The object aimed at," he said, " was to obtain
a large-minded man, whose view of the state of things at
present was favourable to the Beaconsfield administration,
but who would be guided in the future by his own independent judgment." Mr. Roebuck held also "that he
must be a good speaker; if he had any past political life
his course must prove him free from any partisan views—
to be, in short, a real Liberal, beyond the influence of mere
party, and guided only by what he believed to be the
interests of England." In the same letter Mr. Roebuck
said he found age growing too much for him ; and felt that
he could not in future adequately perform the duties of a
member of Parliament. " As to what I say about myself,"
he added, " I must beg of you and my other friends to
believe me when I say that I have come to the conclusion
that I here speak of, very slowly and with great pain, and
very reluctantly ; but if my friends think my aid absolutely
necessary, I would, as far as possible, assist them ; but let
them judge kindly of me, and remember that seventy-six
years is no light weight."

It was not until the summer of 1879 that Mr. Roebuck's
lingering cleavings to Parliament were finally abandoned,
and that he decisively decided not again to ask the constituency to retain him in his charge. This resolution was
kept a secret from all but his most intimate friends. It
was desired that the announcement should come from
Mr. Roebuck's own lips. He intended to make his retiring
speech an occasion for reviewing his whole career, and
arrangements were being prepared with a view to have
this valedictory ceremony in the January of 1880.

*To William Fisher (Sheffield).*

*Ashley Place, November* 21, 1879.—I agree with every word
of your letter, and leave it entirely with my friends as to the
time of the announcement. I always intended that it should be
given in public meeting, on which occasion I proposed to give

a summary of my political career. What, then, I would propose is as follows : (1) That my friends should settle upon what day the announcement should be made. (2) That timely notice should be given of a public meeting, called by myself, asking my constituents to meet me, in order that I might address them in regard of the coming election. (3) That the time and place as settled by my friends should be canvassed at the same time. So much for business. My health has slowly recovered from the effects of malaria, and amongst the most painful of which was a most trying depression of spirits, accompanied by a feeling of general *malaise*—no special pain anywhere, but everywhere a sense of suffering. This has gradually worn off, and I am now, though weak, without pain, and with a general feeling of comfort. I hope you will give me due notice of the time when I am expected at Sheffield. I shall, as usual, be attended by my two faithful guardians [Mrs. and Miss Roebuck], who, with myself, will, I hope, be able to face any weather that may happen. It is here now so dark with a snow-storm that I can hardly see to write.

Mr. Fisher, in reply, cordially invited Mr. Roebuck and his " two faithful guardians " to make his house their home during the visit. Mr. Roebuck's acceptance of that invitation was the last missive received from him by any friend in Sheffield, and, indeed, was probably the last letter he ever wrote. It was dated November 25. On the evening of that day (Tuesday) he was present at the usual dinner of the Benchers of the Inner Temple. The night was a severe one, with very low temperature, and, having venturesomely gone without the warm fur coat he was accustomed to wear in wintry weather, he took cold. He lost his voice, and was troubled with a severe cough. Early on the morning of Thursday the 27th he had a choking fit, caused by failure of the heart's action. Sir William Gull was called in, and Mrs. Roebuck, writing on the 29th (Saturday), recorded the medical verdict that " The lungs are safe, but he is very weak." Still, no serious results seem to have been apprehended, for Mrs. Roebuck added, " We have five weeks before the meeting, but, from the severity of the attack, it will not be prudent to expose him to the winter's cold."

Along with that letter there was delivered a telegram announcing that the end came at half-past one on Sunday morning, November 30. He had become alarmingly ill on the Saturday night. He suffered a great deal of pain, but in the last hours became easier, and he passed away peacefully. He was in the 78th year of his age.

He was buried in the quiet churchyard of Bushey, Hertfordshire — where, for more than forty years, his brother-in-law, the Rev. William Falconer, M.A., had been rector—amid a large concourse of friends and admirers. The voice of criticism was hushed in the general sorrow, and tributes of respect laid upon his grave were tendered as heartily by his political antagonists as by his warmest adherents.

# CHAPTER XXX.

MR. GLADSTONE, who was at that time in the midst of his Midlothian campaign, made a noble return for the many invectives Mr. Roebuck had levelled at his character, his statesmanship, and even his honesty :—

Mr. Roebuck was a man of distinguished mental powers, and as a speaker, as a Parliamentary orator, he had not only many distinguished qualities, but he had some most valuable and telling qualities in a degree perhaps superior to almost any man, if not to any other man, of his generation. Mr. Roebuck, I need not say, was not in sympathy with me; or, rather, I was not in sympathy with him. On the contrary, I have the misfortune to believe that I held a singularly low place in his estimation ; but, while recognizing those talents on the part of Mr. Roebuck which all the world admired, while aware of and lamenting the later course and colour of his political opinions, I wish to take this, the very first opportunity, of stating my full and firm belief that in his later, as well as in his earlier, career, Mr. Roebuck was governed from first to last by principles of integrity and of patriotism. I hope that the honour due to integrity will ever be done to him. That the particular form in which his patriotism developed itself should be imitated by others I must confess, with all due respect and sympathy, I do not desire. Now the grave has closed over a very able man ; and it will be good for us all that on this occasion we should exercise ourselves particularly—for of late years many of us have been vexed with the particular direction of his political course—we should exercise ourselves in yielding to him that tribute of respect which is always due to honesty of purpose. I, like Mr.

Roebuck, have had what I do not hesitate to call the misfortune, the necessity—the conscientious necessity—of changing the political connection in which I began my public career. We changed in very different directions. I must assume, and I do believe, that Mr. Roebuck was well assured in his own mind of the soundness of the policy that of late he was supporting. I assure you that in that one particular of firm conviction, of absolute reliance—of strong reliance, I will say—upon the soundness of a certain policy, I do not yield to Mr. Roebuck, although, unhappily, the policy of which I approve is different.

The press of all sections paid full tribute to Mr. Roebuck's great merit and unique personality. He was, it was said, essentially a critic, an Ishmaelite, " the zebra of politics," a good hater, but, most of all, a hater of hollow pretexts and a scorner of shams—a man of angles and peculiarities, uncomfortable to friends and dangerous to opponents.

The newspaper which, in Sheffield, was chiefly responsible for Mr. Roebuck's rejection in 1868, and which continued in strong opposition to his public course to the end, wrote—

Mr. Roebuck had his faults, but we prefer not to see them now. He made mistakes, but we wish to forget them at this moment. He offended many sensibilities, but they may be left to find their own consolation. What we desire most to keep in mind are the aspects in which Mr. Roebuck showed to the greatest advantage, the fields in which he best served the country of which he was so proud. The picture that first rises to the mind's eye at the mention of Mr. Roebuck's name is one which appeals strongly to English sympathies. It is the figure of that physically feeble being who, bent in body but aggressive in mind, delighted fearlessly to confront odds that seemed overwhelming. The dauntless bearing of him who faced an angry constituency, and sent it away admiring and repentant, could not but command respect. The frail old man who quietly braved Mr. Campbell Foster's torrent of invective that memorable summer evening in Paradise Square, contrasted dramatically with the burly Boanerges who raged

against him. Mr. Roebuck was always at his greatest when he
played the part of Horatius—

> "Facing fearful odds
> For the ashes of his fathers,
> And the temples of his gods!"

A very large part of Sheffield's pride in Mr. Roebuck arose from
the conviction that in him she possessed something unique. She
had got what no other constituency could rival. Others might
approve themselves in patient attention to necessary detail; others
might excel in statesmanlike prudence, in wise foresight, in the
genius that builds up, and in half a hundred qualities that the
member for Sheffield lacked—but still they were not Roebuck.
His splendid self-confidence was unrivalled. His powers of
destructive criticism were inimitable. His egotism was sublime.
There was something almost pathetic in the unwavering faith with
which he regarded his country as England by the grace of
Roebuck; and these two monopolized his field of vision. The
manner in which he put Roebuck first and England second, and
the magnificence with which he was apt to trace all his country's
greatness to a judicious obedience to the Roebuckian behest, were
characteristics which often proved irresistibly tempting to the
satirist and the scoffer. But they had their seat in an intense
patriotism, and in an overpowering intellectual impatience. Even
now the pens which were eagerest to snatch political capital out of
the latter-day developments of Mr. Roebuck's fierce repudiation
of the trammels of party, his restless frettings at the mere sight
of those traces in which he would never run, are quick to write
down his life as a palpable failure, or to damn it with the question-
able praise that one such man is abundantly sufficient. Admirable,
we are told, as a Roebuck may be as a unit, this unapproachable
entity is far too inimitable for a repetition to be tolerated; and
while we mourn a real loss, we may be thankful that this is the
first and the last of the race. Such language it is not our
intention to endorse. When we are told that Mr. Roebuck's
career was a failure, we are fain to admit that it fell far short of
the splendid possibilities that were open to the brilliant young
disciple of Jeremy Bentham and of Joseph Hume; but it gives us
greater satisfaction to remember that Mr. Roebuck himself shared
not in that dreariest of all beliefs of hopeless failure now expressed

2 B

by his once admirers. He was very far from thinking his life a
failure. On the contrary, he was never tired of expressing the
satisfaction with which he contemplated its well-rounded completeness, and the joy its harmonious oneness, its symmetric
consistency, afforded to him. It was no grief to Mr. Roebuck to
find himself—to employ his own expression—" as he usually was,
happily in a minority." On the contrary, he rather preferred it,
for then he knew he was right. "I believe," he said, "taken as
a whole, that my life has been a success." It may not, indeed,
have been an ideal career in the estimation of the disciples of
"sweetness and light." It was not a career to be imitated of
those whose chief desire is to live in peace and charity with all
men. Mr. Roebuck had scant patience with these. His notion
of the duties of life took no account of euphemisms, or expedi-
encies, or the veiling of opinions. He said what he thought in the
sharpest, directest, most incisive words in the English language ;
and since his thoughts seldom glowed with admiration for the
greatness of friend or foe, they were apt to prove unpalatable.
This *nil admirari* attitude of mind has many uses. It is wholesome
for public men, and systems, and institutions to be exposed to
the tonic blasts of keen criticism.

The *rôle* of the candid friend or bitter foe was that for which
nature intended Mr. Roebuck ; and there is no denying that he
did the work better than it had been done since the days of Swift,
better than it is likely to be done for many a long year to come.

"Perfectly independent?" said the *Spectator.* Yes—

Thorns in the flesh are always independent of the organism
in which they create so much disturbance ; and it is, in fact, their
independence, quite as much as their sharpness, which creates the
disturbance. Mr. Roebuck was, almost by essence, a thorn in
the flesh of the party to which he nominally belonged. Whatever
good he did in public life—and he did some very good things,
especially in the earlier part of his career—he did by well
establishing himself as a thorn in the tenderest region of his
party's organization, and shifting about there freely, as that
party moved. It was as a thorn in the flesh of the Liberals that
he long ago exposed the scandals of our government of Canada.
It was as a thorn in the flesh of the Liberals that he exposed the
scandals of the administrative collapse in the Crimea. It was

as a thorn in the flesh of the Liberals that he denounced Lord Palmerston's tendency to fraternize with French Imperialism during the earlier years of Louis Napoleon's *régime*. We can well believe that Mr. Gladstone's administration from 1869 to 1874 would have been rather the better than the worse for such a thorn in the flesh, to remind it of its liability to the universal doom ; nay, that Mr. Roebuck's rejection for Sheffield in 1868, though a very wise and loyal protest on the part of Sheffield against Mr. Roebuck's strange vagaries, was not ultimately advantageous to the Ministry which it numerically strengthened. For, certainly, if Mr. Roebuck ever served his country well, it was by giving voice to the irritation with which the country regarded certain errors of Liberal Governments. But even this function—a valuable one in its way—it cannot be doubted that Mr. Roebuck overdid. He believed so very much in "the contrary," he was so very sharp in his fault-finding with almost every attempt to carry out a Liberal policy, sometimes even when, as in the case of the disestablishment of the Irish Church, he had been deeply pledged to the same policy himself in earlier life, that his warnings came without authority, and his invectives without force. Mr. Roebuck's Radicalism was, indeed, more of a constitutional, political irritability than of a constitutional sympathy with popular policy. He could not choose but be the "candid friend" of any party to which he belonged. And if he had ever joined the Tories formally, he would have been as serious a thorn in the side of Lord Beaconsfield as he was, for the last twenty years, in the side of Lord Palmerston and Mr. Gladstone. It was his mission to scold allies, rather than to assail foes. The rather warm partisanship for capital, and hostility * to labour, which marked his speeches in all the struggles between capital and labour, was no doubt due to the feeling that, nominally at least, it was the labourer for whom he appeared. Perhaps his bitter attacks on the United States of America were due to the same feeling that they were a people of cousins, and that, as a relative and friend of the family, he was bound to confess the disagreeable impressions made upon him. Possibly the same explanation may be given of his curious advocacy of the cause of Austria against that of Italy, as no

---

* He had no hostility to labour—as labour—for he realized clearly that labour and capital could not get on without one another.

doubt it may of the much more defensible and intelligible attack on Lord John Russell for his Ecclesiastical Titles Bill, and of not a few of his raids against the "ribaldry" of the press. The cause of Italy, the cause of the Northern States, the cause of a free press, the cause of Protestantism, were probably all causes which, in his heart, Mr. Roebuck felt bound, by his principles, to advocate; but for that very reason he resented the bondage in which he found himself, and eagerly looked round for an excuse to pour forth his displeasure at certain aspects of these causes which fretted and oppressed him. The antagonistic currents of feeling in Mr. Roebuck were certainly excited more by faults in organizations to which he belonged than by faults in organizations to which he did not belong. There are men who are much more apt to imagine faults and blunders in any system for which they are responsible than in any system for which they are not responsible, and Mr. Roebuck was one of them. When the late Mr. Hadfield and he jointly represented Sheffield, they might have been termed the curds and whey of the Liberal party, Mr. Hadfield furnishing all the solid and nutritious elements of steady-going Liberalism, Mr. Roebuck all those which are of advantage chiefly in case of a sudden attack of cold, when the Liberal party had need of such remedies as a hot and biting fluid, administered to an invalid with his feet in hot water, might provide. And yet Mr. Roebuck was not prone to find fault, or even suspect fault in England, though he was prone to find and suspect fault in the party which, for much the greater part of his political life, administered the government of England. The fault he most commonly found with that party was precisely this—that they did not always take for granted that the aggrandisement of England in the earth was the one chief end of political, diplomatic, and international effort. . . . Indeed, Mr. Roebuck, though he loved to pick holes in the party to which he regarded himself as belonging, and the Government entrusted by that party with power, never, apparently, dreamt for a moment that English power, if it were attained, might be indifferently used. . . . The more there was of English power, the better he was pleased, though with those who wielded English power he was seldom pleased at all. He seemed to be persuaded that, in the hands most likely to wield it, English influence would certainly be abused, and yet to desire earnestly to see it grow and swell. It was a very odd state of mind. Mr. Roebuck was, indeed, a political misanthrope, who compensated himself for attacking almost all possible English Governments, by making an idol of England, steadily ignoring the fact that the Government which was pretty sure to be installed in England would be, in his opinion, cowardly, feeble, and bad.

One who had enjoyed many opportunities of hearing Mr. Roebuck's speeches, wrote—

Among the orators of the platform or of Parliament, there has been no man, within living memory, who possessed such a mastery of crisp, vigorous, nervous English. His sentences were perfect and pointed. Like a rapier, rather than a two-edged sword, they pierced to the heart of a question, and often and often has the telling accuracy of the thrust delighted his friends and thrown discouragement into the ranks of his enemies. Perhaps it was in the House of Commons that Mr. Roebuck's oratory was most telling in his best days ; for he had caught the House of Commons' tone, and that fastidious assembly appreciated both the sharpness and the polish of his style. Even when his voice had to a large extent lost its power, his utterance was so distinct, his action so dignified, that, when he rose to address it, the House was hushed.* There was in him nothing of the garrulousness of age ; his incisive style and epigrammatic energy seemed untouched by time. His speeches were rarely long, and in nothing superfluous. There was a classic grace about his eloquence that formed a remarkable contrast to the slip-shod utterances of less notable men. His speeches were always refreshing, for there was a certain crispness about them strongly in contrast with much of the Parliamentary eloquence of the day. Even the best oratory of

* It was Roebuck's "perfect delivery" that most impressed so unfriendly a critic as Kinglake. "Placing unbounded confidence in himself, and troubling his mind very little about any one else, he had a hardiness beyond other mortals, a compact and vigorous diction, that was good enough, yet not too good, for his purpose, and, above all, a matchless delivery which made up—much more than made up—for want of stature and voice ; because it made him seem like one filled with a sense of his ineffable power " ("Invasion of the Crimea," vol. vi. p. 357). Kinglake admits that Roebuck "had the ear—the rapt ear "of the House, although he attributes the welcome ever given to "an accomplished denouncer who was sure to be vicious and brief," to anticipations of mischief and amusement.

our time runs into a wordy diffuseness, and from this error Mr. Roebuck was singularly free.

The *Daily News* once said—

He was probably the best example that our generation has known of simply good speaking—speaking which, if it does not rise to the height of oratory, never sinks into slovenly chatter, or semi-articulate growling, nor adorns itself with the false glitter of declamatory rhetoric. The shape and the substance were admirably suited to each other. Mr. Roebuck's speech was simply his thought and feeling made audible—often it reflected the thought and feeling of others who were too prudent to give them expression. The words in which he clothed his meaning were just the words in which he made it distinct to himself. For this reason he was a pointed speaker, without being a witty one, and, without being imaginative, he had a sufficient faculty of illustration to aid clear statement and exposition. For this reason also, he was always a short speaker. He never acquired, because he never had any necessity for, the dangerous gift of amplification. Qualification and parenthesis, and copiousness of epithet, and all the verbiage which makes sentences involved and speeches long, are usually the result of inability to choose the few suitable words which would have done promptly all the business for which the *posse comitatus* of ill-drilled and straggling phrases is called out. The inability to choose the right words, and the consequent necessity of enlisting five times as many as are necessary, is the result of indistinct and confused thinking. Mr. Roebuck never wasted words, and he was therefore always able to find a suitable provision for them when necessary. Mr. Roebuck was above all things a distinct and precise speaker. This gift was, no doubt, due in part to the natural character of his mind, but also in a great degree to his training as a disciple in that school of thought in which Bentham, and John Austin, and James Mill were masters, and which was cultivated in the Socratic dialogues of which Mr. Grote's room in Threadneedle Street was the scene, whence proceeded some of the most valuable speculations and researches of the time. If Mr. Roebuck escaped the peculiar vices of slovenly thought and language, which are the besetting danger of Parliamentary debate, his deliverance may in no slight degree be attributed to the delicate weighing of ideas and the precise use of words to which he was trained by his philosophical associates.

In private life Mr. Roebuck did not readily unbend to comparative strangers. His courtesy to mere acquaintances, though perfect, was somewhat cold and distant. Yet anyone who came to him with an honest desire for information was never snubbed or laughed at; however trivial the question might appear, the answer was given with painstaking care and kindness. And to his intimates, and in the domestic circle, he was a model of gentleness and kindness. His tone so quiet; his manner of such an almost silken softness, that he seemed one of the mildest of mortals, as he was one of the most charming, instructive, and delightful of companions.

# INDEX.

Harding, Mr., 130
Harfield, Mr., 27
Harrison, Frederic, 318
Harrison, Samuel, 109
Hartington, Marquis of, (Duke of Devonshire), 280, 352, 357
Harvey, D. W., 94, 95
Harwich, corruption at, 145
Hawes, Sir B., 180, 210, 225, 235, 263
Hayter, Sir W. G., (Wells), 235
Health of Towns Bill, 181
Heaton, Mr., (Leeds), 235, 236
Herbert, Sidney, (afterwards Lord Herbert of Lea), 227
Hetherington's *Despatch*, 82
Hill, Marcus, 182
Hill, Matthew Davenport, 228
Hill, Sir Rowland, 363
Hobhouse, H. W., 42, 43, 48, 49, 66, 145
Hobhouse, J. C., 84, 104; and Nottingham, 145
Hogg, J. W., 154, 197
Holyoake, G. J., 27 n., 125 n., 126
Hood, Thomas, 7 n.
Houghton, Lord, 106, 136
House and window tax, 56
Howe, Mr., 121
Howick, Lord, 147, 156. *See* Grey, 3rd Earl.
Hudson, George, 226
Hudson's Bay Company, 263, 271
Hume, Joseph, introduces Roebuck to Bath, 30, 31 n., 42, 369; on pensions, 56; political knowledge society, 59; pamphlets, 61, 76; preaches mildness, 72; on House of Lords, 73; Radical dissatisfaction with, 80, 81, 83, 85-90, 93, 94, 102-104; and Montrose, 142; on Portugal, 181; challenged by Peel, 195; and Ferrand, 197, 203, 230; on Eastern policy, 232; on property tax, 248
Hungary, 231, 293
Hunt, William, 72
Hutt, W., 102

### I.

Ibbitt, William (Sheffield), 299
Imperial Titles Bill, 348
Import duties, Peel's reduction of, 167
Income tax, 139, 140; for Ireland, 155, 169, 171, 172
India (*see also* Afghan, Scinde), 213; law of Bengal, 240; transferred to the Crown, 270; Oude confiscation, 271

Inns of Court monopoly, 44
Ireland, right of self-government, 96; O'Connell's policy, 149, 150; discontents, 150, 330; repeal, 150, 177, 178; condition of, 151,—in 1847, 169, 171,—in 1875, 348; income tax, 155, 169, 172; Maynooth grant, 156; Devon Commission, 169; Potato blight, 226; scramble for English money, 224 n.; abolition of lord-lieutenancy, 267, 268; true union, 273, 274; Home Rule, 293, 345, 346; real cause of troubles in, 300, 345; their cure, 273, 274, 300, 345; Fenian conspiracy, 309
Irish Church, 58, 64, 66, 149, 150, 318-320, 331, 332, 335, 337, 371
—— clergy (R.C.), 345
—— Coercion Bills, 54, 55, 64, 80, 149, 167-169, 177, 347
—— landlords, 169, 171, 178, 224 n., 318; Land Improvement and Drainage Bill, 224; Land Act (1871), 335
—— municipal corporations, 78, 83, 95, 96
—— Parliamentary Voters' Bill, 234
—— Poor Law, 169, 171, 172, 176, 178
—— railways, loans to, 171, 172, 181, 182
—— Registration Bill, 129, 134
—— State Prisoners and Transportation for Treason Bill, 228
—— Sunday Closing Bill, 349
—— Tithe Bill, 79
—— in America, 281, 322
Italy, King of, 290
Italian unity, 204, 279, 290-294, 301

### J.

James, Sir Henry, (afterwards Lord James), 353, 354
Jay, Rev. William, 185, 186
Jerrold, Douglas, 172
Jessop, Thomas, (Sheffield), 340
Jewish disabilities, 226, 233
Jocelyn, Lord, 195
Johnson, Dr., 141
Johnson, Reverdy, 321, 322
Justice, administration of, 44

### K.

Kaffirs, treatment of, 248, 253
Kean, Charles, actor, 4, 5
Kearsley, J. H., (Wigan), 98

THE END.